# Early Native Literacies
## in New England

*A volume in the series*

Native Americans of the Northeast: History, Culture,
and the Contemporary

# Early Native Literacies in New England

## A Documentary and Critical Anthology

Edited by

Kristina Bross and Hilary E. Wyss

⌒:⌒

*University of Massachusetts Press*

AMHERST

LC 2008003196
ISBN 978-1-55849-648-4 (paper); 647-7 (library cloth)

Designed by Dennis Anderson
Set in Adobe Jenson Pro by dix! Digital Prepress
Printed and bound by The Maple-Vail Book Manufacturing Group

Library of Congress Cataloging-in-Publication Data

Early native literacies in New England : a documentary and critical anthology / edited by
Kristina Bross and Hilary E. Wyss.
p. cm.
Includes bibliographical references and index.
ISBN 978-1-55849-648-4 (pbk. : alk. paper)—
ISBN 978-1-55849-647-7 (library cloth : alk. paper)
1. Algonquian Indians—Material culture.   2. Algonquian Indians—Colonization.
3. Algonquian Indians—Communication.   4. Algonquian languages—Writing.
5. Algonquian languages—Texts. 6. Written communication—New England—History.
7. New England—Antiquities.   I. Bross, Kristina.   II. Wyss, Hilary E.
E99.A35E37 2008
974.004'973—dc22
2008003196

British Library Cataloguing in Publication data are available.

# Contents

# Illustrations

ix

# Acknowledgments

THIS PROJECT emerged from our sense that the extraordinary range of materials relating to colonial Native America that Native tribal historians and
university scholars have unearthed warranted a far larger audience than they
have hitherto received. The richness, subtlety, and depth of Native textual production in early New England and the window that these texts open to a world
often misunderstood or forgotten is astonishing. Our sense of the significance
of these materials and their interest to others was affirmed through two remarkable panels on Native literacy at the 2003 conference of the Society for
Early Americanists (SEA)—one organized by Sandra Gustafson, the other by
Joanna Brooks and Hilary Wyss.

We are grateful to a number of people who made this anthology—inspired
by the SEA panels—possible. First, we thank our contributors, whose initial
enthusiasm and ongoing commitment to the project have inspired us. The community of early Americanists who attended various panels and presentations
that in some way related to this project—held by SEA, the Omohundro Institute for Early American History and Culture, and the American Studies Association—provided not only important feedback and fruitful suggestions but
also a passion for the project that helped sustain us when our own began to flag.
The graduate students in Kristina Bross's English 553 class read an early draft
of the anthology and provided helpful commentary. Three research assistants
at Auburn University—Antonia Bowden, Jill Parrott, and Melissa Pojasek—
contributed the invaluable service of collecting resources and providing superb
editorial support. Our thanks go as well to research assistant Elyssa Tardif for
her help in making last-minute revisions. To our editors at the University of
Massachusetts Press—Clark Dougan, whose unwavering commitment to this
book made what sometimes felt like an endless process endurable, and our series editors, Barry O'Connell and Colin Calloway—we are profoundly grateful.
Our anonymous readers also gave us much useful encouragement and advice
on the form and function of the project. Carol Betsch and everyone at the press
have been unfailingly helpful and enthusiastic. In particular, our copy-editors,
Joan Vidal and Mary Bellino, saved us all over and over from the mistakes and
gaffes that invariably arise when so many texts and scholars are brought together in a single project. Their patience and rigor have unquestionably made
the collection stronger. Any remaining mistakes are ours alone.

Various libraries and historical societies opened their doors to us and generously granted us permission to reprint or photograph rare and fragile materials. Special thanks go to the University of Nottingham Department of Manuscripts and Special Collections, the Connecticut Historical Society, the Newberry Library, the Rauner Special Collections Library of Dartmouth College Library, the Massachusetts Archive, and the Historical Society of Pennsylvania for permission to print the transcription of Hendrick Aupaumut's journal. A number of journals and presses granted us permission to reprint materials: we are grateful to Cornell University Press, the *New England Quarterly*, and the University of Massachusetts Press.

*HW*: On a more personal note, I thank Kristina Bross, my co-editor, whose warmth and humor made this a wonderful experience. I also thank James Truman, my friend, partner, colleague, and husband. From graduate school to this day he remains my best reader and strongest advocate. I am forever grateful to him. Finally, I thank our children, Anna and Cameron, whose love of books and whose matter-of-fact acceptance that I write them still delights my heart.

*KB*: Having Hilary Wyss as both friend and mentor during the compilation of this anthology made the continual stream of e-mails, phone calls, and conferences an intellectual and emotional fix that, although the project has ended, I am not prepared to forgo (fair warning, Hilary). As always, Steven Wereley makes this life of mine possible; he is, by turns (as necessary), refuge and backbone. Finally, my part in this book is for Kate, whose gift of narrative is already awesome, and for Grace, who lives out the promise of her name.

# Introduction

IN 1769 a young Narragansett woman named Sarah Simon spent an agonizing afternoon trying to explain to the white minister responsible for her Christian education just how far short of providing a new spiritual framework for her life his efforts had fallen. Her letter survives in the Dartmouth College archives. In 1794 Hendrick Aupaumut, a Stockbridge/Mahican tribal leader who had served as a go-between for the United States and certain western tribes, created a narration reflecting the oratory that was the signal feature of his diplomatic efforts among the Delawares, Miamis, Shawnees, and others. His work, discovered among private papers in the nineteenth century, can be found in the archives of the Historical Society of Pennsylvania. Sometime in the late eighteenth or early nineteenth century, an unknown Mohegan woman took an old issue of a Hartford, Connecticut, newspaper and carefully lined a woodsplint basket into which she had woven traditional colors and patterns. Her basket sits on the shelf of the Connecticut Historical Society. In the winter of 1659, a Massachusett man named Samuel Ponampam described his encounters with the Christian God to an English missionary, who included this "conversion narrative" in a printed tract touting the success of his evangelism. Sometime between 1771 and 1775, Samson Occom, a Mohegan missionary now best known for a sermon published upon the execution of a fellow Native, Moses Paul, wrote a very different sermon on drunkenness and white vices. The surviving unsigned fragment of his work is included in the Samson Occom Papers at the Connecticut Historical Society.

The written and material archive of early Native authors exists piecemeal and often overlooked in museums, manuscript collections, and print from the colonial period. Too often, access to these works is limited by outdated archiving practices, the fragility of the materials, or a history of scholarly disinterest.[1] This critical anthology seeks to address these problems in two ways: (1) by bringing together texts and images that reflect the wide range of "literacies" that represent the authorship of Algonquian peoples in southern New

---

1. Until relatively recently, important sources of Native writing, such as the marginalia in Indian Bibles, were liable to be viewed, at best, as unimportant or, at worst, as graffiti whose presence lowered the value of rare books. Ives Goddard and Kathleen Bragdon, editors of *Native Writings in Massachusetts*, write, "In spite of the occasional attention that the Massachusett documents had received . . . knowledge of their existence remained vague and incomplete and was confined to a few

England during the seventeenth and eighteenth centuries, and (2) by including brief explorations of the primary texts to help close the critical gap between these resources and the contemporary reader. Thus, signatures, wills, baskets, pictographs, petitions, confessions, and sermons are paired with short essays that provide the contextual material through which they can be understood as markers of literacy in colonial New England.

The focus of this collection is the range of materials through which Algonquian individuals and communities in southern New England up to roughly the year 1800 expressed their identity in a colonial context. *Algonquian* is a (primarily linguistic) term that is understood to include Algonquian-language speakers with similar cultural backgrounds who lived along the eastern seaboard of the United States: For our purposes, we focus on the region that stretches from what we now know as Massachusetts to Rhode Island, Connecticut, and Long Island—an area that includes the Pawtucket, Massachusett, Nipmuck, Pocumtuck, Narragansett, Pokanoket, Niantic, Mohegan, Pequot, Mahican, Montaukett, and Wampanoag people. *New England* in the colonial period referred to the four colonies (Massachusetts, Plymouth, Connecticut, and New Haven) brought together in a loose coalition by the Articles of Confederation in 1643. By the eighteenth century, Algonquian peoples who lived in this area were often simply called the New England Tribes, a name that recognized both the close interrelations of these tribal groups and their existence as members of a new colonial order.

We have narrowed this anthology geographically and temporally to enhance coherence of the materials and to explore the richness and variety of a group of interconnected Native cultures often flattened into a stereotype of "Indianness." We are aware that our decision to limit the materials in this way emphasizes a colonial historical narrative, reflecting the colonizers' idea of "New England" rather than the Native residents' cartography. Nonetheless, we hope that our efforts will serve as a useful corrective to colonial literary histories that have heretofore excluded Native voices. We mean to contribute to the ongoing challenge to the myth—so cherished by white Americans of the nineteenth century and so persistent even today—of the "vanishing Indian," who tragically disappeared from the eastern seaboard. By including materials from the period that is most severely underrepresented in Native American literature courses, this collection offers students the opportunity to view Native American literature not as a nineteenth- or even twentieth-century invention but as a part of

---

specialists and interested individuals. The information appearing in print was fragmentary, anecdotal and inaccurate" (xvii–xviii). Moreover, when older books were rebound, they were often trimmed of their marginalia (see ibid., 374, 416, 458).

a continuing and living tradition that reflects earlier moments of contact and colonization.[2]

## Algonquians, English, and Literacy

When the English settlers came into contact with the Algonquian people of New England in the early 1600s, a significant range of practices and beliefs both separated and united the Native inhabitants of New England. In addition, there had already been extensive contact with French, Dutch, and Spanish traders. From approximately 1616 to 1619—almost certainly as a result of these encounters, which took place shortly before the English arrived—the region was devastated by a massive epidemic; some estimates put the mortality rate at up to 90 percent.[3] Repercussions from this and other epidemics throughout the colonial period reverberated throughout Native communities of the region.

Although it is difficult to speak generally about the range of cultural practices that were already in place when the various colonists arrived, it is likely that most of these groups lived in more or less hierarchical societies where the hereditary leader, or sachem, ruled not by innate power but by consensus, and with the help of members of the elite families of the community. Hunting and farming, the primary means of sustenance, were performed through a gendered division of labor wherein men did most of the hunting and women did most of the farming. Because entire communities followed seasonal migrations within a recognized regional land base, housing generally consisted of wigwams constructed from bark and woven mats that were easily constructed and moved. The powwow, the central religious figure, was recognized for his or her ability to communicate with the spirit world. Religious practitioners also took on the role of healer.[4] Through tattooing, weaving, carving, dyeing, and countless other techniques, Native peoples marked out their relationship to kin, com-

---

2. Writings from this period are particularly underrepresented in literature courses. In *Teaching the Literature of Early America*, James Ruppert's essay on Native American materials devotes approximately one of its thirteen pages to historic Native American materials (that is, written texts); the rest is devoted to an introduction to oral materials. We recognize that because oral texts pose a greater challenge to scholars trained in traditional Western genres, they require extensive treatment; however, in our discussions with colleagues, we have found that even the more familiar forms of Native American Christian sermons, speeches, and confessions are perceived as difficult to integrate into new and existing courses.

3. Bragdon, *Native People*, 26.

4. In addition to subsequent chapters in this anthology, see ibid. and Salisbury, *Manitou and Providence*, two excellent studies of early Algonquian peoples of New England; for more detailed entries on specific groups and periods, see volume 15 of the *Handbook of North American Indians*, edited by Bruce Trigger (in a series edited by William Sturtevant).

munity, and spirit world, communicating across time and space about all that mattered to them long before and well after the arrival of European colonizers.

Because these cultural practices were not associated with anything that clearly resembled European literacy, however, scholars have long believed that the earliest literature of colonial New England was limited to what Anglo-Americans wrote and that the indigenous cultures that Anglo-Americans first encountered in New England were strictly oral in nature. Although oral exchange certainly played a central role in Algonquian cultures of the Northeast, recent scholarship has worked to complicate this overly neat division between oral and literate culture. Certainly stories, religious beliefs, and political exchanges were expressed orally and transmitted from one generation to another in a form that was highly ritualized and clearly central to preserving the immediacy and intimacy of communal life. At the same time, material objects played—and continue to play—a significant role in Algonquian communicative practices. Burial goods, basket patterns, pictographs, mats that line the interiors of wigwams, and even utensils reinforce oral exchanges with physical inscriptions whose functions, although quite varied, always communicate something to members of the communities in which they are produced.[5] In fact, to insist on an oral/print cultural divide in the seventeenth and eighteenth centuries is nonsensical in any number of ways: Puritans employed oral practices (and adapted Indian oral traditions to their own literature, as Laura Arnold Leibman argues in her essay herein), and Indians used various inscription technologies from their own traditions and readily integrated these practices into pen-and-ink inscriptions.

When we shift our focus from Western cultural assumptions about the supremacy of alphabetic literacy, however, there is much debate over what actually constitutes writing: Are carvings or painted images part of literary systems? Are pictures? Clothing? Tattoos? Weaving? Is there a difference between what one study calls "complex iconography" and a "writing system"?[6] Indeed, the question of what, exactly, constitutes "reading," "writing," and even "text" is central to this collection. Our decision to include material objects as

---

5. Tribal historians Melissa Jayne Fawcett and Gladys Tantaquidgeon have pointed out the ways that Mohegan basket weavers, even well into the eighteenth century, communicated among themselves about community identity and the political divisions within their tribe through painted basketry motifs that represented tribal unity and dispersal ("Symbolic Motifs," 98–101, 115–16). In her brief essay about Wampanoag home-building practices, Linda Coombs, of the Wampanoag Indigenous Program at Plimoth Plantation, explains how significant meaning in Native productions is tied up in the technologies of production: "To Native thinking, the ceremonial cannot be separated from the practical. The homes are much, much more than a list of materials or the utilization of certain techniques" ("Ancient Technology").

6. Boone and Mignolo, *Writing without Words*, 6.

well as products of "pure" alphabetic literacy reflects our sense that an overly strict definition of literacy unnecessarily restricts the full exploration of all early American literature, especially early Native literature. Moreover, it is important to recognize the fluid intersections of various ways of writing. As Lisa Brooks argues, "Transformations occurred in Native writing when the European system of recording and sending words entered Native space. Birchbark messages became letters and petitions, wampum council records became treaties, journey pictographs became written 'journals' that contained similar geographic and relational markers, and finally, histories recorded on birchbark and wampum became written communal narratives."[7] Most of the texts included in this anthology register such transformations. It is our contention that new scholarship must open the door not only to markers of such re-visioning but also to evidence of new uses of Western modes of writing.

## A History of Early Native Alphabetic Literacy in New England

Whereas today we may recognize various structures of literacy embedded within Algonquian culture, English colonists showed less interest in exploring such alternative forms. Because indigenous systems were illegible to colonists, the colonizers dismissed and diminished such markers, as they destroyed, outlawed, or co-opted relics, ceremonial practices, hand-crafted goods, and technologies. The attempted erasure of indigenous literacy systems is one of the terrible legacies of conquest. However, the persistence of such systems and their integration into European models of literacy, as seen in journals, baskets, artifacts, wills, petitions, and other texts included in this collection, is a testament to the cultural resilience of the Algonquian people of New England. As it turns out, the Algonquians of early New England were remarkably adept at incorporating new forms of literacy and adapting their own familiar forms to new materials and concepts.

Incorporating new forms of literacy was no small task for indigenous people in colonial New England, and the fact that, among others, Mohegans, Narragansetts, Pequots, and Wampanoags maintained their indigenous cultural practices in the face of English (and later U.S.) colonialism is nothing short of remarkable. As students of the "New England tribes" know well, Christian evangelism, particularly as practiced by Puritan missionaries such as John Eliot, was one of the most potent forces working against Indian cultural survival. Eliot immigrated to Massachusetts in 1631 and shortly after his arrival became the minister at Roxbury, where he served until his death in 1690. Although

---

7. L. Brooks, "The Common Pot," 12.

missionaries argued that theirs was an errand of Christian benevolence, their work was made possible by (and helped to justify) military conquest. Some scholars have argued that the devastating Pequot War of 1636 to 1637 cleared the way for Eliot's evangelism by breaking Indian resistance to the colonizer's presence and by completing the devastation of kinship ties and other means of cultural stability begun by the waves of disease introduced by contact with the earliest European explorers.[8] Indeed, Eliot's first Indian translator was a Pequot War captive.[9]

Eliot began his evangelical work among Indians in the mid-1640s. He believed, as did most leading Puritans in New England, that his evangelical project had to be accompanied by a "civilizing" mission: that Indians had to be humanized before they could be Christianized. To that end, he helped to institute laws meant to supplant traditional customs and settle converts and their kin into "praying towns," which the English intended as communities that would give praying Indians limited self-rule while ensuring colonial control over a previously "wild" people. Between 1650 and 1671, some fourteen praying towns, including Natick, were established.

This phase of evangelical colonization in New England came to an end in 1675 with King Philip's War. During this widespread conflict (some 5 percent of settler colonists and up to 40 percent of Native residents were killed),[10] Native alphabetic literacy came under intense colonial scrutiny. For some colonists, the conflict proved the folly of Eliot's attempts to Christianize a "savage" people. In his history of the war, the Reverend William Hubbard recommended the extermination, rather than the attempted assimilation, of Indians. Indeed, for some colonial observers, the fact that enemy Indians employed their literacy skills in service to King Philip became proof positive that Indians would turn the most Christian of skills to diabolical ends.

Setting aside such Indian-hating judgments, what can we see as the legacy of the earliest Native alphabetic literacy in New England? Eliot believed (in good Protestant style) that literacy would be an important and effective evan-

---

8. The Pequot War, although brief, was decisive, ending in a massacre of Pequot women, children, and noncombatant men at present-day Mystic, Connecticut. Colonial law forbade Pequot survivors to identify themselves as Pequots, and captives were sold into slavery; many were shipped away from their homes to the West Indies. For a general history of the war, see Cave, *The Pequot War*. For arguments by scholars who contend that the Pequot War and the colonial mission effort were bound together, see Jennings, *The Invasion of America* (especially "'We Must Burn Them'" and "Apostles to the Indians"), and Salisbury, "Red Puritans," 31. On conversion as a response to death and disease, see D. Morrison, "A Remnant Remaines," in *A Praying People*, and Robert James Naeher, "Dialogue in the Wilderness."

9. See Tooker, *Eliot's First Indian Teacher*.

10. On the devastation of the war, see Salisbury's introduction to Rowlandson's *Sovereignty and Goodness of God*, 1.

gelical tool. Working with his Indian "assistants" John Sassamon, Job Nesuton, and James Printer, he created a written form of Massachusett, along with an accompanying grammar primer, which was widely used well after his particular mission ended and which made possible many of the materials collected in this anthology. Indeed, the achievements of Eliot and his translators in the mission field most notably include the publication of an "Indian library," made up of religious documents—including the first Bible printed in North America—in the Massachusett language.

For Eliot and other New England missionaries, appropriate conversion involved replacing Native religious and cultural practices, which missionaries either misunderstood or devalued, with English Protestant religious practices, civil organizations, and English ideologies. David Hall's *Worlds of Wonder, Days of Judgment* and works by other scholars have emphasized the link between alphabetic literacy and Christianity in Protestant New England, where primers served as catechisms and the Bible was an introductory reader.[11] For white Protestants in New England, religion was linked to literacy, which was linked to culture or, more specifically, to English culture. Not surprisingly, then, given the close connection between Christianity and literacy training, many of the Native-authored documents of the seventeenth and eighteenth centuries are religious in nature. From marginalia in the Massachusett-language Bible to church records to Native confessions, Christianity suffuses much of the written work of early Native authors.

It is tempting to dismiss such texts as inauthentic and reflecting solely the English colonial perspective. Yet as culturally arrogant as Eliot and other missionary writers were, their work provided a means by which Christian Indians could speak their experiences in ways that ensured their survival and continue to make those experiences available to modern readers. Thus, whatever the intentions of English missionaries may have been, along with the particular set of publications that Eliot and his cohort produced, what emerged from the attempt to codify the Massachusett language in the mid-seventeenth century was a mechanism useful to Native communities that existed within a colonial world. Indeed, as Ives Goddard and Kathleen Bragdon, modern scholars of the Massachusett language, argue in *Native Writings in Massachusett*, "From the time of their first introduction in the mid-seventeenth century . . . the functions of reading and writing were modified [by Native readers and writers] to fit native needs, and defined according to traditional concepts."[12]

---

11. See for example, Patricia Crain's *The Story of A* and E. Jennifer Monaghan's *Learning to Read and Write in Colonial America.*

12. Goddard and Bragdon, *Native Writings in Massachusett*, 20.

A variety of Native-authored works were produced throughout the seventeenth and eighteenth centuries in the alphabetically rendered Massachusett language. Despite the preponderance of religious texts, moreover, some of the most intriguing documents from the period are those that merge various systems of literacy in secular productions such as treaties, deeds, and wills. Unlike their English neighbors, Massachusett speakers imbued many of their documents with distinctly oral elements. Thus, although such legal documents met the criteria for validity under English law, they also contained elements of traditional Native practices,[13] making them in many ways multicultural documents legible within several cultural systems. These elements are particularly evident in the Wampanoag communities of Martha's Vineyard, which were at once enmeshed in the colonial world and developing in their own particular way on an island occasionally removed from such devastating events of colonial history as King Philip's War. In 1727 the missionary Experience Mayhew produced an unprecedented biographical study of more than one hundred Wampanoag residents of Martha's Vineyard;[14] this work together with the carefully maintained land deeds and other transactions between the Wampanoag population and the colonial settlers number among the extraordinarily rich resources of Martha's Vineyard for the study of Algonquian literacy practices, both written and other.

Even after the practice of translating and printing Massachusett-language texts slowed almost to a standstill in the early eighteenth century and as Algonquian communities became increasingly fragmented through devastating economic hardship, disease, and the relentless encroachments of English colonists, alphabetic literacy in Algonquian communities persisted. Handwritten documents in Massachusett continued to be exchanged for much of the rest of the century and traces of a literacy practice that was valued in Algonquian communities are evident in the English-language petitions included in this anthology.

Our focus on the usefulness of literacy to Algonquians who lived under colonization in no way mitigates the violence that underpinned English efforts to bring literacy to Native individuals and their communities. However well Indian writers deployed their new literacies, we must recognize the strong elements of colonial exploitation that circumscribed English efforts. Especially

---

13. Ibid., 14–16.
14. See Leibman's forthcoming edition of Experience Mayhew's *Indian Converts* and Silverman's *Faith and Boundaries*.

in the transcribed and translated documents that characterize much Native writing from the colonial period, we must be alert to questions of coercion. As David Murray argues in his essay herein, "Even in cases involving the most honest and benevolent intentions, the act of 'speaking for' brought with it the limitations and contradictions of the paternalistic and protective stance that successive white authorities adopted." Certainly such limitations and contradictions are present in the statements that most obviously reflect the mediation of English writers: testimony in criminal trials and confession narratives in which white writers paraphrased or transcribed the statements of Native peoples. Even here, however, we may find valuable additions to the early archive of Native literature.

Reading early church, court, and execution statements against the grain for evidence of the experiences and even authorship of Native peoples is an exercise in caution. Every word can be seen alternatively as a marker of self-expression—buried though it may be—or as a signal of white biases and audience expectations. Even so, the struggle to understand these texts as part of the corpus of early Native writings can focus contemporary readers on the need for constant attention to such issues in this and all early modern literature. In fact, even texts that individuals wrote themselves, which seem to meet Western standards of authorship or form, should be read as part of a continuum that contains many other forms and means of expression, unquestionably including autonomous writings. Obviously coerced statements, on one hand, can be read for traces of resistance and, on the other, can alert us to the limitations that seemingly independent writers faced.

Nowhere is this reading practice more important than with documents produced by students or former students in the missionary boarding schools of New England. Arguably the most significant—certainly the most widely known—examples of early Native writing come from these schools. These institutions, infamous in the nineteenth century for their cruelty, were introduced quite early in New England as a "solution" to what the English perceived as the unsettled lifestyles of Indians. Nothing short of the erasure of indigenous culture was contemplated. In 1734 John Sergeant, a missionary to the Mahicans (later known as the Stockbridge Indians in western Massachusetts), devised a boarding school plan whose purpose was (in his own words) "to take such a *Method* in the Education of our *Indian Children*, as shall in the most effectual Manner change their whole Habit of thinking and acting; and raise them, as far as possible, into the Condition of a civil industrious and polish'd People."[15]

---

15. See Sergeant, *Letter to Dr. Colman.*

In 1754, the white minister Eleazar Wheelock founded a charity school in Lebanon, Connecticut, based on Sergeant's (unsuccessful) plan. Wheelock's enthusiasm was drawn in part from his previous success with a Native pupil, the young Samson Occom. Disregarding the fact that Occom had come to him of his own volition as a nineteen-year-old already familiar with reading, writing, and the tenets of Christianity, Wheelock became convinced of the utility of a school like Sergeant's. He writes, "I am fully perswaded from the Acquaintance I have had with them [Indians], it will be found to be very difficult if not impossible to cure them of such savage and sordid Practices, as they have been inured to from their Mother's Womb, and form their Minds and Manners to proper Rules of Virtue, Decency and Humanity, while they are daily under the pernicious Influence of their Parents Example."[16] Wheelock's solution was to limit contact between parents and children, educate Native children alongside white charity students, and turn himself into the patriarch and disciplinarian of all—but especially his "Indian children."

Letters from Wheelock's students at Moor's Charity School in Lebanon, Connecticut, and later in Hanover, New Hampshire, have been preserved by Dartmouth College. The bulk of the letters are written by the boys and young men who were students in Wheelock's school and who eventually became teachers in Native communities: Among them are such figures as Joseph Johnson (Mohegan), David and Jacob Fowler (Montaukett), and Hezekiah Calvin (Delaware). Some letters also exist from the young women who attended the school for a certain period. These serve as a moving testament to the loneliness and other difficulties experienced by the students in Wheelock's school. Whatever his own assessments were, it is clear from these surviving letters that the Native perspective was quite different.

Wheelock's school, which was hardly an ideal situation for Native Americans, was the most visible and active missionary effort to reach Native populations in the mid-eighteenth century. It came as a shock, then, when (in the early 1770s) Wheelock publicly pronounced the effort a failure, moved his school to Hanover, New Hampshire, and focused on educating white students as missionaries in the newly founded Dartmouth College. His decision prompted reactions of surprise and dismay from many, not least his former student Samson Occom, who accused Wheelock of misappropriating funds and betraying Indians generally. It was arguably as a response to this betrayal that Joseph Johnson, Samson Occom, and other of Wheelock's former students went on to found a Native Christian community called Brotherton in upstate New York in the 1770s and early 1780s. This community, which found a home on

---

16. See Wheelock, *Plain and Faithful Narrative*, 25.

land donated by the Oneida Tribe, was formed explicitly to give voice to Native Christians without the dominance of white missionaries.

Shortly after the American Revolution, Brotherton was joined by the community of New Stockbridge, led by Hendrick Aupaumut. Aupaumut, born in 1757, was not a boarding school student; he was a member of the Native community of Stockbridge in western Massachusetts to which Sergeant had ministered until his death in 1749 and in which Sergeant had attempted (and failed) to establish his own boarding school. Although the town had been formed explicitly as an experiment in cross-cultural exchange, the experiment quickly unraveled as white landowners sought to expand their holdings through shady transactions that were to the distinct disadvantage of their Indian neighbors. Shortly after the American Revolution, and after years of growing tensions between the English settlers and the Native population of Stockbridge, Aupaumut and most of the remaining Stockbridge Indians concluded that their future was no longer in that community; they believed that it lay instead in the Christian Indian community then being formed in upstate New York.

Any exploration of early Native literacies in New England must recognize above all the extraordinary contribution of the Brotherton and New Stockbridge founders to early literature. Their writings included here illustrate how effectively these indigenous leaders used their familiarity with English cultural practices (most notably alphabetic literacy) to forge what they saw as a stronger, "better" Indian community that could balance various knowledge systems, including more traditional literacies. It is with these writers that our brief chronology of early Native literacies ends. It is, however, one goal of this collection to persuade readers that the significance and vitality of early Native texts has never ended. The texts and essays in this collection attest to the many ways that Native literacies were, are, and will continue to be an important part of American culture and literature. Although the texts in this anthology have heretofore rarely counted as literature, it is our strong belief that they should.

## Structure of the Anthology

We began our introduction by noting the fragmented nature of the early Native archive, the many special collections, museums, and state archives where early Indian materials can be found today. Modern anthologies cannot (and this collection does not aim to) bring together scattered materials into one "master" archive. The ongoing work of tribal historians, academic scholars, linguists, and others, however, attests to the fact that new understanding can come from unexpected places. Literary scholars can learn about Native tropes from discussions of baskets; Wampanoag linguists can revitalize their twenty-first-century language by drawing on Eliot's mission writings of the 1660s.[17] We hope, then, that by presenting a range of materials for our readers, we expand the ways of knowing not only about the Native past of New England but also about the basis for its future.

The reader will encounter the primary texts collected in this anthology in three or four ways. First, we have organized the selections into chapters focused on separate tribal groups. From the many ways that we could have organized these texts (chronologically, generically, and so forth), we have chosen to group two or three texts with their accompanying essays in their specific cultural context. Each chapter, then, can serve as a free-standing exploration of the literary practices of a particular group, set within the more comprehensive study of early New England Native literacies that the collection presents as a whole.

Within these chapters each document or artifact is prefaced by a brief headnote describing its physical characteristics or the means of its production. The headnote is followed by the edited text, which is sometimes accompanied by a photograph of the original. Finally, each text is accompanied by a short critical essay that situates the text in its cultural, historical, and literary context and offers an expert reading of the text. The accompanying essays, which are intended as a means for the uninitiated to explore these materials, also provide strategies for introducing them into the classroom. None of the essays is meant to offer the final word on any text; they represent, instead, a variety of approaches and interpretations—even some that conflict.[18] Although we perceive this collection as speaking most directly to students of literature, the contributors are drawn from a variety of disciplines, and even those scholars who are most closely aligned may differ in their approach to mediation, the definition of literacy, or the glossing of primary texts. The result is a productive friction that suggests possible readings of long-neglected primary texts, inviting new readers of the texts to construct their own understanding of early Native literacies.

We have asked the contributors to use as light a hand as possible in editing the primary texts. In general, spelling and punctuation have been preserved. For manuscript materials, insertions and strikeouts have been indicated. The result may at times seem inelegant, but we believe that minimal editorial in-

---

17. See Hinton and Hale, *Green Book*.

18. For ways of theorizing alternative Native literacy systems, see Warkentin, "In Search of 'The Word of the Other,'" 1–27; Boone and Mignolo, *Writing without Words*; McMullen and Handsman, *Key into the Language of Woodsplint Baskets*.

tervention yields a primary text that allows readers and researchers to gain the clearest and closest view of the original document.[19]

Finally, those who are interested in a Native past must look to modern Native communities. From the Internet to books, articles, film, novels, powwows, community ceremonies, and many other forms, Native people of contemporary New England have much to say about the ways the past informs the present and the future. We hope that this anthology will serve in some small way to educate all of us to listen and learn in that ongoing conversation.

---

19. For a comparison of different editorial styles, contrast the edition of Samson Occom's "Temperance and Morality Sermon" prepared by Heather Bouwman and included herein with the version that Bouwman edited with several graduate students included in the Early Americas Digital Archive.

# 1 · The Mohegans

BEFORE ENGLISH contact, the Mohegans of Connecticut—certainly one of the most widely recognized of the New England tribes today (thanks, in no small part, to the Mohegan Sun Casino)—were closely tied to the Pequot Tribe, having migrated with them from the upper Hudson River Valley some time around 1500. They split from the Pequots under the leadership of their sachem Uncas, who brought the Mohegans into alliance with the English colonists against the Pequots in the infamous Pequot War of 1637. Throughout the 1630s and 1640s, using his English allies to reinforce his position against neighboring tribes, Uncas led his people against the Narragansetts. During King Philip's War, from 1675 to 1676, the Mohegans, who remained loyal to the English, suffered significant losses. By the time of Uncas's death in 1683, substantial portions of Mohegan land had been sold or leased to colonists, and the tribe was struggling to survive. Even so, today Uncas is remembered as an extraordinary leader who dedicated his life to protecting his people against encroachment and establishing the importance of the Mohegans, or "Wolf People," as a distinct group.

By the mid-eighteenth century, the tribe was divided over a series of issues related to succession and land use. Much to the resentment of many Mohegans, the colonial Connecticut government was using a heavy hand to direct tribal affairs. In 1769 the tribe refused to accept as sachem Ben Uncas III, who was backed by the colonial government. They preferred no sachem to one not only assigned to them by outsiders but also seemingly inclined to sell off Mohegan lands. The tribe was embroiled in a series of disputes related to lands that had been put under the protection of the family of John Mason. Mason, a local colonist, had tried to protect Mohegan interests before he finally turned over the deed to Mohegan land to the government of Connecticut. It was in this tumultuous mid-century period that Samson Occom converted to Christianity and sought out the spiritual and intellectual support of the Reverend Eleazar Wheelock. Eventually becoming an ordained minister and a fierce advocate for the rights of his people, Occom was one of the founders of the Brotherton Community in upstate New York.

Despite the significant reduction in its population throughout the nineteenth century, the Mohegan Nation is today a vibrant, federally recognized tribe whose community centers on the Mohegan Church, a structure built in

1831 to maintain the land base of the Mohegan people and to celebrate their commitment to Christianity as a means of preserving their Mohegan identity. Among those who were central to this effort was Occom's sister, Lucy Tantaquidgeon. In 1931, John, Harold, and Gladys Tantaquidgeon established the Tantaquidgeon Indian Museum down the road from the church. It still stands today as a community resource celebrating what Melissa Tantaquidgeon Zobel has called "the lasting of the Mohegans." [1]

## Suggested Reading

Brooks, Lisa. "The Common Pot: Indigenous Writing and the Reconstruction of Space in the Northeast." Ph.D. diss. Cornell University, 2004.

"Brothertown Indian Nation." Brothertown Indians of Wisconsin website. Available at http://www.brothertownindians.org. Accessed 25 and 30 June, 2006.

Fawcett, Melissa [Melissa Tantaquidgeon Zobel]. *The Lasting of the Mohegans.* Uncasville, Conn.: Mohegan Tribe, 1995.

Mohegan Tribe website. Available at http://www.mohegan.nsn.us. Accessed 15 and 30 June, 2006.

Oberg, Michael Leroy. *Uncas: First of the Mohegans.* Ithaca, N.Y.: Cornell University Press, 2003.

Occom, Samson. *The Collected Writings of Samson Occom, Mohegan: Literature and Leadership in Eighteenth-Century Native America.* Ed. Joanna Brooks. New York: Oxford University Press, 2006.

---

1. See Fawcett [Melissa Tantaquidgeon Zobel], *Lasting of Mohegans.*

Figure 1-1. Letter of Instruction from Oanhekoe, sachem of the Mohegan Indians, 14 July 1703. (By permission of the Honorable Michael Willoughby and the University of Nottingham Department of Manuscripts and Special Collections.)

Letter of Instruction from Oanhekoe
Sachem of the Mohegah Indians in New
England, Dated the 14th July 1703
To Mr Nicholas Hallam of Connecticut in the
Indian Language.
The Interpretation is as follows.

My Loving Neighbour, Mr Nicholas Hallam,
I am informd you are bound for Old
England.   Lett me request you to make me
& my Condition known to the Great L. Anne
& to her Noble Council, first of our
Hereditary Right to ye Soyll & Royaltys
of our Dominion & Territorys before
the English came into ye Country, insomuch
that all due Loyalty & Obedience by
your People is not conferrd on us by the
English, but by ye Gods, who gave us a
Token as an Earnest & pledge of our
Happy Reign here, & allso (as our Old
Seers construed) a more ample Reign in ye
othe Region:   Wherefore the Gods had
sent to that Royall Family one of
their own Tobacco pipes, which strange
Wonderment was taken upon the Beach
at Seabrook, or thereabouts, it being
like Ivory with two Stemms & the Boll
in ye Middle.   This Strange Pipe, not
made by man, is kept Choicer than
Gold from Generation to Generation.
It animates all the Royall Soeiety with
a full perswasion that ye said Token is
sufficient Evidence that they shall

sitt amongst y^e Gods in the long Hunting-
house & there smoak tobacco, as the
highest point of Honor & Dignity, & where
there will be great ffeasting of Fatt
Bear, Deer, & Moose, all Joy & Myrth
to welcom their Entertainment &c.
Allso in y^e Reign of King Charles the
Second of blessed Memory, his Majesty
sent us a Token vizt. a Bible & a
Sword, which present we thankfully
accepted, & keep them in y^e Treasury
as choice as we do y^e aforesaid Gods Pipe,
hoping it may be a Safeguard & a
Shield to Defend us, & we in process of
Time may reap great benefitt thenby,
& attain to y^e Knowledg of the true
& Living God. But of late I meet
with great Descouragements & know not
what will become of our People by reason
of Oppression.       The Court of Hertford
I understand have given all my planting
& Hunting land away to Colchester, &
to New London. So that if I Obtain
not Relief from y^e Great Queens Ma^ty
my People will be in Templation to
scatter from me, & flee to the Eastward
Indians, the ffrench's ffriends, & the
English's Enimys.      Pray S^r remember
my Love & Service to y^e Great Queen
Anne

# Letter of Instruction from
# Oanhekoe, Sachem of the Mohegan Indians in
# New England, 14 July 1703

## OWENECO

The letter is in black ink written on two sheets of folio (6 inches by 12 inches). The writing is fluent and regular, with abbreviations and orthographic conventions that suggest a familiarity with such forms. Oweneco's "mark" at the end appears to be drawn in the same hand or by someone equally confident with a pen.

To Mr. Nicholas Hallam of Connecticut,[2] in the Indian Language.
The Interpretation is as follows:

My Loving Neighbour, Mr Nicholas Hallam,
    I am informd you are bound for Old England. Lett me request you to make me & my Condition known to the Great Q. Anne[3] & to her Noble Council,[4] first of our Hereditary Right to ye Soyll and Royalltys of our Dominion & Territorys before the English came into ye Country, insomuch that all due Loyallty & Obedience by our people is not conferrd on us by the English, but by ye Gods, who gave us a Token as an Earnest & pledge of our Happy Reign here, & allso (as our Old Seers Construed) a more ample Reign in ye othe[r] region: Wherefore the Gods had Sent to that Royall Family[5] one of their own Tobacco pipes, which strange wonderment was taken upon the Beach at Seabrook,[6] or thereabouts, it being like Ivory, with two Stemms to the Boll in ye Middle. This Strange Pipe, not made by man, is kept Choicer than Gold from Generation to Generation. It Animates all the Royall Society[7] with a full perswasion that ye

---

2. Nicholas Hallam and his brother John were prominent local figures who had already challenged the powers of the Connecticut courts and appealed to the Privy Council over their mother's will.

3. The reference is to the queen of England (1665–1714).

4. Her Majesty's Most Honourable Privy Council was—and still is—the most important body of advisors to the monarch.

5. As sachem, or leader, and son of the influential figure Uncas, Oweneco presents his family as the equivalent to the hereditary monarchy of England. The early colonists began this convention of treating sachems as equivalent to kings or sovereigns and referring to them as such.

6. One of the first white settlements in the area, it was usually referred to as Saybrook.

7. See note 5.

Said Token is Sufficient Evidence that they shall Sitt amongst ye Gods in the Long Hunting-house[8] & there Smook Tobacco, as the highest point of Honor and Dignity, & where there will be great ffeasting of Fatt Bear, Deer, & Moose, all Joy and Myrth to wellcom their Entertainment &c.

Also in ye Reign of King Charles the Second of Blessed Memory,[9] his Majesty sent us a Token, vizt. A Bible & a Sword, which present we thankfully accepted, & keep them in ye Treasury as choice as we do ye aforesaid Gods Pipe, hoping it may be a Safeguard & a Shield to defend us, and we in process of Time may reap great Benefitt thereby and attain to ye Knowledge of the true & Living God. But of late I meet with great Descouragements, & know not what will become of our People by reason of Oppression. The Court of Hertford[10] I understand have given all my planting & Hunting Land away to Colchester & to New London. So that if I Obtain not Relief from ye Great Queens Ma[jes]ty my People will be in Temptation to Scatter from me, & to flee to the Eastward Indians,[11] the ffrench's ffriends, & the English's Enimys. Pray Sir remember my Love and Service to ye Great Queen Anne & he[r] Noble Council.

July 14[th] 1703

Oanhekoe [His mark]

The true Interpretation of Oanhekoe's Grievance & Narration, by me John Stanton[12] Interpreter Gent[leman]

---

8. Oweneco is envisaging the afterlife as a more comfortable version of earthly life. Algonquian Indians built dwellings with a frame made from bent young trees and roofed with bark and grasses, often housing more than one family.

9. The reference is to the king of England (1630–85).

10. Hertford, Colchester, and New London were developing townships. The many individual agreements between their members and the Indians resulted in a morass of conflicting legal claims. The local courts were based on English law, and the colony of Connecticut as a whole was under a charter from the English Crown. Complications arose when the independence that the colony believed it was granted under this charter conflicted with the larger authority of the Crown to contend with foreign nations, including Indian tribes. Consequently, Oweneco appeals to the queen and the Privy Council as the final authority above the local courts. Confusing matters was the fact that he and others made many private land deals while acting as sovereign head of state.

11. Queen Anne's War (1702–13), one episode in the long-running rivalry between the French and English as colonial powers, saw attacks in Maine by Abenakis and Iroquois, abetted by the French.

12. John Stanton (1614–1713) was a prominent citizen and the son of the well-known interpreter Thomas Stanton.

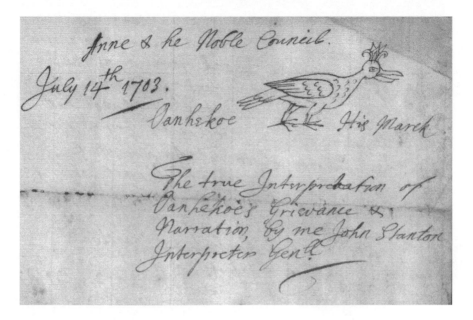

## Letter of Instruction from Oanhekoe, Sachem of the Mohegan Indians, 14 July 1703

### DAVID MURRAY

This letter, which was designed to play a part in a political process, raises interesting questions about the representation of Indian views under circumstances in which English is the language of legal and political power and the unequal power relationships between white people and Indians have been exacerbated and perpetuated by language differences. Since written English was—and still is—the means of access to virtually all areas of influence and power, Indians who lacked English skills and literacy depended on white intermediaries or facilitators to be heard or to have any political agency in their dealings with the increasingly dominant white settlers and their governments. These intermediaries (some Indians and people of mixed blood also acquired the skills to assume this role) had their own agendas, which are often difficult to disentangle from those of the people for whom they were speaking. A missionary, for instance, may have wanted to enhance the Christian sentiments of the dying Indian whose deathbed statements he recorded and published. A translator may have subtly adapted Indian ideas to European perceptions in an effort to present them in an understandable way. In some cases, of course, Indian statements and agreements were simply fabricated, but even in cases involving the most honest and benevolent intentions, the act of "speaking for" brought with it the limitations and contradictions of the paternalistic and protective stance that successive white authorities adopted. The stance entailed the assumption that Indians needed help not just in expressing their views in English but also in knowing what they really wanted and where their best interests truly lay. Since much of the early Indian writing and self-representation that has survived is inevitably the result of such paternalistic intervention, it is the—usually invisible and often underestimated—role of the facilitators that must be considered and that has become of increasing significance for critics and historians.

With Indian views historically silenced or misrepresented, there is an understandably increasing desire to identify an authentic Native "voice" in Indian texts of the past. Because of the problems outlined here, however, it is crucial to pay careful attention to the many processes of production of any Indian text. These texts can range from an actual written piece that is entirely authored and authorized by a literate English-speaking Indian to an account constructed through processes of translation, editing, and rewriting over which the Indian speaker has no control. The question then becomes whose text it is and how we are to read it. Increasing awareness that texts of all sorts can benefit from the kind of rhetorical and stylistic analysis and inquiry formerly afforded only to literary texts has allowed (1) a wider range of materials to be treated critically and (2) the question of whether or to what degree a piece of writing is "by" a particular Indian to be explored more productively and less subjectively.[13]

This particular letter, ostensibly from the Mohegan sachem Oanhekoe (or Oweneco, as it is often written) to his neighbor Nicholas Hallam, allows us to identify quite explicitly some of the elements of its creation. Some additional historical context will also help us to weight these elements in deciding to what degree the letter can actually be considered Oweneco's. First of all, the letter acknowledges the presence of a translator, "John Stanton Interpreter, Gent[leman]," a well-known and trusted figure, whose name appears listed as interpreter in the records of many meetings and transactions. Second, it gives evidence of the presence of a white facilitator or intermediary, Nicholas Hallam (described as a neighbor), who will take the letter to London and present a petition to the Privy Council on behalf of the Mohegans. The role of such intermediaries was, of course, sometimes that of honest broker. In other instances, however, although their actions were allegedly performed on behalf of

---

13. To some extent, Arnold Krupat's work on autobiography pioneered the necessary critical skepticism about authorship and production. For later discussions, see D. Murray, *Forked Tongues*, and Wyss, *Writing Indians*. For a more general discussion of the problems of identifying suppressed voices, see J. C. Scott, *Domination*.

and in the name of Indians and were supported by written statements allegedly authored by Indians, neither the actions nor the written statements were clear to the Indians at the time.

Although the letter is addressed by Oweneco to Hallam, it is clearly designed not as a means of communication between the two but as a message for a third party. This is a formal convention, which can be considered a way of authorizing Hallam to make Oweneco's case. When we consider that Hallam may well have initiated and even written the letter, however, it takes on the strange characteristic of a letter written to himself. In any case, what we have is a document that we may suppose to have originated through Hallam's suggestion. Perhaps he proposed that he take to London a letter from Oweneco explaining his grievance and authorizing Hallam to make his case (a letter that is presumably phrased and written by or with the translator Stanton). Somewhere in this process Oweneco spoke in Mohegan, but we do not know when this occurred or what he said. In what sense, then, is the letter Oweneco's? The ultimate sign of authenticity for documents is, of course, the signature or mark (I return to this later), but the larger questions are to what degree in such situations we can identify the presence or voice of an individual Indian and what means we can employ to do so.

One method is to find out as much as we can about the circumstances surrounding the production of the letter, so let us begin this effort with some context. Oweneco, the son of the famous Mohegan sachem Uncas, inherited the lands and powers of his father along with many complex relationships with his white neighbors. In negotiating the changing political situation after the Pequot War and King Philip's War, during which Indian property and rights were whittled away, Uncas and his heirs found it necessary—in fact, indispensable—not only to trade and sell land to white settlers but also to seek the protection of well-disposed white neighbors. This situation hinders our ability to weigh the proportions of paternalism or coercion involved. Not surprisingly, historians have disagreed over the motives of the key figures,[14] several of whom—most notably John Mason (of Pequot massacre fame, or infamy), his descendants, and the missionary James Fitch—were given, or took, control of the land on behalf of Uncas and later Oweneco.

One major problem for the Mohegans was how to ensure their fair treatment under the law. Without knowledge of English, they could never be sure of fair representation, even by their allies. As the Mohegans' lawyer pointed out,

---

14. Francis Jennings (*The Invasion of America*) was one of the first to question the motives and the language of the colonizers. For a very useful account of the background politics of the period, see St. Jean, "Inventing Guardianship."

the English "had the penning" of all their documents and no doubt "took care to express matters favorably for their own interest."[15] In the case of Oweneco, this general problem was exacerbated by his weakness for alcohol, under the influence of which he was prone to put his signature to documents that he later regretted having signed. The Mohegans persistently complained of his irresponsible behavior when he was drunk. According to records, he rewarded two men who rescued him from drowning while he was inebriated by giving them land. At one point he even assigned his rights to members of the Mason family, whom he trusted, to prevent being exploited in the future. Here again, of course, we must remember that all his recorded statements come via the same processes of mediation, so the line between abuse of his trust and paternalistic protection may not always be clear. Nevertheless, Oweneco seems to have both actively sought the protection of his interests by certain white figures and experienced exploitation by whites. His behavior remained problematic, and he seems to have ended his life as somewhat of a vagrant.

Oweneco's letter is interesting historically because, although it deals with one particular dispute between the colonists and the Mohegans, it appeals to the larger authority of the Crown. The Mason family was eventually unable to prevent the actions of the Connecticut General Court and the governor, who took power over those areas of land reserved for Mohegans under earlier agreements. Thus, a decision was made, perhaps by Mason or Hallam (the bearer of the letter to London), to draw up a petition to Queen Anne and her Privy Council. The letter would be the authority and justification for Hallam to represent the views of Oweneco and the Mohegans. When Hallam appeared before the Privy Council in December 1703, however, there is mention only of his presenting a memorial, which made the Mohegan case in almost the same language as the letter (not a surprising circumstance, since it is likely that he composed some of each). Later he submitted a detailed affidavit, and eventually a commission was formed, which decided in favor of the Mohegans. This action, which reasserted the power of the Crown over that of the colonial governments, was an important one in the ensuing and long-running Mohegan land controversy. It can also be viewed as having a larger historical significance in that it set the pattern not only for later disputes between the states and the federal government but also for the role of the Crown in Canadian legal disputes over Native rights. For our purposes, however— to avoid neglecting Oweneco in our account of the larger narrative and thereby repeating the historical neglect of the Indian actors themselves—Oweneco himself must be the focus.

---

15. Quoted in St. Jean, "Inventing Guardianship," 374.

In order to explore the actual role of Oweneco in the letter, it is worth examining just what the letter does. In language and style of address, it adopts the conventional English forms of courtesy and formality, appearing to be clearly addressed over the head of Hallam to the Queen and Privy Council. The point of the complaint really appears only in the final few sentences, which also contain the very clear warning that if the grievances are not redressed, Oweneco will be unable to command the loyalty of his people. Oweneco's people, he warns, will defect to the eastern Indians, who are (as he pointedly reminds Queen Anne via Hallam) allies of the French and enemies of the English. Self-interest, in addition to justice, is suggested—with perhaps a touch of a threat—as a reason for action by the Crown.

If the main political point of the letter becomes apparent only at the end, then what is the purpose of the rest of the letter? The first part takes pains to establish the relationship between Oweneco as sachem and the monarch in England; it is carefully balanced between an assertion of his own status and a polite recognition of the ultimate powers of the Queen. The first and crucial claim is of Oweneco's hereditary right to his lands—a right that precedes any recognition of his rights under the English Crown ("not conferrd on us by the English, but by ye Gods"). Most interesting here is the *way* he demonstrates his credentials and rights—by the display of objects and their related stories. The "Token" of his rights to land and power is a pipe of sacred origins, given to express the generosity of the gods to the Mohegan royal family, now and in the future, when they will sit feasting on "Fatt Bear, Deer, & Moose." It is one of the gods' "own" pipes, a "strange wonderment" found on the beach and "not made by man," and it has been kept "Choicer than Gold from Generation to Generation." The possession of this object and the relation of its origin are crucial credentials in establishing Oweneco's legitimacy in Indian eyes. Oweneco then moves on to demonstrate his legitimacy in English eyes by invoking an existing political alliance, or at least a connection, with Charles II, which he does through the parallel method of using an object and a story. The Bible and sword presented by Charles (the importance of which, like that of the pipe, lies in their origins and symbolic significance) are explicitly associated with the pipe. The Mohegans "keep them in ye treasury as choice as we do ye aforesaid Gods Pipe." Established here is a parity that falls short of the subservience that might be expected, and by the same token the "Gods" coexist with "the true & Living God" of the Christians, to whom the Mohegans may be brought "in process of Time."

Altogether, some two-thirds of the letter is taken up in this establishment of credentials. This, I believe, is extremely significant in our estimation of the degree to which the letter is by Oweneco and the degree to which it is by

Hallam or others. I would argue that the presence, indeed the dominance, of this Indian form of validation reflects Oweneco's input. Hallam would have had a much clearer sense of the need to put forth the grievance clearly and early, as is confirmed in the Privy Council records. There is no mention of the actual presentation of Oweneco's letter; the petition that Hallam presents on behalf of the Indians is very close to the wording of the last part of the letter, but it omits the content of the first part altogether. Hallam's statement that the Mohegans have "acknowledged the Kings and Queens of England as their Sovereigns, and have been ever ready to pay all due Obedience and to yield Subjection to them"[16] is not quite the same as the parity suggested in the letter. In addition, Hallam presents a moving account of the desperate situation of the Mohegan people that goes beyond the diplomatic niceties; he describes encountering fifty or sixty Mohegans, driven from their land, in the snow, "in a very poor and naked Condition, many of them crying lamentably."[17] This can be seen as part of a larger pattern, continued over the centuries, of presenting the Indians as objects of pity rather than—as the tone of the letter conveys—as equals demanding no more than their rights.

The final significant element of the letter is the signature or mark. The convention of requiring a mark by those who were unable to write reflects the importance of proving the physical presence and agreement of the person in whose name the text is written. Clearly, however, even this convention is subject to abuse, since those who cannot read do not know for certain the content of the document to which they put their mark.[18] Because of Oweneco's importance as sachem and his close involvement with white people, a number of letters and deeds bear his mark. It is interesting to compare them with the mark that appears on this letter. In general, the marks of signatories in the Northeast seem to be pictorial representations. John De Forest, who describes the marks as "totems,"[19] provides a number of examples, including marks by Oweneco. Here, as in most of the marks by Oweneco that I have seen, we have a bird drawn in rudimentary form. Each bird is different, as the examples in Figure 1-2 indicate.

But when we look at the letter under examination, we see a mark that

---

16. Hallam, Memorial Relating to the Complaints of the Mohegan Indians.

17. Hallam, Affidavit.

18. In some cases this issue is recognized in phrases such as this: "The above written Instruction was distinctly read over to the several Indians subscribing, and they carefully understood the same before signing" (Penobscot Indians, Letter to Joseph Dudley, 1713.).

19. *History of the Indians*, 163, 494. The word *totem*, which has a complex history, is taken from forms of the word used by the Chippewa to describe family or residence groups, and the visual aspect of the word seems to have been secondary to that sense. It is not clear that all marks, even in Algonquian groups, were totemic.

Figure 1-2. Oweneco's marks

consists of an altogether different creature, one drawn with great aplomb and topped with what seems to be a crown! We can, therefore assume, I think, that this mark is the work of the writer of the letter rather than the work of Oweneco, which suggests that the letter may be a contemporary copy of an original to which Oweneco put his usual simple mark. Another possibility is that this is the original but that the writer decided it would be better to have a rather more "royal" signature for presentation to the queen.[20]

In what sense, then, can we say that this is Oweneco's letter? As I have argued, the weight given to Indian rather than European forms of establishing credentials together with the assumption of equal sovereignty (both of which are absent from Hallam's petition) suggest Oweneco's own agenda, an agenda that was followed by the actual producers of the written text. Even so, we can make only an informed estimate of Oweneco's role. In this particular case, we do not even have Oweneco's mark, which—misleading though it can often be as evidence of full authorship—is usually seen as the indisputable trace of physical presence. We have, instead, a copy of a lost original, which would itself have been ambiguous evidence of Oweneco's authorship and understanding.

We might be reminded of Gary Snyder's *Myths and Texts*, a series of poems dealing with Indian myths and the texts created from them. Near the end, after encountering what we take to be Coyote's voice, we find the word *signed* followed by an empty bracket, where we would expect his mark or signature. Like the trickster Coyote, the actual presence and voice of this particular Mohegan Indian may ultimately elude us. Nevertheless, we have seen possibilities for marshaling evidence about forms of expression, along with historical evidence, to make informed estimations about where this voice may, and may not, be found.

---

20. This copy of the letter found its way, at a later date, into the hands of a member of the English aristocratic Willoughby family, in whose papers (lodged at the University of Nottingham) it was located; it seems to have been collected as a mere oddity (Nottingham, Mi C 37/1). I have been unable to locate either an original from which this version may have been copied or any other version or copy.

# Diary, 1773

## Joseph Johnson

This diary is currently housed in the Manuscripts and Archives Division of the New York Public Library, Astor, Lenox and Tilden Foundations.[21] Measuring 4.5 inches by 7.125 inches (11.5 centimeters by 18 centimeters), the diary consists of seven sheets of paper sewn down the middle with brown thread, forming fourteen pages. It is attached to Johnson's farewell sermon to the Farmington Indians, which he delivered on his last day at Farmington (1 February 1773). The diary and the sermon are sewn together with white thread; this may have occurred at a later date, since the first page of the sermon is considerably worn.

The handwriting of the diary is very regular, with entries running the full length of the paper, leaving no margins on the page. Johnson occasionally separates entries with an extended horizontal line. The first page of the diary is quite worn, especially at the bottom; the diary is stained throughout and occasionally marked with inkblots and smudging, but there are virtually no revisions or alterations to the text of the diary. As is typical of a daily record, the handwriting, spacing, and even heaviness of the ink vary somewhat among the entries.

Wendsday, the 18th of November, AD 1772

Notwithstanding the good Entertainments with which I was Entertained the Evening past, they asked me only Seven pence. It is about Sunrise, So I go. This morn, I Crosed the Hartford ferry just before nine. I payd only one Copper for my ferrage. I Breakfasted at the house of the Rev[d] M[r] Patten Son in law of the Rev[d] Doct[r] Wheelock. I was recieved very kindly by him, and his wife, as if I was one of the family.[22]

I tarryed in Hartford about 1 hour and an half, then I Sat out for to vizit the Farmington Indians. I went 3 Miles. There I was much at a stand whether to

---

21. The diary is reprinted by permission of the Manuscripts and Archives Division, the New York Public Library, Astor, Lenox and Tilden Foundations. This edition is drawn from L. Murray, *To Do Good*, with permission of University of Massachusetts Press. Punctuation absent at the ends of sentences has been inserted, some internal punctuation has been deleted, and lowercased first words of sentences have been capitalized. Words have not been altered, inserted, or deleted. For full editorial practice, see ibid., 8–9; and for more complete annotation, ibid., 151–67.

22. The Reverend William Patten (1738–75) was the husband of Ruth, Eleazar Wheelock's step-daughter.

call at Famington or no, as my design was to go to the Mohawk Country. There I Stood at a Stand some time. At last [. . .]²³ Came 3 men. I enqured of them, whether it was much out of the way, to go by Farmington, to go at Canaan, through Norfolk. They told me, that now it was the nighest way I could go from here. So I concluded to go by Farmington, the more because I was desired by the Rev ᵈ Samson Occom. So here I [. . .]I dined Seven miles from Hartford at a Tavern, where much people were Exerciseing in a Military way. I arrived at Farmington about 3 in the afternoon, dined again, at one Elijah Wiempy's.²⁴ I desired the Indians to meet together, that I might read the Rev ᵈ Samson Occoms Sermon, Preached at the [. . .] of Moses Paul who was Executed the Second . . . of Septe[. . .] 1772 at N[. . .].²⁵

This afternoon I spent, that is the remainder at the house of Elijah Wiempey. This Evening Several Indians assembled themselves together at the house of Thomas Occurrum. I read the Sermon, which Mʳ Occom Preacht, at the Execution of Moses Paul; they heard with much Solmnity, after that we Sang, after that I spoke little of the goodness of God to all his Creatures, to us in a Perticular manner. Than I Acquainted them of a Proposal, which Mʳ Occom proposed Concerning my keeping a School amongst them if the School was void of a Teacher. They all rejoiced, to think of the Proposal. They Continued asking me if I could Content myself with them, so after we had Prayed; we Concluded the ensueing Day to go their overseer, to get his Approbation and to Confirm all. So we retired, much satisfyed, in the Exercises of our Meeting, to our several homes. This evening, I tarry at Elijah Wimpeys.

Thirdsay, the 19 ᵗʰ of November, AD 1772

I spent chief of this day in walking about the fields of Elijah Wiempy's. This Evening was Examined by their Overseer, Rev ᵈ Timothy Pitkin,²⁶ preaching at the town of Farmington, and he said I was Capable of the bussiness. I read, & wrote, before several. Some of the headmen of the Indian tribe was present.

---

23. Ellipses in brackets signify illegible text.

24. Elijah Wimpey (1734–ca. 1802), who was married to Jerusha, was a veteran of the French and Indian War; he later became a trustee of Brotherton, New York.

25. The last line of the first page of the diary, which is without a cover, is worn off, as are various words toward the bottom of the page. Occom's sermon at the execution of Moses Paul, from the text "For the wages of sin is death" (Rom. 6:23), went through many editions after its initial 1772 publication in New Haven; see also Johnson's letter to Moses Paul, published in March 1772 (reprinted in L. Murray, To Do Good, 141–46).

26. The Reverend Timothy Pitkin (1727–1812) served as Farmington's minister from 1752 to 1785.

Fryday, the 20<sup>th</sup> of November, AD 1772

This morn, I wrote for the tribe a Letter to the Rev<sup>d</sup> Samson Occom.

    This day had Convenient Opportunity to send Letters to my Native home. Sent two. One I wrote here, the other, at the house of the Rev<sup>d</sup> M<sup>r</sup> Timothy Pitkins. I sent for my [Vester?], I tarried in the town till after Sun set. Than I returned to the house of Elijah Wiempey, whire I at present reside.

Saturday, the 21<sup>st</sup> of November, AD 1772

Nothing to the Purpose this day. In the latter Part, I went a guning, kill'd one fowl.

The First Lords Day from Home
Sunday, the 22<sup>d</sup> of November, AD 1772

Went to hear M<sup>r</sup>. Pitkin. The after part of the day he preach't from Hebrews XII.14, follow peace with all men, and holiness, without which no man Shall See the Lord.

Monday, the 23<sup>d</sup> of November, AD 1772

This morning Opened a School in Farmington, among the Indian tribe. Had 9 Indian Children. At Even, I went over to the town, to See M<sup>r</sup> Culver. I returned to Elijah's.

Tuesday, the 24<sup>th</sup> of November, AD 1772

This day had 10 Indian Children.

Wendsday, the 25<sup>th</sup> of November, AD 1772

This day had 11 Indian Children, and one English lad, Named Simeon Barny. This day afternoon I recieved a Letter from the Rev<sup>d</sup>. M<sup>r</sup>. Samson Occom & from Jacob Fowler Schoolmaster at Grotton.[27]

Thirsdday, the 26<sup>th</sup> of November, AD 1772

Kept School as Ussual, nothing remarkable.

---

27. Jacob Fowler (Montauk, 1750–87?) had been a fellow student of Johnson's at Eleazar Wheelock's school.

Fryday, the 27th of November, AD 1772

Kept School as Ussual. At Evening held a Meeting at the house of Samuel Adams, a Singing Meeting.[28] At the close we Concluded to have A singing Meeting twice in a week, that is, Tuesday night, and Fryday night, also we agreed further to spend Some time for Publick worship together, and we appointed, and Set apart, the Sabbath Evenings for that purpose, that is to Sing, pray, and give a word of Exhortation or Spend Some part of it in Reading some books of Edification.

Saturday, the 28th of November, AD 1772

Kept the school in the forepart of the day, in the after part, went over to the Town. Got Paper.

Sabbath Day, the 29th of November, AD 1772

I spent Chief of the time in reading. Very stormy indeed. This Evening, we meet together at the house of Thomas Occurrums. We sang, Prayed, & Conversed about Approaching Death, and the Consequences, if we die Christless, and the great happiness if we have an Interest in Him, which alone Can make us have any Pleasing thoughts of Death, Judgment, & a happy Eternity. Before we parted, I heard several of the grown Persons read, both Sex, Married and Single. I tarried at Elijahs. 2nd Sunday.

Monday, the 30th of November, AD 1772

This day had 16 Scholars, of which 3 were English. This day I left Elijah Wiempys, and board at the house of Solomon Mossucks.[29]

Tuesday, the 1st Day of December, AD 1772

Kept School as Ussual. At Even, we had a singing meeting, which was attended with much Earnestness; had a very full Assembly.
    Concluded with Prayer as Ussual.

Wendsday, the 2d of December, AD 1772

Kept School as Ussual. After I had dismissed the children, I sat in the School house Some time. About dusk one of the chiefs of this town, and one of the young men, brought a Stragling man to me, and desired me to Examine him.

---

28. Samuel Adams (1734–ca. 1800) was the son of Adam, a Quinnipiac. Samuel was married to Hannah Squamp (Wangunk) and had served in the army in 1756 and 1762. His son Solomon married Olive Occom, Samson's daughter.
29. Solomon Mossuck (1723–1802) and his wife, Eunice, both church members, were the parents of Daniel, who attended Wheelock's school and later fought in the American Revolution.

I thought myself not Capable, not knowing the Customs of People Enough. However I did my best, and upon Examination, he enform'd us that he was a Spanish Indian, and was a Servant man to one M^r Durfy of Stonington in this Government, and he further told us, that before he Came away, his Master abused him very much, and gave him leave to go away, not telling him when to return, and it was with much difficulty, we got So much Inteligence from him. We took several methods, Sometime intreating, at another threatening, for he Seem'd to be somewhat delirious, or in other words Crazy. But I did my uttermost Endeavour that he should not be abused, as it seemed to me that all there design, was to make a sport of him. But I remembered Joseph & his brethren, how Joseph Said, for I fear God, do this.[30] And I remembered Our Saviour, when he was brought before Pilate, he answered not a word. My heart was arous'd with Compassion towards the Pitifull Object, and as I had Considerable Influence in this Place I endeavour'd to use it, for his safety. And after we had Examined him, at the school house, alone, he was led to another place, whire another of the chiefs dwelt. There I Spoke boldly, on his behalf, and desired them to require no further Inteligence from him, and use him as becoming rational Creatures or Christians. For my part I must be gone, So[?] I went out, & they Said they would not abuse him, and would harken to all my advice, & words. As Soon as I went out I got about 2 rods from the house, one of the chiefs followed me, and Said, I'll go with you. So he accompanied me, to the place I went, and he Conversed all the way, as we walked. He told me, that he was very intimate with my father in time of war. He exprest much Regard for him, and Said he was My fathers waiter, and told of Several Engagements, where he accompanied my father. He gave my father, the Tittle of Captain in all his Discourse,[31] and after all he acquainted me most freely the Special regards he had for me also, and assurd me that I had more that loved me now, truely than Ever I had my life time before. He said that all was well pleased that I made a Stop here to Spend the winter with them, and many Expressions of Love He Shewed me, till we returnd. Also he told me, what they had privately talked Concerning me, what they proposed to do if I would Comply, &c. &c. &c. One thing I intend to remember for time to Come, about 3 Cows

---

30. "And Joseph said unto them the third day, This do, and Live: for I fear God" (Gen. 42:18). When Joseph's brethren came to him to buy corn in time of famine, they did not recognize the brother they had sold into exile out of jealousy. Eventually, Joseph forgave them and invited them to live with him.

31. Johnson's father, also named Joseph, served for the British in the French and Indian War. In 1757 he was given a special commission to choose and lead twenty-six Indian scouts in an investigation of Lake George; he was promoted to sergeant in 1758. For a letter he wrote to his wife, see L. Murray, *To Do Good*, 25–26.

and worth nothing, took her out of the mire, had nothing but Jacknife, &c. &c. &c.[32]

### Thirsday, the 3ᵈ day of December, AD 1772

This morning after we had tended family worship, I made 3 gamuts or Singing Books, that is, Cut them out, & sewed them together. I began to write down the rules in one. The indians are all desireous of haveing Gamuts, but I am in Continual hurry. Nevertheless, I purpose to furnish them with Singing books as Soon as time will admit.[33] I just dismissed my Scholars who was very regular the day past, and Several Seem to be in Earnest, to learn. I cant help but take Special notice of Indians in this town, and therefore I enter few lines, here, that for time to Come I may look & remember.

I confess that the Lord has prospered my ways, and guided my doubtfull Steps hitherto. Here he has brought me, and placed me amidst a strang Nation, and he has given me favour in their Eyes. I have been used with much Respects in the Several places whire I have been, but much more here. I fear more than belongs to me, but God grant me Grace in my heart, that I may Serve him So much the more here.

Our Custom in the school is to Pray morning & Evening. This Even, I talked to my Scholars before we Sang about our duty to god, and Sat before them the rewards of God to those that Serve him, & Love Him, & so on. Spoke of the Day of Judgment, & the Transactions of that day, as is made known to us by the word of God. They atten'd with great solemnity, and reverence. So we sang, Prayed, & then dismissed them. But now it is almost dusk, alone now I think of Mohegan. Friend my mind runs all over Mohegan as I used to, when I personally was there—but I end hoping in due time to be there once more.

It is too dark for me to write much more, but I believe I Can read my own writing. I am as Ussual, the Mohegan Indian, now keeping a School among the Indians at Farmington, in good health, & Endeavouring to use it for the good of my fellow Indians, &c. &c. &c.

---

32. The handwriting here is very unclear, as is the sense. The story about the three cows may be a parable to illustrate the chiefs' plans for Johnson, or it may be a story about Johnson's father's ingenuity and kindness.

33. Published gamuts, or musical instruction books, must have been expensive enough that it was worth Johnson's time to make them by hand. Examples of the genre with which Johnson might have been familiar are William Tansur's *American Harmony* (1769) and *A New and Complete Introduction to the Grounds and Rules of Musick* (1764).

Fryday, the 4<sup>th</sup> Day of December, AD 1772

Last Evening I went to the house of M<sup>r</sup> Wodsworth [34] & Solomon Mossock accompanied me. There I spent the Evening, heard his daughters Sing Several Tunes, and Sang Some at there desire, myself. Very pleasant Evening.

This morning Something airish, kept School as ussual, now it is noon, I have just now dismissed the Scholars. Before School I wrote down the Musical Characters. I bord now at Solomon Mossocks, & must go to dinner. Thus much for the forenoon. This evening held a singing meeting at the house of Thomas Occurrum. Several indians convened together and Some white People. Held the meeting something late. After Prayers we seperated.

Saturday, the 5<sup>th</sup> Day of December, AD 1772

Very pleasant. Rose very early, wrote Considerable before School in My gamut, the first part. Now I am in health, in Continual hurry, my time is fully employed in one sort of exercise or another. Neither do I forget home.

I make it my bussiness on Saturday, always to Catachize the Children, or Scholars, old & young, of both Sex, also Converse about things Eternal, of God, Christ, and the holy Spirit, of things beyound the Grave, &c. Spent chief of this afternoon in writing, and in drawing lines, for my gamut. This evening is very pleasant. I went abroad.

Spent the Evening with Elijah Wiempy. Drank tea, &c. After I left him, I went in to the house of Landlord Wodsworth, & delivered him his Singing Book, & he desired me to set down and warm me. I tarried a Short Space. So I went to my lodging.

Sabbath Day, the 6<sup>th</sup> of December, AD 1772

Very pleasant indeed. I went to meeting, the forepart of the day. I sat below, and the Preacher Preach't from these words.

Jesus saith unto him, I am the way, and the truth, and the Life, no man cometh unto the father but by me. St. John XIV.6. The way blocked up by Sin made accessable now by Christ, in His Life, in His Doctrine, in His example, in his Obedience, in his Death, in His resurrection, in His Exaltation, & in His Intersession.

In the afterpart of the Day, the preacher preach't from these words and grive not the holy Spirit of god, whireby ye are Sealed unto the day of Redemption—

---

34. William Wadsworth was a Tunxis overseer in 1768, and Hezekiah Wadsworth was overseer in 1776. Johnson refers to "Landlord Wodsworth" in his next entry—an interesting title given that the Tunxis had challenged William Wadsworth's claim to land in 1738.

By reason of grieving the Spirit we are given up to ourselves, & ripen for quick destruction. He laid down several ways how we grieved Gods Spirit—

Spoke in great Earnest all the day long, a faithfull Servant of Jesus Christ.

At Evening we held a Conferance at the house of Thomas Occurrums. Had a very Solemn Time, many tears Shead. Some Said they valued Such meetings more than other, that is the singing meetings. After prayers with which we did Conclude, I heard Several read, grown Persons, married persons, to the number of ten, and it is my Custom every Sabbath evening to hear them read the word of God . . . tend prayers, Sing, Converse, and read Some book for our Edification, & Exhortation . . .

Monday, the 7 th of December, AD 1772

Began to prick out some tunes in my gamut. Kept School as Ussual.

Tuesday, the 8 th of December, AD 1772

Still prick't out more Tunes, & kept School as Ussual. This Evening held a Singing School at the house of Samuel Addams.

Wendsday, the 9 th of December, AD 1772

Prick't out as usual & kept School.
I came to Samuel Adams on Monday and am to board here 1 week. Monday night I was over to the Town, & the white people had a Singing Meeting.

Thirsday, the 10 of December, AD 1772

Prick't out Tunes as Ussual, & kept School.

Fryday, the 11 th of December, AD 1772

Did as Ussual, kept School, Prick't out.

Saturday, the 12 th of December, AD 1772

Kept School as Usual. Catachised the children, gave them warning to keep the Sabbath, in the fear of God, & dismised by Prayer. I Spent most part of this after noon in finishing My Gamut. About Sun 3 Quaters of an hour high I went out in the woods for little diversion or rather for Recreation and I killed one Squiral. This Evening I went to Mr Wodsworths and Spent the Evening there, Singing, Conversing, &c. &c. So Ends the week.

The Lords Day, Decmber 13 th , AD 1772

This morning went to the Town to meeting. M r Pitkin Preached from these words but as for me and my house I will serve the Lord. Spok chiefly to heads of families, and urged family Prayers, morning & Evening, & keep up Strict government in thir houses.

In the after part of the day, he preached from these words. But thou, when thou prayest, enter in to thy Closet, and when thou hast Shut thy door, pray to thy father which is in Secret, and thy father which Seeth in Secret, Shall reward thee openly. Exhorted one & all to Secret prayer and to neglect it upon their peril, both morning & evening, and other proper times when in a Suitable frame.

And further he Said tho all those that keep up Duties, both Publick, & Secret prayer are not True Christians, yet those that live in intire neglect of prayer are Certain no Christians, and told in to have Stated time for our private retirement, & let no friend, or Bussiness hinder us, & much more.

Monday, the 14th of December, AD 1772

Began another Gamut for Samual Adams. Last night had a Conferanc, held it at the house of Samuel Adams. Very Serious one, I hope. I went to Chearlses this Evening to board the week.[35] Kept School as Usual, &c. &c.

Tuesday, the 15th of December, AD 1772

Last night I was over to the town, & was at the house of the Revd Pitkin—& [also?] two different Shops. Ricieved two Psalters for the use of the School.

Gave one to Sarah Robins, the daughter of Hanah Robins.[36] Something Cold, but very pleasant for the time of the year—almost nine. Just done breakfast. I am in good State of health. [At?] night I ricieved Couple of Letters from Groton, one from Mr Jacob Fowler Schoolmaster there, & the other from the two Daughters of Mr Samson Paukanop Deacon there, all which I love most tenderly, and desire to See, perhaps more than I do my family amongst the Scattered Indian Towns, or Tribes, I fear more than my only Sister.[37] So I end hoping in due time to see all well. However, I hope if never in this world, we may by the grace of our Lord meet together before him in his blesed presence, never more to Seperate, but live, love, praise together to all Eternity, which may god Grant of his infinite, free, Soveriegn mercy may be our happy portion. Through Jesus Christ our Lord and blessed Redeemer who ever liveth. Amen & Amen, &c. &c.

---

35. Charles Wimpey, the son of Elijah, was allotted land at Brotherton in 1804.

36. In May 1777, Ruth and Hannah Robbins owned nine acres of land at Farmington between them.

37. Samson Pauquenup (or Poquiantup) was Samson Occom's cousin. His daughter Esther was married to Jacob Fowler's brother David; two of her sisters, probably unmarried at this time, were Eunice and Prudence. Johnson's sister Amy, who had also studied at Wheelock's school, was married to Joseph Cuish from Niantic (see L. Murray, *To Do Good*, 25–26, 131–35).

So I depart and must go to my Calling, or to School—
After School I wrote more to the two Daughters of Sampson Pauquenup.
This Evening held a Singing School at the house of Samuel Adams.
Broke up Considerable late. Looks likely for storm.

## Wendsday, the 16th of December, AD 1772

Continued my Letter to the girls. It Snowed little, the night past, looks very
likely for Storm. So I must go. Just as I finished the Business of the forenoon,
it began to rain very hard. Tarried some time after the exercises were over, at
lenght ventered out.
Now I am here at the house of Charl[. . .] Came here on Monday, 14th In-
stant. This Evening Pricked out Several Tunes for Samuel Adams.

## Thirsday, the 17th of December, AD 1772

Very pleasant after a Storm[38]—Sun rises fair—this morn before breakfast I
wrote from the original, an Extract from the girls Letter—after yt went to the
School—Dismissed at 12—began soon—Scholars behaved very well During
the School time, but when we Came to dismiss by Prayer to God—I charged
them to be Silent—Solemn Considering to whome we was Praying—as they
had several times before been disorderly—in time of worship—I threatend them
and warned them faithfully Sundry times before. So at this time also—So after our minds were Composed we Prayed—but after Prayer—I was Enformed
that 3 different Persons had been Disorderly—Alas how to be freed from the
unwellcome task I Could not see So forth with I ordered them one by one be-
gining at the Eldest—to the Younger So faithfully I made them a Sad Example
of Disobeying the School Orders.
Hoping from my heart—as this is the first—So may it be last in this School
so long as I Continue here—
I Spoke freely to all the rest—that they a warning take—for I assure them
that I will no Distinction make—
And what was inflicted on these 3 at this time was very lite—Their Names
are—Elijah Wiempy Junr.—and Luke Mossock—& Lucy Mossock[39]—So
now I am about to Prick out more Tunes for Samuel Adams—
Well I remember home—O mohegan O Mohegan—the time is long before

---

38. Because Johnson's unusual use of dashes in the following passage suits the outpouring of emo-
tion and the rhythm of speech, the punctuation has not been adjusted. Joanna Brooks (*American
Lazarus*, 69) has identified here two full verses from Isaac Watts's hymn "My Soul Come Meditate the
Day" and adapted portions of Psalm 137.
39. Elijah Wimpey Jr. (1765–ca. 1812) married Elizabeth Peters and stayed at Brotherton until
his death. Luke and Lucy would be children of Solomon and Eunice.

I Shall be walking my wonted places which are on thee—once there I was but perhaps never again, but Still I remember thee—in you is lodged my father & Mother Dear—and my Beloved Sisters—and brothers—

Keep them in thy womb O Mohegan, till thou dost hear the Voice of God— O Mohegan give up thy Dead—then no longer Prisoners Shall they be unto thee—the joyfull hour is Approaching. My Soul Come Meditate the Day and think how near it stands when you must leave—this house of Clay—and fly to Unknown Lands.—Hast my beloved fetch my Soul up to thy blest aboad fly for my Spirit Longs to see—my Saviour—and my *God*—Mohegan is a lonsome place, oft have I sighed—but sighed in vain—desired, but desired in vain—Cast down—but no one to Comfort me—in destress—no one to relieve me—no friend to open my heart and vent my Sorrows—I opened my mouth to the open air—and told the Stones my Sorrow. Thus o Mohegan have you treated me— and thinkest thou—I can forget thee—or thy inhabitants—thinkest thou—or thine inhabiters that I am desireing to be on thee or with them—far far from me be such a thought—but Still there is a precious few in thee, which Causes my mind often to Meditate of thee—Perhaps in due time I may once more Come on thy borders—but first I have to go, to distant Lands; and far Country—and Differant Nations I have to walk through—before I see thee. Thus O Mohegan I must bid you farewell, and Shut the door of my Heart against thee—for I have a truer friend—to entertain in My Heart—So good night—

Spent chief of this Evening in Pricking out Tunes—for Samuel Adams.

## Fryday, the 18th of Dcember, AD 1772

This Evening held a Singing meeting at the House Elijah Wiempy. As I was going I met Hunters returning 4 in Number—Poor luck. Soloman Dideson, any of the Company. This Evening considerable Stormy—and Dark. Got home before any to Chearlses—there Slept—1772.

## Saturday, 19th of December, AD 1772

Kept School as Ussual. Of Dismission I went to Chearlses at diner after that I went to Elijah's, borrowed his Gun Powder and Shot. Than I went into the woods. Chearls & Elijah Jun$^r$. accompanied me and one Ca[. . .] I Shot twice killed two Squirrels Chearls one Squirrel, and that all the Game. As we re- turned we came to Eijahs again. Tarried a Short time, & in that Time Came Joseph Sunsaman, of Grotton[40] and I was much pleased to see him. Tarried a small time. Then Charles & I went home.

---

40. Joseph Sunsaman (Cinnamon, Senshemon) was a prominent Pequot Christian; he later moved to Brotherton.

Sunday, 20ᵗʰ of December, AD 1772

This morn I Saw in my first wakings, in my drowsiness, as it were the likeness of a lamb that had been Slain. Stand in at the foot of my Couch, and these words Seem to be set home upon my heart. He was Oppressed—and he was Afflicted, yet he oppend not his Mouth. He is brought as a lamb to the Slaughter, and as a Sheep before her Shearers is dumb, So he openeth not his Mouth. Isaiah LIII.7. Also, in Revelations V.6 and in the midst of the Elders Stood a Lamb as it had been Slain. What think you, who ever, here after may peruse these Lines—I am Joseph Johnson who do you think was the Subject of my Meditation—or the Object on whom my Soul Delighted—or what impression think you, was left upon my heart? I felt love glow in an ardent manner in my heart. To whome do you think? Methinks one might guise I awoke in some Uncommon Surprize. So I did—no sonner I awoke but got directly up—and Dressed me and followed the Blessed Lamb out, and there I worshiped him. It was Jesus Christ, who was the subject of My firt Meditation, and the only Object of my Love, & in whom my Soul truly Delighted—who left an Impression Upon my heart which Caused my heart to glow in love to him Even to the Lamb of God who taketh away the sins of the World, who once was Slain, but now Ever Liveth. Now give me leave to join my Voice with the Voice of the Elders—and Angels which are round about the throne, Who are saying with a loud Voice, worthy is the Lamb that was Slain; to recieve power, and riches, and wisdom, and Strength, and Honour, and glory, and Blessing. Amen & Amen. 1772.

Sunday, 20ᵗʰ of December, AD 1772. Far.

Joseph Sunsaman with one Mezen Cam in while we were Eatin Breakfast.[41] Also Robert Ashpo arrived here lat Night toward day.[42] Held a Meeting in the fore part of the Day at the house of Thomas Curricomb. Stormy day. After part we assembled our selves at the house of Sam Addams, again in the Evening at Samuel Adamses. They Seemed to be Earnest. Robert, & Joseph Sunsaman Carried on the Meeting.

Monday, 21ˢᵗ of December, AD 1772

Kept School as Ussual. At Even went to the Town. Got 6 Testaments for the Indians. Left Chearlses, and went to board at Elijahs again, my first Residence.

---

41. People by this name lived in Groton, Mohegan, and (evidently) Farmington.
42. Robert Ashpo was brother to Samuel, a well-known Mohegan preacher.

Tuesday, 22<sup>d</sup> of December, AD 1772

Kept School as Ussual. At Even held a Singing Meeting at Adamses. Here I Slept or rather tarried. I pricked out a Singing Book for Adams and sat up alas[?] all Night, the day Star 3 Quarter of high [?].

Wendsday, 23<sup>d</sup> of Dcember, AD 1772

Began Another Gamut for Hannah Robbins. Kept Scholl as Usual, at Even tarried at Hannah Robbins.

Thirdsday, 24<sup>th</sup> of December, AD 1772

After Breakfast went to school. Was Invited to go to Dinner to one Solomon Mossocks. So at noon I went. This Evening Slept at Elijahs Desputed of Hell. Some Snow fell this Evening.

Fryday, 25<sup>th</sup> of December, AD 1772

Kept School as Usual. Between School Prick't out several Tunes after that read Isaac Frasiers Life.[43] Drank Tea at Andrews.[44] This Evening held a Singing meeting at Adams was Invited to go home with one Solomon Mossock to keep a Christmas, and also by Elijah, but finally I was persuaded to tarry with Samuel Adams.

Saturday, 26<sup>th</sup> of December, 1772

Last Evening Slept with Samuel Adams. Held a Discourse about Several things as we lay—on Regeneration, New birth, Many Called but few Chosen, the Prayers of the Wicked are an Abomination, Tares and the Wheat must grow to gether Untill the Harvest, &c.[45] And Severel other things of Consequence—of

---

43. "The notorious" Isaac Frasier (1740–68) managed to set fire to the jail when imprisoned for thirty-odd counts of burglary. While his trial for burning the jail was pending, he escaped from another jail and committed several more thefts. His deathbed account was both sensational and moralistic (see Frasier, *The Notorious Isaac Frasier*).

44. Andrew Curricom (or Corcomp [b. 1747]) was married to Abigail, and at this time they had two small daughters. He lived at Stockbridge, Massachusetts, during the Revolutionary War.

45. Thomas Kendall, a missionary at Caughnawaga between 1772 and 1774, taught the same parable to a Mohawk man. Kendall's anxiety about his missionary role is a far cry from Johnson's and Adams's easy conversation in bed: "Conversed with Philups & read unto him the 14 Chap. of Mathew concerning the tares & Wheat. Was obliged to in explaining it unto him to use the word wild Persnip instead of tares as he could not understand tares. The other their Land is full of it & likewise their wheat in their feilds. I chose this chapter to shew to him that their was no Purgatory that the Bible New of none, and all the while held the bible before me as a shield as it were & recited him to pasages in old testament where it began with thus Saith the Lord, here, atend, harken diligently &c." (Kendall, *Diary*, entry of 4 August).

grieving the Spirit of God of True Conviction of the different sorts of Concern, but one right, of Death Judgment, & Eternity. So before day fell a Sleep.

This morn after Breakfast went to School, very Cold. Went through the Exercises reading, spelling, & Catachising, Exhorting, & dismissed with Prayer. Begins to Snow. Went to Elijahs. The Snow is turned into Rain. So I End for this Day.

From 26th of December 1772 to the 28th of January 1773. Very Short Account

After I tarried 1 week at Elijahs, I tarried a week at Andrews. On Tuesday 29th of December 1772, I hurt my leg. Ran again a Stick at Even. After I tarried a week at Andrews, I went to live with Meazen. I tarried untill Wendsday the 15th of January 1773. At Even My leg, being much Swelled I was advised to go to Hannahs house, the Sister of Elijah, and they made a Poultice, and put on the Same Evening. On Saturday the 8th of January, I Sent a few lines to Doctr. Timothy Hosmer, and he Sent a few Directions, Bathing, Poulticing, and Diet, abstaining from Spirituous Liquors, &c. &c.[46] On Tuesday Evening 11th of January 1773, was appointed for a Singing Meeting, but Robert Asppoo Came, and Carried on the Meeting.

At the Lords Day, 16th of January, 1773, I got so well as that I went to meeting. Very Cold indeed, walked going, rid coming. On Sunday, the 16th of January 1773 at noon I went to Doctr. Hosmers and he dressed my Leg, and gave me Salve. When I got home. (i.e.) to Hannahs house my leg began to be very painfull, and Swelled Some. I laid down. This Evening had a meeting. On Monday 17th of January, 1773, Came to Samuel Adams, and Tarried 1 week. After that I purposed to tarry at Mossocks but Samual Adams persuaded me to tarry another week with him. Monday 24th of January, AD 1773, at Even I went to pay Thomas Corcamp a Vissit. Sang Some. Afterward returned to S.Ad.

Tuesday Evening held a Singing Meeting at Adams house, very agreable Meeting. Wendsday 27th 1773 finished Susannahs Gamut, the Eighth Gamut I Made.[47]

Now it is the 29th of January, 1773, Fryday. Well in heath, but Sore leg yet, from 29th December, 1772.

---

46. Timothy Hosmer was active as a Son of Liberty and an army surgeon during the American Revolution, after which he moved to Genessee County.

47. Susannah Cronick and Susannah Squinnomow were among those who petitioned to sell their lands at Farmington in 1777.

30<sup>th</sup> of January, AD 1773, Saturday

This day I have kept School 10 weeks. This day Came the Indians for to see what Proficiency their Children made in the 10 Weeks Past. Sang, before Prayers Elijah Prayed in the morning. After Prayer Began to read. The Children look very Promising. The Hearts of Parants were not litle Effected to See their Children Stand in order, like a row of willow young Tender, and fair, Beside a Pleasant fountain, or a living Stream. Much Pleasing to See the Children Earnest to learn. It is my meat and Drink to teach Such Children. For my Part I never Saw Indians So much desireous of Learning. I have been Diffirent Parts of this Continent, among diffirent Tribes of the Natives, Scattered up and Down but I Challenge all Indian Schools and School masters, to Show me the order of their Schools, English or English or Indian. (I mean all [. . .] I have been Acquainted as yet.) My Challange is this, that they Excel this School in Manners, & Proficiency Considering the time, as well as the age of the Schollars, that they have been Under my Care. Also I challenge Schoolmasters to bring the Severel Tribes among which, Perhaps, they have resided for, not only 10 weeks, but 10 Months and Perhaps 10 years, and more against this Tribe, with whome I have resided 10 weeks. My Challenge is this that they Excell this Tribe in Singing, the Musical Art, if you tribes Can attend that Part of Solemn, worship with Deacency.

# Joseph Johnson's Diary, Farmington, Connecticut, 18 November 1772 to 1 February 1773

LAURA J. MURRAY

Joseph Johnson's two diaries from the early 1770s are remarkable and apparently unique documents. Unlike Johnson's other writings, mostly pleas for money or support from white patrons, the diaries seem to have been primarily designed for Johnson's own eyes and conscience. They provide a rich portrait of the texture of daily life in small New England Native communities: the comings and goings, the labor, the sociability, and the nature of Christian worship. In the "Indian towns" of Mohegan and Farmington in this period, white preachers were not the most important promoters of either literacy or Christianity. More

This essay is developed from sections of Laura J. Murray, ed., *To Do Good to My Indian Brethren: The Writings of Joseph Johnson, 1751–1776* (Amherst: University of Massachusetts Press, 1998), with permission from University of Massachusetts Press.

commonly, groups of Native Americans prayed, sang, read, and wrote together regularly in their homes, and Aboriginal community thus conceived became the foundation for an emigration movement to Brotherton, New York. The diaries of Johnson, who was a leader of this project, provide a surprisingly intimate portrait of the strivings and the doubts of a young man who was learning to assume a position of responsibility among his "brethren."

Joseph Johnson was born to Joseph and Betty Johnson, both Mohegans, at Mohegan, Connecticut, near Norwich, in 1751. Johnson's father died fighting for the British in the French and Indian War, whereupon Betty Johnson sent seven-year-old Joseph to the Reverend Eleazar Wheelock's Indian Charity School at Lebanon, just down the road. Although young Joseph already had some familiarity with Christian worship and the English language, Wheelock's school must have been a sobering experience. Wheelock drilled his pupils in humility with respect to both earthly and heavenly superiors as earnestly as he drilled them in reading and writing—and in the hours remaining they were sent out to earn their keep at neighboring farms. Still, the school's proximity to Mohegan permitted Johnson and some of his classmates to visit home from time to time, and at least one of Joseph's sisters also attended Wheelock's school. Although Johnson left Mohegan at a tender age, he was by no means severed from his home.[48]

At age fifteen, Johnson was sent west of Albany, New York, to teach school to the Oneidas. Although Wheelock had established his school in New England, his goal was to train missionary workers there for the conversion of the Iroquois. Accordingly, Johnson taught at Oneida for two and a half winters, under the supervision of the missionary Samuel Kirkland, suffering the recalcitrance of his students, the cold and hunger, and the vigorous demands of his white supervisors. During this time, he wrote many dutiful and despairing letters to Wheelock. In 1769 he quit amid charges of drunkenness and misconduct. For the next two years, Johnson—staying well out of Wheelock's watchful view— worked as a schoolteacher in Providence, Rhode Island, and then signed on to a whaling ship. On 9 October 1771, the very day he stepped off the ship in Providence, he began a "Memorandum" in a small notebook whose last page would not be filled until 7 March 1772. In the early entries of this diary, we are kept in suspense about Johnson's lost belongings and his Newport romance. We see his return home to Mohegan echoed regularly in later diary entries when, for example, Johnson notes, "This Day is 6 weeks since I came home."[49]

---

48. For more biographical information and annotation, see L. Murray, *To Do Good*, 25–29 and 50–54.

49. Ibid., 119.

We learn how Johnson and his family supported themselves: husking corn, clearing land, killing hogs, making spoons and brooms. We follow Johnson's medical treatment for a disease he does not name, and we watch him move from furtive romantic longing to fervent devotion to God. We see the patterns of visiting among Native Christians in neighboring villages. If Christianity provided a fabric of sociability, however, it also made severe demands on its practitioners, and in entry after entry Johnson struggles with his depravity in the face of God.

Johnson's second diary (reprinted in full herein), which was kept at Farmington, Connecticut, through the winter of 1772–73, is quite different from the first diary in substance and tone. The Farmington Johnson was no longer primarily a sinner on the verge of rebirth or relapse; he was a religious and community leader. Whereas in the earlier diary Johnson emphasizes his own unworthiness and God's vengeful judgment (he describes himself in a letter from around that time as "a child in the knowledge of Jesus my Lord, and a babe in Understanding"),[50] in the second diary he is calmly thankful that God "has brought me, and placed me amidst a strang Nation, and he has given me favour in their Eyes." In the Farmington diary, Johnson worries more about alienation from his home community at Mohegan than about alienation from God.

When Johnson left Mohegan in November 1772, he was bound for upstate New York. As he recorded at the beginning of his new diary, however, Providence intervened on the road just past Hartford and offered him a chance to take a leadership role among the Native people at Farmington:

> I went 3 Miles. There I was much at a stand whether to call at Famington or no, as my design was to go to the Mohawk Country. There I Stood at a Stand some time. At last [. . .] Came 3 men. I enqured of them, whether it was much out of the way, to go by Farmington, to go at Canaan, through Norfolk. They told me, that now it was the nighest way I could go from here. So I concluded to go by Farmington, the more because I was desired by the Rev^d Samson Occom.

As Johnson waits at the crossroads for a sign about which road to take, three men come along, as in a parable or *Pilgrim's Progress*, and provide him with a sign that directs him to take leadership among his neighbors rather than wander on alone. The staging at the opening of the diary suggests that when he took the road to Farmington, home to a Native American community including people of Tunxis, Quinnipiac, and Mattabeeset or Wangunck descent, Johnson was suddenly invested with a sense of purpose and responsibility. He also continued to see himself as a humble and sometimes abject apprentice to

---

50. Johnson to "all Enquiring friends," n.d., quoted in ibid., 178.

Samson Occom, however.[51] Occom had initially proposed that Johnson teach at Farmington, and Johnson's public reading of Occom's published sermon at the execution of Moses Paul (a Pequot convicted of murder) served as the first phase of Johnson's audition for the position. "They all rejoiced" to hear Occom's idea, and the next day Johnson "read, & wrote, before several," including the Indian overseer the Reverend Timothy Pitkin and "some of the headmen of the Indian tribe." This performance of literacy validated Johnson for both white and Aboriginal authority figures. Indeed, Johnson's skills in interpreting, reproducing, and performing the written word underpinned all his work at Farmington. The job he took on resembled that of a young Samson Occom among the Montauketts in the 1750s: He "kept School . . . and Carried on the Religious Meetings as often as ever, and attended the Sick and their Funerals, and did What Writings they wanted, and often Sat as a Judge to reconcile and Decide their Matters between them, and had Visiters of Indians from all Quarters."[52]

Johnson's diary depicts a small but closely knit community. The census in 1774 counted only twelve men, fourteen women, and seventeen children at Indian Neck, in a bend of the Farmington River, and if these numbers are remotely accurate, all the Aboriginal people at Farmington would have been active Christians.[53] Teaching, leading worship, singing, collecting and making books, hunting, and boarding with one family after another at weekly intervals, Johnson lived on intimate terms with his hosts, as one particularly evocative diary entry demonstrates:

> Last Evening Slept with Samuel Adams. Held a Discourse about Several things as we lay—on Regeneration, New birth, Many Called but few Chosen, the Prayers of the Wicked are an Abomination, Tares and the Wheat must grow to gether Untill the Harvest, &c. And Severel other things of Consequence—of grieving the Spirit of God of True Conviction of the different sorts of Concern, but one right, of Death Judgment, & Eternity. So before day fell a Sleep.

At the tender age of twenty-one, Johnson rather reveled in the fact that he stood as a man of some "Considerable Influence in this Place." After all, he had spent most of his life thus far under the scrutiny and direction of Eleazar

---

51. For more on Johnson's relationship with Occom during this period, see Johnson's letters to Occom in ibid., especially 180–81, 182–85, 192–93, and 200–201.

52. Quoted in Blodgett, *Samson Occom*, 45–46.

53. *Collections*, 117. In 1761 Ezra Stiles met an Indian woman from Farmington who told him that there were only three men and six married Indian women at Farmington and that Pitkin was their sachem; however, Stiles's informant in 1767 reported that ten or twelve families lived there (Dexter, *Extracts*, 136, 269). On Farmington more generally, see L. Murray, *To Do Good*, 298 n. 10, and Feder, *Avaricious Humour*.

Wheelock, Samuel Kirkland, or Samson Occom. When a chief and a young man brought a "Stragling man" into the schoolhouse, Johnson "Spoke boldly, on his behalf, and desired them to require no further Inteligence from him, and use him as becoming rational Creatures or Christians." Johnson apparently left the building to add finality to his words—and it worked: "So[?] I went out," he recalled, "& they Said they would not abuse him, and would harken to all my advice, & words." On this occasion, as he records it in his diary, Johnson explicitly patterned his leadership behaviour on the scriptures: "I remembered Joseph & his brethren," he writes, "how Joseph Said, for I fear God, do this. And I remembered Our Saviour, when he was brought before Pilate, he answered not a word. My heart was arous'd with Compassion." Some of Johnson's authority at Farmington seems also to have come from the fact that one of the Farmington Chiefs "was very intimate with [Johnson's] father in time of war." As Johnson left the schoolhouse after the "Stragling man" incident, this chief hastened after him. "He gave my father, the Tittle of Captain in all his Discourse," wrote Johnson, "and after all he acquainted me most freely the Special regards he had for me also, and assurd me that I had more that loved me now, truely than Ever I had my life time before." Johnson, who had barely known his father, was clearly very moved by these professions of affection, connection, and trust.

A little more than a week after Johnson's arrival, his flock "Concluded to have A singing Meeting twice in a week, that is, Tuesday night, and Fryday night, also we agreed further to spend Some time for Publick worship together, and we appointed, and Set apart, the Sabbath Evenings for that purpose, that is to Sing, pray, and give a word of Exhortation or Spend Some part of it in Reading some books of Edification." In order to support this style of worship, Johnson embarked on the project of producing instructional music books, or "gamuts." On 3 December, he made three—"that is, Cut them out, & sewed them together." Then, he says, "I began to write down the rules in one." Johnson was probably essentially copying a printed gamut in his possession, but his books also contained tunes. Following an evening at the home of "Landlord Wodsworth [Wadsworth]," where he "heard his daughters Sing Several Tunes, and Sang Some at there desire, [him]self," Johnson made a gamut for this family. Since unlike many of the Indians in the town, the Wadsworths certainly could have afforded to buy a gamut, Johnson's gesture suggests that they were engaged by his repertoire. All together, Johnson made eight gamuts for the men and women of his circle.

For Johnson, however, hymns ran deeper than sharing material with others. Overcome with homesickness for Mohegan, Johnson turned to hymns to express himself. As Joanna Brooks has pointed out, the following passage contains two full verses from Isaac Watts's hymn "My Soul Come Meditate the Day" and adapts portions of Psalm 137, with "Mohegan" standing in for "Jerusalem": [54]

> Well I remember home—O mohegan O Mohegan—the time is long before I Shall be walking my wonted places which are on thee—once there I was but perhaps never again, but Still I remember thee—in you is lodged my father & Mother Dear—and my Beloved Sisters—and brothers—
>
> Keep them in thy womb O Mohegan, till thou dost hear the Voice of God— O Mohegan give up thy Dead—then no longer Prisoners Shall they be unto thee—the joyfull hour is Approaching. My Soul Come Meditate the Day and think how near it stands when you must leave—this house of Clay—and fly to Unknown Lands.—Hast my beloved fetch my Soul up to thy blest aboad fly for my Spirit Longs to see—my Saviour—and my God—Mohegan is a lonsome place, oft have I sighed—but sighed in vain—desired, but desired in vain—Cast down—but no one to Comfort me—in destress—no one to relieve me—no friend to open my heart and vent my Sorrows—I opened my mouth to the open air—and told the Stones my Sorrow.

Hymns had permeated Johnson's emotional core. We do not know why he felt that he had to leave Mohegan—perhaps he left in disgrace, or perhaps political tensions forced him to leave—but it is noteworthy that his language of family and nation is also the language of hymns.

Johnson's reticence about the cause of his exile from Mohegan may be frustrating, but it is characteristic of most diaries. Diarists rarely explain that which is obvious to them. Moreover, there is another dimension to this silence: Johnson's most personal writing—his diaries—would not have been understood as private, so he almost certainly chose to remain silent about sensitive personal or political issues. He claims that he keeps a record of his work so "that for time to Come [he] may look & remember" his promising students. Many missionaries in eighteenth-century New England, however, kept journals at the demand of the missionary societies that paid their salaries. Although we have no direct evidence that Johnson was required to keep a diary for his employer or possible benefactor, the fact that he concludes his writing with grand claims of his successes in the field evokes the genre of the diary-as-missionary-report:

> I have been Diffirent Parts of this Continent, among diffirent Tribes of the Natives, Scattered up and Down but I Challenge all Indian Schools and School masters, to Show me the order of their Schools, English or . . . Indian . . . that they Excel this School in Manners, & Proficiency Considering the time, as well as the age of the Schollars, that they have been Under my Care.

54. J. Brooks, *American Lazarus*, 69.

It appears that Johnson also used his diary as practice for writing letters to potential benefactors or practice for oral exhortation. He signs his name at the end of one homesick entry as if he were writing a letter: "I am as Ussual, the Mohegan Indian, now keeping a School among the Indians at Farmington, in good health, & Endeavouring to use it for the good of my fellow Indians, &c. &c. &c." On another occasion, he reports a dream of a lamb at the foot of his bed and asks:

> What think you, who ever, here after may peruse these Lines—I am Joseph Johnson who do you think was the Subject of my Meditation—or the Object on whom my Soul Delighted—or what impression think you, was left upon my heart? I felt love glow in an ardent manner in my heart. To whome do you think? Methinks one might guise I awoke in some Uncommon Surprize, So I did—no sonner I awoke but got directly up—and Dressed me and followed the Blessed Lamb out, and there I worshiped him. It was Jesus Christ, who was the subject of My firt Meditation, and the only Object of my Love, & in whom my Soul truly Delighted.

It is quite startling to come across this direct address—"What think you, who ever, here after may peruse these Lines"—and to think that perhaps Johnson imagined unknown readers, even perhaps from sometime in the future, to inquire into the "Object on whom [his] Soul Delighted." Reading this passage eerily puts us in the position of Johnson's eager students or exacting mentors.

It is not clear why Johnson left his Farmington position after only ten weeks. In a letter to Samson Occom dated a week after the last diary entry in December 1772, Johnson reported plans to go to Oneida, to Dartmouth College, and to Boston "upon Some Bussiness for this Tribe." [55] By early April, he was back teaching at Farmington again, and it appears that he stayed there for another year, all the while petitioning Eleazar Wheelock, Andrew Oliver of the New England Company, and the governor of Connecticut for funds to support the school. It would seem, therefore, that he left because the tribe or its overseer could no longer pay his salary; there is no indication of conflict or dissatisfaction on either side.

The diary is bound with a portion of Johnson's farewell sermon, which offers a taste of another, primarily oral, genre in which Johnson was fluent. Rather than explicate a particular text, the sermon ranges through Christ's life, telling a story—one that, although Johnson expects will be familiar to his audience, he deems worthy of repetition. The tissue of the New Testament quotations in the sermon is held together and made immediate by Johnson's exhortations

---

55. Quoted in L. Murray, *To Do Good*, 181.

to his listeners to "hear" and "Behold" the final events of Christ's life. The occasion of Johnson's own departure would certainly have intensified the emotional impact of the sermon. Johnson begins by urging the people to "attend diligently, and hearken what a Departing friend has to say to you, before he depart, and you See his face no more, nor hear his Voice Sounding amongst you as Usual, Either Exhorting or weeping or making melody to God." In a flight of language reminiscent of the New Testament, Johnson reminds his brethren, "No more will you See his [Johnson's] tears of Compassion, and Sorrow, flowing from his pitying Eye, no more Entering your houses, seting at your tables, no more will he rest his weary head upon your Pillows." In this context, Johnson later asks his audience to "hear what a depearting Lord Says unto his Beloved deciples, to Comfort them, and he Says unto them, Never the less, I tell you the truth, it is Expedient for you that I go away: for if I go not away, the Comforter will not Come unto you. But if I depart I will Send him, unto you."[56]

It is suggestive to read this sermon in the context of the plans being made, during these months, by several groups of Christian Indians from Connecticut, Rhode Island, and Long Island to emigrate to Oneida land in upstate New York. Six weeks after Johnson preached his farewell sermon at Farmington, representatives of the "seven Tribes" met at Mohegan and committed to the emigration. Although Occom served as the primary political and religious leader of the resettlement, Johnson was its major practical facilitator. We may speculate that at the time of his first departure from Farmington he was already bolstering his confidence, and others' confidence in him, by ventriloquizing Christ and by assuring his listeners, "It is Expedient for you that I go away: for if I go not away, the Comforter will not Come unto you." This assumption of Christ's role may seem arrogant; however, to the Christian itinerant, subsuming one's life into that of Christ was the ultimate act of humility.[57] The men and women of Farmington would have heard this echo, and it appears to have resonated truly for many of them. In April, when he was teaching once again at Farmington, Johnson wrote a letter to Occom declaring, "Were all the School masters used with the Same respects and tenderness as I have been, and Still am used, how chearfully would they spend their time."[58]

56. Ibid., 165, and manuscript diary, NYPL.
57. In a sermon to the Oneidas, David Avery, a white student of Wheelock's, compared himself overtly to Christ, stating that his parting words were like the dying words of Christ (Avery, "Valedictory Address"). In a sermon written on 23 May 1774, Johnson developed an allegory between the life of the Old Testament Joseph and the life of Jesus (Occom Papers, Connecticut Historical Society), and in a letter to the New York Congress, 5 July 1775, Johnson compared himself to "Joseph of old" (L. Murray, To Do Good, 267). Thus, he may even have conceived an elaborate set of Old and New Testament allegorical relationships.
58. Ibid., 200.

In October, Johnson wrote a letter, signed by eight men from Farmington, to "All Our Indian Brethren," urging them to remember the commitments to emigration that they had made in the spring and requesting that they send representatives to see the land and make formal arrangements with the Oneidas. The letter assures, "Our kind Women sends a word of Encouragement, and Says that they will make little yoke hegg [dried corn] to give to the travelers."[59] Through 1774 and 1775, having written many letters of appeal and traveled extensively, Johnson secured a deed for land near Oneida and persuaded both white and Native people of the importance of the emigration plan. All the while, he was trying to prepare himself more fully for the ministry and struggling to support himself and his family (he had married Occom's daughter Tabitha in December 1773). Preparations for the emigration became more and more difficult as the discontents of the American colonies developed into full-blown war against Britain; during this time Johnson worked hard to assure both the British and the Americans that it was in their interest to let him travel back and forth between New England and New York. Sometime in this chaotic period, Johnson died, at the age of 25; we do not know where or why. By way of obituary, all that remains is a comment from another of Wheelock's former students: "The Churches this way who had a taste of Mr Johnson's ministerial Gifts feel for the public in the loss of that zealous, pious and very promising Indian Preacher."[60]

The other emigrants persisted in their plans. Although the first group of Brotherton settlers was forced back to Massachusetts and Connecticut to wait out the Revolutionary War, they ventured west again in 1785. In his documentation of the founding of the town, Occom noted that Elijah Wimpey of Farmington was one of the town's first trustees and Andrew Acorrocomb, another Farmington man, one of its first fence viewers.[61] Johnson would have been pleased with the fruits of his months of labor and Christian fellowship at Farmington.

59. Ibid.

60. McClure, Letter to Eleazar Wheelock.

61. Quoted in L. Murray, *To Do Good*, 308. Towns often appointed fence viewers to adjudicate boundary disputes.

# Mohegan Wood-splint Basket

The Mohegan *manu'da*, or basket, pictured here is in the collection of the Connecticut Historical Society. It is 12 inches wide, 17 inches long, and 11 inches high. It is rectangular in shape, with sides that curve slightly inward. The rim is double reinforced and single wrapped, creating a sturdy durable frame. The cover is slightly concave, perhaps from age, with sharply defined corners. The warp and weft of the splits are of medium width. The basket is decorated on three sides in Mohegan pink and green, and it is fully lined with pages from an 1817 Hartford, Connecticut, newspaper.

Figure 1-3. Mohegan Painted Wood-splint Storage Basket. (Courtesy of the Connecticut Historical Society, A-1853, Hartford.)

# The Cultural Work of a Mohegan Painted Basket

STEPHANIE FITZGERALD

In steed of shelves, they have severall baskets, wherin they put all
their householdstuff: they have some great bags or sacks made of Hempe,
which will hold five or six bushells.

—Roger Williams
*A Key into the Language of America*

The Mohegan word for painting, *wuskuswang*, is the same word used for writing, inducting painted baskets in a long textual tradition that includes decorative birch bark etching, beadwork, wampum belts, and the written word. These
practices comprise systems of signification that were and are read as texts.
Because they do not conform to Western conceptions of writing, they have
been dismissed, ignored, and largely excluded from the historical record, thus
obscuring the long history of Native texts and textualities. Most scholarship
on Native decorated artifacts has focused on material aspects. More recently,
Hertha Dawn Wong has argued for texts such as pictographic signatures,
painted plains tipis, and winter counts as forms of precontact autobiographical
narratives.[62]

To consider early Native painted wood-splint baskets as texts is to decenter
or problematize current critical conceptions of early Native literacies and textualities. What would a history of Native print culture look like if it included
three-dimensional texts such as baskets or tipis? How does the inclusion of
forms previously not considered texts change conceptions of literacy and communicative practices? How do we begin to read a basket's narrative? This essay
undertakes the project of opening a theoretical discourse that will work toward
a paradigm for reading alternative Native textualities.

Indians made baskets and other woven objects long before European and
other settlers reached American shores, and they continue these cultural practices to this day. The baskets and other objects are often covered with symbolic
designs containing insightful readings into the particular culture from which
they originate. According to the specific cultural context, the designs may take
the form of figures, geometric shapes, or floral patterns. Baskets, which were
and still are ceremonial and utilitarian objects used for transportation and
storage of items, prayer ceremonies, and traditional games, function as com-

---

62. Wong, *Sending My Heart Back.*

municative devices. In sum, by touching every aspect of daily Native life, both past and present, basketry is imbued with cultural and spiritual power.[63]

Both the variety of design patterns and symbols on Mohegan baskets of the early nineteenth century and Mohegan cultural memory support the theory that basket patterns were used as communicative or narrative devices.[64] In 1995 a heavily decorated Mohegan elm bark box was repatriated from the Peabody and Essex Museum in Salem, Massachusetts. Upon seeing a photograph of the box, tribal elder Gladys Tantaquidgeon recalled it as looking "like the one from Oneida."[65] Further research determined that the box had been sent by minister Samson Occom from the Mohegan community in Brothertown to his sister Lucy at Mohegan as a record of the journey. Bearing inscriptions of the Trail of Life and Path of the Sun design patterns, the box embodies the continuity of Mohegan cultural traditions and identity in a time of tremendous change.

The decoding of the text of a basket requires shifting from a Western to a Native perspective and situating both the basket and its text within a specific tribal context. Size, form, style, and varying degrees of decoration all play a role in the making of the meaning and function. Mohegan people made several different kinds of wood-splint *manu'dag*, or baskets. They range from carrying baskets with handles to small sewing baskets and decorative wall pockets to coarse draining baskets and the typical rectangular covered storage basket such as the basket in Figure 1-3. Wood-splint basket making was not a solitary effort; it was one that involved contributions of labor from within the community. The selection of an appropriate log, the soaking process, the separation of the wood rings, and the preparation of the splints are all required before the actual weaving of a basket can begin.[66] The weaving of Mohegan baskets was generally a communal winter activity. It was performed by women to the accompaniment of stories and songs, which in turn become part of the basket, joining together two traditions, oral and textual.[67] Once a ready supply of baskets was completed, they were sold door to door by their makers or by family members on routes that often covered the entire length and breadth of New England.

---

63. See, for example, Porter, *The Art of Native American Basketry*, and Mowatt, Morphy, and Dransart, *Basketmakers*.

64. McMullen, "Woodsplint Basketry Decoration," 114.

65. Fawcett and Tantaquidgeon, "Symbolic Motifs," 135.

66. For a more detailed explanation of the basket making process, see Tantaquidgeon, "Basketry Designs," 43–33, and Richmond, "Schaghticoke Basket-Making," 130.

67. Frank Speck and Jesse Moses provide a brief account of Mohegan communal basket making in "Some Mohegan-Pequot Legends," 183. Native men did not become involved in the weaving of baskets until the later part of the nineteenth century, when economic conditions forced them to seek new avenues of entry into the cash economy. See Turnbaugh and Turnbaugh, "Weaving the Woods," 90.

Many of these basket sellers, noted for characteristics ranging from wit to storytelling to musicianship, became legendary figures in the communities they visited.

Few late nineteenth-century northeastern Native baskets were signed by their makers (a practice that is culturally Western).[68] The narrative that unfolds in the textual surface of a basket is not an individual creation; it belongs to the tribal community. Authorship, then, is communal rather than individual, and the resulting narrative belongs to the community as a whole.

The Mohegan covered *manu'da*, or basket, pictured here is lined with an 1817 Hartford, Connecticut, newspaper, thereby fixing the date of the basket at 1817 or earlier. Newspaper linings were common practice during the nineteenth century.[69] Laurel Thatcher Ulrich has considered a similar covered storage basket—probably Mahican or Schagticoke, based on its distinctive construction and design—lined with pages from the *Rutland* (Vermont) *Herald* dated from 1821 to 1822. Placed by the owner of the basket, using a wheat paste compound, the paper lining protects the contents against not only the rough inner surface of the wood splints but also dust and insects.[70] Ultimately, the newspaper linings are intended not as a means of communication but as protection for the basket contents. To read the Mohegan narrative of the basket, we must make a critical move that elides the Western print symbolic system in favor of traditional Mohegan communicative practices: We must turn to its surface.

The basket is decorated on three sides, painted free hand in Mohegan pink (a mixture of red and white lead) and green, using a handmade twig brush. The design pattern consists of traditional Mohegan symbols: three four-domed medallions and a linked chain of stylized leaves, strawberries, dots, and trellises. The chain forms a triangular-shaped stockade around the green center medallion, which is outlined in a series of pink dots, with a pair of pink spirals flanking the top dome. Below, the medallion is enclosed by two green leaves outlined in Mohegan pink with green dots. On either side of the stockade are two additional four-domed medallions painted in the opposite color scheme: Mohegan pink with pairs of green spirals flanking the top domes. The entire front wall of the basket is framed by a chain of alternating half domes in Mohegan pink and green.

---

68. Circa 1870, one basket maker marked several baskets with the initials "J.H.S." A number of other baskets have been attributed to this individual through, for example, distinctive construction techniques (see McMullen, "Woodsplint Basketry Decoration").

69. The earliest known example of a newspaper-lined wood-splint basket is a Mohegan basket that was lined with an 1808 Hartford, Connecticut, newspaper. As Laurel Thatcher Ulrich points out, other baskets from this period were lined with religious publications dating to the 1820s (see Ulrich, *The Age of Homespun*, 352).

70. See ibid., 342.

The designs are not only aesthetically pleasing but also deeply culturally significant. The artistic renderings displayed on the basket are representations of both the abundant natural landscape and the Mohegan cosmology. As the Mohegan elder Gladys Tantaquidgeon explains, "To the Mohegan, designs and life are more than simple representations of nature. There is a spiritual force that flows through all things, and if these symbols are true representations of that force, this spirit should be expressed in the designs."[71] Thus, Mohegan basket design patterns contain spiritual connotations that serve to reinforce their aesthetic value and provide meaning for those who can read the basket text. For example, one prominent Mohegan design, the Trail of Life symbol, explains the "east-to-west passage of spirits," following the path of the sun.[72] The significance of these two cardinal directions is found in other aspects of Mohegan life, such as the eastern- and western-facing openings in the ceremonial arbor.

A spiritual force is present in this Mohegan *manu'da*. One of the primary symbols of the basket, perhaps the most important symbol found in Mohegan culture, is the four-domed medallion. It is thought to represent the four directions, or four cardinal points, as well as the interrelationship of the soul, earth, and universe.[73] Through the use of this symbol, the basket pattern offers a view into traditional Mohegan belief and cosmology. The stylized leaves and strawberries represent not only the Mohegan land but also the plant beings and the food and medicine they provide, which signifies the interdependent relationship between the people and the land. The dot element represents the Mohegan people. The trail design that encloses the central medallion may symbolize the Trail of Life or the Path of the Sun. Together, the symbols and designs of the basket text create a narrative for the reader to decode.

In an analysis of similar basket designs, Ann McMullen has suggested that the inscribed texts are political commentaries on the move to Brothertown by a faction of the Mohegan Tribe, spanning the years from the 1770s to the 1820s. "The message," she writes, "was that people would lose their Mohegan identity when they left the tribal lands."[74] Any text is open to multiple readings, but this particular analysis reflects a non-Native bias. I offer here an alternative rooted in traditional Mohegan cosmology.

Mohegan oral tradition holds that "the People" came from the East, over a desert, and then crossed "the great fresh water." Forced out by their enemies, the Mohawks, they eventually moved on to the eastern side of the Connecticut

71. Fawcett and Tantaquidgeon, "Symbolic Motifs," 99.
72. Fawcett, *Medicine Trail*, 41.
73. Tanataquidgeon, "Basketry Designs," 24.
74. McMullen, "Woodsplint Basketry Decoration," 123.

River, the site of the present-day Mohegan Nation.[75] I read the design pattern of this basket as a possible retelling of the Mohegan original migration story. The combination of traditional symbols such as the Trail of Life pattern with the four-domed medallions creates a fusion of Mohegan history and cosmology. It is no cause for wonder that a basket of this era might depict the migration story. In 1775, some forty-two years before the confirmed date of the basket, Samson Occom, the Mohegan minister and tribal elder, led a group of Mohegans and Long Island Indians to create a settlement at Brotherton, New York, to escape both white influence and white infringement on Indian lands. This move, like the later move from New York to Wisconsin in the 1820s, caused factionalism within the Mohegan community. Mohegan history, in the tradition of most Indian nations, is one of migrations and removals. Thus, this basket bears witness to the particular cultural and historical moment that it inhabits.

The basket represents multiple layers of meaning on several different levels. As a material object, it possesses a utilitarian function. For the non-Native, it is also a Mohegan cultural artifact. Through its utilitarian function, it serves to reinscribe Mohegan history and cosmology into everyday life. As a gendered cultural form, the basket is the embodiment of the role of women in passing on not only the basket-weaving tradition but cultural knowledge as well. Finally, as a text, the basket assumes primacy over its newspaper lining, reducing it to a utilitarian function devoid of communicative practice.

---

75. Speck and Moses gathered at least two versions of the Mohegan migration story from tribal members in the early part of the twentieth century (see "Native Tribes and Dialects of Connecticut," 216–17).

# Temperance and Morality Sermon

## SAMSON OCCOM

This eight-page undated sermon[76] appears in a hand-sewn booklet whose pages measure 6.5 inches by 8 inches. Occom writes on both sides of the page and leaves virtually no margin. The manuscript begins *in medias res* and breaks off before its conclusion; it is missing at least the first two pages and the last page. The extant middle section is reprinted here. The sermon can be found in the Occom Papers, Index # 79998, folder 26 (microfilm pp. 398–402), Connecticut Historical Society, Hartford, Conn. This sermon is reprinted by kind permission of the Connecticut Historical Society, Hartford, Conn.[77]

[. . . ]whe{n} he drowned his Reason he loses all that Time and he is fit for no Service at all, either for himself, for his Family,{[and?]}[78] for his Country, and how much more is he unfit to Serve God, —And yet, (to astonishment) he is just fit to Se{r}ve the Devil, Yea Drink itself is the Service of the Devil, and

---

76. The notes in this edition are based on a collaborative edition I produced with several of my graduate students at the University of St. Thomas (Occom, "Temperance and Morality Sermon," ed. Bouwman et al.), available online at the Early Americas Digital Archive, http://www.mith2.umd.edu/eada/ (Ralph Bauer, site editor). I am especially indebted to Margret Aldrich, Nicole Brudos Ferrara, Keri Henkel, Sara Hoffman, and Marilyn Paulson for their research on Cook's voyages, on syphilis, and on the deity Cauktuntooct.

77. I have used a very light hand in editing this sermon. Square brackets, [ ], indicate missing words that I have inserted for readability; square brackets with an enclosure followed by a question mark indicate an uncertain reading of a word or letter. Curly brackets, { }, indicate interlineations, which Occom sometimes indicated with a caret and sometimes simply wrote above the line. (He also wrote carets for which he neglected to write interlineations.) I have included the carets where they appeared in the original. Like most writing of the time period, Occom's capitalizations are varied and frequent by today's standards. Complicating matters is the fact that many lower and uppercase characters, particularly his "C," "G," "A," and "S," are similar in appearance. Capitalization versus lowercasing was therefore often a judgment call on my part. Occom's punctuation is sparing, and he often finishes sentences with a comma, a dash, or a comma-dash combination; frequently, if the sentence finishes at the end of a line, he uses no punctuation. I have inserted punctuation (in square brackets) sparingly and for readability only. Occom's spelling remains intact, except where I have—once again for readability—silently changed the old English "f" to "s" and occasionally altered spelling in square brackets. I have silently emended repeated words, crossed-out words, and words broken at the ends of lines (Occom tended to write to the very end of the line and to break words in odd places to make the most efficient use of the page).

78. Occom includes a strange mark here that looks somewhat like his shorthand for "and."

This fits him for all manner of Service to the old [Geeny?],[79] and ma{n}y has undone thimself{es},[80] and their families by Drunkness, —and this Practice is Condemn'd by all Consciencd People, and it is in the Power of mankind to break off from this acursed Sin if they will, and they know it, it is in Vain to Say I Cant Help it, and it is a folly to blame the Devil[;] does the Devil Cary the Man to Tavern and there Call for the Liquor for him, and does [he] ^ {take} the Cup, and pour down in his Throat, and does the Devil pay for the Liquor, and does he repeatedly Call for Drink and keep pouring of ^[it] in his Thr[oa]{t} till he has made him Drunk; if this is the Case then the man is Clear of Sin and Blaim, and the Devil is Guilty of ^ {that} Sin, —But let us See a little farther does not the Drunkard Use that natural Power & understanding Which god has given him in his persute after Strong Drink? dont he think and Consider Where he can get Liquor, and when he has found a Place in his mind, he will [?][81] use them Leg, which ^ {god has} giveen him, and direct his Course to the Place where he expects to get Liquor, and when he is got there, he will [use] that ^ {tongue} and Speech, which God ^ {has} given him, and Call for Liquor, and when it is granted; he takes [the?][82] Cup with his own Hands, and he pours it down in his ^ {own} Throat and he Uses the power of Swallowing, and Swallows down his Liquor and he will repeatedly Call, and pour down the Liquor till he has Transformd himself, from a Rational Man to worse than a Natural fool.—Now is it not in the Power of this Man to break off from this Course of Life—I am persuaded he Can, —Such a man that will Contrive and follow all ways, to get Strong Drink, and take Pleasure in it, is properly a Drunkard, —a man may be ^ {over}taken Some Times, but if he is asham{d} of it, and Repent of it, is not a Drunkard, —[83]

Let us Trace another Practice, which is Universal, among the People Calld Civilized Nations; That Cursing {s?}wearing and Profaining the Name of god; it is so common amongst all Sorts of People, that it is become Innocent and in-ofensive, but let it be never So Common, it is of the Same Nature as it ever was, it is the most ^ daring, ^ {Heaven & God Provoking} Sin that man is Capable

---

79. The word looks like "Geeby" or "Geeny"; the "n" appears to have been overwritten with a "b." Brooks reads this word as "Greedy" (Occom, *Collected Writings*, 226).

80. The "t" at the beginning of this word and the "es" at the end (to transform the word from "himself" to "themselves") appear to have been added later. It also appears that "their" was originally "his" and was later overwritten.

81. A word here appears to have run off the end of the line; one letter, perhaps a "y" for "yet," is partly visible.

82. The bottom of this page of the original is torn.

83. Because—except in two cases noted later—Occom used all the white space available on the page, there are no paragraph breaks in the original text. None of his text is indented. I have inserted paragraph breaks for readability, where Occom clearly changes subjects.

of Commiting, and it is the most ^ {un}profitable Sin, it neither Cloathes the
Body nor feeds it, Why is a rational man so in Love with Such Language is it
^ {so} Comely, is it decent, is, it graceful, is it Credible is it manly, is it gentteel,
is it Godly, and Chistian Like, Why no, I think every Considerate Person must
Say no, ^ {by} no ^ {means},—well, then it must be, uncomely, indecent dis-
graceful uncredible inhuman ungenteel, ungodly unchrstian, unholy, Yea ^ {in}
thruth, it is {everything [sinful?]} Devilish, and Hellish Language, it is from the
Bottumless Pit and it is fit for ^ {no} Creature but Devils, and I Verily believe
the Devils dont Cuse and Sware and Profane the Name of god, as mankind
does; It is Amazing to hear, how expert the White People are in Swaring, Men
Women and Children, of all ages Ranks and Degrees, it Seems to be a mother
Tongue with them, or are there Schools where they go to Learn this Language?
Now, is it in the Power of Man to leave of Swaring, or is it not? I am glad there
is no Such Language among the Indians, it is not because, that it {is} incable of
it, ^ {But} it is Horred, they will not Use Such Language.—I will tell ^ {you}
amazing Truth among them, they have ^ {very} Great Veneration for the Name
of the great god, in their perfect Heathenism they Calld god, Cauktuntooct,[84]
which Signifies Supream Independent Power, and they had Such Regard for
this Name, they woud not Suffer their Children to mention that Name, they
Say it was too great for Children to Mention—and in the Evening when it is
Time to go to Bed, an old man (who is apoited for that purpose), will go round
the Town, with a loud Voice, Calling upon the young People and Children to
desist making Noise and go to Sleep, and not to Disturbe god, Now how is it
amonst those that are Call'd Christians; {dont ye hear ye [Christians?]}[85] Don't
you think these Heathen Indians will rise up against ^ {you} at the last Day not
only for this Sin, but for many others also—Yea, don't they Testify against you
now in this Life, —But you will reply and Say: are they so Clear of Sin as to
rise up against us; no by no means; but you have learnt them many of the Sins
they are Guilty of, and they are Ignorant Heathens, and You are Christians,
and have [had?] all Learning, and great knowledge, and ^ {therefore} you ought
to go before them in all Holy Conversation and Godliness—But in Stead of
that, I am af{r}aid you Lead them {in} the Downward Road in all manner of
abominations;

　　And {many} Diseases, Eupopians Brought into this Country, that the
Natives were intirely Ignorant before, Such as what they Call in Genteel Lan-

---

84. Or possibly it reads *Cauhtuntooct*. One of the great Narragansett deities, Cautantowwit was
known as the creator and ruler of humans. He was thought to be generally benevolent, and he gave humans their first bean and corn seeds to grow (Simmons, *Spirit of the New England Tribes*, 38–39, 41).
85. If this is the word *Christian*, it is abbreviated—it is only four or five letters long.

guage, Venerial Disease, in Common Language French Pox.[86] Captain Cook in {his} Voige Round the World, Says that there was a Vesel in a ^ {Place} Called Otaheite,[87] about fifteen ^ {months} before him, and had left that a Cursed {common} disease among the poor Indians, which they were utterly Ignorant of before; The Captain was so Honest ^ {as} to Say If hee Could have learnt their Specific[88] for the Venereal Disease, if ^ {such} they have it would have been of great advantage to us, for when hee left the Island it ^ {had] been Contracted by more than half the People on Board the Ship, but he was not quite so Honest as to Say whether he had it himself—Vol. 1: 146: p [.] This was only return{g} the Compliment, and they ^ {had} no Room to Complain, and it was only giving back what they had receivd from the Europians and I Suppose there {was} no difficulty in returning it,[89]—But Since we have begun ^ {upon} this Practice which is Called, Whoredome, let us take notice of {it} a little, I Suppose it is Universal among all Nations, and it is Universally Condemnd by Rational People, it is abominable, inhuman and Beastly Practice, and it is more abonable when it is Supported and Countenanced by polite, Learned, and Christian People, but some will Say or Ask, who allows Such Practice, the Eng[lish] how many Baudy or Whore Houses are there in that Nation, and I Suppose it is just so among the French, these are Calld Christian Nations and the most Learned Nations in the World at this Age of the World; and I never heard of any Such House amongst the Indians in this ^ {great} Continent; Certainly Common Sense Condemns such Practices and the Heavenly Artilery is leaveld against it and the Thunders of Mount Sinai are Roaring against it, Yet men will persist in it, —The grand Question occurs again, is man a Rational Man, unable to turn from this detestable, Filthy, Shameful, and Beastly Practice? Or Can he desist, and become a Chaste Creature? I immagine to hear an Answere Universaly from all Rational Men, Saying, O! Yes O! Yes, we [can.]

---

86. The "French Pox" is syphilis, a contagious sexually transmitted disease that had, at the time, no cure. There is some debate as to how Native American populations became infected with syphilis; one theory is that sailors on Columbus's ships brought a form of the disease to the Americas, which then mutated into a more potent strain to which Europeans had no resistance and made its way back to Europe (Andreski, *Syphilis*, 7).

87. Otaheite is Tahiti.

88. "Specific" means "remedy" or "cure."

89. Upon landing in Tahiti during his first voyage around the world (1768–71), Captain James Cook had his men checked by the ship's physician to make sure they were free from venereal disease. When Cook's men came down with syphilis after visiting Tahiti, no one was quite sure where the disease originated. One theory is that the French, who were on the island a short time before Cook, exposed the islanders to syphilis (see, for example, Cook, *Journal of a Voyage*, 57, *Journal During his First Voyage*, 76–77; Withey, *Voyages of Discovery*, 101–3). In the previous sentence, Occom seems to be referring to a specific volume of Cook's journals; I have been unable to locate the edition to which he refers.

Why don't he trun then, it is because he will not—he C{h}uses to go to Hell
in his own way, and if he will, who can he Blame?—Mariage is Lawful, and
Honorable, but god will Judge Whore Mongers and all Adulterous[90]

Another Practice which is very previlent everywhere amongst all Nations
and all Sorts of People [is] Contention, Quarriling, and Fighting, there is
Scarcely any ^ [thing] else, but Whispering, Backbiting and Defaming one
another—this Breeds Quarrliling, & Wars[.] Certainly this is unbecoming
Rational Creatures, it [is] Condemn'd by the Light of Nature, and it is utterly
Condemnd by Scripture, and it is what we don't like from our fellow men, and
if we dont like it, why should we give it to our fellow men, and if we dont like
Such Treatment, and can blame others for it, then we must believe, it is in their
Power, to treat us and their fellow men better, well, if they Can, then Certainly
we Can too; and ^ {why} don't we do it; I have took a particular ^ {notice}
of the words Speaking against one another; Speaking again{st?} another must
mean, belying ^ {one another}, If I Speak the Truth about my Neighbour, I
don't Speak against him but for him, to make this plain let us take tow Neighbours; one, is everyway agreable to his Neighbours, he is kind, benevolen{t}
loving, obliging, just and Honest in all his dealing, with his Neighbours, he is
a man of Truth, and uses no bad Language, he do{es} not defame his Neighbours, —now if I shoud till of his real Charac{ter} woud that be Speaking
against him, why no by no means, it is Sea^{p}king for him; but if I Shoud
give him Contrary Characters, that is Speaking ^ {against} him, because I dont
give him his True Character.—But the other Neighbour is right to the reverse,
he is every ^ {way} disagreea[ble?] to his Neighbours, he is Moross and Cross,
unkind Turbellent, he Cheats in his Dealings all he can he Curses and Swares,
Defames his Neighbour[s?] and Sets his Neighbours by the Ears, Sews the
Seeds of Discords, and he will lie for a Copper as for nothing, —now upon
Ocation, If I shoud call his true Character, will that ^ {be} Speaking against
him? I think not, but if I shoud Say that he is a Clever kind just and Honest
man, I shoud Say that of him, which he is not, and therefore I Should Speake
against him in so saying, Dont you think so?—there is another way of Speaking against my Neighbour, that is, when I See my fellow Creature take a miss
Step, and directly, I ^ {take the} ocation, to blaze it abroad, and exaggerate
the matter, and make it Seven Times worse than it really is; this {is} Speaking
against my Neighbour, in a Very bad Sense; it is discovering his Nakedness to
the world, Ham like Concerning his Father, for which he was Severly Curst by

---

90. The end of this line, unlike most others in the text, contains a couple of words' worth of blank
space, as if Occom meant to write in more later, or perhaps this blank space was intended to indicate
a pause or end of paragraph.

his Father [91]—Now is it not in the Power of men to Treat one another better? I think they Can, and if they dont, then they ^ {are} under blame, —[92]

Love is everywhere Commend[ed] and Command[ed] [in?] the Holy Scrip-tures, and it is Certainly Beutiful and agreable amongst Rational Creatures, and it is in our Power naturally to Love and to be kind to one another; and it is the Strength of a Kingdom and Nation to live in Peace and in Love, it is the Beauty of a State, City Town or Family to dw[ell] together in Love, Peace, and Unity—The Scripture commands People to Provoke one another to Love and to good works—But I think in these Days, People in general are Provoking one another to Hatred & to Evil Works[.?] if it is in our Power to hate one another, then there is equal Power to Love one another & if [we] don't Love one an-other, then we are Self Condemn'd it is very Natural for mankind [to] Love to be lovd, and usd well, Well let us Practice that Rule upon our fellow men{Well Well},[93]—I might go on mentioning ^ {many} Practices amongst the Children of men, but what has been said is quite Sufficient to Lead the minds of men, to Consider the Conduct of their fellow men, and also their own Conduct, —It is very Common amongst all Nations, and amongst {*}[94] all orders, Ranks and Degrees of men; and amongst all ages, both men Women and Children to find Fault with each other {yea it is [?][95] unfit not to find falt},—and it is Very well that {with one another} we can See so far, [Th?]is must lay a foundation for us to see our own Conduct; and this makes it very plain, that we all ^ [have] Power to do well, and if our Conduct has been bad; we believe, it is in our Natu[r?]al ^ [power] to do better,—it is a Universal Doctrine, and it [is] the [Provo?]king of all, that have any understanding to their fellow men, to do well, or to do better, this is the Universal Creed of all mankind; From hence [ar]ises this Dayly Preaching,—The Kings of the [ea]rth woud have their Subjects do well or better, [th]e People woud have their Kings do well, all that have any Power and Authority over the People woud have them do well, the People find fault with their Ruler; and woud have [him] do better, the Minsters of the

---

91. Ham, son of Noah, saw and reported his father's drunken nakedness; for this disrespect, Noah cursed him (Gen. 9:22–27).

92. Occom leaves enough room for a word or two at the end of this line; perhaps it is meant as a paragraph break.

93. "Well, Well" appears under "well, Well" in the previous sentences. The words do not appear to be an insert (they have no logical place for insertion) as much as a reminder of emphasis—perhaps a reminder to play on the multiple meanings of the word *well*.

94. An asterisk appears to have been written beneath the dash after "Conduct."

95. Between "is" and "unfit" is a small notation, perhaps shorthand, which looks somewhat like an uppercase cursive "L." I have been unable to match this symbol with those listed in shorthand texts; it resembles Mason's shorthand for "conceived," but it may also be Occom's own symbol.

gospel exhort their People to do [be]tter, [an]d the People woud have their Ministers [??] [96] better. Husbands woud have the[ir]. . . . [97]

## Samson Occom and the Sermonic Tradition

HEATHER BOUWMAN

Anyone who is familiar with Samson Occom today knows him primarily for two pieces of writing: his sermon preached at the execution of a fellow Native, Moses Paul (1772), and a brief narrative of his life (written circa 1768, it was not published in his lifetime). These are his only writings selected for reprinting in the most commonly used anthologies of American literature.[98] Yet Occom wrote widely, mastering several different genres; among his extant works are diaries, speeches, hymns, a history of the Montaukett people, an herbal medicine booklet, two short autobiographical accounts, political writings, numerous letters, and some twenty sermons.[99] Occom was up to his elbows in the written word. For this reason I suggest that we take our studies beyond his two commonly anthologized texts, to review a wider array of his writings, and consider what studying his unpublished works adds to our picture of Occom. What new insights can we gain from studying the Temperance and Morality sermon (included here)? How can Occom's personal history; the literary, social, and historical contexts of the sermon; and theoretical perspectives be brought to bear on this narrative? In what ways can various kinds of extratextual knowledge help unlock the sermon to readers and expose the sorts of literacy in which Occom was engaged?

We may find that the context in which Occom writes opens new windows on the content of his sermon. When Occom penned this sermon, he was experiencing some of the more difficult years of his life and some of the best of his publishing career. Although we cannot specify the exact date of the sermon, we can pinpoint it as written after 1771 (the conclusion of Captain Cook's first voyage, which is mentioned in the sermon), and most likely before 1775 (the conclu-

---

96. Three words appear to be missing here.

97. The text runs to the bottom of the page and cuts off; there was clearly at least one more page to this manuscript, but it is missing.

98. See *The Norton Anthology of American Literature*, vol. A; *The Heath Anthology of American Literature*, vol. A; *Harper American Literature*, vol. 1; Castillo and Schweitzer, *Literatures of Colonial America*; and Mulford, Vietto, and Winans, *Early American Writings*.

99. Reprinted in Joanna Brooks (Occom, *Collected Writings*).

sion of his second voyage, which is not mentioned in the sermon); the sermon was almost certainly delivered before the conclusion of the Revolutionary War, since it refers to white colonists as the "English" rather than as the "Americans." Briefly, these are the issues that Occom faced at the time: After successfully touring England from 1765 to 1768 to raise funds for the Indian Charity School of Eleazar Wheelock (his former teacher and current mentor), Occom returned to find that Wheelock did not have a second high-profile assignment in store for him. Rather, Wheelock wanted Occom to become a missionary to the Onondagas in New York, and when Occom refused (citing concerns about his health and the well-being of his growing family),[100] Wheelock charged him with being prideful. For his part, Occom strongly criticized Wheelock's use of the substantial funds he had raised in England for Indian education, charging Wheelock with funneling the funds into white education. He and Wheelock exchanged sharp words, culminating in Occom's famous 1771 letter in which he writes that his "alma mater" has become too "alba mater"—too white. To make matters worse, Occom had lingering personal problems: his struggles with illness beginning in 1768 and continuing at least through 1773;[101] the death of his son Aaron in 1771; and the continuing effects of a lawsuit in which he had participated in the 1760s. (The "Mason affair" a lawsuit over Mohegan land, alienated Occom from some of his white supporters and some of his fellow Mohegans and most likely cost him preaching and teaching opportunities and financial support.)

One of his biggest professional hurdles during this time was that (beginning in March 1769) he was being charged with drunkenness, mostly by Wheelock, his old mentor, whose motivation may have been professional jealousy and racism. Over a two-year period, Wheelock wrote several letters leveling these accusations. The letters were addressed to Occom as well as to prominent supporters (including George Whitefield, the famous English preacher, and John Thornton, the secretary of the English missionary society that financed both Occom and Wheelock). At first Occom denied any drunken behavior, and then, in a surprising switch, he confessed an act of drunkenness to his presbytery. In late 1769, after investigating Occom's report of the incident, the

---

100. Wheelock was supposed to watch over Occom's family while he was in England, but he had let them go poor and hungry. Moreover, as William Love explains, Wheelock's son Ralph had offended the Onondagas deeply with his patronizing and high-handed tactics when he had visited them in the 1760s, and Occom may have opposed the idea of cleaning up Ralph's mess (Love, Samson Occom, 161).

101. Love writes that Occom began a long struggle with illness in 1768 (ibid., 162). Occom discusses his health in general terms in some of his letters—for example, in a letter of October 1772 (reprinted in Collected Writings, 101) and in his letter to Susannah Wheatley in September 1773 (Collected Writings, 106).

presbytery concluded that Occom had not, in fact, been drunk. Meanwhile, Wheelock continued to claim that Occom was engaging in drunken behavior; he even wrote to Occom's English supporters in 1771 to suggest that they discontinue their financial support of Occom. Although the charges were never proved (even with Occom's confession, he was absolved of any blame), they followed him all his life. Even during the Brothertown years (beginning in 1785),[102] people gossiped that Occom had a drinking problem, perpetuating the rumors that had begun with Wheelock's original charges. (It is perhaps important to note here that—amid bitter disagreements and accusations about the drunkenness charges, Wheelock's use of the English funds, Occom's refusal to become a missionary to the Onondagas, and Wheelock's perception of Occom's pride—Wheelock and Occom apparently ended their correspondence in 1774. There is no record of any further correspondence between them.)

Of course, many of Occom's personal problems led to financial problems. Because of his participation in the Mason lawsuit and his trip to England (both of which his Boston financial supporters had reacted to with disapproval), perhaps because of the drinking charges, and certainly because of his break with Wheelock, Occom struggled to make a living. During this period, his only employment was as an itinerant preacher, living hand-to-mouth, and "tilling his lands" for support (as Wheelock put it in 1769).[103] Beginning in 1772, his financial burdens were somewhat relieved when he once again received support from the English Trust),[104] but Occom did not have a permanent position as preacher or teacher during this period, and funding was always undependable.

In the Temperance and Morality sermon reprinted here, it is conceivable that Occom's references to drinking and to talking against a neighbor may have not only held personal resonance but also served as a kind of public defense, a way for Occom to argue his side of the issue: What does it mean to be drunk? What does it mean to speak critically of a neighbor (or mentor)? Also significant, however, is that these sermon passages show Occom participating in and extending what was already a life being lived in print. Occom's battles with Wheelock and his part in the Mason controversy both took place in written documents; the charges of drunkenness and the resolution of these charges also took place in writing. Significantly, during what were certainly bleak years

---

102. In 1785, after years of planning, Occom helped a group of Indians from the "Seven Tribes"—the towns of Charlestown, Farmington, Groton, Mohegan, Montauk, Niantic, and Stonington—move to the less crowded western side of New York state, where they established the town of Brothertown. Occom paid lengthy visits to the town each summer, returning to his family at Mohegan for the winter months; he finally moved to Brothertown permanently in 1789.

103. Quoted in Love, *Samson Occom*, 156.

104. Blodgett, *Samson Occom*, 146.

for Occom personally, he made his publishing debut: His well-known sermon on the execution of Moses Paul, often cited as the first text written by a Native American specifically for publication, came out in 1772. Then in 1774 he published the first edition of his hymnbook, which contained several hymns that he authored. These were his most successful and productive publishing years. Occom was taking his place in the world of print, a world that, in a sense, had already authored him as the "Indian preacher" who had toured England and as the "Mohegan preacher" who had been Wheelock's most successful student.

Even during these difficult years (perhaps especially so), Occom's public life was a life of print, and in his writing he shapes this life with a good knowledge of how print conventions work. Although many of Occom's sermons were apparently never written out in full—Occom worked from notes and (often fairly sparse) outlines—the Temperance and Morality sermon, a rare exception, is fully scripted (although the opening and closing pages have since been lost). Occom was, by all reports, a gifted impromptu speaker; in this case, however, he opted to rely on the power of the pen. This sermon, unlike his transitory extemporaneous sermons, has the longevity of the written word, a power with which Occom was certainly well acquainted after his letter-borne arguments with Wheelock, his paperbound legal battles, and his own successful sermon publication. The Temperance and Morality sermon is a document that, by its very existence, recognizes and participates in the power of print.

Yet the document is, in many ways, also an oral document. The sermon, collected in the Samson Occom Papers at the Connecticut Historical Society, appears to be not a "fair copy" but a first draft, with insertions and corrections throughout. Occom wrote quickly, using dashes, for the most part, to show end punctuation or (especially at the end of a line) omitting end punctuation altogether. The entire eight pages of preserved text are contained in one long paragraph that contains little white space; Occom was apparently trying to conserve paper. Although Occom often preached using notes or outlines, of the seventeen to twenty Occom sermons owned by the Connecticut Historical Society (depending on how the fragments are counted),[105] most are written out (a few are in outline or partial outline form). Occom preached frequently, sometimes as often as several times a week, and he probably reused his written sermons; he also most likely did a great deal of extemporaneous preaching. Although his journals suggest that most of his preaching was exegetical, several of the sermons at the Connecticut Historical Society contain social criticism. Perhaps Occom decided to write out the Temperance and Morality sermon and other sermons of social critique because he was concerned about perfecting

---

105. Brooks counts twenty sermons. See Occom, *Collected Sermons*.

the wording, or perhaps he had a strong interest in preserving these sermons for posterity.[106] Perhaps the Temperance and Morality sermon was delivered often, or perhaps it was delivered to an important group of supporters—all good reasons to write it out and take the time to edit it.[107]

Internal evidence suggests that the sermon is addressed to a mixed or white audience; it shows Occom's awareness of his audience and his appeal to racially diverse listeners. The Moses Paul sermon, so often cited as a marvel of preaching before a mixed audience, was not by any stretch of the imagination the only sermon (or even one of only a few sermons) that Occom preached before a mixed group. Occom's diaries from 1774 to 1775, for example,[108] indicate that he addressed a wide range of people in his journeys as an itinerant preacher. Of the sixty-one days represented in the diary,[109] Occom preaches at least thirty-seven times (and possibly another five or six times where it is difficult to determine whether he is preaching or simply momentarily addressing the crowd). Of these preaching experiences, he specifically notes addressing white crowds on three occasions: At Stockbridge he preaches "first to the English, and Just before night to the Indians"; at Fort Stanwix he preaches "all Day to the Whites"; and at the Hollow he preaches at "the House of ... a young Dutchman," where he "had a great Number of People."[110] In many other instances, he specifies having preached to mixed congregations—or, at least, to audi-

---

106. Some of Occom's sermons that include social critique are fully scripted, but so are some of his exegetical sermons. We can only speculate why he would write out one sermon and not another. Two important factors, of course, would have been adequate time and access to paper—neither of which were in large supply in Occom's often itinerant life. It is possible that he wrote out sermons more frequently when he was at home than when he was traveling.

107. I was caught in a dilemma between editing Occom's text for clarity (making it as accessible as possible) and editing it for accuracy (making it as true to the source as possible). Generally, I would argue for accuracy—for as "literal" a transcription of the text as possible. In a work in which the author himself (I am certain) would clean up the writing before heading to the press, in which it is clear that the text is a rough draft that the author did not, in its present form, intend for publication, however, I waver. Would I publish Mark Twain's rough first draft of *Huckleberry Finn* as the novel? If I did, would I expect readers to see Twain's full genius in the writing? What would I want them to get out of reading the book in its rough form? In Occom's case, I hope that readers find the text itself compelling, and I hope that they remember the oral nature of the text as they analyze and (inevitably) evaluate it.

108. Occom may have kept diaries consistently throughout his life, but the only diaries that have been preserved are partial and pertain primarily to his travels; he writes very little about his home life. Although there are occasional detailed and evocative entries on weddings, dreams, visits with friends, and the like, for the most part, the diaries function as travel and preaching records. Many of Occom's journals (and letters) are included in Blodgett, *Samson Occom*; Love, *Samson Occom*; and Richardson, *Indian Preacher*. J. Brooks has recently edited an outstanding and much-needed comprehensive collection of Occom's writings (*Collected Writings*).

109. July 8–August 14, 1774, and December 22, 1774–February 9, 1775. Reprinted in Occom, *Collected Writings*.

110. Ibid., 275, 277, 280.

ences that, although not always identified racially, appear to be mixed. At New Lebanon, for example, he preaches to a group that includes "governor Franklin and a gentleman from the west Indies and others and Some Ladies,"[111] and on several occasions he notes that he preached to Indian audiences with white missionaries present. He preaches to many different kinds of people, including a "Seven Day Baptist" with a Moravian wife, friends and acquaintances including the "good Doctor Tarbell," a "Baptist Brother," a "multoe man,"[112] and at the homes of both Indians and white colonists. Most of the time he does not feel the need to specify the race of his listeners (presumably because the diaries are not intended for publication and he does not need the personal reminder—or perhaps simply because he considers the race of his audience unimportant).

This pattern of preaching to mixed audiences (racially, nationally, and denominationally) continues throughout Occom's life. In the diaries of his travels around Brothertown, New York, from 1785 to 1787,[113] Occom notes that he preached before white audiences (of various nationalities), mixed white/Indian audiences, and mixed Indian audiences (Brothertown Indians, Stockbridge Indians, Oneidas, and others); he writes that at one wedding at least ten languages were spoken.[114] The Temperance and Morality sermon, like the Moses Paul sermon, shows that Occom used his position as an Indian preacher to address various constituencies in his mixed audiences. Several critics have discussed Occom's tactical use of multiple audiences in the Moses Paul sermon,[115] but it is important to note that it was not unusual for Occom to address white listeners. Rather, this was part of a larger pattern—evident throughout his sermons—of playing to multiple audiences and addressing white constituents as well as Indian constituents in complex and multilayered ways.

It would be useful to ask how Occom's criticisms both critique and play into white Christian sermonic traditions: In other words, what kind of "literacy" does he achieve in the sermon form? In the Temperance and Morality sermon, as in many of his other sermons, Occom has a savvy grasp of how to address multiple audiences. While he preaches to one constituency (white people who swear, for example), other constituencies are listening. A multifaceted audience is always implicit in sermons: The preacher may address a particular kind of sinner or a particular subset of his congregation, but everyone listens to and can presumably learn from all parts of the sermon—at the least, each person

111. Ibid., 276.
112. Ibid., 278, 276, 280, 282.
113. Occom, *Collected Writings*, 301–85.
114. Ibid., 381.
115. See, for example, M. Elliott, "This Indian Bait," and D. Murray, *Forked Tongues*, for two excellent discussions of Occom's use of multiple audiences.

can develop an understanding of the sins of others and the roles of others. In addition to addressing multiple audiences, Occom understands that the interaction between preacher and congregant is one of solidarity as well as one of authority. Occom's critique of white listeners suggests a bond with them: By speaking to white audience members as "you," he suggests that they are there, part of the family/congregation, listening to his sermon. The purpose of a sermon is to address those who have come to be saved (or those who are already saved but need help along the path to heaven). Whereas you might talk *about* the unsaved, hell-bound sinners of the world, you would talk *to* those who wish to repent, to improve. Thus, we have Jonathan Edwards's famous *Sinners in the Hands of an Angry God* (which was addressed to those who were not yet saved but who wished to be) and Occom's sermon preached at the hanging of Moses Paul (which was addressed in part to Moses Paul, who had reportedly asked Occom to come preach, presumably for the purpose of being saved before his death). The context of the sermon—especially the unpublished sermon—is a church, a so-called family of God composed of actual and potential converts. By addressing white members of this family, Occom indicates at least some solidarity with them.

Of course, he also indicates criticism, as is evident in the text, not only in its many references to English sinners but also (and particularly) in its contrast of English sin with pagan (pre-Christian) Indian goodness (there is no swearing in Indian language; there are no whorehouses in the precontact Americas). In criticizing his listeners, Occom participates in the long-standing preaching practice of pointing out sins and calling sinners to repent. But in putting forth pagan Indians as exemplars of virtue worthy of imitation, Occom veers from the traditional practice of putting forth Christ or the ancient church as worthy of imitation. Here pagans are models that the sinning white listeners should emulate. In this sermon, Occom criticizes white culture as the breeding ground for swearing, venereal disease, and prostitution. Two characteristics of these passages stand out to me: (1) how Occom plays with language (swearing as a "mother tongue," the "genteel language" of "venereal disease"), his delicious sense of irony mobilizing the passages to make their social critique, and (2) the social critique itself, which throughout the sermon is anything but subtle. Whereas critics have uncovered the subtle criticisms implicit in the Moses Paul sermon—criticisms sometimes so subtle that we may wonder if they really exist—the Temperance and Morality sermon opts for a bold attack.

One point of note, then, in this sermon, especially as it compares with the Moses Paul sermon, is how strongly Occom speaks his criticisms of white colonists. Referencing Homi Bhabha's writings on mimicry, David Murray writes of Occom's "forked tongue" in the Moses Paul sermon, in which the colonized is like but not *quite* like the colonizer, responding not with total agreement to the colonial agenda but with (as Bhabha writes elsewhere) "sly civility."[116] Whereas the Moses Paul sermon fits quite well into Bhabha's notion of sly civility, however, and suggests that the speaker can offer a criticism of the colonist through his very acceptance (or appearance of acceptance) of the colonists' terms (Christianity, civilization, reason, and so on), the Temperance and Morality sermon states at several points that Indian culture is simply better than white culture. There is, in the swearing and adultery sections of the sermon, in particular, no real attempt at either slyness or civility. Rather, Occom speaks blatant criticisms of white people, and he does so to their faces ("you" are sinners, he tells them).

The Temperance and Morality sermon thus suggests layers of colonial discourse. Classic postcolonial theories—particularly those theories arising from discussions of (Asian) Indian or African literature—overlook the fact that, at the time of Occom's writings, his white listeners may very well have viewed themselves as the "colonized": unrepresented and deserted by the European English, constantly seen as the backward, hick little brother at political and social gatherings, taxed without due representation. Christian Indians—by now often living in their own, not-quite-traditional-Indian, not-quite-white communities—would have viewed themselves as political, cultural, and religious entities different from those of traditional Indians, a different layer in the colonial strata. Traditional, pre-Christian Indians, referred to in this sermon in quite positive ways but unlikely to be part of the audience hearing the sermon (and never addressed as "you"), constitute yet another layer. When Occom sets up a comparison between colonists ("English" and "French") and Indians (who, he says, never knew either swearing or whorehouses), he underscores a real set of problems in colonial American discourse: There are no "Americans" as yet, and there are no precontact Indians whom Occom can talk about on a first-hand basis. He is forced to create: For the colonists, he creates as stand-ins the worldly "English gentleman" and the "French explorer" figures; his criticisms of them are aimed at "you," his white listeners. Contrasting these sinning colonists, he offers not Christian Indians (who presumably know English and thus English swear words and who have at least a theoretical knowledge of the existence of whorehouses) but precontact pagan Indians. The historically real Christian Indian (and, one might argue, the historically real colonist) does not appear in this text; that figure is supplanted by the pre-Christian Indian of Occom's imagination (and by the English gentleman and French explorer); the only Christian Indian in the text, it seems, is the narrator. In this sermon,

---

116. Bhabha, "Sly Civility."

the figures who appear (the English gentleman, the French explorer, the pagan Indian) are created for rhetorical purposes and suggest that Occom is making the Other even more "other" (English or French, pagan) to provide his contrast and thus his critique.

The Temperance and Morality sermon is not a sermon about sameness, not a sermon that offers sly civility or mimicry; rather, it is a sermon that declares difference and uses the creation of that difference as a mode of critique. Occom's sermon shows his deep knowledge of the sermonic form and his ability to negotiate that form in order to address multiple audiences. Perhaps even more important is how, through the sermon itself, Occom participates in ongoing print debates about his life and how he is defined. Moreover, it is evident that Occom evinces a kind of cultural literacy in his creation of difference and his mobilizing of it to argue, in a Christian sermon, for a new way of envisioning sinners and goodness and a new way of envisioning colonists and Indians.

# Title Pages from Samson Occom's *Sermon Preached at the Execution of Moses Paul*

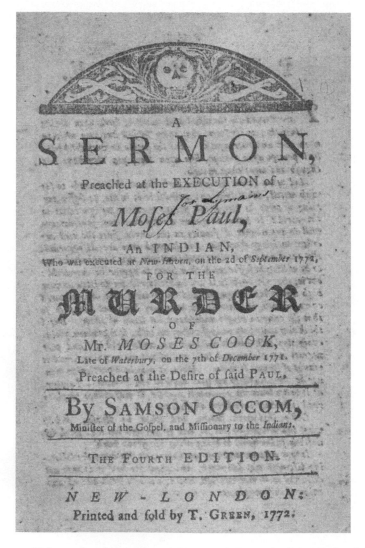

A

# SERMON,

Preached at the EXECUTION of

*Moses Paul,*

An INDIAN,

Who was executed at *New-Haven*, on the 2d of *September* 1772,

FOR THE

# 𝕸𝖀𝕽𝕯𝕰𝕽

OF

Mr. *MOSES COOK,*

Late of *Waterbury*, on the 7th of *December* 1771.

Preached at the Defire of faid PAUL.

## By SAMSON OCCOM,

Minifter of the Gofpel, and Miffionary to the *Indians.*

THE FOURTH EDITION.

*NEW-LONDON:*

Printed and fold by T. GREEN, 1772.

Figure 1-4. Title page from Samson Occom's *Sermon at the Execution of Moses Paul, an Indian,* 4th ed., 1772. (Courtesy of the Edward E. Ayer Collection, The Newberry Library, Chicago.)

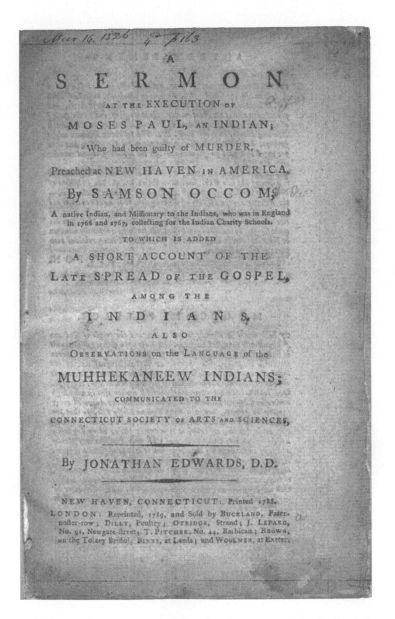

A

# SERMON

AT THE EXECUTION OF

## MOSES PAUL, AN INDIAN;

Who had been guilty of MURDER,

Preached at NEW HAVEN IN AMERICA.

### By SAMSON OCCOM,

A native Indian, and Missionary to the Indians, who was in England
in 1766 and 1767, collecting for the Indian Charity Schools.

TO WHICH IS ADDED

## A SHORT ACCOUNT OF THE

## LATE SPREAD OF THE GOSPEL,

AMONG THE

## INDIANS,

ALSO

OBSERVATIONS on the LANGUAGE of the

## MUHHEKANEEW INDIANS;

COMMUNICATED TO THE

CONNECTICUT SOCIETY OF ARTS AND SCIENCES,

### By JONATHAN EDWARDS, D.D.

NEW HAVEN, CONNECTICUT: Printed 1788.
LONDON: Reprinted, 1789, and Sold by BUCKLAND, Pater-
noster-row; DILLY, Poultry; OTRIDGE, Strand; J. LEPARD,
No. 91, Newgate-street; T. PITCHER, No. 44, Barbican; BROWN,
on the Tolzey Bristol; BINNS, at Leeds; and WOULMER, at Exeter.

Figure 1-5. Title page from Samson Occom's *Sermon at the Execution of Moses Paul, an Indian,* 1789.
(Courtesy of the Edward E. Ayer Collection, The Newberry Library, Chicago.)

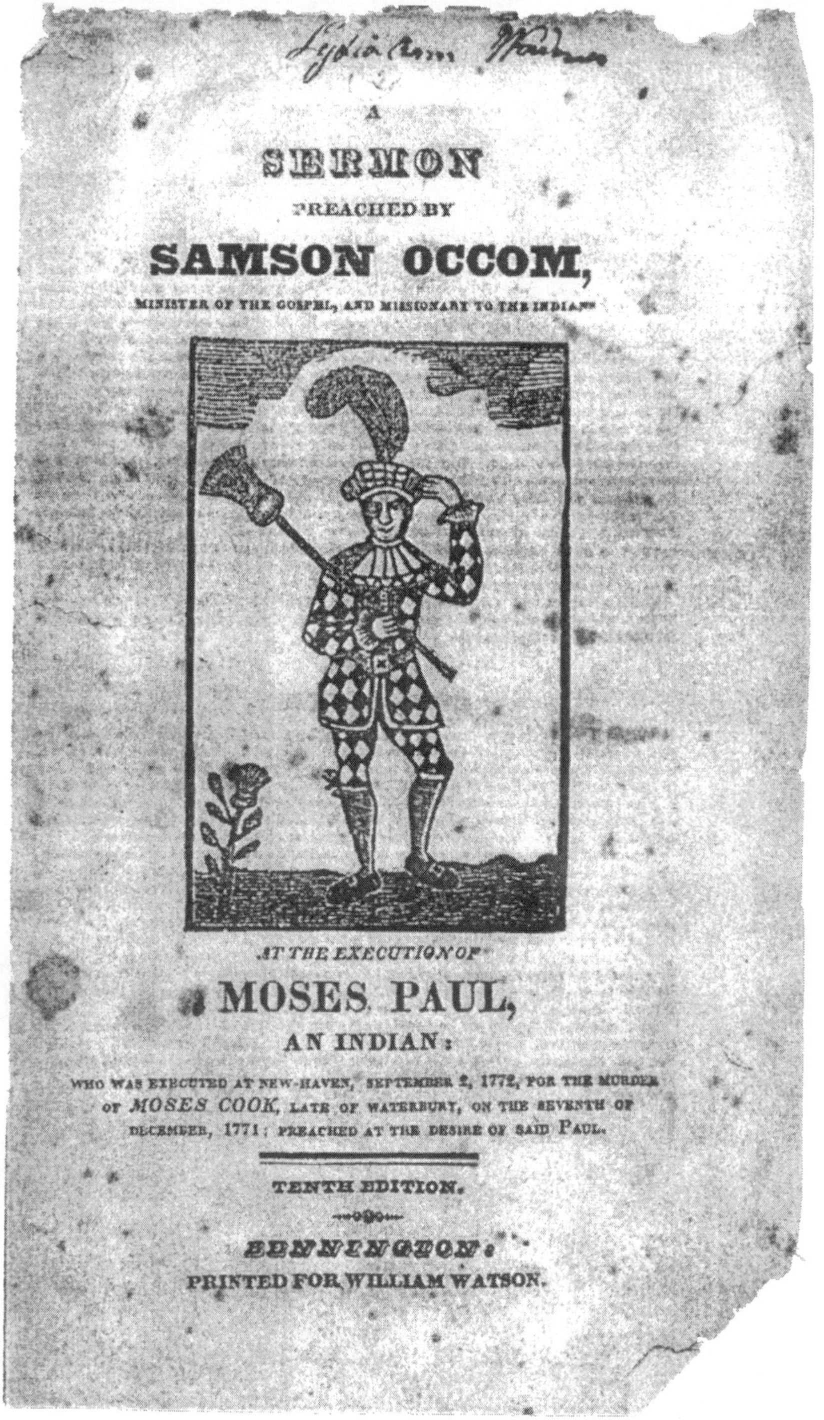

A

SERMON

PREACHED BY

SAMSON OCCOM,

MINISTER OF THE GOSPEL, AND MISSIONARY TO THE INDIANS

AT THE EXECUTION OF

MOSES PAUL,

AN INDIAN:

WHO WAS EXECUTED AT NEW-HAVEN, SEPTEMBER 2, 1772, FOR THE MURDER OF *MOSES COOK*, LATE OF WATERBURY, ON THE SEVENTH OF DECEMBER, 1771; PREACHED AT THE DESIRE OF SAID PAUL.

TENTH EDITION.

BENNINGTON:

PRINTED FOR WILLIAM WATSON.

Figure 1-6. Title page from Samson Occom's *Sermon at the Execution of Moses Paul, an Indian*, 10th ed. (By permission of the Houghton Library, Harvard University.)

# Samson Occom and Native Print Literacy

PHILLIP H. ROUND

Of all the Native literacies discussed in this volume, perhaps none has been more often misrepresented or misunderstood than print literacy. To some degree, that misunderstanding lies in the definition of print literacy itself. Unlike simple literacy, often tracked in historical records by signature evidence, print literacy encompasses a broader array of cultural skills—the ability to understand and manipulate the meanings of different typographic fonts, to interpret and to employ illustrations, and to navigate the physical properties of printed texts. Well into the nineteenth century, Native Americans were considered "an unlettered people,"[117] yet several northeastern tribal communities had been engaged in reading and writing books since the seventeenth century.

Samson Occom lived at the center of this emerging world of Native print literacy in eighteenth-century New England. From the time he picked up his first primer until his death in 1792, Occom was, in many ways, a man of the book. His 1766 portrait, which was painted in England at the request of Lord Huntington, portrays him seated at a table with his right hand outstretched on an open Bible in front of a bookcase full of beautifully bound volumes. Occom himself bound books to supplement his income, and his diary is full of references to books that he purchased, was given, had borrowed, or had recommended.[118]

Occom's famous Personal Narrative, one of the earliest autobiographical sketches written by an American Indian in English, focuses on the challenges and opportunities that print literacy posed for the Mohegan convert. Penned in December 1765, while Occom sat in Boston disconsolately awaiting the departure of a ship for England, the Personal Narrative presents the author's life as a rebuttal to the charges of those who publicly questioned whether he was fit to be a minister. As was usual for a Native convert, such interrogation was most often directed toward his "Indianness." "Some say I cant talk Indian," Occom lamented to Wheelock. "Others say I cant read."[119] In what would become a familiar story for American Indians engaged in Euro-American literacy,

---

117. This is the phrase used by Supreme Court Justice John McLean in his concurring opinion for *Worcester v. Georgia* in 1832. Although that finding supported Cherokee tribal sovereignty, McLean's language continues the Marshall court's policy of characterizing the Cherokee as uncivilized and in a state of "pupilage" (Chief Justice John Marshall's words).

118. Love, *Samson Occom*, 148–50.

119. Letter to Eleazar Wheelock, 6 December 1765, reprinted in J. Brooks, *Collected Writings of Samson Occom*, 74.

Occom's ethnicity was at the center of the conflict. Yet the words he used to describe the attack on his character are telling: They focus on literacy—both Native language and European print—as an index of Occom's identity.

Occom's response to these charges is equally revealing. Rather than answer them publicly—or ignore them completely—he penned an autobiography. Writing an autobiographical sketch, even in the "privacy" of manuscript, was a way for Occom to face "the world." The public arena in which he found himself, at the age of forty-three, demanded of him an accounting of his education and upbringing, even though he had been ministering to Native converts since the age of twenty-seven and had been ordained in 1758. Although, he says, he began his life "a Heathen in Mmoyanheeunnuck," by the age of seventeen, Occom "began to think about religion," and he "began to learn to read." [120] At age nineteen, he went to live with Wheelock, and there he spent three years "learning." Occom ends his first draft at this point, with a desire for Christian conversion realized through a weekly course in "reading." Literacy, faith, and identity become inextricably intertwined in his simple page-long declaration of a "true account" of his education. Occom's story is paradigmatic of a whole generation of literate, Christian Native converts, for whom both vernacular and English print literacy framed their public utterances, a generation in which tribal oral traditions and European manuscript culture offered spaces for resistance and self-fashioning.

Recent scholarship on the history of the book has begun to recognize the centrality of print literacy to "the contact between the representatives of a literate European culture and those of a wholly oral indigenous one." [121] D. W. McKenzie, one of the founders of modern Anglo-American book studies, observes that the history of the book provides a theoretical framework for moving from simple questions of textual authority "to those of dissemination and readership as matters of economic and political motive." Such questions are paramount in the case of non-Europeans colonized by Europeans because of the central role played by "oral, manuscript, and printed texts in determining the right of indigenous peoples subjected to European colonization and to the commercial and cultural impositions of the powerful technologies of print." Viewing Native literacy through the lens of book history also better prepares us to recognize "the continuing reciprocities of speech and print in the evolution of [Indian] texts." [122]

Yet this "reciprocity" was neither evenhanded nor equal for Native Ameri-

---

120. Autobiographical Narrative, First Draft, 28 November 1765, reprinted in ibid., 51–52.
121. McKenzie, *Bibliography and Sociology of Texts*, 79.
122. Ibid., 1, 5, 130.

cans. As Sidonie Smith and Julia Watson have observed, "The language of writing, the means of publication—publishing house, editor, distribution markets . . . are associated with the colonizer's domination." Indian books and manuscripts find themselves immersed in what Philippe Lejune has succinctly described as "the vicious circle imposed by the market of cultural goods."[123] In this vein, literary scholar Laura Donaldson does well to caution, "English alphabetic writing has become so thoroughly naturalized that its function as a colonial technology has remained obscure." Donaldson argues that "writing worked alongside these more overt weapons of conquest" to "re-configure aboriginal cultures and bodies in ways functional for Euramerican imperialism."[124]

Armed with a heightened awareness of the role of literacy in New World colonization and exploitive colonial practices, we must still come to terms with recent literary studies such as Hilary Wyss's *Writing Indians*, which clearly demonstrates "the crucial role of literacy in forming colonial Native subjectivity."[125] In order to reposition Native print literacy in this complex array of European colonialism and Native agency, we must examine the earliest examples of Native print literacy from the point of view of European colonial practices and the complexities of colonial Native subjectivities.

By the last decades of the seventeenth century, for example, Massachusett-speaking converts had gained a literacy rate of almost 30 percent in Native-language syllabary texts. In communities such as Mashpee, Natick, and Gays Head, printed and written texts in Massachusett were "produced in the normal course of conducting the daily affairs of the Indian communities." The documents that have survived from the period mark uses of writing and print that swing from the sacred to the secular, the public to the personal. Deeds are most common, but among the records that Ives Goddard and Kathleen Bragdon have catalogued are also "records of town meetings, . . . depositions, wills, petitions, letters, notes, arrest warrants, a power-of-attorney, a notice of banns, . . . [and] marginalia in books."[126]

The table of contents from the 1685 edition of *Mamusse wunneetupanatamwe up biblum God* (The Holy Bible in Massachusett) exemplifies the complex weave of Native ideas and language with European concepts and print that constituted early Native literacy. The *Indian Bible* (as it is known in most scholarship) is justly famous for being the first Bible printed in North America, but when viewed as an expression of Native print literacy, it also reveals how, as Kristina Bross has observed, "the vernacular Bible made Indian readers

123. Smith and Watson, *Women, Autobiography, Theory*, 47; *On Autobiography*, 197.
124. Donaldson, "Writing the Talking Stick," 47.
125. Wyss, *Writing Indians*, 6.
126. Goddard and Bragdon, *Native Writings*, xvii.

possible."[127] The word *Book* in the italicized headings in the table of contents, like the word *God* on its title page, is left untranslated. This interpenetration of English and Massachusett, and the untranslatable state of such words—like the discovery of European books among the traditional grave goods in Algonquian burial sites in the Northeast—suggests a complex intermingling of European and Native, English and vernacular modes of signification.

Similarly, the text itself, as an article of production and consumption, has long been viewed as the sole work of John Eliot and a colonial and Christian imposition from "outside" Native societies. Yet to see the *Indian Bible* this way is, as Bross points out, to erase "the participation of the praying Indians in its production."[128] Recent works by Kristina Bross, Hilary Wyss, and Jill Lepore have pointed to the centrality of Native participants such as James Printer, who functioned (in the words of Wyss) "as cultural half-breeds inhabiting that dangerous no-man's-land between identifiable cultural positions."[129]

Thus, profound anxiety was also woven into this new possibility of print literacy for many Indian readers, and the marginalia penned in Massachusett in many extant copies of the *Indian Bible* show that vernacular print provided both a protected space for self-expression and affirmation of community and at the same time sheltered doubts and self-loathing. Some converts wrote proudly, "This is my hand," and "this book is right," as they interacted with print for the first time. Others, however, found the experience daunting. "I do not like very much to read," one Native reader wrote, "for I am too pitiful in this world."[130]

Native vernacular print was also partly integrated into the larger ongoing cultural project in the colonies that Patricia Crain has labeled "the alphabetization of America."[131] The *Indian Primer* (published in Boston in 1720)[132] exemplifies how vernacular print guided Native readers toward the more subtle forms of literacy entailed in typography. As a text that owed its existence to European education manuals such as *The New England Primer*, the *Indian Primer* exhibited to its pupils an array of alphabets in roman, italic, and black letter type on its opening pages. The facing page "translation" not only showed Native readers how to form letters in the Massachusett syllabary to match their English semantic equivalents; it also showed them how to shape the typographic tone of the utterance to master European typographic convention. In this way,

127. Bross, *Dry Bones*, 68.
128. Ibid., 54.
129. Wyss, *Writing Indians*, 12. See also Lepore, *The Name of War*.
130. Quoted in Goddard and Bragdon, *Native Writings*, 439.
131. Crain, *Story of A*, 4.
132. See E. Mayhew, *Indian Primer*.

the *Indian Primer* served as a disciplinary educational technology, "introducing the alphabet into a nonalphabetized culture and to a nonprint audience."[133]

Taken together, Native language texts such as the *Primer* and manuscript and printed works and marginalia such as those described and catalogued by Goddard and Bragdon, found meaning in Massachusett communities as they supplemented and extended existing cultural values. In societies where "skilled speech and status were interrelated," written and printed rhetorical style and formal protocols were practiced as extensions of these modes of sociability. Bragdon finds that in Native New England, "writing was inherently social, and that reading and writing were 'inextricably' linked to speech." These works, "not merely remnants of the oral mode that survived into writing," describe a print literacy that embodies "the ongoing sociability and orality of literacy among the Massachusett speaking people."[134]

By the time Occom began to study with Wheelock in 1753, there was also a growing body of English-language primers, spellers, and devotional manuals that were directed at Native peoples. Occom's diary recounts how many of these books shaped his emerging skills as a writer and orator. He asked his English patrons to send copies of Benjamin Keach's *Tropologia* (1681) to other Native ministers, for he considered it "the best Book for the Instruction of the Indians of Humane Composure [he] ever saw."[135] He also recommended Alexander Cruden's *A Complete Concordance to the Holy Scriptures of the Old and New Testament* (London, 1738) and was given Matthew Poole's *Annotations upon the Holy Bible* (1683) by one of Wheelock's correspondents. In his own library, Occom held works such as Thomas Horton's *Forty-six Sermons* (London, 1674) and a 1685 edition of Eliot's *Indian Bible*.

Armed with these print sources and practiced in catchizing his Indian students in the Mohegan language, Occom developed a public speaking style that was becoming well known and was much sought after in the early 1770s. By 1772, when he was asked to deliver an execution sermon for a fellow Native American who had been convicted of murder, Occom was probably the most famous English-language Indian orator in North America. After he delivered his sermon, Occom was immediately asked to publish it—a common practice for many Euro-American ministers after they had delivered a particularly noteworthy public sermon or address. Like his public performances, Occom's first published work turned on the sensational prospect of an Indian convert

---

133. Crain, *Story of A*, 42.
134. Goddard and Bragdon, *Native Writings*, 122, 123.
135. Letter to Andrew Gifford, 19 October 1772, reprinted in J. Brooks, *Collected Writings of Samson Occom*, 101.

speaking to another Indian on the evils of drink. Soon, however, it became much more than that. The resulting publication attained status as not only a milestone in the history of American Indian print literacy, as the first book published by a Native author, but also an important watershed in the history of American religious publishing, with nineteen editions subsequently published in both the colonies and England.

Occom's *Sermon at the Execution of Moses Paul*, first published by Timothy Green in New London, Connecticut, in 1772, marks a crucial point at which the varied experiences of Native people in the Northeast coalesced with European print to produce the first "Indian" book. As we have seen, Occom's foray into Anglo-American print culture did not come out of nowhere, and a close reading of the physical properties of this text shows that the technology of movable type was becoming, for many Native people, an integral part of the larger practices of cultural literacies explored in the other chapters of this anthology. The title page of an early edition of Occom's *Sermon at the Execution of Moses Paul* (Figure 1-4) announces its subject through not only its content but also its typography. The death's head motif at the top of the page locates the pamphlet in an established Puritan literary genre: the execution sermon, a genre that plays an essential role in what David Hall has called the region's "Protestant vernacular."[136] The words *Sermon, Moses Paul,* and *Murder* leap from the page, because the typography imparts to each word a special meaning beyond its semantic signification. Black letter type sets off *Murder* from the rest of the page in a gothic effort to sensationalize the pamphlet. Although the modern reader might prefer to think that Occom's "Indian" identity sold this work to popular readers, the typography of the title page does little to support that idea. Murder, after all, will sell out. Occom's title page sets up his sermon to be what Hall has termed a "steady seller,"[137] an irresistible blend of prurience and piety.

Only the Introduction, which follows the title page, exposes the author's vexed relationship (ethnic, political, racial) to a material object that has effectively signaled its own authority and sensationality (read: "steady-sellerness") in typographical ways. Here Occom writes, "The world is already full of books. . . . What folly and madness it is in me to suffer anything of mine to appear in print, to expose my ignorance to the world." Yet in spite of this hesitation and doubt, Occom's text goes on (both in material form and rhetorical structure) in exemplary execution sermon style, with typography—especially italic type—underscoring crucial points in the orally delivered address to add

136. Hall, *Worlds of Wonder,* 5.
137. Ibid., 48–52.

emphasis and immediacy to the printed work. When, for example, Occom addresses his fellow Native Americans directly ("my poor kindred"),[138] the type is set off in italic, as is his later apostrophe to Paul himself.

In addition to the way the sermon is set on the page, the text exposes the role that print played in forging social relationships between Indian converts and Anglo-American Christians in early America. Marginal notations written here and there in this copy of the 1772 edition and title page autographs show how such texts were disseminated, who read them, and how readers reacted to them. Joseph Lyman, a Connecticut cleric and supporter of missionary work among the Indians, owned this edition. In its final pages (not pictured here), there is a telling handwritten exclamation that brackets the printed text: *Amabam Audiebam* (O Everlasting Love! O Hearken unto this Everlasting!).[139] The reader's marginal interjection suggests the powerful interactive response that even the printed text could engender in late eighteenth-century readers.

Evidence drawn from outside the printed work suggests that it also enjoyed popularity among Native American Christian converts. In Farmington, Connecticut, in 1772, Joseph Johnson convened a group of fellow Christians "that [he] might read the Revd. Samson Occoms Sermon."[140] The work so affected Johnson that he wrote and published his own response, *Letter from J—h J—n . . . to Moses Paul* (1772). Later, when he was on a missionary trip to the Mohawk, Johnson again gathered a group together to hear him read the sermon. Johnson's diary notation suggests that perhaps this reading was at the request of the Mohawk community: "I being desired to make a short stop here, in order to read unto these Indians the Sermon."[141] On the basis of his reading and the "exercises" that followed, the community asked Johnson to stay the winter and teach the children.

By the final decades of the eighteenth century, print was fairly common in Indian communities from the Five Nations in the North to the "Civilized Tribes" of the Southeast. In 1798, for example, the Society for the Propagation of the Gospel reported that it had circulated more than 300 volumes to Native converts and others within its jurisdiction. Of these, 38 were Bibles, 84 were testaments, and the rest were divided between 150 spelling books and 85 primers.[142] Occom's and Johnson's letters suggest that there was an even greater demand for good-quality print among Native converts than the society could supply. More than once, Johnson and Occom pled for small-print-run

---

138. J. Brooks, *Collected Writings of Samson Occom*, 192.
139. This copy of the sermon is part of the Ayer Collection at the Newberry Library in Chicago.
140. Quoted in L. Murray, *To Do Good*, 151.
141. Quoted in ibid., 187.
142. Thacher, *Brief Account*, 3.

favors—"half a Dozen of Smal Quarto Bibles, With good Paint and Papers and Binding"[143]—that might carry a fledgling Christian community through its first tentative stages of formation. By 1808, when Abiel Holmes delivered his sermon and report to the society, some fourteen thousand books had been distributed in the District of Maine alone over the previous five years. Among the Bibles, testaments, and hymnals, there were two thousand primers and spelling books.[144]

Long after the death of its author, Occom's sermon was republished, offering readers in the nineteenth century new meanings—for the death of Moses Paul and for Indian identity. The nineteen editions printed from 1772 through the first half of the nineteenth century, offered publishers and booksellers many opportunities to exploit Occom's popularity for their own purposes. In 1789 a New England publisher produced an edition of the *Sermon* that appended Jonathan Edwards Jr.'s treatise on Indian languages (Figure 1-5). In this case, Occom's work enables that of Edwards, in some ways passing the authority of the "Indian" authenticity of the first text onto the second, white-authored work.

In 1810 a reprint of Occom's *Sermon* appeared in Bennington, Vermont. Its title page illustration (Figure 1-6) undercuts the authority of the Indian author by employing the parodic image of a mountebank, or zany—that festive and theatrical jester-like character who, as Crain notes in her study of American alphabetic literacy, "descends from the commedia dell'arte *zanni*, the artful scheming, and bumbling clown."[145] It is not clear from this engraving whether Moses Paul or Occom is the object of the satire, but since "scholars and pedagogues are the mainstay" of this tradition and since this figure began to appear regularly in nineteenth-century primers in association with the education of children, it seems possible that the Bennington edition attempts to turn Occom's learning and literacy against the Native people as a mere parroting performance of white literate practices.

Toward the end of his life, in 1785, Occom moved to Oneida country in upstate New York. His first act upon resettlement was to write to the missionary society requesting many "necessaries" that the community was lacking. His request signals the continuing importance of books to Native Christian communities in the late eighteenth century: "Our most Humble Petition and Request is, this once, to help us a little, in our settling, in this wilderness, we extreamly want a grist mill and saaw mill and we [are] very destitute of all

143. Letter to Robert Keen, September 1768, reprinted in J. Brooks, *Collected Writings of Samson Occom*, 83.

144. Holmes, *Discourse*.

145. Crain, *Story of A*, 76.

manner of Husbandry tools and we should be glad and thankfull for a little Liberary." [146] From this "little liberary" and others like it across Indian country at the dawn of the nineteenth century, American Indian authorship, political agency, and tribal histories flourished in a new medium of print that combined the long-standing traditions of the Native ancestors with pressed type on a paper page.

---

146. Brotherton Tribe letter to U.S. Congress [1785?], reprinted in J. Brooks, *Collected Writings of Samson Occom*, 148–50.

# 2 · The Narragansetts

NOT TECHNICALLY part of New England in the original colonial sense, the Narragansetts were at the center of a network of Algonquian peoples, with the Pequots and Mohegans to their west, the Wampanoags to their east across Narragansett Bay, and the Nipmucks, Pawtuxets, and Massachusetts to their north.

According to Narragansett tradition, the deity Cautantowwit created humanity. Dissatisfied with his earlier stone creations, Cautantowwit broke the original man and woman and made a second version of humanity from a tree. From the great Cautantowwit, humans received corn and beans; Cheepi, a force of darkness, connected them to a spirit world and was therefore central to powwows or healers. Guided by a cosmography that shaped their world view, the Narragansetts lived for generations in a world defined by the interrelationship between spirits (or *manitou*), the people themselves and their neighbors, and the natural world, whose cycles shaped their annual movements from coastal to interior villages.

When the English arrived in the region in 1620, the Narragansetts, Pequots, Mohegans, and Wampanoags already had an extensive history of forming and dissolving alliances. When the Wampanoags befriended the English, the Narragansetts and the Pequots formed trading alliances with the Dutch. As English power in the region increased, however, Dutch influence declined. When the dissenting Puritan Roger Williams settled in the area of what is now Providence, Rhode Island, in 1636, perhaps he seemed a useful source of English trade to the Narragansett sachem Canonicus. In the spring of 1637, the Narragansetts threw in their lot with the English and their Mohegan and Niantic allies against the Pequots in a decisive (and devastating) battle that destroyed Pequot control of much of Connecticut. In 1643 the Mohegans and the Narragansetts narrowly avoided full-scale war after the Mohegan sachem Uncas killed the Narragansett sachem Miantonomi.

Initially, the Narragansetts took a neutral position in King Philip's war, but they were drawn into the hostilities (in what is now known as "the Great Swamp Fight" of late 1675) when the English destroyed a Narragansett winter camp. By the early eighteenth century, Narragansett settlements were limited to a few smaller communities in southwestern Rhode Island near Charlestown and North Kingston, which were often mixed with Niantic and other Native peoples from New England and beyond. It was not until 1766 that the first schoolhouse was built to serve the Narragansett community, despite missionary efforts reaching back to at least 1733. The first Christian congregation on the Narragansett reservation was established in 1745 by the ordained Indian minister Samuel Niles, the first of several Native preachers to minister to the Narragansett community beginning in the eighteenth century. In fact, according to the tribal website, the three-acre tract of land on which the Indian Church is located "is the only original parcel of land that has never been out of the possession of the Narragansett Tribe." [1]

Today the Narragansett Indian Tribe is based in Charlestown, Rhode Island, with a Narragansett Indian longhouse as the center of tribal activities and a school and museum that form a core element of cultural continuity.

## Suggested Reading

Herndon, Ruth Wallis, and Ella Wilcox Sekatau. "The Right to a Name: The Narragansett People and Rhode Island Officials in the Revolutionary Era." *Ethnohistory* 44, no. 3 (1997): 433–62.

Narragansett Indian Tribe website. Available at http://www.narragansett-tribe.org. Accessed 30 June 2006.

Simmons, William S. "Narragansett." In *Handbook of North American Indians*. Vol 15, *Northeast*, edited by Bruce G. Trigger, 190–97. Washington, D.C.: Smithsonian Institution, 1978.

Sweet, John Wood. *Bodies Politic: Negotiating Race in the American North, 1730–1830*. Baltimore: Johns Hopkins University Press, 2003.

---

1. Narragansett Indian Tribe website.

# The Case of Sarah Pharaoh

These three documents form part of a court proceeding for infanticide that was heard by the Superior Court of Judicature (the highest court) of the colony of Rhode Island in 1730. The depositions (testimonies given under oath) were copied from local court records onto sheets of paper included in the packet of file papers that make up the case record. They are archived in the Rhode Island Supreme Judicial Court Records Center in Pawtucket, Rhode Island. These evidences were taken by county justices of the peace called in to conduct an investigation into a suspected infanticide. Although written as statements, they were probably the result of questioning, which may have been conducted through an interpreter. Few Narragansetts were fluent in English at this time; therefore, interpreters were commonly employed in court proceedings. When an interpreter was used, however, the intervention was usually noted in the record, and none is specified in the depositions under examination.

## Deposition of Mary Sambo (against Sarah Pharaoh)

The Deposition of An Indian Woman belonging To South Kingstown Called Mary Sambo being Strictly Charged by Us the Subscribers to Speak the Whole Truth And to omit Nothing that was Meteriall to To [sic] Prove the Soposed Murder And She Said She Would Tell all She Knew About it & that Living in a house or Cottage on Coll. Christopher Allens Land an Indian Woman Called Sarah Faraoh came to her Cottage about Seven weeks agone & there Tarryed a prette while and while she was there She perceived the said Sarah Faraoh To Look burley as She thought & charged her with being with Child. But She denyed being with child & Kept a blanked wraped about her, & Soon after She perceived her Shift Near her brest to be wet and She thoght with milk but could not say it was, & while She was there She saw by the fire in the place where She The sd Sarah had sat Several Cloders of blood and Then She went and Looked in the bed where She had Lain and perceived also the Same Sight there & then asked the sd Sarah the reason of it and what the matter was with her & whether it was Common for women to be so Said Sarah replyed it was Common for women to be so that had not been well a great while as She her Selfe had Not and further saith Not Taken in South Kingstown in Kings County this 16th day of March A: D: 1729 Before Rowse Helme Assist: [Assistant]

## Examination of Sarah Pharaoh (on the Reverse
## of the Same Paper as the Sambo Deposition)

The Examination of An Indian Woman belonging to South Kingstown Called Sarah Faraoh being Examined on Suspition of Murdering of A Certaine young Child Which was found Dead on Collo Christophr Allens Land in sd Town Who Declairs that the Child was None of hers and that She had Not bin with Child Sence her Boy was Borne, Which She Sayeth Was Above Four Yeares Agoe: And further She Sayeth that Some Time the last Spring She Told An Indian that She was with Child and that She Wanted to Drink Some Rum but She Now Declares that What She Told sd Indian Was only Jeasting Talk Taken in South Kingstown in Kings County this 16th day of March A: D: 1729 Before Rowse Helme Assist: and Christopher Allen, Justice of the Peace

## Deposition of Indian Hannah

Indian Hannah Who Commonly Lives With Robert Potter in South Kings-town being an Old Indian Woman Who Was Called before Us the Subscribers to Declair the whole Truth of What She Knew Concerning Sarah Faraohs being With Child And She Declared that Sarah Faraoh Come to her . . . in the Latter Part of Last Mowing Time[2] And told her that She was Not Well and was Much out of Order and Desired sd Hannah to Get Some Roots for her to Take but sd Hannah says She Made her this Reply & Told her She Thought She was with Child and if so The Taking sd Roots Would Kill the the [sic] Child and She must be Hanged for It She Further Says that Indians Often Use that Sort of Roots When they Are in Travil[3] Which Soon Cause them to be Delivered/Taken in South Kingstown this 18th Day of March A: D: 1729 before Rowse Helme Assist/ Christo Allen Justice of the peace

~:~

---

2. "Mowing Time" refers to late summer or fall, when hay is being mowed for winter.
3. "Travil" signifies "travail," "labor," or "childbirth."

# The Dreadful Case of Sarah Pharaoh

## Finding Native Women's Voices in an Eighteenth-Century Infanticide Case

### ANN MARIE PLANE

Mary Sambo, who was called to testify in a case of infanticide in 1730, "Said She Would Tell all She Knew About it." Two other Indian women, "Indian Hannah," a healer, and Sarah Pharaoh, the accused, gave testimony as well.[4] Although additional witnesses in this southern Rhode Island community were also called, it is the involvement of the three examined here that makes this case particularly useful to scholars of Native American women's history, American colonial legal history, and Native American speech and literacy in early America.

It is arguable that these documents are out of place in a collection that focuses on Native literacy. After all, other than the mark (a vertical line) that Sambo placed, in lieu of a signature, on a bond for her appearance, none of these women can be said to have written a word—not here and, as far as we know, not at any time in their lives. That, however, is precisely the dilemma that faces scholars who are interested in women's writing in general and Native American women's writing  in particular. Of the few documents that reveal aspects of women's lives in the seventeenth and eighteenth centuries, all but a handful were written by men. Of the documents that speak to the experiences of Native American women—certainly among the records I combed for a larger study of Native American marriage in southeastern New England during the seventeenth and eighteenth centuries—not one was actually penned by a Native American woman.[5] Thus, although purists may wish to adhere to a strict definition of "women's writing," doing so both elides and erases women in general and Native women in particular from the pages of history.[6] Such distortion of the past has dominated understandings of the colonial world for several centuries, but with the dawn of the twenty-first century, this myopia has been challenged with great force and ingenuity.[7] Accepting a broader definition of "writing," therefore, let us take a look at what Mary Sambo, Indian Hannah, and Sarah Pharaoh have to say.

What brought these three Indian women into court was a shocking discovery. Benjamin Lad and three of his friends, all boys about fourteen years old,

---

4. See R. v. Sarah Pharaoh.
5. See Plane, Colonial Intimacies, 10–11.
6. Ulrich, "Of Pens and Needles," 200–207.
7. Merrell, "Colonial Historians and American Indians," 94–96.

had been sent by Christopher Allen "A Looking for fox holes in order to dig after them, it being a place known to be Plenty of foxes." They came across what they called "an Indian barn," a large pit dug into the ground, which was used by New England Natives to store maize over the winter—by safely tucking it, protected by layers of sand and woven mats, into the "barn"—until it was needed for food or seeds. At the side of this unused pit, however, they saw fresh marks. "Looking therein, We Saw Something, which we soon discovered to be a dead Infant Child being Naked." [8] They removed the body, and hurried away to report their discovery to Allen, the landowner.

It was common in this part of southern Rhode Island for land to be divided into huge acreages under the control of a few wealthy landowning families. With the other residents in some way beholden to these great families, this landholding pattern was quite different from that found in most of the rest of colonial New England. Nevertheless, these farms were not devoid of a diversity of people. Although a few white men held most of the lands, a variety of tenants and laborers populated the region. In addition to being home to English-speaking smallholders, artisans, and tenants, King's County, Rhode Island—whose workforce was one of the most diverse in New England—included an unusually high concentration of African and African American slaves, Irish farm laborers, Indians, and people whose parents hailed from more than one of these groups.[9] Thus, although each woman was, where possible, identified by the white landowner "with whom" she lived, it is clear from reading the depositions that Sambo and Hannah did not live as dependents within a white household; they maintained their own independent residences. (Hannah is described as one "Who Commonly Lives With Robert Potter," while Sambo is described as "Living in a house or Cottage on Coll. Christopher Allens Land.") Most important, although the white guardians of Charles Ninegret, the Narragansett sachem, played a large "advisory" role and regularly arranged for much of his acreage to be rented out, Ninegret was still—legally speaking—autonomous, retaining title to substantial portions of the county.[10] The three women were probably Narragansetts, although during this period the term *Indian* applied to other New England Natives and even sometimes to imported Spanish Indian servants.

The Pharaoh court case involved many of these different elements of King's County society. The record of the investigation gives an unprecedented glimpse

8. Depositions of Benjamin Lad, Ichabod Sheffield Jr., Samuel Potter, and Nathaniel Sheffield, March 16, 1729/30.

9. E. Channing, *Narragansett Planters*, 10 n. 1. See also Plane, *Colonial Intimacies*, 123.

10. Plane, "Customary Laws of Marriage," 186–87.

into the webs of kinship and connection that linked individuals and families to the land and to one another in unusually rich and otherwise largely invisible ways. The case file is not large. There is a summary of the charges in the Superior Court record book for the March 1730 session. Because the modern calendar was not adopted until later in the century, the new year began in mid-March, so although the depositions are dated 1729, the whole investigation took place locally between 15 and 18 March 1729/1730 (i.e., 1730) and was forwarded to the superior court in Newport for its session beginning on the last Tuesday in March 1730, after the new year had turned.[11] In addition to the indictment, the depositions by the three Indian women, and the deposition by Lad and his friends, there is a warrant for a coroner's inquest, the verdict of the coroner's jury, Sambo's bond to appear and give testimony, and the order to the constable to transport Pharaoh to jail in Newport. It appears that the superior court in Newport dismissed the case, as the back of the formal indictment is marked simply "ignoramus 1730." Sambo, Pharaoh, and Indian Hannah do not appear elsewhere in the Rhode Island court record, although they may have made a mark in the lengthy account book reckonings that large landowners—such as Colonel Allen—kept with their long-term tenants.

Even so, this cache of documents is a remarkable find. It is rare enough to have a fully realized deposition from a single Indian deponent; to have multiple sources in which the individuals paint a picture of their daily lives, describe their interactions, and contradict one another is a historian's veritable gold mine. The words of Sambo, Indian Hannah, and Pharaoh are, of course, constrained by the conventional forms of eighteenth-century legal testimony. Thus, although Sambo begins by noting that she will "Tell all She Knew About it," this was surely a formulaic response, since she was "Stricktly Charged" by her examiners "to Speak the Whole Truth And to omit Nothing that was Meteriall to . . . Prove the Soposed Murder." Each woman gave her testimony before Rowse Helme, one of the governor's assistants (representatives) for the county. Colonel Allen was most likely also present for all three cases. He is noted in two of the depositions; and although the Sambo document itself refers to "us the subscribers" (seemingly more than just Helme), he is not listed by name in Sambo's case. Perhaps the two officials decided that it would be better for Allen not to sign off on the examination of his own tenant. Whatever the legal niceties, another document makes the practical implications clear—Allen stood "as surety" for Sambo's later appearance in court as a witness. If she failed to give testimony, Allen would have to forfeit his money, and she would owe Allen. Her freedom to speak openly about what she knew was, therefore, limited in

11. *R. v. Sarah Pharaoh*, File Papers: Indictment.

some significant ways by her prior obligation to her landlord. Indian Hannah and Sarah Pharaoh could not have failed to experience similar constraints on their own testimony.

Despite the constraints, the experiences of these three Indian women—along with their individual circumstances, concerns, opinions, and disagreements— emerge forcefully in these documents. Clearly, Pharaoh wants something specific from Sambo and Indian Hannah. Clearly, the two women want to absolve themselves of any responsibility for wrongdoing. Sambo's interactions with Pharaoh are related in a way that foregrounds her suspicions of Pharaoh's pregnancy and the due investigation of her suspicions in the way that any English woman would have recognized. Midwives and ordinary women of child-bearing age were expected by English courts to keep a watchful eye on younger or less protected women and bring suspicions of note to the authorities.[12] Midwives and healers (and it would appear that Indian Hannah was known for such talents) were expected to use their knowledge to ease suffering, not to abet abortion or infanticide (actions for which, as Hannah reports, Pharaoh "must be Hanged"). Did these Indian women understand their responsibilities under English law? Or, what is more likely, did the process of developing a statement—a process that might involve considerable give-and-take between examiners, witness, and such intermediaries as a landlord, a relative, or (even at this late date) a translator—create the appearance of diligent investigation when, in fact, ignorance, indifference, or even outright collusion might have been the truer characterization of the relationship between Pharaoh and each of her Indian neighbors?

Even if the full truth of Sambo's and Hannah's reactions to Pharaoh can never be known, each deposition reveals much about the day-to-day world in which these women lived. This was a world in which it was not unusual when an Indian woman "Tarryed a prette while" in the home of another Indian family, in which Indian women were frequently the householders, separate from any menfolk; in which some women, like Indian Hannah, became known as especially talented healers, herbalists, and midwives; in which the signs of pregnancy and parturition—a "burley" physique, postpartum blood clots, breast milk leaking onto a linen shift—were telltale signs of a familiar narrative. This was a world in which an Indian woman had to support herself by her own labor. Children were as much a hindrance as a help as she struggled to keep her head above the mountain of debts that dogged most eighteenth-century workers. One or more children might better be bound out as household labor to an English family—which, in fact, many Native parents found themselves obliged

12. Ulrich, *Good Wives*, ch. 4; Ulrich, *A Midwife's Tale*, 149–52.

(by circumstances, finances, or the law) to do.[13] Tellingly, there is no mention of the presence of Pharaoh's four-year-old boy—only the assertion that she had not been with child since his birth.

In fact, all three women exhibit considerable sophistication in their understanding of the uses of their testimony. Pharaoh recognized that denial was her best option, and, given the level of oppression that the women faced, her response represents a significant challenge to colonial authorities. Since confession might well lead her to the hangman's noose, she steadfastly denied that she had been with child—despite the considerable evidence (requests for abortifacient roots, telltale spots of blood and milk, the dead body of a baby) and the willingness of her compatriots to testify against her.[14] Sambo's testimony was assembled into a coherent narrative by the English justices, but her deposition still bears traces of the original questions and answers of her interview. She comes across as a diligent, responsible matron, questioning Pharaoh's "burley" shape, examining the places where she had lain or sat, and questioning Pharaoh as to "the reason of it." Similarly, Indian Hannah seems well aware of the colonial laws governing midwifery—either she or her examiner made it clear that she refused to obtain certain roots for Pharaoh, knowing full well that they might cause her to run afoul of the colonial authorities, for whom infanticide was a capital crime.

These depositions reveal both the many voices and the unique circumstances of Native women. At the same time, they expose their subjects' inevitable enmeshment in colonial legal structures. The literacy of the Native women is one steeped in familiarity with colonial hierarchies, legal institutions, and labor systems. These are not conventional forms of literacy, of course; rather, they are very specific forms, forged only after long acquaintance with the dangers posed by colonial authority. There is no single voice here; there is a multiplicity of voices, rising together—each with disparate strands—to forge a single chorus.

---

13. See Murray and Herndon, "Markets for Children in Early America," 356–82.

14. See Hoffer and Hull, *Murdering Mothers*, 60–64. On abortion during this period, see also Dayton, "Taking the Trade," 19–49.

# Letter to Eleazar Wheelock, 1769

## Sarah Simon

Sarah Simon's letter is in the Dartmouth College Archives among the papers of Eleazar Wheelock. It is written on one sheet of paper, measuring approximately 12 inches by 7.5 inches, which is folded in half to produce four surfaces for writing. The last side is addressed as follows:

For—
The Re[end] Mr Elezer Wheelo[k][DD]
    Att
    Lebanon

The letter is marked throughout with inkblots and misspellings, signaling the lack of experience of the writer. In addition, words spill off the left-hand side of the page, many words are hyphenated, and (where the author reached the end of the sheet of paper and opted to finish at the beginning of the next line) some words are simply cut off. There is a great deal of space between the lines—enough for Simon to insert revisions and corrections above the sentence in question. The handwriting is generally neat, but the letter concludes rather abruptly, with lines spaced more closely and a signature squeezed into the final line of the letter, which is written at the very bottom of the page.

Lebanon Crank[15] ye
16th 1769

Re[end] and Hon[rd] Sir

I have been this some time back thinking upon things of Religion, and I think thay do not look so {^plain to me}[16] as I have seen them {^and} I have grat many wicked thoughts and I do not knowe what I Shall do if I do not ask Somebodys advise about it for I feel very bad about it; I have thought a grte while that I would Come and talk with {^the} Dr but then I thought again that

---

15. "Lebanon Crank" is the name of the area of Lebanon in which Moor's Charity School was situated and the area in which most of the students boarded. Today it is the town of Columbia, Connecticut.

16. I have left the spelling as it appears in the original, and I have marked the author's inserted passages with a caret in curly brackets, {^}. In the original, the caret is written under the line and the inserted word or words (which are shown here in curly brackets) appear above the line.

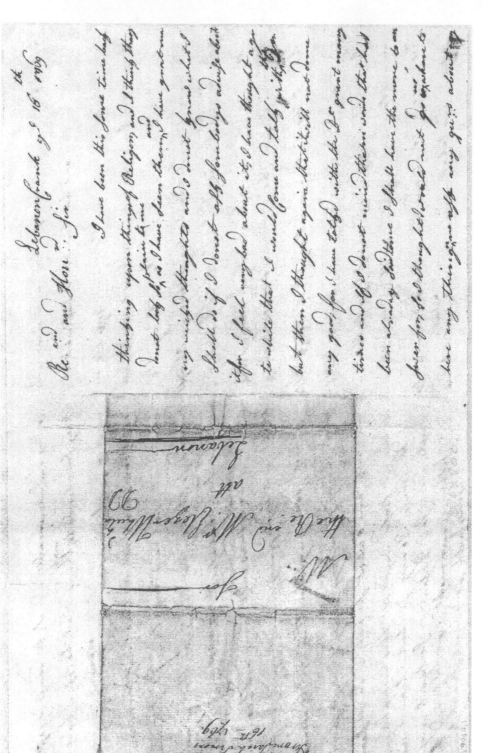

Figure 2-1. Sarah Simon, letter to Eleazar Wheelock, 1769. (Courtesy of Dartmouth College Archives.)

but I fear it is the work of satan and I have until it till I am undone for him and I believe that satan is happier with me than anybody else in this world even when I go to bed he keeps all my thoughts away upon something else and every temptation he lies before me till I however would not till my body of its beams I was at home this often same all alone also thinking upon those things now and saying what I should do and I thought of a day while and I hope that when any one was at left almost every thing they brought go to them minister and engross fathers and their lead you into its and then I think it is applied what to love and I take your advice and depend to

is this unacountable or fact, the Devil is just any sometime to think that he be life when once you are in perfection and I don't keep up together and I seem to see all the true Christian men meets with such a struggle with satan so and I see that who are far from that I am a christian because the Devil is whatsoever me more than he is with any one else found on I go to to pray but till me that I will not do my goodnature will round any thing for me to go every thing to put its back and o what shall I do I fear too me o God would all this weighty given if I could Do any good but I fear I will last. S.S. I desire to submit myself to the

Dutifull Servant Lawrence Hartshorne

it will not do me any good, for I have talkd with the Dr grant many times and If I do not mind them words that has been alraday said to me I shall have the more to answer for; so I thought I would not go {^no} where to here any thing {^or} no ask any qu ns about any but I fear it is the works of Saton; and I have missed it till I am undone for Ever and I believe that Saton is besser [17] with me than any body els in this world Even when I go to Read he taks all my thoughts away upon something Els and many temptation he las before me I thought I never would not till any body of it but as I was at home this after noon all alone I was thinking upon thise things and wondering what I should do and I thought of a book I have Read onse that when any one was at last about any thing thay must go to thare minister and inquire of them and these {^will} lead you into it, and then I think it is my duty to Come and take your advise. And I {^what}[18] want to know is this am {^I} uncureable or not, the devil is jest Redy sometimes to {^make me} think that becase I have made a perfertion [19] and do not {^alwas} keep upright. and it seems to me all the true Christan never meats with such a struggle with Saton as I do and so that maks me fear that I am a Christan becase the devil is so bese with me more than he is with any one Els for when I go to try to pray he till me that it will not do any good nither will it merat any thing so he trys Every thing to put me back. and o what shall I do it seam to me I Could writ all this night to you if it would do any good but I fear it will not. —So I Desire to subscrib my Silfe your most humble and Ever Duty full searvent Sarah Simons

# Writing Back to Wheelock

## One Young Woman's Response to Colonial Christianity

HILARY E. WYSS

The mid-eighteenth century saw increased possibilities for Native education, as religious enthusiasm spread in both Anglo-American and Native circles. Communities of Mohegans, Niantics, Narragansetts, Pequots, Montauks, and others all hired schoolteachers who generally taught girls as well as boys. And

---

17. Possibly "busier." See the passage later in the letter where the word "bese" seems to echo this sentence in that "the devil is so [busy] with me."

18. "What" seems to be inserted in the wrong place: The passage is probably meant to read, "And what I want to know is . . ."

19. It is unclear what the perversion is that Sarah Simon refers to here. Wheelock's students repeatedly confessed to such sins as drinking, fighting, and lewd behavior, but there is no further record of what Simon considers (or thinks Wheelock will consider) "a perfertion."

while missionary societies were often focused on the education of Native boys, Native communities—many of which had far more girls than boys available for anglicized schooling practices—were clearly interested in tending to their female students and employing Native women as educators. As one observer reported of the Pequots of Stonington, "They generally inclined to have a *school mistress*, and an *Indian*; Urging that their children were chiefly *Girls*. I knew not whether this wd be agreable to Commissioners, however, allow'd them to make trial. Several were propos'd, but they could not unite in any."[20]

Native girls had other educational possibilities as well: In the eighteenth century, they were also included in plans for boarding schools such as John Sergeant's Stockbridge Boarding School and Eleazar Wheelock's Charity School in Lebanon, Connecticut (albeit hardly on an equal footing with their male counterparts).[21] Indeed, at Wheelock's co-educational school, Native girls attended class only one day a week; the boys, in contrast, were in class at least five days a week. Whereas boys generally lived at the school, girls spent most of their time boarding with local families, learning the art of housewifery.[22] Even so, Wheelock's female students learned to write: Approximately six letters clearly authored and written by female students from the Connecticut school have been preserved among the hundreds of letters by and about Wheelock's Indian students, and Wheelock's ledger books indicate regular purchases of paper for "the female school."[23]

Yet writing, the symbolic system most intimately attached to English power structures, was not self-evidently of benefit to Native women. Whatever educational opportunities were available, the reality for Native women was that they had very few opportunities to participate in English colonial structures to their fullest abilities. As wives, daughters, and servants on Anglo-American terms, Native women—unlike in most Native communities—were accorded virtually no political or legal rights.[24] Indeed, although women were increasingly included in writing instruction through the eighteenth century, colonial presumptions about its suitability for "masculine" pursuits such as business,

---

20. Joseph Fish to Andrew Oliver, 5 November 1757. See Love, *Samson Occom*, 188–206, for more specific information on schoolmasters and Native communities.

21. In the first in a series of tracts describing his school, Wheelock explains his plan to educate Native missionaries to prepare them to serve not only as ministers and teachers with distant tribes but also as examples of proper (that is, English-style) living. As part of that plan, he explains, "a Number of Girls should also be instructed in whatever should be necessary to render them fit, to perform the Female Part, as House-wives, School-mistresses, Tayloresses, etc." (*Plain and Faithful Narrative*, 15).

22. Szasz, *Indian Education*, 222.

23. Wheelock's ledger books, Dartmouth College Archive.

24. See Plane, "Putting a Face on Colonization" 140–65; Bragdon, *Native People*, 170–83; O'Brien, *Dispossession by Degrees*, 100–101.

ministry, and politics meant that, as a consequence of their gender, women were barred from its most obvious economic benefits.[25]

In the missionary circles through which Native women received their literacy instruction, the boarding school was the environment that most emphatically positioned them as secondary figures—lesser, certainly, than the Anglo-Americans who controlled their access to education but also lesser than their male counterparts. Women were expected to be appendages whose primary function was to aid their spouses, a perspective that Wheelock repeatedly emphasized to his students, particularly the seventeen or so girls who spent time at Moor's Charity school in the decade during which it was in operation in Lebanon, Connecticut. Their own needs and desires were irrelevant to the situation. For at least some young Native women, the double abjection of their position was untenable; many left Wheelock's school after only a few months, and only one student, Hannah Garret, ever fulfilled Wheelock's plan, by marrying one of the male students of his school.

Sarah Simon (Narragansett), one of the few eighteenth-century Native girls for whom a set of self-authored ruminations on self and identity has been preserved, serves as a dramatic example of the difficulties of being a Native girl in Wheelock's school. The surviving writing of Simon, who entered Wheelock's school in December 1765, is a poignant reminder that whatever promise education held out to young Native women in the eighteenth century, in the end it offered a structure through which they could define only what they would not be rather than what they could be. Sarah was one of five children sent by their mother (also named Sarah Simon) from the Narragansett community of Charlestown, Rhode Island, to Wheelock's school; she was one of the approximately sixteen pupils who were Narragansetts. Letters to and from these students indicate that they remained close and generally looked out for one another. Letters also suggest that Sarah and the other pupils went back and forth between the school and the Narragansett community (Sarah was home, for example, for at least part of 1767). Yet life in Charlestown, Rhode Island, was not easy for Natives in the mid-eighteenth century, and the connection with Wheelock's school removed them from tensions involving an increasingly unpopular schoolmaster, devastating legal battles, religious feuding, and a town government aggressively working to erase evidence of its Native population.[26]

Simon's writing reveals a rather tortuous relationship with all that Whee-

<hr />

25. As E. Jennifer Monaghan points out, because the *presumption* in colonial New England was that writing was better suited to boys, it was construed as a masculine activity ("She Loved to Read," 507; "Literacy Instruction," 66–67).

26. Herndon and Sekatau, "Right to a Name," 437, 452–54; Simmons, "Narragansett," 195–96; Simmons and Simmons, *Old Light*, xxxii–xxxvii, 126–29.

lock's charity school offered her. Clearly, at least part of the transition for young Sarah must have been the shift from a home in which women dominated to a school in which men did. Although evidence is sketchy, scholars suggest that Narragansett society may have been organized along more or less matrilineal lines; certainly, the Simon home, headed by the widowed Sarah Simon, was dominated by a matriarch.[27] The letters between Wheelock and the widow Sarah Simon suggest that Sarah the daughter initially fulfilled a role as her mother's deputy.[28] Her reports persuade her mother to send along the boys. (Her mother writes, "I've great satisfaction, in the account my daughter Sarah has given me of Your pious care of those Children which are under Your tuition," and at another point Wheelock writes to Sarah's mother, "I receivd your James not to please myself but at your earnest Desire by your Daughter Sarah, who told me you had given him to me to bring up and despose of as my own Son").[29] Sarah also seems to have mediated for her brothers early on, as they made their way through the school. Yet she receives little reward for this role, and as her brothers become increasingly important members of Wheelock's school, her own role diminishes substantially.

Certainly as a pupil in Wheelock's school, Sarah would have been expected to engage in the practice of writing; from the moment of their first arrival, Wheelock's students signed confessions, documents, and letters, whether or not they were able to write them. One hapless young woman was required to put her mark to a document on the very day of her arrival, confessing the sin of drinking at a tavern several days before—an act, according to the confession, that is "much to the dishonour of god & very prejudicial to the design & Reputation of this school."[30] Writing was intimately connected to Wheelock's disciplinary system; through signed confessions, Wheelock monitored his students, controlled their actions, and demanded that they reconceptualize their thoughts and deeds in terms of sin and damnation.

Throughout her letters—in all there are three, although she is mentioned in other letters as well—Sarah Simon's tone is consistently humble and submissive. Her first surviving letter—written in May 1768, two and a half years after her arrival—tells Wheelock that she is unwell and that perhaps some sea air (her home in Rhode Island is on the water) might do her good. She closes

27. For more on the role of women in Narragansett society, see Simmons, "Narragansett," and Herndon and Sekatau, 442, 445.

28. Edward Deake, the schoolmaster for the Narragansetts from about 1765 to 1776, was probably the scribe for several letters from the Simon family (McCallum, Letters, 225, 227, 231). For information on Deake, see Love, Samson Occom, 195–96, and Simmons and Simmons, Old Light.

29. Quoted in McCallum, Letters, 227, 225.

30. Ibid., 232.

with "but then if the Docktor [Wheelock] is not willing I have nothing more to Say for I would not do any thing to displease Mr Wheelock not for nothing at tall."[31] No response is recorded, but approximately a month later Edward Deake, the schoolmaster for the Narragansetts, warns Wheelock that one of his former students "has been some time among ye Indians in this place" and that he is spreading rumors about Wheelock's mistreatment of his pupils—namely that "Mary Secutor, & Sarah Simon have been kept as close to work, as if they were your slaves, & have had no privelidge in ye School Since last Fall, nor one Copper allow'd ym for their labour" and that James Simon is being bound out to a farmer rather than educated in the school.[32] In a rage, a few days after his receipt of this letter, Wheelock writes the widow Sarah Simon a long, defensive letter in which he justifies his treatment of her children and then imperiously concludes, "Your Daughter Sarah carries herself very well, but I think it not best she should come home to visit you till the Fall."[33]

In her next letter, written a year later, Sarah begs Wheelock to allow her to go home, for, she says, "I wont very much to See my Mother I understand she has mete with trouble latly and She wants to see me and she is not able to come to See me. . . . I do not think that she is long for this world . . . for she is very weekly and always Sick. My parent is very near and Dear to me: and being I do not desine to Ever to go home and live with hir again, I desire to beg that favour to go and see hir as ofen as the Doctor is willing I should for I don't want to ofand the Doctr in the least. But I feel willing to do any thing Sir that you think is bast for me."[34]

Through these letters, Sarah Simon is using writing in the way she is meant to: With all the markers of humility and deference appropriately deployed,

---

31. All of the letters from Wheelock's students cited here, including Sarah's, are available in their original form on microfilm from the Eleazar Wheelock Collection at Dartmouth College. They are also included in McCallum's *Letters*, from which they are cited.

32. Quoted in ibid., 65. John Daniel, a Narragansett parent, had pulled his son Charles from the school in November 1767 after learning that he was to "live with a good farmer a year or two" (quoted in ibid., 209). He writes in a fury to Wheelock, "I always tho't Your School was free to ye Natives; not to learn them how to Farm it, but to advance in Christian Knowledge . . . but to work two Years to learn to Farm it, is what I don't consent to, when I can as well learn him that myself and have ye prophet of his Labour, being myself bro't up with ye best of Farmers" (quoted in ibid., 231).

33. Quoted in ibid., 226. Although it is unclear whether Wheelock's former student was mischaracterizing the treatment of his students, it is worth noting that at no point did Wheelock refute the facts of the case—that the girls were getting little instruction and that both the boys and the girls were spending much of their time in labor. Wheelock, unlike his students and their increasingly alarmed parents, seems to have felt that this was the most appropriate training for the young Native people put in his charge.

34. Quoted in ibid., 229. Sarah Simon the mother lived on; she is recorded as having received a blanket from missionary Joseph Fish in 1771 and again in 1773 (Simmons and Simmons, *Old Light*, 73, 97).

Sarah's writing suggests that along with literacy skills, she has learned her proper place in the world. Even so, she does not fully accept her place; she is quite literally asking for permission to resituate herself or to reposition herself in her community. The fact that she is even asking suggests that she holds out hope that one way or another she can reconcile the various elements of her life and that through skillful negotiation she can work out a way to retain her connections to her home while fulfilling Wheelock's expectations for her.

The final document from Sarah that we have—the one reproduced here—is another letter to Wheelock, three smudged and blotted pages written in 1769, in which she seems to be admitting her defeat at the hands of Satan. Unlike the "confessions" that Wheelock was in the habit of requiring periodically from his pupils, clearly written by Wheelock, signed by Native students and witnessed by Anglo-American men, this is no perfunctory apology. It is instead a heartfelt questioning of all that Wheelock's school represents, and despite Sarah's concluding phrase, "So I Desire to subscrib my Silfe your most humble and Ever Duty full searvent Sarah Simons," it reads far more like a critique of his ability to help her in any way. As a record of her own reading and writing habits (she tells Wheelock of a book she once read; she spends an afternoon alone at home drafting a letter), the letter is simultaneously marked by her inexperience as a writer (in the most literal sense of the inkblots and the occasional awkward phrasing) and by her ongoing struggle to incorporate literacy skills into her life in a meaningful way. Ironically, underneath her despair over the state of her soul is a declaration of independence, a terrified and heart-wrenching realization that she is not meant to participate in the world that Wheelock has created.

Perhaps the most striking element of the letter is the absence of any reference to the Bible. In her spiritual crisis, Sarah Simon does not refer to the Bible as a source of comfort—a revealing oversight for a young woman who has spent the previous four years in a charity school whose stated purpose is to bring Indian children just like her to a clearer sense of Protestant Christianity. She does tell us that when she tries to read, Satan "taks all [her] thoughts away upon something Els and many temptation he la[y]s before [her]." Reading, she suggests, leads one away from piety—a view that is a far cry from Wheelock's insistence on literacy as a precondition for true religion. Even when she does actually refer to a book, it directs her away from reading and toward verbal exchange. She tells us, "I thought of a book I have Read onse that when any one was at last about any thing thay must go to thare minister and inquire of them and these {^ will} lead you into it, and then I think it is my duty to Come and take your advise."

Her experience with Wheelock, however, has led her to believe otherwise.

She writes, "I have thought a grte while that I would Come and talk with {^the} Dr but then I thought again that it will not do me any good, for I have talkd with the Dr grant many times and If I do not mind them words that has been alraday said to me I shall have the more to answer for." Despite the advice from her book, her strong inclination is that verbal exchange will not work—perhaps because Wheelock talks *at* her instead of actually addressing the problems as she sees them. Whatever the case, it seems clear to her that a meeting is out of the question—it will only compound her problems or give her "the more to answer for."

The production of this text was clearly no small task for Sarah Simon. Her unsteady handwriting, the inkblots throughout, the phonetic spelling of certain words, and even the way the words seem to run off the edge of her pages suggest that, despite her years at Wheelock's school, she was not an experienced writer. Indeed, she tells us that she wrote the letter under very specific (and probably quite unusual) circumstances: She was alone, she had an afternoon stretched before her, and she was clearly in spiritual crisis. She tells us that she originally had no intention of revealing her struggle to anyone, but she felt that she was morally obliged to reach out to Wheelock. Her document very clearly delineates the ways in which she is willing to do so.

The shape of this document is that of a letter; there is a date in the upper right hand corner, the opening salutation "Rev$^{end}$ and Hon$^{rd}$ Sir," and a closing phrase followed by her signature. The condition of the letter—folded and addressed on the outer page—indicates that it has been sent rather than personally taken to Wheelock. To frame this document as a letter is to imply a very different kind of exchange from the verbal exchanges she has read about in her book. Like a verbal exchange, a letter presumes a response; a confession, in contrast, is a statement rather than a conversation. A letter, however, also presumes that each party will have the opportunity to say what he or she has to say. On one level, then, writing provides Sarah Simon the only real possibility of voicing her position to Wheelock—especially since that position is clearly quite different from what Wheelock has in mind for her. In a startling departure from her previous letters, which are filled with flattery for Wheelock and self-abasement for Sarah, here there are no apologies, and no negotiations—only a single question, one to which Simon seems to already foresee Wheelock's answer: "And I {^what} [what I] want to know is this am {^I} uncureable or not."

Indeed, what this document most vividly suggests is that for Sarah Simon, religion is constructed as a battle between Satan and Wheelock for her soul. God is absent from the equation; there is no positive force that drives the Christianity that Wheelock has offered her, only the possibility of failure, of sin and damnation. The stern and unforgiving Wheelock presents her with directives that she cannot follow, advice that she cannot take, and rules that are too rigid; Satan, on the other hand, offers her seductive arguments and behaviors that feel comfortable to her. Satan is always there, listening to her, guiding her, conversing with her, whereas Wheelock is so distant that her best hope of communicating with him is to mail him a letter.

As Sarah Simon's afternoon of writing and contemplation turns into night, she becomes increasingly despondent: "O what shall I do it seam to me I Could writ all this night to you if it would do any good but I fear it will not," she reports bitterly. Finally, despite its promise to give her a voice to speak to Wheelock, writing has failed her. The exchange between Wheelock and Sarah must be framed in his terms, but those terms provide only a vocabulary for what she cannot be, not what she is.

Whereas Simon's letter announced her failure as a Christian on Wheelock's terms, her home community offered a strikingly different version of Christianity. An observer writes of a Sabbath meeting "at Narragansett" in 1768 (a year before Sarah Simon drafted her letter to Wheelock), in which Native "exhorters," or lay ministers, "attempted generally to describe the christian life, & did it, by giving a relation of their own religious experiences, which were mostly visions, dreams, impulses & similitudes." Speaking in both "English & . . . Indian," these Native preachers "were all very earnest in voice & gesture, so much so that some of them . . . seemed transported with a kind of enthusiasm." The emphasis throughout seems to have been on the forgiveness of sins and on the joyful attainment of heaven by Christians. The description continues, "One of the Exhorters addressed me . . . & said 'this is the way that we Indians have to get to Heaven. You white people have another way. I don't know but your way will bring *you* there, but I know that our way will bring *us* there." [35] Indeed, one of the long-standing tensions in the Narragansett community was between the white missionary Joseph Fish, who insisted on the importance of literacy and rigorous training in "true" religion, and Samuel Niles (Narragansett), a nonliterate preacher whose version of Christianity celebrated a more intuitive understanding of grace. [36] Sarah Simon's rejection of reading and writing as solutions to her religious crisis echo the sentiments of the Narragansett religious community to which she may well have returned. The Christian practices of the Native ministers, rooted in oral expression and indigenous lifeways, stood in stark contrast to those of Wheelock and Fish. Although leaving Wheelock's

---

35. Maclure, *Diary*, 189–90.
36. Simmons and Simmons, *Old Light*, xxviii–xxix; xxx–xxxi.

school may have curtailed Sarah Simon's economic prospects, we can only speculate on what religion held out for young Sarah, who by 1769 was so clearly ready to abandon Wheelock's rules.

There is no record of what happened to Sarah Simon thereafter. In terms of the archives, she simply disappeared into silence, having recorded her disillusionment with the power of words—written or spoken by a Native woman within an English power structure—to bring her any sort of satisfaction. Her last letter is dated 1769, and although the month in which the letter was written is unknown, Wheelock's daybook records boarding expenses for Sarah Simon ending in May or perhaps November 1769.[37] The last mention of Simon by name is a charge on 27 January 1770 for hiring a horse for a journey to Narragansett—possibly Sarah Simon's final journey home from Wheelock's school before he moved it from Connecticut.[38]

---

37. The November 1769 notation in Wheelock's daybook mentions boarding expenses for unnamed "hired girls," in contrast to the "Indian girls" he refers to before this date, who were boarded by David Huntington and his family (Wheelock's daybook, Dartmouth College Archive).

38. Wheelock's ledger book has a note on 6 November "To the Journey of Mr Allen's Horse to Narraganset to carry Sarah Symons home July 12th" and immediately below that a record of payment for "cash and expenses of Peter & for her" on the same date. At the bottom of the same page, posted for 27 January is a notation for cash paid to a Jo Hunt "for 2 Journies of his Horse to Narraganset by Hez Calvin & Sarah Symons." It is unclear when these journeys actually took place, but after November 1769, although Wheelock continued to pay off outstanding debts associated with the "female school" for up to a year, he ceased recording new charges for it.

# 3 · Natick

WE HAVE titled this section after the name of the first "praying town," Natick, established by Christian Indians and John Eliot some twenty miles west of Boston. The title acknowledges that no one traditional term fully represents the people included in this chapter. Unlike the groups named in the other sections of this anthology, Natick Indians have a specific colonial origin: The Natick Indian identity emerged in 1650, with the founding of Natick as the first praying town in New England. Although the inhabitants were drawn from the Massachusetts, the Pawtuckets, the Nipmuks, and other groups, they are most often associated with the Massachusetts. In time, the people who chose to live in Natick became a unified community, and the success of Natick as a missionary enterprise led nineteenth-century antiquarians and early ethnographers to designate Natick as the name of both a tribe and a language.

Although estimates of the numbers of "praying Indians" in New England in the seventeenth century range from sixty-four to eleven hundred, the cultural significance of these Christian Indians exceeded their numbers, since white colonists depended on them to help justify their existence to supporters in England. Missionaries could point to Natick as a tangible sign of their efforts to further Christ's kingdom on earth. For Native peoples of the region, Natick offered a strategy for survival, albeit perhaps one that required exceptional acculturation, as Eliot demanded that converts abandon most traditional lifeways.

Despite any accommodation to English demands, Natick was, as Jean O'Brien writes, "an Indian place." Founded on land occupied by John Speen and his family, Natick attracted inhabitants—Christian or not—because it was within their homelands, offered those whose immediate family had succumbed to war and disease the opportunity to associate with friends and other relations, and involved building a new Native community (albeit one within the "institutions of the imposed English colonial order)."[1] At least until the mid-eighteenth century—when residents were systematically dispossessed and dispersed—becoming a Natick Indian meant survival and persistence.

Because of their close association with Eliot's mission, Natick Indians were known from the beginning for their alphabetic literacy, and if Mohegan writ-

---

1. O'Brien, *Dispossession by Degrees*, x.

ers from the early colonial period are better known for their sermons, hymns, and letters, Natick Indians arguably made possible the alphabetic literacy of other Native peoples in the region. Natick Indians learned to read and write as a requirement of their Christian faith, but they used their literacy for their own purposes. Written texts range from marginalia in Bibles to wills, deeds, town and church records, and letters. Natick Indians became translators and printers, collaborating on the translation and publication of the first Bible ever printed in North America: *Mamusse Wunneetupanatamwe Up-Biblum God.* Although Eliot is listed as the author for most volumes in the "Indian library," he could not have produced its Massachusett-language primer, confession, logic primer, and religious tracts without the assistance of leading Christian Indians, most likely Natick residents. A few Natick Indians probably attended Harvard, where Christian Indians from Martha's Vineyard produced Latin compositions.

King Philip's War, from 1675 to 1676, was devastating for the Christian Indians of New England. Despite their decades of allegiance to the Bay Colony, Natick Indians became the objects of English suspicion and hatred, and they were subsequently rounded up with other converts and held on Deer Island in the Boston Harbor. After the war, Natick was reestablished, but within tighter colonial controls. Nevertheless, interest in print literacy continued, and a second edition of the Massachusett Bible was issued in 1685. Massachusett-language texts (although not necessarily written by Natick residents) would be produced well into the eighteenth century.

The continuing legacy of Natick includes the use of the Indian Bible as an invaluable resource for language revitalization. In particular, the Wôpanâak Language Reclamation Project has relied on, among other resources, the print legacy of the Natick Indians. In recent years the Praying Indian Tribe of Natick has worked to reestablish its community. In 2005 the group held a powwow—the first since the days of Eliot—and in 2006 the tribe held a Memorial Day ceremony to honor Christian Indians who fought in the Revolutionary War.

## Suggested Reading

Feldman, Orna. "Inspired by a Dream." *Spectrum*, Spring 2001. Available at http://web.mit.edu/giving/spectrum/spring01/inspired-by-a-dream.html. Accessed 30 June 2006.

Kellaway, William. *The New England Company, 1649–1776: Missionary Society to the American Indians.* New York: Barnes and Noble, 1962.

Miller, A. Richard. "1651–2001: 350th Anniversary of Natick, Massachusetts and the

Natick Praying Indians." Miller Microcomputer Services. Available at http://www
.millermicro.com/natprayind.html. Accessed 12 May 2006 and 30 June 2006.

O'Brien, Jean. *Dispossession by Degrees: Indian Land and Identity in Natick Massachusetts,
1650–1790*. New York:Cambridge University Press, 1997.

Praying Indians of Natick and Ponkapoag Official Tribal Website. Available at http://
natickprayingindians.org/. Accessed 20 June and 30 June 2006.

# Confession Narrative, 1656

## Samuel Ponampam

This document is taken from John Eliot's *A Further Account of the Progress of the Gospel amongst the Indians in New England*,[2] one of a series of publications commonly known as the Eliot Tracts. These pamphlets, published in London, were designed to tout New England's Indian evangelism and solicit funds from English readers. Generally written in letter form by eye-witness observers, they recounted the attempt to convert Indians to Christianity. The letters were sent to the officials of the New England Company, an organization headed by prominent Englishmen and created to administer colonial missionary enterprises. Once in London, the letters would be edited into pamphlet form, usually with a preface or an afterword written by an interested observer in England rather than by a colonist. The pamphlets seem to have been popular reading. One bookseller listed *Tears of Repentance*, in which several other Indian confessions appeared, as one of his most "vendible" books.[3]

Ponampiam[4]
*He was next called forth, and thus spake.*
I Confess my sinnes before the Lord, and his people this day. While my Father lived, and I was young, I was at play, and my Father rebuked me, and said, we shall all die shortly.[5] [In private we asked him what ground or reason moved his Father so to speak? he answered, it was when the English were new come over, and he thinketh that his Father had heard that Mr *Wilson*[6] had spoken of the flood of *Noah*, how God drowned all the world for the sinnes of the people.] Then I was troubled, and thought sure what God saith, shall be, and not what man saith; but I quickly forgot this, and thought not of any good. That same Winter the pox came; all my kindred died, only my Mother and I lived, we came to *Cohannit*, by *Dorchester*, where I lived till I was a man, and married. All those daies I sinned, and prayed to all gods, and did as others did, there I

---

2. Eliot, *Further Account*, 54–57.
3. See London, *Most Vendible Books in England*.
4. Elsewhere in this tract, and more commonly, the spelling is Ponampam.
5. In an earlier confession in this tract, Ponampam reports that this incident took place when he was "about 8 years old" (Eliot, *Further Account*, 20).
6. The reference is to John Wilson, pastor at Boston Church.

lived till the Minister came to teach us.[7] When I heard that they prayed, my heart desired it not. Sometime I prayed among them, and sometime I neglected it. I feared to pray because of the *Sachems*, therefore I put it off, for the fear of man. Afterward I considered in my heart, to pray to God, not because I loved the word, but for other reasons. I heard that Word, Mal. I. *From the rising of the Sun to the going down thereof, my name shall be great among the Gentiles, and in every place incense shall be offered unto my name, and a pure offering, for my name shall be great among the heathen, saith the Lord of hosts.* Then I was troubled in my thoughts about running away, yet then I thought if I should go to another place, they must pray also, and therefore I cannot flie from praying to God, therefore I tarried, and when others prayed, I prayed with them, only I still feared man; after I heard the same word again, to perswade us to pray to God; and I did so, but not for Gods sake, only it was before man. I remembred the Sabbath, and I heard Mr *Mathews* also preach of it,[8] and therefore I thought I would keep the Sabbath, but still I feared man. Upon a Sabbath, they wished me to teach what I remembred, that the Minister had taught. I did so, and we had talk about what I said, and we fell out. Thereupon I went away, and left praying to God. I went into the Countrey, but I remembred my wife and children, and quickly returned, but not for Gods sake. Again the Minister preached on I *Chron.* 28.9. *And thou Solomon my son know the God of thy Fathers, and serve him with a perfect heart, and with a willing mind, for the Lord searcheth all hearts, and understandeth all the imagination of the thoughts; if thou seek him, he will be found of thee, but if thou forsake him, he will cast thee off for ever.* This greatly troubled me, because I had left praying to God, and I had deserved eternall wrath. Then I desired to pray, I begged mercy, but I knew not what to do, for my sins were many, my heart was full of originall sin, and my heart was often full of anger; but then I was angry at my self, for I found my heart quickly carried after sin. Afterward, through the free mercy of God, I heard that word, *He that penitently believeth in Christ shall be pardoned and saved*; then my heart did beg earnestly for pardon and mercy. I heard *Joh.* 15.[9] *Whatever ye ask the Father in my name, he will give it you*; therefore my heart did now greatly beg for mercy in Christ and pardon. Afterward I heard *Mat.* 5. 28. *Who ever looketh upon a woman to lust after her, hath committed adultery in his heart.* Then my heart was troubled, because many were my sins, in my eies, and heart, and actions too. My heart did love the having of two wives, and

---

7. The minister was John Eliot.

8. The reference is possibly to the Reverend Marmaduke Matthews, or it may be a misspelling that refers to Thomas Mayhew.

9. Here and later this refers to the book of John.

other lusts of that kind:[10] Then Satan said to me, You are a great sinner, and God will not pardon you, therefore cast off praying and run away, it is a vain thing for you to pray. Here you want land, but in the Countrey there is land enough, and riches abundance, therefore pray no more. My heart did almost like it, but I heard that word, *Mat.* 4. *Satan tempted Christ, and shewed him the Kingdoms of the world, and the glory thereof, and promised to give them to him, if he would worship him.* Then my heart said, that even thus Satan tempteth me to cast off praying to God; and therefore my heart desired to believe that word of Christ, *Thou shalt worship the Lord thy God, and him only shalt thou serve.* Then I prayed again, but still I was full of sin, and very weak I was, and I loved sin. Again I heard, *Joh.* 14. *I am the Way, the Truth, and the Life, no man cometh unto the Father but by me.* Then I fully saw that Christ only is our Redeemer, and Saviour, and I desire to believe in Christ; and my heart said, that nothing that I can do can save me, only Christ: therefore I beg for Christ, and a part in him. Then said my heart, I give my heart and my self to Christ, and my wife and children, let him do with us what he will. Then my mother and two children died, and my heart said, What Christ will do, so be it; I have given them to him, and I begged pardon and mercy, if God will please to pardon me a poor sinner, blessed be his name.

## Temptation in the Wilderness
### Samuel Ponampam's Confession

KRISTINA BROSS

"Literacy" in seventeenth-century New England had many meanings—to English colonists no less than to Native inhabitants. The ability to read did not necessarily imply the ability to write. Manuscript and print circulation posed various challenges to the colonial community as a whole, and oral traditions were bound up with print technologies just as surely for the Puritan taking notes at a Sunday meeting as for the "praying Indian" writing out copies of scripture in longhand to be read to new or prospective converts. It is in this nexus of reading, writing, thinking, and speaking that I locate the confession narrative of Samuel Ponampam.

Eliot, that central figure of colonial evangelism, began transcribing the con-

---

10. One of the cultural changes that English missionaries demanded of Christian converts was monogamous marriage.

This essay is adapted from Bross, *Dry Bones and Indian Sermons,* ch. 3.

fessions of Christian converts in 1649 to persuade observers both at home and in London that his efforts were bearing fruit and that the praying Indians to whom he ministered were ready to gather together in their own church. This move would have had important religious and political effects. Since Bay Colony Christians were gathered in independent congregations, a praying Indian church would have unprecedented autonomy. Moreover, the Christian identity of some Algonquians was being used in legal arguments over land. Thus, there must have been a great deal of pressure on Eliot and others who were transcribing praying Indian confessions to represent their words as unimpeachably orthodox.

What would an "orthodox" relation of religious experiences have looked like in the 1640s and 1650s? Narratives of conversion as requisites for membership in Puritan churches have been documented as early as 1554, and by the 1630s publicly related narratives were an issue for serious debate in New England.[11] Notwithstanding any disagreement about the place and purpose of the confessions in Puritan churches, the contours of the genre can be discerned in the surviving narratives, and New England became a place where a successful confession opened doors to Christian communion—doors to social and religious belonging.

In general, the form of the confession, as Edmund Morgan has argued, had a flexible but clear "morphology," which included stages of intellectual understanding of God's word: "holy desperation" (which involves feeling one's sinfulness), grief for one's sin, and finally assurance of God's grace.[12] Charles Cohen has argued that praying Indian confessions—the earlier ones at least— lacked that final sense of assurance and were more concerned with the "legal" elements of conversion—Sabbath breaking, dress, deportment.[13] Here we are faced with the problems of mediation: If praying Indian confessions are distinct from those of other Puritans, can the differences be chalked up to individual agency, to a particular Christian Indian culture, or to Eliot's eccentricities as a minister, missionary, and translator? All three explanations most likely figure into any reading of praying Indian confessions. Nevertheless, even the transcribed and translated form of Ponampam's printed confession can be understood to reflect the dialogue between the convert and English missionaries. By attending to the context of the religious contact zone of the mid-seventeenth century and in particular by considering the impact of printed scriptures on the praying Indian community, we can better understand Ponampam's highly

---

11. See Caldwell, "Origins," in *Puritan Conversion Narrative.*
12. E. Morgan, *Visible Saints,* 90.
13. C. Cohen, "Conversion among Puritans and Amerindians," 233–56.

mediated conversion narrative as an example of early Native rather than English colonial literature.

Mission literature records two attempts by Indian converts to form their own church. The first trial, in 1652, was conducted in the praying town of Natick and therefore required the several Puritan elders who came to hear testimony to travel. These logistics perhaps further emphasized the measure of praying Indian autonomy that an Indian church would create. Whether for this or other reasons, the trial failed. In 1659 a second trial of the "pillars" of an Indian church was held in the English town of Roxbury, Massachusetts. This time, the converts prevailed, and in 1660 the first praying Indian church was formed.

A close look at the several versions of each man's testimony—testimonies delivered ("rehearsed") more privately before church officials as well as testimonies given before a wider audience—reveals several common elements: references to family (both to the "heathen" status of parents and to the heartbreaking loss of children, spouses, friends, and kin to violence and disease) and, especially, the close and consistent use of scripture as inspiration for and proof of conversion. The latter element can help us place Ponampam's confession in a tradition of early Native literacy.

Praying Indians first encountered Christian scriptures in paraphrases used by Eliot in his proselytizing sermons, later in translations of scripture that circulated in manuscript form, and eventually in the first Bible printed in North America—a translation entitled *Mamusse Wunneetupanatamwe Up-Biblum God.* Eliot's initial scriptural paraphrases made a strong impression on those who heard them. In his confessions, Ponampam refers especially to Eliot's use of Malachi 1:11: "For from the rising of the sun even unto the going down of the same my name shall be great among the Gentiles; and in every place incense shall be offered unto my name, and a pure offering: for my name shall be great among the heathen, saith the Lord of hosts." This passage the missionary rendered as "From the rising of the Sun, to the going down of the same, thy name shall be great among the Indians, and in every place prayers shall be made to thy name, pure prayers, for thy name shall be great among the Indians." [14]

Ponampam found this scripture important, although probably not in the way that Eliot would have wished. In each of Ponampam's five recorded confessions, he refers to Malachi 1:11, and he paraphrases it in the first three. [15] Clearly,

---

14. Quoted in Winslow, *Glorious Progress,* 82.

15. See Eliot and Mayhew, "Tears of Repentance": *"That all from the rising of the sun to the going down thereof, shall pray unto God"* (240); *"But then I heard Gods free mercy in his word, call all to pray, from the rising of the Sun to the going down thereof"* (241); *"That al shal pray from the rising to the sitting Sun"* (242).

the verse held meaning for him. In the final transcribed confession, Ponampam reports that Eliot had preached on this text on more than one occasion: "I heard the same word *again*, to persuade us to pray to God; and I did so." Although Eliot believed the verse to be an effective evangelical tool, as Ponampam ponders the application of the scripture to his own soul he finds reason to doubt its truth on a personal level. Although he says that he was persuaded to pray, he registers the coercive elements of Eliot's translation. Ponampam's initial decision "to pray," it seems, meant that outwardly he would conform to Christian practices; however, he testifies in an earlier confession, "I considered whether I should pray, but I found not in my heart that *all* should pray."[16] Ponampam's accounts suggest that he took away from Eliot's preaching his message about the inevitability and totality of Indian Christianization (*all* shall pray) but that he doubted him. At best, Eliot's proclamation of universal conversion proved unsettling, as Ponampam reveals in his third recorded confession: Upon "considering of that word, that all shall pray, I was troubled."[17]

In Ponampam's last confession, we find an elaborate treatment of scripture and its application to his experiences. Whereas the bare bones of his later successful confessions are evident in the 1652 rehearsals, in the intervening years, he was able to flesh them out by attending Eliot's meetings and reading translated scripture. Scriptural literacy is even more important in the later confessions, and these accounts give us some sense of Ponampam as a reader and exegete. Ponampam was a lecturer in the praying Indian community, and the tracts record five versions of his confession (three from the first trial, recorded in *Tears of Repentance* [1653], and two from the final, successful trial, published in *A Further Account of the Gospel among the Indians in New England* [1660], the last of which is reproduced here). By the time Natick's leading Christians tried to form their own church in 1659, Eliot had translated a great deal of scripture. Although the Bible in full would not be printed until 1663, the New Testament was nearly complete (it was published in 1660). Ponampam seems to have received a copy in 1662, when he began to write his name and various dates in the margins, but as a lecturer at Natick, it is likely that he had access to manuscript materials. Moreover, Indian converts gave proof of their increased Christian understanding in sermons recorded in John Eliot's 1659 pamphlet *A Further Accompt of the Progesse of the Gospel*, published the same year that Ponampam's confession (along with those of his fellows) finally met with the approval of the English elders. (These confessions were published a year later in Eliot's *A Further Account of the Progress of the Gospel*.)

---

16. Quoted in ibid., 242, emphasis added.
17. Ibid., 242.

Thus, it is not surprising that in both of his 1659 confessions, his version of Malachi 1:11 more closely conforms to the King James version than to Eliot's paraphrase. Ponampam explicitly identifies it by chapter and verse in the confession included here. As his quotation of Malachi comes closer to the standard English version, so too, in terms that are increasingly clear, do his accounts depict his troubled sense of Christianity and conversion as inescapable. In the first confession recorded in 1659, he reports his response to Eliot's sermon:

> My heart did not desire [to pray], but to go away to some other place. But remembring the word of God, that all shall pray to God. Then I did not desire to go away, but to pray to God. But if I pray afore the Sachems pray [that is, before Indian leaders convert], I fear they will kill me, and therefore I will not pray. But yet when others prayed, I prayed with them; and I thought, if I run away to other places, they will pray too, therefore I will pray here.[18]

The confession painfully describes not a spontaneous conversion upon hearing the Word, but the deliberations of a colonial subject with too few choices, in a world that Eliot's Malachi translation seems to fit all too well. Those who were not praying Indians literally had nowhere else to go—"from the rising to the setting Sun."

Ponampam is even more direct in his last confession: "Then I was troubled in my thoughts about running away, yet then I thought if I should go to another place, they must pray also, and therefore I cannot flie from praying to God, therefore I tarried." Of course, Ponampam is confessing a great sin—the desire, however swiftly quashed, to hide from God. He seems to be suppressing the desire because he foresees the fulfillment of Eliot's colonial prophecy that soon all Indians would "pray." Once again, his self-description reflects painful realities. Hemmed in by Christians, there is no escaping conversion.

Thus, we can see the influence of Eliot's paraphrase of Malachi on Ponampam's decision to remain a part of the praying Indian community. The verse convinces Ponampam to stay put, to remain with the Praying Indian community. However, it seems the verse had only qualified success as a tool of conversion—perhaps because Ponampam perceived Eliot's sermon as manipulative, if not at the time of delivery, then later when he had access to another version. Ponampam decided to pray "but not for Gods sake, only it was before man." In other words, he turned to prayer for political reasons, making an outward show "before man" in order to become a part of the praying Indian community. However effective the verse had been in convincing him that he could not flee from God, it was not instrumental to his heart-felt conversion:

---

18. Quoted in Eliot, *Further Account*, 20.

He did not pray "for Gods sake." Moreover, Ponampam's words imply a connection between his understanding of the English settler's use of this text for the work of colonization and conversion, on one hand, and his recognition of the consequent political utility of "praying before man," on the other.

This perceptive account of the motivations for Eliot's use of Malachi 1:11 and of Ponampam's testimony as to its limited effect on him appears in the mission record only after the convert reportedly leaves off the scriptural paraphrase (which he must have learned from Eliot and which is described as accurately quoting from the King James Bible version of the verse). Even if initially Ponampam's encounter with scripture seems to have resulted in a confession of hypocrisy that ran counter to Eliot's many assurances of the Indians' true conversions, Eliot may have had good reason for describing Ponampam's "mistakes" in interpreting God's word. In other words, even as it seems to undercut Eliot's reputation as missionary, Ponampam's ability to work through his error and come to true faith certainly implies his readiness for full church membership. It is a conventional confession of error, and so the confession survives in the mission literature. Alternatively, however, we might read this statement as a direct challenge to Eliot's accounts of his missionary successes and a testament to Ponampam's discernment of the coercive tactics of colonization and conversion. His testimony comes close to casting doubt on the missionary's ability to separate sincere conversion from dissembling. The apparent convert saw through the tactics of evangelism and initially rejected them.

Indeed, it is not until Ponampam applies a different scripture of his own choosing to his desire for escape that he can report an experience of salvation. His testimony on the effects of Matthew 4 exemplifies the potential for Puritan Indians to illuminate their own experiences by reading the Bible and thus escape the control of colonial interpreters. Ponampam's confession describes a time when he considered moving to Connecticut to escape the rigors of the life of the converted Indians. While debating the move, he finds a verse to guide him: "This merciful word of God I heard, That *Satan led Christ into the wilderness to tempt him,* and so I thought hee would do me."[19] He elaborates his reading in another confession, imagining that Satan, speaking directly to him, says, "You are a great sinner, and God will not pardon you, therefore cast off praying and run away, it is a vain thing for you to pray. Here you want land, but in the Countrey there is land enough, and riches [in] abundance, therefore pray no more." This imagined offer strongly attracts Ponampam until he remembers a gospel lesson: "My heart did almost like it, but I heard that word, *Mat. 4. Satan tempted Christ, and shewed him the Kingdoms of the world, and the glory thereof,*

---

19. Quoted in ibid., 22.

*and promised to give them to him, if he would worship him.* Then my heart said, that even thus Satan tempteth me to cast off praying to God." Ponampam's confession of his temptation and his triumph over it must have been accepted by the English who heard him because it signaled to Puritan elders the successful repudiation of a traditional Indian lifestyle. Mission literature had impressed on its English readers that before colonization and evangelism Indians were wandering in the wilderness, both spiritually in their ignorance of Christ and literally as a nomadic people. Ponampam's application of Matthew 4 to his own temptations demonstrates his internalization of that assessment, and the elders took it as proof that they could now trust him with church estate.

Once again, however, Ponampam's interpretation also illustrates that he recognized how few viable choices were available to him in 1659. He sees that from a Puritan perspective the "Countrey" beyond English settlement is the site of the "wilderness" of sin. He is in the process of embracing Puritanism, so presumably he is prepared to accept that perspective. But there are reasons aside from the spiritual that also explain why Ponampam considers and then rejects removing to Connecticut. The "Kingdoms of the world" with which Satan tempts Ponampam are Indian lands. In offering him such "kingdoms," Satan, like so many English colonists, fails to register either kinship ties or hostilities among various Indian peoples. Thus, it is not surprising that this dialogue with Satan indicates Ponampam's separation from the English Puritans who seek to convert him while refusing to embrace him, who refuse his rights to Bay Colony land and tell him, "You are a great sinner and God will not pardon you," as they push him outside the bounds of New England to lands that are already claimed and occupied. In addition, the dialogue underscores his alienation from those who are not praying Indians and possibly from his own earlier life. He recognizes clearly that although the English audience might see Satan's alternative of running away to "the country" as a real possibility for "heathens," it is not a viable option for him. The "wild Indian" identity, assumed to be his by English magistrates particularly fearful of Indian apostasy, in no way belongs to Ponampam, who is settled in a praying town and beginning to embrace a Christian identity.

The most striking aspect of this passage in Ponampam's confession is how it seems to disturb the colonial mission's construction of the Christian Indian through "colonial mimicry."[20] New England Puritans demanded that praying Indians assume a Christian identity, but one that kept them perpetually in between—almost regenerate but never quite fully so—thereby necessitating continual infusions of money, goods, and missionaries from the metropolitan

---

20. Bhabha, "Of Mimicry and Man," 86.

center (whether London or Boston). As Ponampam inserts himself personally into scripture, however, he varies the pattern established by Puritan typology for praying Indians, reversing English colonial commonplaces and radically extending the message of Eliot's translation of Malachi 1:11. Note that in his confession, Ponampam creates his Puritan identity by casting his difficulties into recognizably Christian—and colonial—terms. In good Puritan fashion, he mimics the identity so central to the colonial articulations of New England, asserting his centrality within a Christian belief system that, when translated by English settlers into the colonial register, marginalizes him. In this way, Ponampam, in turn, translates Matthew 4 into a colonial text, but his version reflects his displacement, both physical and spiritual. Ponampam sees his encounters with Satan and his temptations as taking place not in the "wilds" outside but within the bounds of colonial charters.[21] In his translation of Matthew 4, English "civilization" becomes his personal "wilderness," in which he encounters Satan and risks temptation.

Ponampam's appropriation of Puritan tropes and genres disrupts the colonists' understanding of themselves as claiming either a vacant wilderness or the devil's territories. Ponampam so successfully adapts the conventions of the confession genre to his experiences that he and others like him threaten to displace the English elect as saintly colonists.[22] His decision not to run away seals his own claim to a physical place in the colonies, to lands set aside for praying towns, even as his repudiation of Satan seals his claim to a Christian identity. The radical extension of the disturbance suggested by Ponampam's confession will be the appropriation of prayer, psalm singing, and scripture to their own ends by Indians warring against English settlers during King Philip's War.[23]

To be sure, Ponampam's reading of Matthew 4 is itself not a "point of revolution" in which he overturns the colonial mythology so central to Puritan New England.[24] After all, as Robert Allen Warrior has argued, Canaanites, not Israelites, are the readier type for Indians displaced by English settlers.[25] Nevertheless, it is with such readings that "praying Indians" created Christian

<hr>

21. Robert Naeher, quoting James H. Merrell, argues that in the face of European colonial invasion, "native Americans came to view their world as 'every bit as new as that confronting transplanted Africans or Europeans'" ("Dialogue in the Wilderness," 363).

22. Bhabha characterizes such disruptions as undermining what the colonizer has assumed to be immutable. Ponampam's narrative may "so disturb the systematic (and systemic) construction of discriminatory knowledges"—such as the identification of the elect by public confession of faith—"that the cultural, once recognized as the medium of authority, becomes virtually unrecognizable" (*Location of Culture*, 115).

23. See Bross, "Satan's Captives," in *Dry Bones and Indian Sermons*.

24. The term "point of revolution" is from Cheyfitz, *Poetics of Imperialism*, 125.

25. Warrior, "Native American Perspective," 285.

identities that served their needs and through which they performed a Native Christianity potentially unrecognizable to their English proselytizers.

For his part, Ponampam created a narrative that called into question those English observers who doubted the sincerity of the praying Indians and feared that their "unsettled" lifestyle might tempt them to "escape" English law and religion by running away to Connecticut or other "kingdoms of the world." In Ponampam's interpretation of Matthew 4, only a Satan would see such an escape as possible for a praying Indian. Through this use of the Indian Bible, Ponampam has fully "translated" himself into the gospel experience—or, rather, translated the gospel into his own experiences—and appropriated one of the most cherished English Puritan tropes: New England as Israel in an American wilderness. Indeed, he chooses the antitype itself for his own identity. Like Christ, he has encountered Satan in the wilderness, and like Christ he emerges triumphant.

# Natick Indian Petition, 1748

The Natick people's petition in defense of their fishing rights, housed in the Massachusetts Archives, is available on microfilm. The two-page manuscript document is composed of a preamble that addresses Massachusetts governor William Shirley, identification of the petitioning party, the body of the petition, and thirteen signatures or marks of Natick Indian men. The document itself thus conforms to the typical style of petitions submitted to the Massachusetts General Court and is formulaic in those respects. It appears that nine of the Indian men signed their own names to the document (their penmanship suggests a range of familiarity with English writing). The actions taken by the governing bodies are noted at the end of the document. Apart from several inkblots that make deciphering the content somewhat challenging, the eighteenth-century orthography is fairly legible. The petition is housed in the Massachusetts Archives Collection, Collection at Columbia Point, Boston (v. 31, pp. 574–75).

To his Excellency William Shirley Esqr. Capt. Genll. and Governor in Chief, in and over his Majesties Province, of the Massachusetts Bay, in New England, To his Majesties council, and House of Representatives in [the] Court assembled,[26]

The Petition of the Indian Inhabitants of the Parish of Natick in the County of Middlesex in Sd Province[27]

Humbly Shows

That although all possable care was taken by the Genll Court of Sd Province at the first, to give and grant unto us the great Priviledges of Fishing, by ordering our Sittuation so as that certain Ponds, Convenient and good for Fishing, are included within the Bounds of sd Parish, which Ponds have been of great advantage to us, and supplyed us with Fish of various Sorts, Especially with Ale-wives in plenty, whereby our families have been in a great measure

---

26. Original spelling and punctuation have been retained. Shirley was the colonial governor at the time the petition was filed.

27. Natick is located about sixteen miles west and south of Boston. Parish status carried particular political rights and responsibilities, such as levying taxes and sending representatives to the General Court.

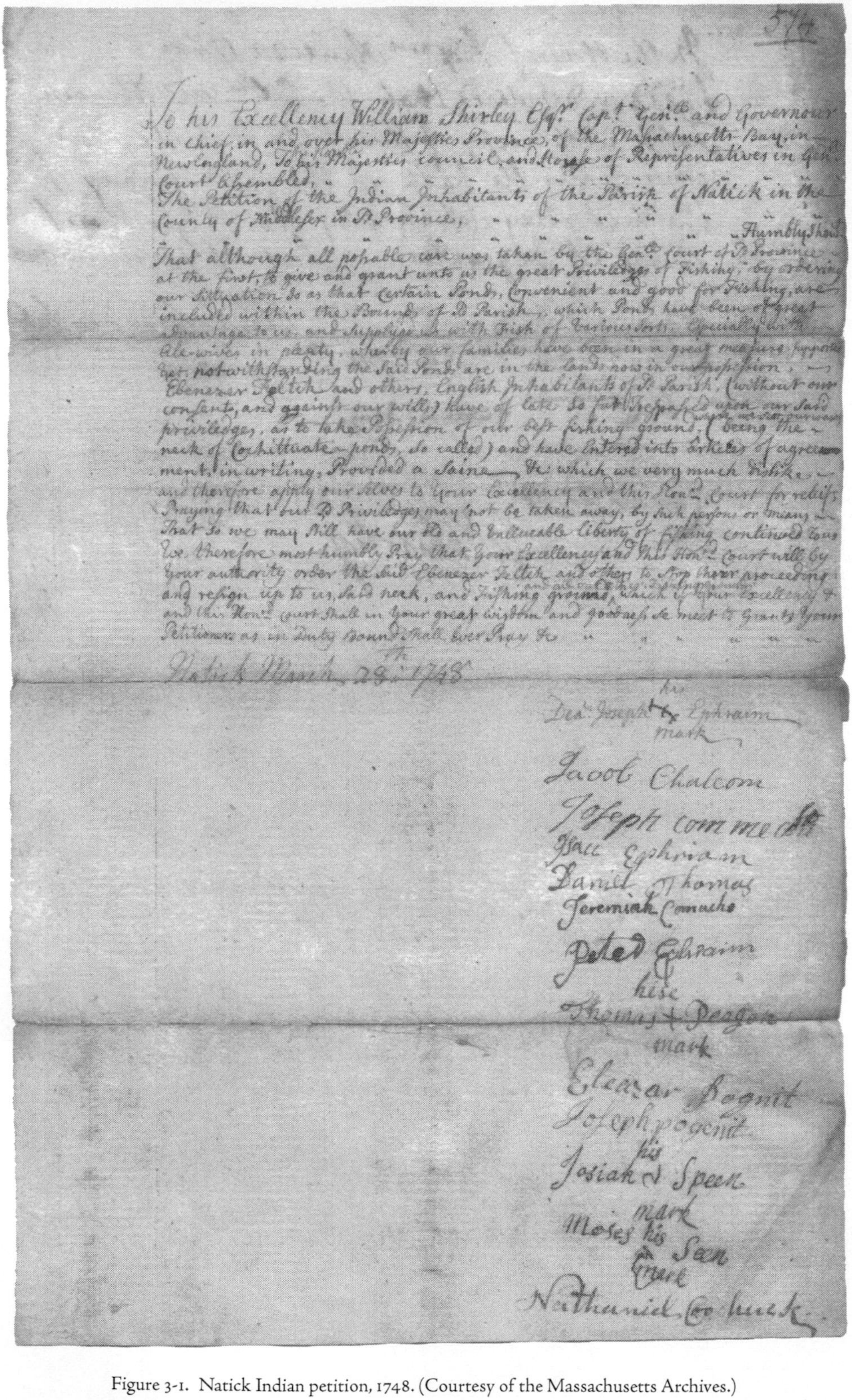

Figure 3-1. Natick Indian petition, 1748. (Courtesy of the Massachusetts Archives.)

575

In the House of Represents April. 22. 1748
Read and Ordered that the Pet.rs serve Ebenezer
Felch with a copy of this Pett.n that he show
cause if any he hath on the first fryday of
the next May Session why the Prayer thereof
should not be granted        Sent up for concurrence
                                              T Hutchinson Spkr

In Council April 23.d 1748
Read & Concured          J Willard Secry

Consented to
                W Shirley

Supported Yet, notwithstanding the said Ponds are in the lands now in our possession—Ebenezer Feltch [28] and others, English Inhabitants of Sd Parish, (without our consent, and against our wills) have of late so far Trespassed upon our Said priviledges, as to take Possession of our best fishing ground, where we sett our weirs [29] (being the neck of Cochittuate ponds, so called) and have Entered into articles of agreement, in writing, Provided a Saine,[30] &c: which we very much dislike—and therefore apply our selves to Your Excellency and this Honrd Court for relief, Praying that our Sd Priviledges may not be taken away, by such persons or means—That so we may still have our old and valluable liberty of fishing continued to us We therefore most humbly Pray that Your Excellency and this Honrd Court will by Your authority order the said Ebenezer Feltch and others to stop their proceeding and resign up to us, said neck, and Fishing grounds, and all our other Fishing grounds which if your Excellency & and this Honrd Court Shall in Your great wisdom and goodness Se meet to Grant Your Petitioners as in Duty Bound Shall Ever Pray &c.

Natick March 28th 1748

Deac Joseph Ephraim [his mark] [31]
Jacob Chalcom
Joseph Commecho
Isaac Ephraim
Daniel Thomas
Jeremiah Comacho
Peter Ephraim
Thomas Peagon [his mark]
Eleazar Pognit
Joseph Pogenit
Josiah Speen [his mark]
Moses Seen [32] [his mark]
Nathaniel Coochuck

---

28. Ebenezer Felch arrived in Natick by 1744 at the latest and served for nineteen years as surveyor and sometimes clerk for the Indian proprietors of the town. The fact that just four years prior to this petition he had petitioned the General Court to defend Indian rights to the community wood supply suggests the complexity of relationships in Natick. (See O'Brien, *Dispossession by Degrees*, 169–71.)

29. Weirs are fish traps commonly used by the Indians in New England.

30. The reference is to a large fishing net.

31. Unless otherwise indicated, all names were signed.

32. This is most likely *Speen* rather than *Seen*.

In the House of Reprs April.22.1748
Read and Ordered that the Ptrs serve Ebenezer Felch with a copy of this Petn
that he shew cause if any he hath on the first fryday of the next May Session
why the Prayer thereof should not be granted. Sent up for concurrence
T Hutchinson [____] [33]
In Council April 23rd 1748
Read & Concured
J Willard [____] [34]
Consented to
WShirley

# "Our Old and Valluable Liberty"

## A Natick Indian Petition in Defense of Their Fishing Rights, 1748

### JEAN M. O'BRIEN

In 1748 thirteen Natick Indian men endorsed a brief yet revealing petition to
the Massachusetts General Court. Created nearly one hundred years before,
this most "successful" of "praying towns" became a hotly contested terrain
that pitted Indians against aggressive English people who had become their
neighbors. All but exclusively an Indian place until the middle decades of the
eighteenth century, Natick at midcentury included ever more English people as
Indian landowners sold off portions of their individually owned land in order
to raise capital to make improvements on their farms, put money at interest to
earn a livelihood, or (increasingly) discharge debts that left them to the mercy
of English legal entanglements. The changing demographic and geographic
situation of Natick both represented particular Indian visions for securing a
place in the social order of English colonialism and produced the conditions
whereby Indian struggles for autonomy within that order would be undermined in the community. Over the course of the eighteenth century, Indian
power within the town would be challenged, as English people worked aggressively to control the land base, the resources, and the political and religious
institutions of the town. [35]

---

33. This indicates an illegible abbreviation for *speaker* (speaker of the House of Representatives).
34. This indicates an illegible abbreviation for *secretary*.
35. O'Brien, *Dispossession by Degrees*.

Petitions to the Massachusetts General Court are an important resource for understanding Indian responses to English colonialism in Natick and other Indian communities. In Massachusetts, petitions to the court constituted a standard means of pleading a cause to the colonial governing body. Indian access to this process can be understood as part of the larger assimilation project, which sought to impose English ways on Indians brought within the colonial social order as "friend Indians."[36] The Massachusetts Archives includes hundreds of petitions written by, for, or on behalf of Indian people in the seventeenth and eighteenth centuries, and Natick petitions are conspicuous in this important body of evidence. Most of the Natick petitions, especially petitions from the eighteenth century, concern Indian land. These land petitions were produced in compliance with colonial regulations that governed Indian land transactions, which required General Court approval for any land transaction that involved Indian sellers.[37] Adopted, ostensibly, to provide protection for Indians from the fraudulent activities of the English, such bureaucratic mechanisms preserved the notion of propriety and legality in Indian dispossession. Because the bureaucratic process required Indians to provide reasons for selling their land, court records also often richly reveal the dramatic cultural transformations that Indians underwent as they resisted the physical and cultural encroachment of English colonialism. Land petitions frequently provide graphic descriptions of Indian lifeways—including economic pursuits, material culture, religious and cultural choices, and demographic situations.

How should we read Indian petitions produced in colonial Massachusetts? What do we make of Indian uses of literacy in English in an imposed bureaucracy that sought to secure the English social order? What can we know about Indian uses of English forms of writing given the surviving record?[38]

On the most general level, Indian participation in the English bureaucracy plots power relationships as they had been transformed in the colonial context. Crudely speaking, the very fact of Indian participation tells us whose regulations would govern relationships between Indian and English people. Whose language becomes the official language of diplomacy and governance reveals much about who holds the balance of power. One might interpret Indian petitions as evidence that they had succumbed to the colonial order and placidly accepted the imposition of the institutions that upheld that colonial order.

There is, however, more to the story than that. From a different angle, Indian

---

36. Ibid., 65–90.
37. Ibid., 71.
38. On Indian literacy in New England, see Goddard and Bragdon, *Native Writings in Massachusett*; L. Murray, "'Pray Sir, Consider a Little,'" 15–41; Nelson, "'(I Speak Like a Fool),'" 42–65; and Wyss, *Writing Indians.*

participation in the colonial bureaucracy can be viewed as proactive: Indians selectively adopted particular aspects of English culture in order to resist their complete effacement by an aggressive and expansive English presence. This Indian petition offers a rich and subtle example of Indian resistance within the potentially suffocating constraints of English colonialism.

The document is written in English, and it appears that whoever took down the text also wrote Deacon Joseph Ephraim's name, the first to appear under the main body of the text. Ephraim's mark, which he left on the document in place of a signature, is identical to those that he left on other documents—it somewhat resembles a capital "E" slanted diagonally between his first and last names.[39] Three other Indians also made marks within their names, but the handwriting differs from that of the body of the text. Nine of the thirteen petitioners signed their own names to the document, which demonstrates that they had at least some competence in writing in English and suggests that at least some could read enough to understand and thus authorize the content of the petition. It is impossible to know definitively who wrote the document; nowhere is the author identified. A cursory glance strongly suggests, however, that none of the Indian signatories was the writer, since their signatures do not resemble the handwriting of the main body. The additions to the document tell us that the petition was read in the House of Representatives, whose members decided a course of action to which the council and then the governor subsequently consented.

In some of these respects, the 1748 petition resembled other petitions emanating from Natick. They are all penned in English, most likely by a number of different English scribes. The petitions include a smattering of signatures by Indians, but in contrast to this particular petition, the overwhelming majority left their marks on the documents. During the course of the eighteenth century, at least twenty-two Natick Indians attached their signatures to petitions to the General Court; the number of signatures on this petition would suggest a higher degree of familiarity with writing than the full set of petitions reveals. Of the wider group of signatories, only two, one of whom is represented on this document, signed petitions with handwriting that even vaguely resembled the signatures they attached to them.[40] In reading these documents, it is crucial

39. See, for example, Massachusetts Archives Collection, v. 31, p. 136, 1726 (hereafter cited as MA) and MA v. 31, p. 574, 1748.

40. I have standardized the spellings of Indian names. Examples of signatures are Jacob Chalcom, Joseph Comecho, Isaac Ephraim, Daniel Thomas, Jeremiah Comecho, Eleazar Paugenit, Joseph Paugenit, and Nathaniel Coochuck (MA v. 31, p. 574, 1748); Daniel Speen, Samuel Paugenit, and Uriah Coochuck (MA v. 32, p. 90, 1750); Samuel Lawrence (MA v. 32, p. 607, 1755); Benjamin Tray (MA v. 31, p. 136, 1726); John Ephraim (MA v. 31, p. 375, 1742); Jeffrey Henry (MA v. 31, p. 389, 1741); William Thomas (MA v. 31, p. 459, 1743); Ebenezer Ephraim (MA v. 31, p. 488, 1743/4);

to know that they are heavily mediated in these ways. Nevertheless, they reveal much about the experiences of Indian people in New England.

In its structure and form, this petition—and many other petitions—might support the notion that Indians and their Indianness had been eclipsed. Written in English, mostly likely by an Englishman, the petition also follows the conventions of address of individuals of low status addressing a governing body in a rigidly hierarchical society. It begins with formulaic language of address, acknowledging the official structure of power in the colony and summoning the attention of the colonial governor, William Shirley, and the two houses of the legislature that would hear and act on the petition. The "Indian Inhabitants" situate themselves as residents in a place defined in English terms: the "Parish" of Natick in the "County of Middlesex in Sd Province." The salutation indicates their technical position of submission to a colonial regime. Their petition "Humbly Shows" their reasons for addressing the court, and it ends similarly, by humbly praying that the court take action to address their grievance against English encroachment on their rights in Natick. The final phrases of the text employ the standard language of submission and compliance, leaving determination of the dispute to "your Excellency & and this Honrd Court [who] Shall in Your great wisdom and goodness Se meet to Grant Your Petitioners as in Duty Bound Shall Ever Pray &c."

Evidence from the body of the petition might also be used to support the notion of Indian submission. At the beginning, the petitioners point out that the General Court had purposely situated Natick's land to Indians "to give and grant unto us the great Priviledges of Fishing" by including "certain Ponds, Convenient and good for Fishing . . . within the Bounds of sd Parish." This construction semantically locates the power to regulate land possession with the English governing body—it is the court that grants Indians the "priviledges of Fishing" and the possession of the ponds where Indian families take the fish that "in a great measure" support them. Furthermore, by the very act of petitioning, the defenders of Natick's fishing rights signal acceptance of the court as the final arbitrator in their dispute.

A closer look, however, yields a more complex story. Further into the body of the text, the petitioners describe their fishing rights as an "old and valluable liberty" rather than a gift in the form of a specific grant from the General Court. Although such language does not directly controvert the notion that Indian fishing rights originated with the English, it might be read as an assertion of

Benjamin Wiser (MA v. 31, p. 557, 1747/8); Peter Brand (MA v. 32, p. 312, 1752); Samuel Abraham (MA v. 32, p. 243, 1753); and Cesar Ferrit (MA v. 32, p. 429, 1753). Those whose signatures resembled the body of the text somewhat are Nathaniel Coochuck (MA v. 31, p. 471, 1743) and Benjamin Wiser (MA v. 31, p. 557, 1747/8, and MA v. 33, p. 55, 1758).

Aboriginal rights that long antedated the arrival of the English. This subtle turn of phrase can be interpreted as an affirmation of Indian precedence as the grounds for Indian complaints against encroaching English people, whose access to Indian fishing grounds could hardly be regarded as an "old and valuable liberty." Yet by foregrounding the English "grant" of these grounds and rights, they announced the security of those rights within the colonial order.

The continuation of earlier Indian ways of belonging on the land is also visible in the petition, offering further evidence of Indian resistance against the English regime. The fact that Indian families "have been in a great measure Supported" by the "Fish of various Sorts" suggests the persistence of an Indian economy quite different from the English inland agricultural economy. English inhabitants might have included fishing as a marginal activity, but in no English communities other than ports and fishing villages would fishing be a principal economic focus. Also important is the fact that the petitioners portray their fishing rights as collective: The English are trespassers on "our Said priviledges, as to take Possession of our best fishing ground." They call on the court to protect their "old and valluable liberty of fishing" by forcing the English to give up their pretentious seizure of "said neck, and Fishing grounds, and all our other Fishing grounds."

The very fact of the petition's existence underscores Indian resistance. In spite of the formulaic language of submission, the angry and resilient tone of the complaint is unmistakably present in the text. The petitioners stridently argue that in spite of the protections of their rights put in place by the commonwealth, "Ebenezer Feltch and others . . . (without our consent, and against our wills)" have trespassed on their fishing grounds at the neck of Cochituate Pond. The culprits in this injustice are boldly flouting Indian rights in Natick. They "have of late so far Trespassed upon our Said priviledges, as to take Possession of our best fishing ground . . . and have Entered into articles of agreement, in writing, Provided a Saine, &c: which we very much dislike." The petitioners cast the behavior of the trespassers as audacious. They attempt to bolster their physical seizure of Indian fishing grounds through the use of literacy, in the form of "articles of agreement" that presumably authorize their seizure.

This literary self-authorization is countered, however, by the Indian petitioners' own knowledge of the power of writing. Even though, in the technical sense, the document was most likely produced by an Englishman, its explicit intent is to use the institutions of English colonialism to defend Indian rights. We can only speculate on the scribe's motives: Was it a local person knowledgeable about political matters, who earned a few shillings for his work, or one of the government-appointed guardians of the Indians honestly discharging his responsibilities, or perhaps a scheming neighbor who envisioned his own enrichment somehow resulting from his advocacy of the petitioners in this case? We simply do not know. Although we probably cannot know the precise context that produced the text, however, we can certainly recognize that the Indian petitioners understood the power of the written word as a weapon in a continuing legacy of Indian resistance in New England.

Who were these savvy petitioners? By gathering information from other Massachusetts General Court petitions; town, church, and vital records; land transactions; and other governmental records, we can learn a great deal. The petitioners were all landowners in Natick, and all but two were either descended from or original proprietors or freeholders when an English-style land system was initiated in the town in 1719. The other two had married into proprietary families. At least half actively engaged in the market economy, buying and selling land in order to establish English-style farms. Seven of the thirteen had been baptized, and four had attained full communion in the congregational church. Joseph Ephraim, who was born around the time of King Philip's War, in 1675, had been selected as a deacon in the church and raised a large family in Natick. Peter and Isaac, two of the signatories, were his sons, and another, Jeremiah Comecho, had married his daughter Sarah. The Speens were descendants of a founding family whose members relinquished their traditional ownership of Natick's lands for the founding of the community in 1650. Other kin ties connected the signatories with one another and with many other families.[41] In sum, the petitioners represented important Natick families. Significantly, even while their own lives embraced many English cultural, religious, social, and economic practices, they wrote to defend communal fishing rights for Indian people as central to the sustenance of Natick.

Taken as a whole, the text resembles what Laura Murray found in her analysis of the correspondence of the Indians David Fowler and Hezekiah Calvin with Eleazar Wheelock, their teacher and erstwhile benefactor. Their posture was an "elaborate combination of deference and defiance that is determined by the specific and immediate conditions of their writing as well as by the overall

---

41. Original Indian Record Book (hereafter cited as OIRB), Morse Institute Public Library, Natick, Mass. (proprietors and freeholders); Thomas W. Baldwin, comp., *Vital Records of Natick, Massachusetts to the Year 1850* (hereafter cited as NVR) (Jacob Chalcom married Leah Thomas, daughter of proprietor Solomon Thomas; Nathaniel Coochuck married Mary Tabumso, descendant of proprietor Hannah Tabumsug); O'Brien, *Dispossession by Degrees*, 151–62 (market economy); Peabody and Badger Records, Church of Natick, 1725–1795, Typescript copy, Massachusetts Historical Society, Boston, Mass. (baptisms/church membership); NVR (Joseph Ephraim's family); MA v. 32, p. 614, 1755 (Joseph Ephraim's age); OIRB (Speen grant); O'Brien, *Dispossession by Degrees*, 126–67 (kinship in the community).

lines of their relationship with Wheelock."[42] Like Wheelock's students, Natick Indians balanced protest with prostration in defending their rights within the colonial relationship. Struggling within a colonial regime that threatened to overwhelm them, New England Indians in Natick and elsewhere resisted the aggressions of their neighbors by understanding and using the power of literacy in English and using English forms of deference to push for individual and collective Indian rights.

What came of the dispute? The official record is mute. Neither the Acts and Resolves of the Massachusetts Council nor the Journals of the House of Representatives reported a response from Felch. If we take the summons for Felch to explain why the petition of the Indian inhabitants of Natick should not be granted at face value in combination with Felch's apparent failure to answer, then we must conclude that the Indians prevailed in the dispute. Did Felch understand that he had no grounds to counter the petitioners' accusations? Did he decide that the Indians were powerless to stop the audacious violation of their property rights even with the weight of the colonial establishment stacked against him? We cannot know. The proprietors' records of Natick do, however, allow us to flesh out this story of Indian fishing rights into the 1760s. The Indian proprietors of Natick had retained collective ownership of much of the land on the edges of Cochituate Pond even as they had, by that time, divided into individual ownership nearly every acre in Natick. This fact suggests that the Indians continued to regard their "old and valluable" fishing rights as a communal good that was not subject to ideas of individual ownership and that they could best protect this resource by the continuation of collective ownership. In 1763, however, Felch finally got his way. When the Indian proprietors made a final division of their few remaining common lands, they gave Felch 10.25 acres bordering on Cochituate Pond "for [his] nineteen years Service as their Survyer."[43]

---

42. L. Murray, " 'Pray, Sir, Consider a Little,' " 32.
43. O'Brien, *Dispossession by Degrees*, 168–71.

# 4 · The Pequots

THE CENTER of Pequot communal life was the area between the Thames and the Mystic rivers in present-day Connecticut. At the time of colonization, the Pequots numbered approximately thirteen thousand, and they controlled some two thousand square miles of territory. Undeniably a powerful force in colonial New England, they were a commanding presence before European contact as well. This long-standing dominance may be one reason that Mohegan and Narragansett leaders allied against the Pequots during the colonial period despite their earlier association with them in trade and kinship networks.

Like the Wampanoags, Narragansetts, and other groups in the area, the Pequots followed a traditional cosmology guided primarily by Cautantowwit, the creator, and Cheepi, a spirit who linked the living and the dead. These groups understood themselves to inhabit a world infused by the spiritual; powerful people, animals, and objects were referred to as *manitou*.

Largely thanks to European colonial prejudices, the Pequots have been known historically as brutal aggressors. Although recent linguists link the name Pequot to elements of the landscape, and the archaeologist Robert Grumet notes that modern Pequots connect the name to an Algonquian word for "ally," colonial English writers used the translation "destroyer," a stigma that contributed to the tragic events and aftermath of the 1637 war. The conflict, sparked by trade and land disputes among the Pequots, the Mohegans, the Narragansetts, the Dutch, and various English colonists, led to the burning of the Pequot fort at Mystic by English militiamen—a massacre so terrible that Bay Colony settlers felt compelled to defend the act in print—and a swamp fight that ended Pequot military resistance. Colonial authorities secured their victory by forbidding survivors to call themselves Pequot and by forcing captives to work as their servants or selling them in the West Indies.

The war may be considered a defining aspect of Pequot history; however, contrary to the assumption of many historians, it failed to achieve the extinction of the Pequot people. In fact, Pequot survivors immediately began to leave their enforced servitude, reclaim their identities, and establish settlements in New England. Eventually, they acquired reservation lands at Noank, Stonington, and (in 1666) Mashantucket, a settlement that the Pequot Nation holds to this day. Most Pequots converted to Christianity during the Great Awakening in the first half of the eighteenth century. William Apess, a well-known early nineteenth-century Pequot writer, published the Christian testimonies of several Pequot women in 1833. His other writings include an autobiography and pointed criticisms of English colonial history and its continuing racist legacy.

In the 1980s the Mashantucket Pequot Tribal Nation successfully sued for land reparations and federal recognition. Today the nation operates several prominent businesses, including the Foxwoods Resort and Casino. The Mashantucket Pequot Museum and Research Center offers an especially rich resource for Native American scholarship and, through its website and exhibits, helps to tell the continuing story of the Pequot people.

## Suggested Reading

Apess, William. *On Our Own Ground: The Complete Writings of William Apess, a Pequot.* Ed. Barry O'Connell. Amherst: University of Massachusetts Press, 1992.

Cave, Alfred A. *The Pequot War.* Amherst: University of Massachusetts Press, 1996.

Hauptman, Laurence M., and James D. Wherry, eds. *The Pequots in Southern New England: The Fall and Rise of an American Indian Nation.* Norman: Unversity of Oklahoma Press, 1990.

Mashantucket Pequot Museum and Research Center website. Available at http://www.pequotmuseum.org/. Accessed 30 June 2006.

# Pequot Medicine Bundle

The object in question here, a Pequot medicine bundle, consists of a torn and folded page from a King James Bible and the front left paw of a bear which were contained in a small bag made of woolen trade cloth. This bundle was buried with an eleven-year-old Pequot girl in her community cemetery on what is today the Mashantucket Pequot Reservation. A portion of this bundle was preserved because of its contact with an iron object, which turned the organic materials into iron salts. The original size of the object is difficult to determine; it is estimated that the bag measured 5–6 inches by 5–6 inches. In 1993 the funerary objects which had been disturbed during the construction of a private home were reburied with the human remains at the tribal cemetery. We have not reproduced an image of any portion of the medicine bundle because of its nature as a funerary object.

# Bundles, Bears, and Bibles
## Interpreting Seventeenth-Century Native "Texts"

KEVIN A. MCBRIDE

The subject of this essay, the academic interpretation of funerary objects from a Mashantucket Pequot cemetery, is a very sensitive—and potentially problematic and offensive—issue for Native Americans. For many generations the Pequots and other Native peoples have struggled with the misappropriation and misrepresentation of their histories, sacred objects, and human remains by anthropologists, archaeologists, and ethnohistorians. More recently, Native people and scholars from various disciplines—recognizing both the opportunities and potential problems in their collaboration—have begun to work together to foster a better understanding of Native histories.[1] Toward that effort, this essay was reviewed and approved by the Mashantucket Pequot Tribal Council and the tribal Historic and Cultural Preservation Committee, whose members provided many important insights. The Mashantucket Pequots have a long and productive tradition of collaboration with both archaeologists and anthropologists.[2] Although the Mashantucket Pequots do not necessarily agree with the perspective or the conclusions herein, they support and recog-

---

1. Kerber, *Cross-Cultural Collaboration*.
2. Jones and McBride, "Indigenous Archaeology."

nize the importance of multiple viewpoints in the reconstruction and interpretation of the past, as long as the process and subsequent dissemination of
information are carried out in a respectful manner. This essay is the result of
our collaboration.

In the third quarter of the seventeenth century, a young Pequot girl was buried in her community cemetery on the Mashantucket Pequot Reservation. The
girl, who was eleven years old when she died, was the oldest member of her age
group, on the verge of becoming a young woman. She, like the other individuals interred in the cemetery, was buried in a traditional manner. She was placed
in a circular grave, the bottom of which was lined with woven mats made from
reed and rush; her arms and legs, bent at the elbows and knees, were drawn
tightly to her chin. She lay on her right side, facing the east, with the top of
her skull and the long axis of her spine oriented toward the southwest. Funerary objects of a personal, symbolic, and ritual nature that were placed with her
reflected her age and gender as well as her role and status within the tribe.

Her forehead was adorned with a headband made of brass and purple wam-
pum-shell beads and sprinkled with red ocher. Several intricately designed
necklaces made from purple and white shell and from brass and glass beads,
incorporating effigies of shell and brass birds, turtles, and amphibians, were
hung around her neck.

As an individual in transition from childhood to young adulthood, she was
provided with objects that reflected both her identity as a child and her emerging role and status as a young woman. Like younger children in her age group,
she received many objects of an ideological, ritual, or symbolic nature, such as
necklaces, headbands, and effigies. Unlike younger children in her age group,
she also received objects that reflected the maturity, responsibilities, and role of
a young woman in the tribe, such as a pestle, a pothook, and an iron hoe.

Of particular interest, and the subject of this essay, was a small bag, a
medicine bundle made from a piece of fine woolen trade cloth that contained
the front left paw of a bear and a folded page from a seventeenth-century
Bible. The bag and its contents were preserved by virtue of their direct contact
with an iron cup or ladle, which partially covered the woolen bag and transformed
the cloth and paper into iron salts, thus creating a pseudomorph (an exact repro-
duction of the form and structure of the original but in a different substance).[3]

The presence of a Bible or other Christian iconography would normally
suggest some degree of involvement with Christianity, perhaps conversion. The
association of the Bible page with the bear paw in the context of a medicine
bundle, however, suggests the importance of further deciphering the "text" of

---

3. Amory, "The Trout and the Milk," 56.

the bundle. The text comprises individual components or contexts that must be read or interpreted both individually and collectively, each of which poses a series of questions. What does the association of the bear and the Bible in the context of a medicine bundle inform us about Native transformation and appropriation of European objects, ideologies, and iconography? What does the medicine bundle inform us about Native strategies for spiritual and physical well-being during a period in which great pressures were being imposed on the Pequot culture and society from land loss, disease, and warfare? What does the Bible fragment inform us about Pequot perspectives on Christianity and the Bible? Finally, what does the "text" inform us about the character and personal history of the girl and her role and status in Pequot society?

## Pequot Mortuary Ritual

The cemetery where the young girl was buried, now known as Long Pond, was used between 1666 and 1720 by the Councilor's Town, one of two Pequot communities at Mashantucket in the late seventeenth and early eighteenth centuries. In 1990 the Mashantucket Pequot Tribal Council authorized recovery, analysis, and reburial for twenty to thirty graves disturbed during the construction of a private home and excavation, analysis, and reburial for twenty-five undisturbed graves on the house lot. An additional twenty to thirty identified graves were to be left undisturbed.[4]

The Pequots buried at Long Pond ranged from as young as one to two years to more than sixty years old. Because of the extensive damage to the graves and the poor preservation of the human remains, few individuals could be identified beyond general age categories (adult/child) or gender. Of the individuals who were identified beyond these parameters, males ($n = 9$) outnumbered females ($n = 6$) and adults ($n = 19$) outnumbered infants ($n = 3$) and children ($n = 3$). The mortality rate among young adults was quite high, representing approximately 60 percent of the cemetery population. The high death rate in this age group suggests a population that was hit hard by disease and perhaps (especially in the case of the men) warfare.

The relationship between the mortuary ritual of the Native peoples of southern New England and their cosmology and worldview has been well documented.[5] The alignment of the deceased, with the head oriented toward the southwest, corresponded to the direction that the soul traveled when it left

---

4. Currie and McBride, "Respect for the Ancestors"; McBride, "Ancient and Crazie."
5. Rubertone, *Grave Undertakings*; Simmons, *Cautantowwit's House*.

the body, to Cautantowwit's house.[6] The arrangement of the body in a flexed or fetal position signified the connection between birth and death, "giving symbolic expression to a belief in the process of continuous renewal between the community of the living and those of the ancestors residing in the afterworld in the southwest."[7]

The objects that accompanied the deceased on their journey consist of personal possessions (e.g., a pestle, an iron hoe, clothing), ritual items (e.g., a medicine bundle, effigies), and social or ideological objects (e.g., necklaces, headbands).[8] The funerary objects (whether of European or Native manufacture), which were associated in significant ways with the individuals with whom they were placed, were selected on the basis of the individual's age, gender, role, and status. The European objects and materials had been transformed, adapted, and incorporated into the daily lives and traditions of the Pequots. In the context of the mortuary ritual, Native and European objects represented links with the community, the individual, and the afterlife and were considered highly symbolic of Pequot beliefs and practices in the physical and spiritual worlds.

On the basis of their elaborate treatment during the mortuary ritual treatment at Long Pond, ethnohistoric evidence, and comparative data from other seventeenth-century Native cemeteries, it is clear that the children—those between the ages of three and eleven years—formed a cohort, a group distinct from that of the infants and adults.[9] Children in the three-to-eleven-year cohort constituted less than 12 percent of the cemetery population, yet they were buried with 95 percent of the ritual, social, or ideological objects (e.g., wampum belts, headbands, necklaces, and effigies).[10] The children in this age group had survived infancy, presumably had been named, and had been ready to assume new status and identities within the community.[11]

The bear paw offering is somewhat unusual; although it has not been identified in other mortuary contexts in southern New England, animal effigies (e.g., representations of turtles, bears, ducks, and amphibians) were common.[12] The bear and other animals represented in stone, copper, brass, and shell are be-

---

6. Simmons, *Cautantowwit's House*. Cautantowwit, the god of the Southwest, is the chief deity of the Native people of southern New England. According to Narragansett tradition, Cautantowwit, the creator of men and women, resided in the afterworld inhabited by the souls of the dead.

7. Rubertone, *Grave Undertakings*, 133.

8. Ibid.; McBride, "Ancient and Crazie."

9. Rubertone, *Grave Undertakings*.

10. McBride, "Ancient and Crazie."

11. Ibid.; Rubertone, *Grave Undertakings*.

12. Ibid.

lieved to be powerful beings capable of transitioning between the physical and spiritual realms of the sky and the terrestrial world and between the terrestrial and underwater worlds.

Children were perceived to be in a state of liminality, existing on the threshold or boundary between the physical and spiritual worlds. The perception that infants, in particular, did not have a firm existence in the physical world was often reflected in mortuary ritual by the presence of bracelets or anklets intended to keep the child tied to the earth.[13] Although older children (between three and eleven years) may have had a firmer existence in the physical world, they had not yet achieved the status, knowledge, and power to travel unassisted from the physical world to the spirit world. This sheds some light on the presence or representation of powerful beings, infused with manitou, that can transition between the physical and spirit worlds.

## Bible

All that remained of the Bible page in the medicine bundle interred with the eleven-year-old Pequot girl were six partly legible words. Because the words "new song" were included among them, Hugh Amory, the bibliographer who conducted the analysis, suspected that the lines were from a psalm and therefore from a Bible.[14] Amory eventually identified the page as containing the opening line of Psalm 98: "O sing unto the Lord a new song, for he hath done marvelous things."[15] Analysis of the size, type, line endings, and margin indicated that the page was from a small-format King James Bible printed in Holland between 1669 and 1680 and most likely imported to Boston between 1675 and 1680.[16]

Typically, seventeenth-century small-format Bibles were personal possessions. Like all Bibles, including the larger-format Bibles, which were used as family Bibles or at the pulpit, personal Bibles were sometimes quite expensive. The most common Bible associated with Native communities in the seventeenth century was the Eliot Bible, which was printed by John Eliot in two editions in 1663 and 1685. Eliot Bibles, which were written in Wampanoag and English, were provided to Native converts to Christianity, primarily to Christian Indian communities ("praying towns") in Massachusetts. Because Pequot and Massachusett were distinct languages and there is no evidence that Eliot visited Mashantucket (or would have been welcome if he had), it is unlikely

---

13. Ibid.; Benard, "Native American Childrearing."
14. Amory, "The Trout and the Milk," fig. 1.
15. Quoted in ibid., 56.
16. See ibid., 60.

that an Eliot Bible found its way to Mashantucket. English missionaries were somewhat active at Mashantucket in the seventeenth century; however, until the Great Awakening of the early 1740s, they had limited or no success in converting the Pequots or any other Native group in Connecticut or Rhode Island.[17] In 1713 and 1714, when the Society for Propagation of the Gospel in the New World sent Experience Mayhew among the Narragansetts, Pequots, and Mohegans to determine the cause of their resistance to Christianity, he was met with hostility or indifference from the communities.[18] It is reasonable to conclude, therefore, that the presence of the Bible at Long Pond does not indicate widespread acceptance of Christianity among the Pequots.

How the the girl, her family, or her community obtained the Bible is an open question, but it is likely that it was acquired by purchase, trade, or gift. Small-format Bibles were generally personal possessions; the larger format was generally used for family or pulpit Bibles.[19] The Bible may have been a gift from an Englishman who was on friendly terms with the Pequots. The question of how it was acquired, however, is less important than how it was perceived by and used in the Pequot community. The fact that a single page of the Bible was found in the medicine bundle suggests that other members of the community may have used other pages from the Bible in similar ways. The use of a single page also suggests that the meaning, use, and perception of the Bible differed fundamentally from the Christian perspective. The inclusion of the page in the bundle transforms the symbolic system of the printed word to another communicative system—that of the Pequot mortuary ritual.

It is possible that the psalm had meaning for the Pequot community or for the young girl. In a personal communication with Jessie Little Doe in 2005, she suggested that the selection of the left paw of the bear and Psalm 98 might have been purposeful, as the psalm contains the words "his right hand." In this context, the bear paw and Bible page reflect a balance between, on one hand, traditional beliefs and ritual and, on the other hand, the new beliefs and power represented by the Bible. Although there is no evidence that the Pequots were literate at this time, this does not preclude their having knowledge of the contents and meaning of the psalm.

The association of the bear paw with the Bible page in the medicine bundle is unusual in that it integrates the manitou (spirit) of objects that represent worldviews and beliefs that are fundamentally different from each other. In the context of the medicine bundle, however, the Bible and bear paw can also be

17. Simmons, "Great Awakening"; Simmons and Simmons, Old Light.
18. J. Ford, Some Correspondence.
19. Amory, "The Trout and the Milk," 61.

considered culturally congruent in that from a Native perspective they were both perceived as objects of power and healing and, perhaps, a way of transcending or communicating between the physical and spiritual worlds. It can also be argued that the Bible had an analogous function in English society, which may have been understood at some level by the Pequots.

Found individually, even in a mortuary context, these objects would not be interpreted in the same way as in the context of a medicine bundle. Although the bear, in any context, would be interpreted as a Native symbol of power and healing, the Bible would normally indicate an interest in or conversion to Christianity. It is the association of the Bible with the bear paw in the context of a medicine bundle that shifts the meaning of the Bible away from that of an English religious text that contains the word of God.

The importance, meaning, and power of the Bible to the English would not have been lost on the Native people of seventeenth-century New England. The Puritans believed in the supreme authority of the Bible as the word of God and as an indispensable guide for spiritual and civil life. The Puritans further believed that their Christian faith delivered them from their enemies (as during the Pequot War of 1637) and protected them from misfortunes including drought, famine, and epidemic diseases such as smallpox. Conversely, of course, God's displeasure resulted in swift punishment that came in many forms. The Puritan belief that the Bible and their Christian faith protected them from the smallpox epidemics of the seventeenth century—which devastated Native communities throughout the Northeast, resulting in a 90 percent mortality rate by the early eighteenth century—was common knowledge among Native peoples. These communities may well have come to perceive the Bible as an object of great power, capable of protecting not only the English but also their own people from myriad misfortunes, including various newly introduced European diseases.

## Manitou and Power

When the Pequots and other Native people first encountered Europeans in the early seventeenth century, they incorporated the strangers and their foreign objects into their own worldview. Native people initially perceived Europeans as culture heroes, supernatural man-beings who had returned from beyond the sea, bringing with them materials and substances of power from the under(water) world.[20] According to Ezra Stiles, when the Pequots saw the first European vessels sailing into Long Island Sound, "they said it was Weetucks a

---

20. Bradley, *Evolution of the Onondaga Iroquois*, 66.

coming again."[21] Weetucks is a local manifestation of a northeastern culture hero who had great power and often came to the aid of humans.[22] As Roger Williams observed, the Narragansetts described Weetucks as "a man that wrought great Miracles amongst them, and walking upon the waters, & c. with some kind of broken Resemblance to the Sonne of God."[23] This statement suggests that Williams (and, by inference, the Narragansetts) recognized similarities between Weetucks and Christ, essentially transforming the cultural and spiritual ethos of the "other" into their own worldview.

This perspective is also evident in the Native appropriation and transformation of European objects such as the Bible and printed text. Williams reported that "when they [the Narragansetts] talke amongst themselves of the English ships, and great buildings, of the plowing of their Fields, and especially of their Bookes and Letters, they will end thus: Manittowock [Manitou] They are Gods."[24]

In the burial of the young Pequot girl, the physical and contextual association of the Bible page with a being of great power (the bear) suggests not only a conceptual relationship between the two but also a process by which Native people transformed and incorporated European objects infused with manitou (i.e., the Bible) into their worldview.

*Manitou*, poorly defined from a Eurocentric perspective as "power," is the spiritual potency associated with an object, with a being, or with natural phenomena. It "was the force which made everything in nature alive and responsive to man. Only a fool would confront life [or death] without it."[25] Manitou can be accumulated by proper ritual and then used by individuals or communities as they make their way through or negotiate between the natural and spiritual worlds.

## Manitou and Bears

Fundamental differences existed between the ways that Native people in southern New England, as elsewhere in North America, and Europeans viewed animals. According to the Native view, animals were different from people but not necessarily subordinate to them. Most animals had a special relationship with people and were connected to them through the spiritual and physical worlds. Manitou were also considered to be "other-than-human beings capable

---

21. Quoted in Dexter, *Extracts*, 83.
22. Simmons, *Spirit of the New England Tribes*, 172.
23. R. Williams, *A Key into the Language of America*, A5.
24. Ibid., 125.
25. Martin, *Keepers of the Game*, 34.

of assuming a variety of physical forms—including animals—and exerting spiritual power in a number of ways."[26] Through appropriate ritual and training, individuals could exert "spiritual levels of control through the medium of an animal" such as the bear.[27]

The bear, held in high esteem by Native groups throughout North America, is often associated with special hunting and healing rituals and is usually addressed with such honorific titles as grandfather, reflecting the power and wisdom of the bear and its similarity to humans. Williams identified the bear as one of only a few animals in the Narragansett (and presumably Pequot) world capable of exerting great spiritual power and described as possessing "divine powers."[28] Rituals associated with bears have been recorded for the many Native groups in eastern North America.[29] Although analogies with respect to beliefs and rituals among the Pequots should not be made lightly, given the broad geographic and cultural distribution of these practices among Native peoples in eastern North America, it seems a reasonable inference that the bear was widely associated with power.

Frank Speck and Jesse Moses have argued for a cross-cultural symbology and ritual among Native peoples in eastern North America that reflects a close connection between the sky world (with its soul spirits) and the terrestrial world (with its living beings).[30] This connection is expressed in rituals whereby "the departed spirits of relatives and friends are believed to be present side by side with the living as visitors from the sky to the earth and the living."[31] The bear sacrifice ceremony, performed in many forms by Native peoples across the eastern woodlands, serves in part to renew the eternal relationship between earth beings and sky beings. The bear, a being that manifests itself as the earth bear and the sky bear, can transcend both the spirit world and the physical world.

## Conclusion

The medicine bundle should be viewed as a Native text whose various elements must be read or interpreted both individually and collectively in order to discern its meaning. The Bible fragment, in the context of the medicine bundle,

---

26. Anderson, "Chickwallop and the Beast," 29.
27. Speck and Moses, *Celestial Bear*, 27.
28. See Anderson, "Chickwallop and the Beast," 29; LaFantasie, *Correspondence of Roger Williams*, 1:146.
29. Hallowell, "Bear Ceremonialism."
30. Speck and Moses, *Celestial Bear*.
31. Ibid., 32.

must be interpreted from a Native perspective, given that it reflects a process of transformation and appropriation of European objects into a Native worldview. Although the Pequots may have understood the literal meaning of the Bible page, the context in which it was found suggests that its original meaning (from an English perspective) was essentially transformed in order to accommodate a Native perspective on manitou and power. The text of the medicine bundle and its contents can be read as representing evolving Native strategies intended to assist the living and the dead as they traverse spiritual and physical worlds forever changed by the arrival of the Europeans.

# The Confession and Dying Warning
## of Katherine Garret

Executed in 1738 for infanticide, Katherine Garret (Pequot) left "under her own Hand" the following final address, accompanied by an anonymous account of her behavior and religious conversion while she was in prison. Timothy Green of New London published both texts in 1738 as supplemental documents to the Reverend Eliphalet Adams's thirty-seven-page execution sermon, under the full title *A SERMON Preached on the Occasion of the EXECUTION of Katherine Garret, an Indian-Servant, (Who was Condemned for the Murder of her Spurious Child,) On May 3ᵈ. 1738. To which is Added some short Account of her Behavior after her Condemnation. Together with her Dying WARNING and EXHORTATION. Left under her own Hand.* Adams (1677–1753) began his career as an Indian missionary and served as a popular preacher at the First Congregational Church of New London. Green (1679–1757) published a wide variety of colonial pamphlets, including religious tracts and execution narratives. A copy of the forty-four-page pamphlet is housed at the American Antiquarian Society in Worcester, Massachusetts; a microform version is available through the Readex Early American Imprints series.

*I Katherine Garret,* being Condemned to Die for the Crying Sin of Murder, Do Own the Justice of GOD in suffering me to die this Violent Death; and also Acknowledge the Justice of the Court who has Sentenced me to die this Death; and I thank them who have Lengthened the Time to me, whereby I have had great Opportunity to prepare for my Death: I thank those also who have taken pains with me for my Soul; so that since I have been in Prison, I have had opportunity to seek after Baptism & the Supper of the Lord & have obtained both. I Confess my self to have been a great Sinner; a sinner by Nature, also guilty of many Actual Transgressions, Particularly of Pride and Lying, as well as of the Sin of destroying the Fruit of my own Body, for which latter, I am now to Die.[32] I thank God that I was learn'd to Read in my Childhood, which

---

I thank my research assistant, Amanda Bennett, for her transcription assistance.

32. Gratitude for imprisonment, exhortations to honor the Sabbath, and the call to obey parents and masters, which are quite commonplace in dying warnings, exemplify how the genre seeks to enforce social hierarchies and gender norms. Infanticide confessions commonly establish a slippery slope from illicit female sexual activity to lying to conceal a pregnancy to murder.

has been much my Exercise since I have been in Prison, and especially since my Condemnation. The Bible has been a precious Book to me. There I read, *That* JESUS CHRIST *came into the world to Save Sinners,* Even the *Chief of Sinners:* And that *all manner of Sins shall be forgiven, One only Excepted;*[33] *For his Blood Cleanseth from all Sin.* And other good Books I have been favoured with, by peoples giving and lending them to me, which has been blessed to me.

I would Warn all Young People against Sinning against their own Consciences; For there is a GOD that Knows all things. Oh! Beware of all Sin, Especially of Fornication; for that has led me to Murder. Remember the Sabbath-day to keep it Holy. Be Sober and wise. Redeem your Time, and Improve it well.

Little Children I would Warn you to take heed of Sinning against God. Be Dutiful to your Parents; For *the Eye that Mocks at his Father and despiseth to Obey his Mother, the Ravens of the Valley shall pick it out, and the Young Eagles shall eat it.*[34] Little Children, Learn to Pray to God; Sit still on the Lord's Day, and Love your Books.

I would also Warn Servants, Either *Whites* or *Blacks,* to be Obedient to your Masters & Mistresses. Be Faithful in your places and diligent: Above all Fear God; fear to Sin against Him: He is our Great Master.

I would also Intreat Parents and Masters to set a good Example before their Children and Servants, for You also must give an Account to God how you carry it to them.[35]

I desire the Prayers of all God's People for me, Private Christians, as well as Ministers of the Gospel, that I may while I have Life Improve it aright; May have all my Sins Pardoned and may be Accepted through CHRIST JESUS. Amen.

Katherine Garret.

---

33. A reference to Original Sin.

34. Prov. 30:17. Although many Native spiritual traditions consider eagles messengers of the Creator and ravens emissaries of the afterworld, a syncretic reading seems unlikely, given that both birds here serve as vehicles of extreme physical violence. If anything, the passage highlights the fact that Garret must refashion indigenous belief and see "other wise" in order to comprehend the Old Testament message of swift and brutal retribution.

35. Garret's warning to masters to improve their treatment of servants is atypical (although such protests would become more common later in the century). Her racial specificity concerning those servants who should obey their masters is also distinctive.

New London, May 3. 1738.

*It may Possibly be Acceptable to the Publick, if some* brief Account *were given of the person, on the Occasion of whose Execution the foregoing Discourse was Delivered.*[36]

SHE was of the *Pequot* Tribe of *Indians* & Descended from one of the best Families among them; In her Childhood she was put into the Family of the Reverend Mr. WILLIAM WORTHINGTON, where she was taught to read well and to write & Instructed in the principles of religion; During her Confinement she often lamented her neglecting to Improve the Advantages she Enjoyed, always speaking honourably of her Master, who was frequent in giving her good Instruction and Advice.

Having Unhappily fallen into the Sin of Fornication & being with Child, it pass'd for a while without Suspicion by any in the family, at length being Question'd about it she deny'd it & turn'd it off, assigning *other causes* for the appearances that were observ'd, so that the suspicions about her were thereby *very much* laid asleep;

When her hour was Come, she was Delivered alone by her self in the Barn; upon search the Infant was found, with marks upon it of Violence, that had been used, of which wounds it soon Dyed.[37]

Upon this she was Committed to the County Goal [*sic*], where she lay Confined for a considerable time, & the longer because the Witnesses who were to

---

36. The "foregoing Discourse" refers to Adams's thirty-seven-page execution sermon (not included here); the pamphlet published by Green opens with the sermon, which is followed by this account, and concludes with Garret's confession and dying warning. Here, we reverse the order of the documents in order to foreground the section written in Garret's "own Hand." Spelling, punctuation, and capitalization, including possible printer errors, remain true to the original.

37. According to handwritten testimony in the *New London Superior Court Files*, Temperance Worthington, the wife of the Reverend William Worthington, testified that earlier that day, Garret had complained of stomach sickness, retired to rest, and later emerged from the barn. Hours later, a child's cry prompted a search, and Reverend Mr. Worthington located an infant under a pile of hay and spotted a bloody wooden block nearby. The Reverend Mr. Worthington stated, "The child was an Indian male child, naked and newly born, and Kate told in my hearing who was the father of it." (The father remains unnamed in the records.) According to William Worthington, Garret confessed to abandoning the infant, admitting that "she was the mother of the child, and that she was delivered of it in [said] barn, and that she hid it in the place above [mentioned], and because it cried, she took it out again, and then laid it there again, and it did not cry, and so she came in." According to Temperance Worthington, "Finally, Kate did confess to me that she did strike ~~murder~~ the child twice on the side of the head with a wood block." (The strikethrough appears on the handwritten testimony.) Despite the alleged confessions, Garret pleaded not guilty at her arraignment. The account suggests that Garret anticipated a more sympathetic response than the one she received from the Saybrook community where she lived and worked.

give Evidence in the case, were, by reason of Infirmity (one of them) not able to travel so far from home to the place where the Court was to be held, to bear their Testimony.

During this space, I have little to observe Concerning her; Only, that when the Court for her Tryal was appointed to be held at *Saybrook*, she seemed to Entertain a full Expectation that she should be Cleared.

But when upon her tryal, the proofs of her Guilt, appeared so plain and full to the Jury and the Court, that she was brought in Guilty and Sentence of Condemnation was pronounced against her, she was thrown into the utmost Confusion & Distress, Her Expressions were rash and unguarded and she scarce forebore throwing blame on all sorts of persons; With this Disposition of mind (tho' somewhat moderated) she was remanded back to her prison.[38]

From this time pains were Continually taken with her, not only to allay this resentment, but to make her Sensible of the Heinousness of her Sin, of her Lost and undone Condition by Nature and her need of an Interest in Jesus Christ, setting forth at the same time the greatness of Gods mercy and that there is forgiveness with him that he may be feared, which pains (together with Gods Blessing, upon her reading the holy Scriptures and other good Books that were put into her hands and her attendance on the Ministry of the Word, on Sabbath and Lecture days, as well as at private Meetings from house to house in the Neighbourhood to all of which she was allowed to come) it is to be hoped were sanctifyed to give her quite another sight and sense of things than she had before: One of her Expressions were, *That she seemed to have been asleep in the former part of her Life and that things appeared to her quite other wise than they used to do.*

The Authority were so favourable to her, as to allow her Large Opportunity (almost six Months from her Condemnation to her Execution) which Time she was diligent to Improve in making preparation for her Death;

Having Never been *Baptized*, she was Earnestly Desirous of that, wherefore pains were taken to Acquaint her with the main principles of the Christian Religion and the Nature of the Covenant of Grace. The understanding of which her former good Education, made more Easie to her. And after some time, upon her *making an Open Acknowledgement of her great and Crying Sins*, taking shame to her self & manifesting her Sorrow on that account; *Professing the Christian Faith & Consenting to the Covenant of grace,* she was *Baptized.*[39]

---

38. To prompt reluctant witnesses to testify, the court moved the trial from New London to Saybrook. Garret's trial was held from 15 November to 17 November, ten months after the infant was discovered. She was executed on 3 May 1738, nearly six months after the guilty verdict and execution order.

39. New London church records confirm that Adams baptized Garret on 29 January 1738 (see Blake, *Later History*).

Soon after, She was Extreamly Desirous to partake with us at the *Lord's Table before she Suffer'd,* And upon its appearing that she understood the Nature & Design of that Ordinance, at her request she was allowed and had the opportunity to Communicate with us *twice.*

In her attendance upon the ministry of the Word her Behavior was Decent & she ever appeared as one *Exceedingly Affected,* Especially when her Case was more particularly touch'd upon whither in *Prayers* or *Sermons.*

When I visited her in her prison, she seldom could part with me, without Desiring that I would Pray with her before I went, which favour she Desired of others also, who Visited her during her Confinement.

Many of her Expressions from time to time were Valuable and worth the Preserving.

Among other things she said, *That it was a Mercy she was found out, otherwise she might have gone on in her Course of sinning & been Eternally Lost. That sin seem'd now like poison to her & those sins in which she was wont to delight, were now Loathsom: That she had found more pleasure in her prison, than Ever she did in the Days of her Vanity. That she was heartily sorry for her sin not so much for the shame & punishment that it had bro't her to, as because thereby she had offended and dishonored God. She could submit to the shame of her Death, It would be soon Over & then she should not know what people talked of her. Some* (she said) *had reported of her things that were false, but she heartily forgave them; She Entertained no grudge or malice against any person on any account, for that alone, she knew, would ruin her, if she did. The Devil was very busie, she said, to hinder her from Praying & Reading, but she did it the more, to spite him* (that was her word) *and the Temptation Vanished & she found Comfort.*[40] She often Expressed her *Concern* lest she should *build upon a sandy foundation.* Being asked from time to time, how Death seemed to her, the nearer it Approached. She answered, *Sometimes More Terrible, sometimes Less Terrible.* And being asked at what times she Observed it to be less Terrible, she replyed, *That after she had been Earnestly seeking to God, the fear of Death very much Abated.* She said, *that her dependence was upon the Righteousness of Christ for her acceptance with God and look'd up on him as a surety who had paid their debts for believers.*[41]

---

40. Such statements documenting the "benefits" of incarceration are typical in "miraculous conversion" narratives. More atypical is Garret's insistence, even after converting and confessing, that people had falsely testified against her. Garret's extreme distress as her execution day approaches might suggest an enduring hope that by earnest preparation, she might earn clemency.

41. Hebrews 7:22 constructs Christ as surety, bound by Covenant to "pay for" our sins. An indentured servant might certainly respond enthusiastically to this economic metaphor of a benevolent Christ, guarantor of earthly debts and obligations. The Indian servant Patience Boston uses a similar economic metaphor for salvation in her narrative, noting, "My Surety, I trust, has paid my whole Debt" (*Faithful Narrative*, 27).

But I forbear gathering up any more of her Expressions, That I be not too tedious.

The Day before her Execution she was Exceedingly Overwhelmed and cast Down, It seemed to be the most *trying time* to her, during her whole Confinement, whither it were Occasioned by the want of her taking her usual rest or food or whether the near approach of Death were Left to be an Uncommon Terror to her.

Every one's Compassions were moved for her, and she was Visited more frequently & by greater Numbers of persons and Prayers more fervently made on her account. Towards the evening *her Master* came from *Saybrook* to take his last farewell of her, with whose presence, the Instructions and Consolations that were given & the Prayers that were made for her, she somthing revived and was Overheard in her Prayers (after the people were, many of them, gone) to *bless God who had sent his Servants that Day to Pray for, to Instruct and Comfort her a poor Dying Creature.*

On the Day of her Execution, she was more strengthened and enabled to attend at the Sermon that was preach'd on that Melancholy Occasion, altho' with some faintings; Upon her retiring to the Prison, when it was Over, she made apt and pertinent remarks, upon the sight of her Coffin, the taking off of her fetters, the putting the rope about her Neck & other such Occurrences. Then she took her Leave of her friends thanking them for the good Offices which they had done her (as she Ever Expressed a grateful Spirit to every one, that at any time, had shewn her any Kindness) She passed on foot in the sad procession, for about a Mile, to the place of Execution & still *went On praying.*

Excepting when the *Rev'd Ministers in the Neighbourhood* (gathered together on the Occasion & who gave her their Company) Endeavoured to fill up the time, by ministring to her Counsels, Comforts & Encouragements, to whom she made satisfactory replyes.

When she was arrived at the place of Execution, (which was surrounded with a Vast Circle of people, more Numerous, perhaps, than Ever was gathered together before, On any Occasion, in this Colony,) she first Commended her self to God's mercy, In a more set and very fervent Prayer. Tho' sometimes the Expressions were more broken and Incoherent.

Next Her Master, Full of Concern and Affection for her, Spread her Case before God; Her Warning left in writing was publickly read to which she added many Other Warnings and Counsels by word of mouth, Lifting up her Voice as she could that she might be the farther heard; We took our Leave of her and she of us in an Affecting Manner;

The few moments she had to live after this, she spent in warm & Devout

Addresses to her Heavenly Father, till her breath was stopt; And with her hands lifted up, as she cou'd, she past out of life, *in the posture of one praying.*

She was of a proper Stature & goodly Countenance and seemed to be Naturally of an Ingenious Disposition;

By her good Behavior all Along she generally gain'd the Esteem and good will of those that Came about her and it is *Charitably hoped,* that she might find Mercy in the sight of the Lord.

May this Example be of use to all Persons in *our times* to keep them from Sinning against God, that every one may *hear & fear* and *do no more Presumptuously.*

Particularly, may all her *Country people,* in their several Tribes, whither round about us or farther off, hearken diligently to the Offers & Proposals of the Gospel that are made to them! Let there be Nothing to Obstruct & Discourage so good a work, May the Time to favour them now Come, the set time let it Come! *Amen.*

# Seeing Other Wise

### Reading a Pequot Execution Narrative

JODI SCHORB

A century before the pathbreaking autobiography of William Apess, *Son of the Forest* (1829), the titles begin appearing sparsely among the annals of what are commonly classified as American criminal narratives: *The Faithful Narrative of the Wicked Life and Remarkable Conversion of Patience Boston* (1735), *A Sermon Preached on the Occasion of the Execution of Katherine Garret* (1738), and Mohegan minister Samson Occom's *Sermon Preached at the Execution of Moses Paul* (1774). From the American print origin of the execution narrative in 1674, nearly a dozen texts by or about Native Americans find their way into the genre.[42] Like narratives of Indians converted to Christianity, a related body of literature that preceded the execution genre in popularity, these rare and

---

42. The first published execution sermon is Samuel Danforth's *The Cry of Sodom* (1674), a jeremiad that marked the execution of a young, white, male servant for bestiality. For narratives by or about Indians, see Boston, *Faithful Narrative;* H. T. Channing, *God Admonishing His People;* Danforth, *Woeful Effects of Drunkenness;* Julian, *Last Speech and Dying Advice;* Moodey, *Life and Death of Joseph Quasson;* Occom, *Collected Writings;* Pitkin, *Sermon Delivered at the Execution of John Jacobs;* and Spalding, *Sermon Delivered Previous to the Execution of Isaac Coombs.*

challenging texts mark some of the earliest ways Native Americans entered into American print culture. Documenting the last days and final words of Native peoples held in colonial jails before they were executed for capital crimes, this body of writings by or about Native captives makes for a compelling variation on Indian captivity literature.

To read these texts well, we need to consider them outside the genre of crime writings and within a longer cultural history of white fascination with the meaning of Indian death. More than a century earlier, Puritan missionaries had popularized a form of Indian deathbed literature that still resonates with later Indian criminal narratives, a genre devoted to recording the dying words and gestures of converted and unconverted Indians. In John Eliot's *Dying Speeches of Several Indians* (1685) and Experience Mayhew's *Indian Converts* (1727), Eliot and Mayhew selected what they felt were good (meaning pedagogically useful) deaths, whereby Indians demonstrated their understanding of Christian principles and seemingly accepted their fate while they hoped for salvation. Laura Stevens argues that during the seventeenth century Indian death becomes "convenient to the stories and longings of America," most directly as missionaries construct dying Indians as "vehicles of affect directed towards various ideological ends." Such deathbed accounts represent Indian death with a blend of "satisfaction and sorrow . . . inevitability and guilt," as they simultaneously celebrate the conversion of heathen souls and mourn their passing. Paradoxically, although such deathbed literature establishes Natives as equals in the eyes of God, it was used to secure funding for colonial projects that dispersed and decimated Indian populations.[43] In this way, according to Stevens, Indian deathbed narratives enact a form of what Renato Rosaldo has called "imperialist nostalgia," in which the dominant culture mourns "the passing of what they have transformed."[44]

More than a century later, such missionary efforts had been largely abandoned. Still, the importance of Indian deaths persisted, even as the meaning of Indian deaths altered. As both "good Christians" and "dying Indians," Katherine Garret, Patience Boston, Moses Paul, and other condemned Indians also serve as "vehicles of affect." As they had a century before, albeit much more subtly, ministers invoked audiences to seek "spiritual comfort from indigenous death."[45] Large-scale population decimation, land loss, and migration into small enclaves had greatly eliminated Indians as a threat to white expansion in

---

43. Stevens, "Christian Origins of the Vanishing Indian," 18, 17, 30.
44. Quoted in ibid., 18.
45. Ibid., 22.

New England. Moreover, funding for large-scale missionary efforts had all but evaporated, fueling Cotton Mather's 1724 lament that a project meant to spread so much zeal had converted so few.[46] Thus, ministers used the experiences of captive converts to revive hope that a historically failed missionary effort might once again become revitalized and succeed. If this meant that certain forms of Indian death continued to provide white observers with spiritual comfort, we must question why—and whether—Natives would willingly and passively participate in this form of imperialist nostalgia. Natives, however, often used their role as vehicles of effect for different ideological ends, often to express persistent feelings of loss and displacement and to voice subtle protests against the effects of colonization.

The core text included here, "The Confession and Dying Warning of Katherine Garret," was one of at least three texts circulated on the occasion of Garret's 1738 execution. A relatively unknown servant to a white minister, Garret suddenly became infamous as "Indian Kate" when, in January 1737 in Saybrook, Connecticut, an abandoned newborn "with marks upon it of Violence" was found in a barn owned by her master, the Reverend William Worthington. The minister's wife suspected that the baby belonged to Garret, and after repeated questioning, Garret confessed to concealing an unwanted pregnancy and hiding the newborn in the barn; she was less direct on whether she intentionally murdered the infant. Garret was subsequently arrested, tried, and convicted of murder.[47] Garret expected to be acquitted, but she was sentenced to death. The verdict was neither decided nor carried out easily: Because witnesses were reluctant to travel to testify against her, the court passed a special act to move the trial location. Moreover, because authorities considered Garret neither sufficiently resigned to her fate nor properly prepared to die, they postponed her execution by nearly six months in order to "allay [her] resentment" and make her "Sensible to the Heinousness of her Sin." Eventually Garret, like the majority of Natives for whom we have criminal captivity narratives, converted to Christianity. Her hanging was the first in New London history. On a fair day in May, Garret sat shackled while the Reverend Eliphalet Adams delivered her execution sermon. A huge crowd gathered to witness her execution; observers describe "a Vast Circle of people, more Numerous, perhaps, than Ever was gathered together before, On any occasion, in this Colony." Ministers and

---

46. In a 1724 letter to the Connecticut governor, Mather expressed his "despondencies" over the "gospelizing of our Indians" and hoped for better success than had been accomplished (quoted in Szasz, *Indian Education*, 192).

47. The investigation was persistent: the Worthingtons presented evidence that Garret had given birth, a midwife was ordered to "search the body of Kate" to confirm the pregnancy, and—strikingly—authorities scalped the corpse to conclude that the infant's skull had been fractured. See n. 37.

Garret used the somber occasion to address the crowd and attach pedagogical significance to her death.[48]

Garret's execution produced three texts—the sermon, the account, and Garret's dying warning (the last two of which are included here). The account, which was most likely penned by Adams, the white minister who delivered Garret's execution sermon, seeks to make Garret legible as a Christian convert. Crafted in the style of the spiritual autobiography, a genre that traces an individual's spiritual growth, the account emphasizes Garret's jailhouse conversion to Christianity and monitors the strength of her newfound faith as she prepares for death. Interest in such accounts grew in the early eighteenth century as the Great Awakening created demand for tales of personal faith conquering doubt and the ever expanding public print sphere responded to audience interest in criminal biography.[49] Written "under her own Hand" and delivered as her direct oratory to her vast audiences, Garret's dying warning seems to promise access to her own consciousness. A quick perusal, however, reminds us that the text is shaped less by Garret's private thoughts than by the demands of the genre. Dying warnings existed as a popular literary form long before Garret climbed the scaffold to speak, and here, as earlier, audiences demanded religious insight from an individual's proximity to death. Thus, while "The Confession and Dying Warning" is written "under her own Hand," the text is nevertheless written for a predominantly white, Christian audience as part of a very structured public ritual.[50]

As a result, although observers admiringly recount Garret's powerful speech, "Lifting up her Voice as she could that she might be the farther heard," her voice remains difficult for modern readers to access. The amount of formulaic content and the degree of editorial control that ministers maintained over Garret's texts create one of the most difficult interpretive challenges to reading both narratives and prompt us to question whether Garret's voice is in there at all. How are we to "hear" Garret, an eighteenth-century female Pequot servant, and what might her voice sound like?

The problem is not unique to these narratives but endemic to the entire genre of early Native American life writing, a genre in which "as told to" narratives abound, filtered and structured by the lens of the white amanuensis

---

48. On Indian death as a pedagogical moment, see Seeman, "Reading Indians' Deathbed Scenes," a study of hundreds of Indian deathbed scenes that offers a useful overview of traditions associated with the *ars moriendi*, or art of dying, the belief that proper behavior before death could ensure salvation.

49. On the popularity of miraculous conversion narratives during the Great Awakening, see D. Williams, *Pillars of Salt*, 7–11, and D. Cohen, *Pillars of Salt*, 66–72.

50. Although white audiences dominated, executions attracted a diverse spectatorship. According to one history, when Samson Occom addressed Moses Paul, there were "many Indians in the crowd" (Banner, *Death Penalty*, 53).

(whether anthropologist, ethnographer, biographer, or historian). This common challenge reminds us that Garret's text, which preceded the advent of the Native life-writing genre by nearly a century, bears more similarities to the later genre than may first appear.[51] The voice we perceive is largely the voice that white editors want us to hear, a voice made legible by a process of translation, even though Garret could speak and read English and allegedly penned the dying warning herself. As a result, potentially important expressions by Garret are omitted, calling into high relief the moments when her "translator" fails or refuses to understand her language. For example, the account, describing some of Garret's words as "broken and Incoherent," declines to record a portion of her direct address to the gathered crowds. At other times, the minister, resolving not to continue "gathering up any more of her Expressions, That [he] be not too tedious," deems thorough attention to her speech unnecessary. On another occasion, the account reveals that while on the scaffold Garret "added many Other Warnings and Counsels by word of mouth" but withholds the content of her impromptu oratory.[52] These textual blank spaces function like the dead letters of the contact zone—Garret sends the letters, but they miss their intended targets.[53]

With this interpretive challenge in mind, readers should become attentive to the ways in which Garret's narrative becomes the literary equivalent of the "frontier" (a term that I borrow from Arnold Krupat, who uses it to refer to the "ground on which two cultures meet" within early Native texts, a ground marked by a history of domination and appropriation).[54] Instead of looking for a solitary "voice" in this text, Krupat urges us to read for voices—shifting, colluding, competing voices that give a text its complex texture and indeterminate tone. Krupat's formulation provides us with a nexus that allows us to read texts such as Garret's dying warning as Indian autobiography, a genre that,

---

51. For more on this genre, see Krupat, *For Those Who Come After*; D. Murray, *Forked Tongues*; and Brumble, *American Indian Autobiography* (especially Brumble's chapter titled "Editors, Ghosts, and Amanuensis," 72–97).

52. Similarly, the narrative of the Indian servant Patience Boston was published with a preface explaining that her story was—tellingly—"taken from her Mouth" (*Faithful Narrative*, i). Boston's amanuenses defend their practice as a necessary corrective to Boston's way of telling. For a detailed reading of voice in Boston's narrative, see Harvey, "'Taken from Her Mouth.'"

53. Here I refer to what Mary Louise Pratt describes as "the perils of writing in the contact zone": "miscomprehension, incomprehension, dead letters, unread masterpieces" ("Arts of the Contact Zone," 590). Pratt argues that such moments are bound to occur when "the subordinated subject single-handedly gives himself authority in the colonizer's language and verbal repertoire" (588). Pratt defines the "contact zone" as "social spaces where cultures meet, clash, and grapple with each other, often in context of highly asymmetrical relations of power, such as colonialism, slavery, or their aftermaths" (584).

54. Krupat, *For Those Who Come After*, 33.

according to Krupat, is defined precisely *by* a process of limited collaboration and shaped *within* the nexus of colonial power dynamics. According to Krupat, Indian autobiography is "constituted as a genre of writing by its original, bi-cultural, composite composition, the product of a collaboration between the Native American subject of the autobiography who provides its 'content' and the Euramerican editor who ultimately provides its 'form' by fixing the text in writing."[55] Extending Krupat's argument, David Murray argues, "This entails seeing [the texts] not as a corrupted and inferior form, but as *a new form which reflects precisely the cultural limitations and contradictions inherent in a situation where oral and literate cultures meet.*"[56] By electing to read Garret's narrative as a mode of Indian autobiography, we can embrace its challenges of voice and form by foregrounding its dual and often dueling voices and agendas.[57]

Garret's early education (during which she learned to read and write), her access to books while she was in prison, and her exposure to eighteenth-century oral sermon culture during her jailhouse excursions would have familiarized her with the expectations of written public confessions.[58] Ministers express hope that reading and attending sermons will reshape her belief system, of-fering her "quite another sight and sense of things than she had before." As a "literate" Indian, Garret would be expected to pay tribute to the knowledge gained from this Christian education; she does so by noting, "I thank God that I was learn'd to Read in my Childhood, which has been much my Exercise since I have been in Prison." Yet in contrast to dying warnings that testify to the clarifying power of specific biblical passages, Garret constructs reading as an opportunity for interpersonal exchange rather than private contemplation. On

55. Krupat, *Ethnocriticism*, 219. See Krupat, *For Those Who Come After* (especially 28–54), for a fuller statement of his theory. Krupat distinguishes Indian autobiography from "autobiographies by Indians," which, in contrast to Indian autobiography, are "self-written lives" (*Ethnocriticism*, 219). For a different approach to the problem of Indian autobiography, see D. Murray, *Forked Tongues*, 65–97. David Murray suggests that Krupat's distinction may be overstated; he argues that because self-authored texts are "equally implicated in cross-cultural complicities and contradictions," the term "bicultural composite composition" can apply equally well to many texts authored "solely" by Native writers (68). On the usefulness of Pratt's term "autoethnography" to describe this relationship, see Wyss, *Writing Indians*, 4, and Gussman, "Politics of Piety," 104.

56. D. Murray, *Forked Tongues*, 68 (emphasis mine).

57. Analysis of vocal multiplicity occurs frequently in captivity narrative scholarship; I adapt my phrase from that of Tara Fitzpatrick, who notes the "dual (and sometimes dueling) voices" of minis-ters and captives in traditional Indian captivity accounts such as Mary Rowlandson's narrative ("The Figure of Captivity," 2); see also Castiglia, *Bound and Determined* (203 n. 4).

58. Ministers commonly gave prisoners biblical passages, sermons, and conversion narratives, in-cluding execution sermons and dying warnings, to help properly prepare them for death. For example, the Indian servant Patience Boston notes that "divers[e] Examples of poor Indians converted, and how they lived, and how they died" were read to her, "by which [she] was refreshed and revived" (*Faithful Narrative*, 17).

the scaffold, for example, she gives thanks to "other good Books I have been favoured with, by peoples giving and lending them to me, which has been blessed to me." Here the blessing lies in the act of giving and lending rather than in the content of the books. Garret's response to the fact that she is the *subject of oral narrative* suggests another kind of benefit afforded by her literacy: The account notes that she was "*Exceedingly Affected,* Especially when her Case was more particularly touch'd upon whither in *Prayers* or *Sermons.*" Thus, Garret's knowledge of the genre, specifically her interest in hearing her own story circulated publicly, most likely motivates her own investment in writing her brief narrative. Penning a dying warning would do more than position Garret as a showpiece of Indian education and literacy; it would allow her to participate in the way her narrative was "touch'd upon" and recorded in history. Clearly, we miss something if we see Garret as a mere puppet lacking agency over her text and her performance on the scaffold.

Some knowledge of generic conventions helps us discern the formulaic from the unique elements in the narratives. Originally delivered as execution sermons—minister-penned jeremiads delivered the Sunday before or the day of a public execution—execution narratives are meant to foreground the signs and consequences of individual and communal spiritual backsliding. Intended to prepare the condemned for impending death and prompt audiences to engage in rigorous self-examination, the execution sermon's emotive rhetorical strategy strives to instill fear, demand repentance, and—just when permanent damnation seems imminent—offer a glimpse of hope for salvation.[59] Concerned with creating in both listening and reading audiences a felt, immediate sense of their impending mortality, ministers tended to downplay distinctions between the prisoner and the general public, muting the potentially sensational details of capital crimes to make the sins of the condemned applicable to all. For example, Adams's execution sermon and Garret's dying warning caution against pride, lying, and fornication—transgressions that audiences were likely to share—with relatively little comment on the infanticide. In this way, execution narratives abstract the body of the condemned into a monument—a figure that carries meaning beyond the individual's material and cultural specificity and transforms the person into a universal communal symbol.[60]

---

59. For the classic statement on the jeremiad, see Bercovitch, *American Jeremiad.*

60. On the history of the genre and the symbolic function of the condemned, see D. Williams, *Pillars of Salt,* and D. Cohen, *Pillars of Salt.* Seeman's study of Indian deathbed scenes offers a fine analysis of the problem of—and productive possibilities for—working with formulaic texts from an ethnohistorical perspective. The study distinguishes between "model" and "unorthodox" elements, wading through the "standard plots and stock phrases" to locate unorthodox moments that "represent fissures through which something closer to the actual experience of dying Indians may be glimpsed" ("Reading Indians' Deathbed Scenes," 18–19).

By the mid-eighteenth century, execution narratives would grow increasingly concerned with the sociology of crime. Ministers and prisoners alike blame poor parenting, neglected education, and poverty for driving individuals to despair. As a result, theological justifications often compete with material and social conditions as explanations for crime.[61] Audience demand for biographical detail tended to imbue the condemned with increasing material specificity, a development that was often at odds with the ministers' attempts to make generic examples of criminals. This trend had important implications for the genre's Native American subjects. Thus, the anonymous account explicitly foregrounds Garret's race and her distinguished tribal ancestry in its opening statement, "She was of the *Pequot* Tribe of *Indians* & Descended from one of the best Families among them." The introduction also supplies details that, although cursory, shed light on her class, occupation, and gender—including her precarious position as a household servant, her role as a reluctant convert to Christianity, her predicament in having to grapple with an unplanned pregnancy that could jeopardize her employment, and her fierce resentment toward the colonial courts over the justice of her sentence. Garret's dying warning anticipates the advent of the sociological wave by decades, and we see a glimpse of this emerging trend when—obliquely suggesting the types of power relationships and working conditions that enticed so many female servants to conceal and murder their infants—she admonishes masters to improve their treatment of servants.[62]

Readers should be attentive to shifts and tensions in the narrative as it alternates between telling a specific story about Garret, turning her into a generic Indian, and universalizing her even further by erasing her racial, class,

61. For example, Samson Occom's 1772 sermon on the execution of Moses Paul—a fellow Indian who, while in a drunken state, killed a man—offers extensive discussion of alcohol and its impact on native communities. Although Occom does not attack white people directly for introducing alcohol, he articulates the milieu of despair under which alcoholism flourishes. Both D. Williams and D. Cohen document the rise of sociological explanations for crime in execution narratives; they also note that, as the century progressed, ministers ceded control of the genre to printers who continued to innovate and adapt the genre to public tastes, giving criminals more voice in the narratives. Williams's assessment of the extent to which criminals have agency in their narratives is more nuanced and cautionary than Cohen's.

62. Despite the harsh New England law that considered an unmarried mother's concealment of the death of an illegitimate newborn as evidence of murder, single women and servants had greater incentive to rid themselves of unwanted newborns. On the surge of single women, especially Indian and black servants, who were prosecuted for neonatal infanticide in Connecticut between 1740 and 1750, see Dayton, *Women before the Bar*, 210–13. For (1) further proof of the disproportionate number of charges against Indian and black people for serious crimes and (2) a discussion of the social usefulness of female crime to enforce female chastity, see Hull, *Female Felons*, 57–58 and 124–25, respectively. On the intersections of race, class and violence in New England infanticide narratives, see Harris, *Executing Race*.

and gendered specificity. As the account progresses, for example, "Indian Kate" becomes *"a poor Dying Creature."* As a sympathetic figure, repentant and most likely redeemed, Garret is someone ministers encourage white audiences to sympathize with and even emulate: an "Example ... to all Persons in *our times."* Yet in the final lines, she is explicitly reinscribed within racial categories, repositioned not as a Christian everywoman but as an exemplary Indian. Appealing to "all her *Country people*, in their several Tribes" to "hearken diligently to the Offers & Proposals of the Gospel," the account concludes with the hope that Garret's example will resonate within tribal communities and encourage widespread conversion.

Despite generic conventions that elide Garret's voice and her material specificity, both her dying warning and the account contain details that help us see Garret in her fuller social context. In fact, Garret's narrative can be read as a direct product of the transformation of eighteenth-century New England Native cultures, capturing the tense and often fragile world of white–Indian relations. Her connection to North Stonington, her precarious place in the white household, her long period of jailhouse confinement, the formal structure of her narrative—all of these mark her narrative as a prime example of what has been called the period of "adaptation and persistence ... in the century following political and demographic subordination" of northeastern Native communities.[63] Whether or not it is accurately recorded, Garret's exclamation *"that things appeared to her quite other wise than they used to"*—a potent phrase for understanding Garret's ambivalent position as speaker—captures the massive process of adaptation and adjustment for the Native. Traditional Indian captivity narratives emphasize how captives confront and adapt to "otherness"; here the word suggests the ongoing process of change that marks indigenous responses to colonial power.[64]

It may be difficult for those modern observers who know relatively little about eighteenth-century New England Native life to see Garret as a Pequot. Scholarship tends to aggravate the problem: Traditional histories of New En-

---

63. Mandell, *Behind the Frontier*, vii.

64. Indian captivity narrative scholarship (which focuses largely on white colonists captured by Native Americans) emphasizes the importance of the captive's liminal state—the period of confusion and strategic adaptation while he or she struggles to negotiate new rituals, social codes, and systems of meaning. Garret's assertion offers an intriguing parallel to Rowlandson's disconcerting admission, "I can remember the time, when I used to sleep quietly without workings in my thoughts, whole nights together; *but now it is otherwise with me*" ("True History of the Captivity," 64, emphasis mine). Hilary Wyss foregrounds the parallels between captivity narratives and Christian Indian tracts, arguing that both are premised on a "disruption of racial or cultural identity" through a "somewhat parallel" process of separation from community and appropriation of "an altered (Christian) identity" (*Writing Indians*, 13). For a fuller reading of the overlap between Indian captivity narratives by whites and Christian missionary narratives by Indians, see ibid., 12–15.

gland Native communities, especially Pequot histories, frequently end in the late seventeenth century, overlooking this crucial eighteenth-century period of "adaptation and persistence."[65] Yet Garret is interesting precisely for the ways she embodies an experience that is typical of eighteenth-century New England Natives: the process of loss and adjustment that accompanied large-scale population shifts from tribal lands into smaller enclaves in close proximity to English towns. During this time, the number of Indians who worked in the English towns and the number of Indian servants in white homes increased.[66] The Garret family experienced this shift firsthand, and surviving records of their family history begin where traditional Pequot histories end. A closer look at the Garret family brings this elided past to the foreground.

A century before Garret's execution, nearby Mystic was the scene of one of the most notorious massacres in colonial history. In 1637 Captain John Mason set fire to the main Pequot fort, killing an estimated seven hundred Pequots, mostly women and children. The 1638 Treaty of Hartford attempted to divide and dissolve the decimated tribe into the Mohegans and Narragansetts, two tribes that had aided the colonists in the attack on the Pequots. From the 1650s to 1670s, Harmon Garret (Cashawasset), the son of a Niantic sachem and longtime leader of the Pawcatuck (eastern) Pequots, fought to wrest the tribe from Mohegan control and reclaim lands. Refusing to abandon land near Groton and Stonington during protracted battles with white settlers, Garret helped secure for the Pequots a permanent reservation at Lantern Hill in North Stonington, land that the Connecticut Colony purchased in 1685 for permanent use by the tribe. After Garret's death, his son, Catapeset Garret (Carapazet, Kottupesit) moved a large network of Pequots onto this land, and there the Garrets remained for many generations.[67]

In the early decades of the eighteenth century, mostly in response to rapid colonial expansion into previously secluded Native enclaves, missionaries renewed largely abandoned efforts to convert Indians to Christianity. The next

---

65. For example, Alden Vaughan concludes his history of the New England frontier with the following misinformation: "The tragedy is that in the long run the red man of New England succeeded neither in amalgamation nor in resistance. Rather, by 1750 the Indian had almost disappeared from the New England scene" (*New England Frontier*, 326).

66. On the changing patterns of New England Indian settlement, especially in eastern Massachusetts, see Mandell, *Behind the Frontier*, who argues that, by the 1720s, the number of distinct Native villages had drastically declined. Tribes resettled instead into more condensed enclaves, suffered increased poaching and trespass by white neighbors, and saw growing numbers of their members become voluntarily and involuntarily employed in bordering white towns.

67. For Garret's petition, see Connecticut (Colony), *Public Records*, vol. 2 (Connecticut 529). On the history of the eastern Pequots, see Campisi, "Emergence of the Mashantucket Pequot Tribe"; Simmons, *Spirit of the New England Tribes*; Deforest, *History of the Indians*; Caulkins, *History of New London*; and DenOuden, "Against Conquest."

three generations of Garrets felt the effects of this movement firsthand, and by the 1740s a sizable portion of the North Stonington community had converted to Christianity.[68] During Katherine Garret's lifetime, missionary efforts focused on removing children from Indian villages and advocating schooling and indentureship as the primary models of socialization.[69] Born in North Stonington, Katherine—in contrast to her North Stonington kin—was not a baptized Christian. Other Garrets were, however, hailed as Christian success stories: While the renowned missionary Experience Mayhew was on an expedition through the Pequot settlement in 1713, two years after Katherine's birth, he recorded his interactions with members of the Garret family, including Catapeset's children, Joseph and Benjamin.[70] Mayhew, who relied on Joseph as interpreter, praised him as "a person of good parts and of very good quality among the Indians."[71] In 1725, when Katherine was fourteen, Connecticut governor Joseph Talcott recommended a plan for Christianization that focused on removing children from their reservation communities to keep them "separate from their parents and under good government";[72] around this time, Katherine, who was not baptized, was indentured into the Worthington household. Although there is no record of Katherine's parentage, her role in the Worthington household must be understood against this backdrop of social change that affected the North Stonington Native community.

When read in this context, Katherine's jailhouse conversion is notable not for happening suddenly but for taking so long. As Garret's employer and spiritual mentor for more than a decade, the Reverend Mr. Worthington was

---

68. Although the Connecticut General Court seemed willing—or at least resigned—to set aside land and coexist with Native communities, it sought to weaken tribal power. In 1717, for example, the Connecticut General Assembly passed "Measures for Bringing the Indians in the Colony to the Knowledge of the Gospel," which advocated dividing and privatizing Indian land so that it would pass from "the Father to his Children," thus diminishing tribal control over land (DenOuden, "Against Conquest," 380).

69. For the fullest analysis of how the rise in servitude impacted Natives, see Plane, *Colonial Intimacies*, which argues that "servitude replaced old-style evangelization as [a] means of assimilating individual Indians to English ways" (102).

70. Katherine's parents are unknown; records reveal only that Benjamin and Joseph had a sister, possibly Katherine, her mother, an aunt, or a cousin. Records of the nearby Stonington Congregational Church show the baptismal records of numerous other Garret descendants. Benjamin (born circa 1701–5) had a son, Benjamin Jr. (born circa 1725), whose daughter, Hannah (born circa 1747) would marry a former fellow student from Eleazar Wheelock's boarding school, David Fowler (Montauk). Hannah and David would become important figures in Samson Occom's Brotherton movement. On Joseph, Benjamin, and Hannah Garret, see Szasz, *Indian Education*, 181–82, 224–31.

71. Quoted in Szasz, *Indian Education*, 181.

72. Quoted in DenOuden, "Against Conquest," 383. Interestingly, the Reverend Eliphalet Adams took the future Mohegan sachem Ben Uncas III into his home as a boarder at the time that Katherine was bound to the Reverend Mr. Worthington.

required to bring Katherine to Christianity, but—for undisclosed reasons—she remained uninterested in conversion. The account downplays the failure of the Worthingtons to provide proper socialization and highlights Garret's conversion as a successful missionary effort. It is telling that the account ends with an impassioned plea to Native Americans; after all, Garret's narrative was written not in the flush of early colonial idealism but amid the prevailing eighteenth-century sentiment that widespread Indian conversion was no longer possible. In this sense, Garret's identity as an Indian becomes crucial to her status as a "monument," for she embodied the dream—in the unlikely form of a confessed murderer—that the conversion project might still take hold and succeed.

Is Katherine Garret's conversion, then, real? Is it forced? Or is it a form of strategic adaptation—the "posture" of prayer—designed, at best, to win her release from prison and, at worst, to hedge her bets against the unknown? Given the history of violence and coercion that accompanied the arrival of Christianity into indigenous communities, some observers may be tempted to dismiss Garret's Christian expressions as no more than colonialist propaganda. Others may eye her last-minute conversion with suspicion, as they would any dying man or woman who suddenly finds salvation. In Garret's case, her conversion grants her some immediate benefits, allowing her to travel from "house to house in the Neighbourhood," attend lectures (which could last eight hours), and to "partake . . . at the *Lord's Table*." Yet readers' skepticism, while understandable, can be disempowering to the very figures that they seek to construe. Citing the work of postcolonial scholars such as Abdul JanMohammed and Edward Said, Dana Nelson cautions against denying that Native peoples may embrace Christianity; she argues that this denial replicates a colonialist mode of seeing by "appropriating whatever subjectivity the native might claim and calling it the achievement of the colonizer."[73] Such dismissive readings regard evangelical discourse as little more than "an instrument of oppression, implemented against the hopeless resistance of Natives."[74]

Still more might be gained by considering Garret's conversion genuine. Recent social and literary histories have argued the difficult but tenable position that Christianity served, ironically, as a force of both dispersal and cohesion during this time, offering many Natives support in times of turbulence and change. Although Christianity was leveraged by courts to separate Native children from parents and weaken tribal control of land, it also (as Occom and Apess testify to directly) helped many Natives endure the hardships of

73. Nelson, "'(I Speak Like a Fool),'" 52.
74. Kelleter, "Puritan Missionaries," 84.

colonization.[75] This religious self-fashioning is strikingly evident in the execution narrative of Patience Boston (Wampanoag). For example, Boston describes Christ empathetically as "buffeted scourged and spit upon . . . *a Man of Sorrows, and acquainted with Grief,*" identifying less with religious dogma than the physical sufferings and emotional isolation of a persecuted Christ.[76] In addition, many narratives rhetorically leverage the Natives' understanding of Christian principles to expose Christian hypocrisy, a technique that Apess would put to effect brilliantly a century later in "The Experiences of Five Christian Indians" (1833). Garret practices a similar strategy in her dying warning, cautioning masters to improve their treatment of servants and reminding them that they must "Account to God" for their behavior.[77] She also refashions social hierarchies by recasting masters into servants: Referring to ministerial visits received in prison, she thanks God for sending "his Servants" to attend to her; later, she reminds all who are gathered that God is "our Great Master."

As a result, even a heavy-handed amanuensis in these sample texts does not prevent readers from perceiving gaps in a minister's interpretive frame or from locating alternative spaces of interpretation. For example, the account tells us that after her sentencing, Garret "was thrown into the utmost Confusion & Distress" and that "Her Expressions were rash and unguarded . . . throwing blame on all sorts of persons." Despite the fact that Garret's "unguarded" language is excised from the text of the account, the recounting of this incident undermines its claim that Garret passively embraced her fate. Similarly, where the minister highlights the forces of faith triumphing over Garret's sinful nature, readers may see Garret's persistent ambivalence and struggle. Her "faintings," her "broken" expressions, her "Exceedingly . . . cast Down" appearance belie the "proper Stature" with which she ostensibly accepts her death. Moreover, portions of her dying warning function less as confession than as a self-vindication

---

75. Mandell notes, "The situation was complete with irony, for the religion introduced by English invaders now acted as a cement for native enclaves, and the transformation of Indian groups was in part facilitated by the faith that offered social and psychological stability in the sea of change" (*Behind the Frontier,* 59). Homer Noley (Choctaw) has demanded recognition for those Native Americans who worked to spread Christianity to Native peoples "because of the strength of their belief" ("The Interpreters," 59). For further arguments about how Christian Indians redefine the terms of Christianity to endure the pressures and violence of colonization, see Gussman, "Politics of Piety"; Weaver, *Native American Religious Identity;* and Wyss, *Writing Indians.*

76. Boston, *Faithful Narrative,* 2. For a different examination of Native identification with the physical body and mental sufferings of Christ, see Joanna Brooks's analysis of Occom's hymnody ("Six Hymns").

77. A lively example of how faith might be used for more disruptive purpose occurs in Patience Boston's narrative, when the ever-quarrelsome Boston leverages her newfound faith to call attention to the dishonor of public execution, saying that she does not want "*Sambo* a negro [to execute her] . . . because it would be a dishonour to the Church of which he is a Member" (*Faithful Narrative,* 32).

strategy commonly found in Native American autobiography—notably her complaint that "*Some . . . had reported of her things that were false.*"[78]

Even phrases that ostensibly function as pedagogical examples of "good death" do not necessarily further the minister's ends. Take, for example, the seemingly pious opening of the dying warning: "*I Katherine Garret*, being Condemned to Die for the Crying Sin of Murder, Do Own the Justice of GOD in suffering me to die this Violent Death." Here, the speaker accepts God's judgment, but—calling her imminent execution "this Violent Death"—seems to question that of society. This phrase gains further resonance when juxtaposed with the text of the sermon preached by Adams. Adams's sermon repeatedly emphasizes a single verse from Proverbs: "A Man that doth Violence to the blood of any person, shall flee to the Pit [i.e., grave], Let no man stay him."[79] Repeating the line throughout the sermon, he emphasizes that *anyone* who does violence to *any* person must be swiftly put to death. Referring to the ensuing moment of execution as "this Violent Death," Garret's opening line begs the question "Who will answer for the violence of Katherine Garret's death?" Garret's opening line might then be viewed as a form of colonial mimicry, repetition with a difference.

Because Pequot execution narratives document real moments when actual crowds gathered to witness literal "Indian vanishings," they can indeed highlight dramatic and oppressive displays of colonial power on the Native body. Yet the texts and rituals of public executions also work in less regimented ways, affording the condemned an opportunity—in mediated form—for autobiography, self-presentation, and even social protest. Despite the highly mediated form of the genre, the narratives—like the bodies of the condemned—are marked by surplus that cannot be contained by formulas, and Natives such as Garret use the narratives to testify directly to the processes of change, adaptation, and struggle that they faced in the eighteenth century. By embracing rather than evading problematic moments in the text, by seeing productive possibilities in its holes and gaps, in its dual and dueling voices, in its claims of seeing "*other wise*," we can rightfully situate Garret's dying warning on the boundaries of the Native American eighteenth-century literary frontier.

78. On self-vindication as a strategy in what he labels "pre-literate traditions" of Indian autobiography, see Brumble, *American Indian Autobiography*, 38–39.

79. Prov. 28:17.

# 5 · The Wampanoags

THE WAMPANOAG people lived in settlements that stretched from southeastern Massachusetts (including Cape Cod, Nantucket Island, Martha's Vineyard, and the Elizabeth Islands) to portions of Rhode Island. According to Wampanoag tradition, Moshup, a benevolent giant, shaped the coastline by moving boulders to facilitate his whale hunting, guided the people to Martha's Vineyard, and protected them in myriad ways. Additional deities marked the Wampanoag spiritual landscape, not the least of whom was Hobbomok (or Cheepi), who provided visions for adolescent boys who were brave or strong enough to seek these visions from him.

By the time of permanent English settlement at Plymouth, Massachusetts, in 1620, the Wampanoags, devastated by recent epidemics, were living in a loose confederacy under the control of the sachem Massasoit. Initially eager to forge an alliance with the newcomers to offset Narragansett aggression, Massasoit saw the uneasy collaboration with the Plymouth settlers become more and more tense, as English settlers continued to pour in and the Wampanoags were increasingly displaced from land that they considered their own. The alliance crumbled in 1675 under the Wampanoag sachem Metacomet (known as King Philip to the English), embroiling much of New England in a major confrontation involving the English settlers and nearly every Native community in the region. The Wampanoag people were split in their allegiances, and by the close of the war in 1676 many mainland Wampanoag communities were fragmented beyond recognition, bearing the full brunt of the vengeance of the English colonists, who ensured the outcome of the war through forced deportation, enslavement, and execution.

The Wampanoags of Martha's Vineyard and its adjoining islands managed to escape this fate by achieving the extraordinary feat of remaining neutral in King Philip's War. Martha's Vineyard (or Noepe, as it was originally known by the Wampanoags), an island off the coast of Cape Cod that stretches approximately 100 square miles, was the homeland of a large segment of the Wampanoag people (and, after 1642, a number of white settlers). Although the Wampanoag community of Martha's Vineyard was in many ways typical of the colonial world, its relative isolation from the mainland of New England and its extended relationship with the Mayhew family marked its unique history.

Traditionally divided into four sachemships (Aquinnah, or Gay Head;

Takemmy, or West Tisbury; Nunnepog; and Chappaquiddick), the Martha's Vineyard Wampanoags had, by the early eighteenth century, established Christian communities throughout the island, most notably at Aquinnah (Gay Head) and at Okokammeh (Christiantown) in West Tisbury. Through the intervention of Mayhew family members, who had a close affiliation with missionary societies in England, Wampanoag converts to Christianity had some of the earliest access to literacy training—specifically literacy in the Wampanoag language, The first school was established in the winter of 1652, and by the time Experience Mayhew wrote *Indian Converts* in 1727, vernacular literacy rates were probably some of the highest in New England. Despite the Mayhew family's professed commitment to Native well-being, however, the Wampanoag people suffered extensive loss of both land and resources throughout the eighteenth century, as the population of the island shifted from Wampanoag to English colonial domination.

Today the Wampanoag Tribe of Gay Head (Aquinnah) is a federally recognized body. Active on Martha's Vineyard, it is committed to maintaining "original Wampanoag lifestyles and values, with a modern lifestyle layered upon the traditional."[1]

## Suggested Reading

Mayhew, Experience. *Experience Mayhew's* Indian Converts: *A Cultural Edition*. Ed. Laura Arnold Leibman. Native Americans in the Northeast. Amherst: University of Massachusetts Press, 2008.

Silverman, David J. *Faith and Boundaries: Colonists, Christianity, and Community among the Wampanoag Indians of Martha's Vineyard, 1600–1871*. Studies in North American Indian History. New York: Cambridge University Press, 2005.

Wampanoag Tribe of Gayhead website. Available at http://www.wampanoagtribe .net/. Accessed 10 May and 30 June 2006.

---

1. "Aquinnah Cultural Center."

# Mittark's Will, 1681/1703

This document was written in Wampanoag before being translated into English by an unknown interpreter (probably Matthew or Experience Mayhew) and entered into the records of Dukes County (Martha's Vineyard) and the Massachusetts Bay Colony in 1703. The English version included here is based on the Massachusetts Bay Colony copy that was edited and reprinted in Ives Goddard and Kathleen Bragdon's *Native Writings in Massachusett*. The rendering included here, however, eliminates most of Goddard and Bragdon's editorial symbols and (in contrast to the Massachusetts Bay Colony version) uses the term *sachemship* rather than *chieftainship*, in accordance with the English translation contained in the Dukes County Registry of Deeds.[2] The once deteriorating manuscript copies of the deed in Dukes County have been professionally restored, a process that involved repairing, de-acidifying, cleaning, encapsulating the documents in mylar envelopes, and then rebinding them. This restoration process, coupled with the clear handwriting of the scribe, greatly facilitated use of the 1703 copies of Mittark's will, which are now merely tattered around the edges.

I am Muttaak, sachem of Gay Head and Nashaquitsa as far as Wanemessit.[3] Know this all people. I muttaak and my chief men and my children and my people, these are our lands. forever we own them, and our posterity forever shall own them. I Muttaak and we the chief men, and with our children and all our common people present, have agreed that no one shall sell land. But if anyone larcenously sells land, you shall take back your land, because it is forever your possession. But if anyone does not keep this agreement, he shall fall and have nothing more of this land at Gay Head and Nashaquitsa at all

---

2. Dukes County Registry of Deeds, 1:349, Dukes County Courthouse.

3. Mittark was the sachem of Aquinnah, or Gay Head, from at least the early 1660s until his death in January 1683. His father, Nohtooksact, a sachem from the Massachusetts Bay area, became the leader of the populous Aquinnah sachemship of Martha's Vineyard through unknown circumstances. During the early 1660s, after Mittark embraced Christianity, he was banished by his people to the eastern end of Martha's Vineyard, the center of Christian Indian life. Only three years later, he persuaded his people to host the Christian mission and returned to Aquinnah. During the next twenty years, he ranked among the most respected Christian Indian leaders on the island. He fathered at least three daughters (whose names are unknown) and a son, Joseph. See E. Mayhew, *Indian Converts*, 21–23, 67, and M. Mayhew, *Conquests and Triumphs of Grace*, 47–48.

Nashaquitsa is a neck of land that connects the Aquinnah peninsula to Martha's Vineyard proper. Squibnocket Pond forms its southwestern border, while Nashaquitsa and Menemsha Ponds run along its northeastern end. The location of Wanemessit is uncertain.

forever. I Muttaak and we the chief men, and our posterity, say: And it shall be so forever. I Ummuttaak[4] say this, and my chief men: if any of these sons of mine protects my sachemship, he shall forever be a sachem. But if any one of my sons does not protect my sachemship and sells it, he shall fall forever. And we chief men say this, and our sachem: if any of these sons of ours protects our sachemship, he shall forever be a chief man. But if any of our sons does not protect our sachemship and sells it, he shall fall forever. I Umattaag, sachem, say this and my chief men; that is our agreement. We say it before God. It shall be so forever.

I Umuttaag, this is my hand, on the date September 11, 1681.
We chief men say this say this [and] our sachem; this is our agreement. [We say it] before God. It shall be so forever. These are our hands.
I John Keeps[5] am a witness and this is my hand concerning the agreement of Ummuttaak and his chief men of Gay Head and Nashaquitsa, all [and] both. I Puttukquannan[6] am a witness. I witnessed this agreement of Ummuttaak and his chief men of Gay Head and Nashaquitsa, both. No one forever [shall] sell it; they [shall] keep it. I Puttakquannan, this is my hand.
I Sasauwapinnoo[7] am a witness. I witnessed the agreement of Ummuttaak and his chief men of Gay Head and Nashaquitsa, all [and] both. I Sasauwampinnoo, by my hand.

Entered feb: 21st: 1709

---

4. For a discussion of the schwa *u*, see Goddard and Bragdon, *Native Writings*, 2:484.

5. The identity of John Keeps is uncertain. He might have been John Gibbs, the first Wampanoag pastor on the island of Nantucket. See Mather, *Magnalia Christi Americana*, 1:567.

6. Little is known of Puttukquannan other than that he had rights to lands along the coastal ponds in the Takemmy sachemship of Martha's Vineyard (see Dukes County Registry of Deeds, 1:271, Dukes County Courthouse). He might have been Pattook, sachem of the Martha's Vineyard subregion of Chickemoo, who served as a magistrate in the Martha's Vineyard Christian Indian courts during the late seventeenth century.

7. The only other appearance of Sasauwapinnoo in the historical record was in 1719, when his grandson testified that he heard him discuss the birth order of two brothers (see Goddard and Bragdon, *Native Writings*, 1:213).

## "We Chief Men Say This"

### Wampanoag Memory, English Authority, and the Contest over Mittark's Will

#### DAVID J. SILVERMAN

Referring to the document included here as Mittark's Will is somewhat problematic, since there was disagreement among contemporaries about whether it truly belonged to Mittark (sachem of the Wampanoags of Aquinnah on Martha's Vineyard during the late seventeenth century) and whether it qualified as a will. The Aquinnah Wampanoags presented the document to English authorities sometime around 1703, claiming that it had been drafted by Mittark in 1681, shortly before his death. In it, Mittark declares that if any of his successors as sachem attempts to sell Wampanoag land, that sale will be null and void and the seller will be deposed from office—or "fall forever," according to Wampanoag metaphorical speech. Suffice it to say that this document was quite unlike the colonists' formulaic wills, which distributed personal property and real estate, but its unorthodox format was hardly the substance of the controversy. The point of the document, not to mention the timing of its appearance, was to challenge the recent sale of the entire Aquinnah Wampanoag sachemship by Mittark's son and successor, Joseph. Mittark's will announced that, despite the fact that the Wampanoag people, in a region increasingly dominated by Englishmen, had become weakened, subjugated, and marginalized, they were not about to allow their territory to be seized with impunity. Since the Wampanoags could no longer redress their grievances through force, they would wield the pen in colonial courts and legislative chambers. For the moment, at least, they had turned literacy from the colonists' advantage into their own.

The Wampanaogs were desperate for the provisions of Mittark's will to be fulfilled, for by the late seventeenth century English land expansion represented their greatest threat. Largely by hosting Christian missionaries from the Mayhew family (whose members ruled the English of Martha's Vineyard) and then using their Christian status and contacts to maintain open political dialogue, the Vineyard Wampanoags (like their close kin on Cape Cod) had avoided hostilities with English settlers since the colonists' arrival on the island in 1642. The Wampanoags' efforts at peace were assisted by their vast numbers on the island—as late as the 1670s, there were as many as fifteen Vineyard Indians to every colonist—offsetting the colonists' regional numerical advantage. Yet the balance of power had radically shifted by the turn of the century. Devastating losses suffered by mainland Wampanoags, Narragansetts, Nipmucs, and other Indians during King Philip's War between 1675 and 1676 eliminated any legitimate threat of pan-Indian military resistance to colonization. Moreover, although during the conflict Martha's Vineyard Wampanoags dutifully cooperated with the English militia to guard the island, most colonists distrusted the Natives, viewing them as hostiles masquerading as Christians. As the colonists' hatred of the Indians increased, the Wampanoags' ability to contain it diminished. In March 1682, their staunchest English advocate, the missionary and chief English magistrate Thomas Mayhew Sr. died, ending forty years of uninterrupted rule on the island during which he had administered the Indian land market and the spread of English jurisdiction with uncommon (if not total) restraint. An epidemic in 1690 and several lesser outbreaks decimated the Native population, reducing it from approximately fifteen hundred in 1670 to some nine hundred in 1703. Combined with growing Native indebtedness to colonial merchants and submission to English courts, these developments inaugurated a rush of Indian land sales that had gutted Native communities on the eastern side of the island by the late seventeenth century.[8]

Aquinnah, widely held to be "the best tract of land on the Iseland and the Valluablest," was a prime target for land-hungry colonists and their leaders.[9] In April 1685, Thomas Dongan, the royal governor of New York (which had included Martha's Vineyard since 1671), created the Manor of Martha's Vineyard on the site of what is now the town of Chilmark, right on the doorstep to Aquinnah. Next he appointed Matthew Mayhew as lord and, to circumvent restrictions against granting himself such privileges, had Mayhew sell him back the manor.[10] Not until Dongan hired Mayhew to purchase Wampanoag lands to lease out to English tenants did this elaborate scheme come to a close. Yet this was just the beginning of the Indians' struggles. Within five years, the minor sachem John Philip had signed away his title to Squibnocket and Nomans Land Island, thereby surrounding Aquinnah with English claims.[11] Then, in May 1687, in a deed apparently signed in New York, the Aquinnah sachem, Joseph Mittark, granted all of his territory to Dongan in exchange for a mere £30.[12] Assuming that Joseph had the best of intentions, he may have believed that the sale would enlist New York to defend Aquinnah against the more numerous and less predictable colonists of the island (consistent with the Indian

8. This history is discussed at greater length in Silverman, *Faith and Boundaries* and "Deposing the Sachem."

9. Guildhall Library, New England Company Records, MSS, 7955/1, p. 37.

10. Dukes County Registry of Deeds, 1:241–47, Dukes County Courthouse; Guildhall Library, New England Company Records, MSS, 8003.

11. Dukes County Registry of Deeds, 1:126, 128, 137, Dukes County Courthouse.

12. Ibid., 4:128; Guildhall Library, New England Company Records, MSS, 8004.

custom whereby weaker communities paid tribute to stronger communities in exchange for their protection). That, however, was not at all Dongan's intent. Dongan wanted to seize for his own profits Wampanoag land that the English judged as excess, land that the Wampanoags needed for hunting, gathering, fishing, and the like. Joseph's miscalculation had sprung a trap set by colonial grandees that threatened to ensnare all of his people's territory.

It would have been suicidal for the Wampanoags to take up arms in the face of this corrupt encroachment, but they had one other potent weapon in their arsenal: the printed word. Since the 1650s, young Wampanoags had been attending local mission schools, taught at first by Thomas Mayhew Jr. and his assistant, Peter Folger, and later by a cadre of educated Wampanoags, including Tackanash, Momonaquem, and Kequish. The schools followed a straightforward curriculum centered on the catechism, reading, and writing, mostly in the Wampanoag language but also, to a much lesser extent, in English. A series of Native-language texts published under the direction of the missionary John Eliot assisted in this work. The first volume of Eliot's Indian library was a primer or catechism, followed in 1655 by the books of Genesis and Matthew, in 1661 by fifteen hundred copies of the New Testament, and in 1663 by another fifteen hundred complete Bibles (or about one for every Christian Indian family in New England).[13] New editions followed, with the addition of inspirational and instructional tracts such as Richard Baxter's *Call to the Unconverted*, Bishop Lewis Bayly's *Practice of Piety*, *The Logic Primer*, *The Day Which the Lord Hath Made*, and a variety of sermons. Handwritten manuscripts, including a Wampanoag catechism authored by Thomas Mayhew Sr., then copied by Native preachers, supplemented this printed material. Alphabetic literacy was entirely new to Wampanoags, but many embraced it with a passion. By 1698 an inspection of Christian Indian communities found, "Most of the Indians belonging to Martha's Vineyard (Chaubaqueduck [Chappaquiddick] excepted) are well instructed in reading."[14] The Wampanoags' enthusiasm for formal education did not last indefinitely, however. Soon after this report was issued, the Indians' missionary sponsor, the New England Company, ceased its Native publications and began encouraging its teachers to carry on instruction solely in English, prompting many Indians to withdraw their children from school. Even so, as late as the 1720s, the missionary Experience Mayhew observed, "Considerable numbers of the Indians have learned to read and write," although "they have mostly done this after the rate that poor Men among the

13. Jill Lepore submits that a complete Native-language Bible was printed for every 2.5 praying Indians; however, she overstates her case, since her figures do not appear to include the three thousand or so Christian Wampanoags of Martha's Vineyard and Nantucket (*Name of War*, 34–35).

14. Danforth and Grindal, "Account of an Indian Visitation," 132.

English are wont to do," and "few of them [are] able to read and understand English Books in any measure well."[15] Mayhew overlooked the fact that the Wampanoags' modest literacy was an achievement that no other Indian people could match and, more to the point, that it met their limited goals. Even Wampanoags with only a basic reading knowledge could engage with the documents of greatest concern to their communities—the Bible, religious tracts, deeds, wills, and court papers. The few fully literate Wampanoags—those who were capable of reading and writing, sometimes in both languages—could shoulder the responsibility of guarding their people against a colonial state whose official documents had become an indelible part of Native existence.

The Wampanoags brought Mittark's will into public view with just such a defense in mind. They knew that despite the English theory that "wandering" Indians had no legitimate land claims apart from their planting fields, in practice colonists depended on Indian deeds to authenticate their titles and satisfy the Natives. Not just any Indian signature would do; colonists relied on the Indians' collective memory to identify the appropriate seller or sellers.[16] Most of this business took place informally and was not recorded. When an Englishman attempted to register an Indian deed long after it had purportedly been signed, however (a fairly common practice), he typically gathered Native testimony that the earlier transaction was valid and then had those who had given corroborating testimony place their signatures or marks on the deed.[17] These documents contain some of the best available evidence about Natives' community life, family ties, and territoriality during the colonial era. Oftentimes, they include such details as the genealogy of the grantor, the names of sachems who permitted the grantor's family to use the land, the identity of witnesses who were present when the sachems made these decisions, rival claims to the land made by other Indians, and the names (and sometimes the status) of those who accepted the deed in question. This collective Indian memory and collective Indian decision making, put to paper, girded much of the colonists' landed property.

A number of these deeds appear to contain transcriptions of the distinctive Native speech.[18] One deed, a 1666 transaction from Plymouth Colony, cen-

15. E. Mayhew, *Indian Converts*, xxiii. See also idem, *Brief Account of the State of the Indians*, 4.

16. On English debates over the necessity of purchasing Indian lands, see Cushman, "Reasons and Considerations"; Shurtleff, *Records of the Governor*, 3:281–82; Eisinger, "Puritan Justification"; and Washburn, "Moral and Legal Justification."

17. For examples of such documents, see Bangs, *Indian Deeds*, 277–78, 335–36, 353–56, 361–62, 448–49, 459, 464; Nahaton, Letter to Daniel Fisher; and Little, "Indian Land Deeds at Nantucket," especially 63–65.

18. The following discussion owes a great deal to Little, "Indian Land Deeds at Nantucket," and Bragdon, "Emphatical Speech and Great Action."

ters on testimony from seven Indians that Watuchpoo and Sampson have the right to sell a parcel of land along the northwestern side of Buzzard's Bay. King Philip, the paramount Wampanoag sachem for whom the war of 1675 to 1676 was named, was one of the witnesses. His declaration reads:

> Know all these present that Phillip have given power unto Watuchpoo and Sampson and theire brethren To hold and make sale of to whom they will by my consent; and they shall not have it; without they be Willing to lett it goe; it shalbe soe by my consent; But without my Knowlidge they cannot safely to: but with my consent there is none that can lay claime to that land which they have marked out; it is theires for ever soe therefore none can safely purchase any otherwise but by Watachpoo and Sampson and theire brethren.[19]

In all likelihood, Philip dictated this passage to the Indian witnesses and had it recorded on the spot, for his entry contains several hallmarks of Indian oratory. It repeats the same theme over and over again to give listeners the chance to commit it to memory, and it lacks the precise language of English legal documents; it assumes that once everyone has heard Philip say that Watuchpoo and Sampson alone have the right to this particular tract, there will be nothing left to parse over. If an Englishman had drawn up this document, he might have simply noted that Philip acknowledged the grantors' rights, but the deed was probably written by John Sassamon, one of the witnesses, who worked for Philip as an interpreter and scribe.[20] His job was to print Philip's words as close to verbatim as possible, and it appears that in this instance he did as he was asked.

Similarities between Mittark's will and the 1666 deed suggest that the will also recorded an actual speech. Both documents contain memory-aiding repetition of important points. They are rife with symbols of the speaker's elite status, such as vacillations between third- and first-person self-references and commands to the audience: "Know this," and "Know all these present." Both rely on chief men as witnesses for their authority. Writings from this period, including English writings, are not known for consistent spelling or grammar, but the Indians' variations appear conspicuously Native. Both documents contain short, easily memorized sentences, in contrast to the colonists' characteristic run-ons. The phonetic renderings of Mittark's name in the will (Muttaak; Ummuttaak; Umattaag) capture subtle pronunciations of the Wampanoag language that few Englishmen knew. Mittark's will, in short, was consistent with other colonial-era documents that were based on Native orations.

---

19. Bangs, *Indian Deeds*, 360–61.
20. On Sassamon, see Ronda and Ronda, "Death of John Saassamon," Lepore, *The Name of War*, 21–47.

The purpose of Mittark's will was as conventional as its form. In 1664 a mainland sachem named Josias Chickatabutt, or Wampatuck, set off a tract of land along the Titicut River for the enjoyment of a small community of Indians in perpetuity. He specified that if the community leader ever tried "to give sell or any way make over any part or parcell of ye said lands unto the English he or they that shall so doe shall by vertue of this prohibition forfeit and loose all his and their Interest in ye said lands and by vertue of this deed the said lands lost of [or] forfeited shall fall to and belong to the rest of ye then Tittecut Indians and their Indian heirs and Assigns for ever."[21] A year later, two Cape Cod sachems formed a Christian Indian reserve called Mashpee that was never to be sold, and in 1669 the sachem Keteanummin of Takemmy on Martha's Vineyard followed suit in an area thereafter known as Christiantown.[22] Around the same time, in Chappaquiddick, on the eastern end of Martha's Vineyard, the Chappaquiddick sachem, Pakeponesso, bypassed as heir his eldest son, Pecosh, in favor of a younger son, Seeknout, for fear that Pecosh "would sell land to the English."[23] Whoever was responsible for Mittark's will had a keen sense of Wampanoag precedents for defending the land.

The will alone was insufficient to challenge Dongan's title; it took the Aquinnah people's formation of a wall of agreement that the will had indeed been written in 1681. The version of the document entered into the public record was accompanied by the testimony of Sasauapinu, one of the original signers, "that this writing was made by Mattaak[,] witness my hand[,] this writing is indeed true septemr 11th: 1681." He was joined by "I Harry Cheife Magestrate Noshouohkamuck," the chief magistrate of the Martha's Vineyard territory of Nashuakemuck, who said that he had "heard Sauapinu and he says this writing was indeed made by old Muttaak[.]"[24] The Wampanoags' attempt to register the paper on the basis of this testimony some twenty years after the fact merely followed the colonists' example of entering deeds for Indian land years, even decades, after they had allegedly been signed. Given the colonists' standard and their dependence on Native memory to authenticate their own titles, how could they dismiss Mittark's land-sale ban?

Then again, how could they accept it? Taking the will to its logical conclusion would entail seizing Dongan's property, displacing colonial tenants, and establishing a precedent that might upset English property rights throughout the region. As if to prove the point, almost simultaneously Wampanoags from surrounding communities presented yellowed papers challenging English

21. Quoted in Bangs, *Indian Deeds*, 328–29.
22. Campisi, *Mashpee Indians*, 78; Silverman, *Faith and Boundaries*, 46–48.
23. Massachusetts State Archives, Suffolk Files, #12965, p. 104.
24. Massachusetts Archives, v. 31, p. 10.

rights at Squibnocket on Martha's Vineyard, Nomans Land Island, Nantucket, Naushon Island (of the Elizabeth Islands), and Assawompsett (in the main-land town of Middleboro).[25] The fact that the Wampanaogs in these locations were linked by strong kin and church ties hinted that their documents were part of an organized protest against English expansion. Proof of collusion, however, was elusive.

In 1703, to the relief of colonial landowners, a committee appointed by Boston designed a foolproof way to dismiss the Indians' challenge. The committee contended that most of the Indians' papers had not "been proved in due Form of Law, nor drawn up in Form as is usual among the English." Regarding the Nantucket "will," they found "by the confession of the scribe that wrote it and by other witnesses, that they did not agree to the time nor place where it was writt ... which gives us cause to believe that they were not true but forged and false." The committee also declared the Natives' writing for Squibnocket "forged and not true." Then outside pressure caused a hairline crack in Aquinnah's solidarity. Upon inquiry, "an Indian called Jonah Hossewit which seemed to be a sober honest man comes before the Committee and said that he wrote that writing long since Mattark's death and by the Testimony of sundry other Indians wee have good reason to thinke that said writing was forged and not true."[26]

Was it, however? After all was said and done, Aquinnah's case still came down to the word of Jonah Hossueit (who in just a few years would emerge as a heterodox Baptist preacher) against that of his neighbors (the vast majority of whom remained Congregationalists).[27] It is possible that his confession was a false attack against religious opponents who had been telling the truth all along. Another scenario is that the Wampanoags drew up the document after Dongan's purchase but faithfully transcribed the proceedings of a 1681 council (like colonists who used oral accounts of Indian land genealogies to justify their own land titles). Or, perhaps, Aquinnah was shrewdly playing the colonists' old game of manipulating the printed word.[28] Whatever the case, the

25. M. Mayhew, Letter to Wait Winthrop; Mandell, *Behind the Frontier*, 72–73; Little, "Indian Horse Commons," and "Sachem Nickanoose and the Grass Contest," Parts I and II.

26. Massachusetts State Archives, Suffolk Files, 31:17. See also ibid., 31:501b, 501c, 505, 505a. In 1712, the Nashuakemuck Wampanoags on Martha's Vineyard would try again to register an ancient will, this time attributed to the deceased sachem Chipnock, only to have it rejected on the grounds of its "being unintelligible and the witness thereto being long since deceased" (see Dukes County Courthouse, Dukes County Probate Records, 1:39, and the original Wampanoag-language document, "Chipnock's Will—1691. Disallowed 1712," Dukes County Courthouse, in a metal file labeled "Petitions: Common Pleas" among a bundle of papers listed as "Titles."

27. See Thomas, *Diary of Samuel Sewall*, 1:465, and Backus, *History of New England*, 1:438–39.

28. Daniel Mandell argues that there is "little doubt" that these were oral agreements later put to paper, but he does not adequately entertain the possibility of Native machination (*Behind the Frontier*, 72–73).

Indians could not win with Englishmen setting the rules. Boston's rejection of the Wampanoags' claims indicated that it would rely on Indian memory only when it suited colonial interests; English authorities were not about to let control of *their* written record slip into Native hands.[29]

The Aquinnah Wampanoags did not regain written title to their land, but they continued to possess it physically. Their rally around Mittark's will frustrated Dongan into selling his rights to the missionary New England Company, which had been concerned that the praying Indians of Martha's Vineyard were about to be "scattered up and down the Continent, and returning to the barbarous Customes of their Ancestors."[30] From that point on, the Company, as landlord, often infuriated the Wampanoags by making such heavy-handed, paternalistic decisions as renting out a huge swath of Aquinnah to an English farmer to raise proceeds for Indian schools and poor relief. Nevertheless, from 1711 until the 1780s, the company effectively halted the sale of any Aquinnah land to outsiders, thus providing the Wampanoags with a safe haven when many neighboring Indian communities were on the verge of collapse. In this sense, Mittark's will had achieved something of a victory.

The Wampanoags had also demonstrated that the supposed division between literacy and orality, between written authority and community memory, was far more permeable than many colonists or their historians have presumed. Instead of being trapped between two diametrically opposed cultures, the Wampanoags melded their ways of speaking and remembering with the colonists' printed word until they had formed a distinctly Indian literacy. "Written talks," such as Mittark's will, could not replicate the moment of speech—the pitch, tone, and cadence of the speaker, his or her gestures and presence, the audience's responses; the ambiance of the setting—but they were reflective of many Wampanoag speech ways. Most important, they embodied the will of a people for whom few other options remained for asserting what had become a basic principle of their survival in colonial New England: "These are our lands. forever we own them, and our posterity forever shall own them." Wampanoags demanded that colonists pay attention to these words and confront their own hypocrisy in accepting Indian testimony only when it served colonial ends. We too should listen to the page.[31]

---

29. For more on this theme, see Barsh, "Behind Land Claims."
30. J. Ford, *Some Correspondence*, 94.
31. This line is a play on Murray and Rice, *Talking on the Page*.

# The Hannit Family in Experience Mayhew's
## *Indian Converts*

The text from which these biographies are taken was published in 1727 by Experience Mayhew, a fourth-generation English missionary who lived on present-day Martha's Vineyard. Titled *Indian Converts: Or, Some Account of the Lives and Dying Speeches of a Considerable Number of the Christianized Indians of Martha's Vineyard in New England*, the book organized its biographies under four headings: "Indian Ministers," "Good Men," "Religious Women," and "Pious Children."

## Chapter I. Example XVII

Mr. JAPHETH HANNIT, *the third Pastor of the Indian Church on Martha's Vineyard, who died July 29, 1712.*

*Japheth Hannit*[32] was born in or about the Year 1638, in the Place now called *Chilmark*,[33] on *Martha's Vineyard*. His Father was an *Indian* of prime Quality there,[34] named *Pamchannit*; which Name being contracted into *Hannit* only, by leaving out the two first Syllables of it, became afterward the Sirname of his Son *Japheth*, and others of his Offspring: a thing very common among our *Indians*.

---

32. Japheth was the progenitor of an important Christian family on Martha's Vineyard: He was the father of Bethia Escohana (E. Mayhew, *Indian Converts*, 102–3), Jerusha Job(e) (wife of Job Soomannah [51–52, 105, 110–13]), Jedidah Hannit (232–34), Jeremiah Hannit (223–24), Joshua Hannit (224), and Hannah Tobe (wife of Elias Wauwompuque [70]). He was also the grandfather of Japheth Skuhwhannan (102–6) and Mehitable Keape, who kept school at Christiantown and whose house was used for church meetings (Pierce and Segel, *Wampanoag Genealogical History*, 1:126–27, 244, 338–39).

33. It was originally known as Nashaukemuck. *Nashowakemmuck* means "the half way house" (see "Annals of Chilmark" in Banks, *History of Martha's Vineyard*, II, 3). The town is in the southwestern part of the island.

34. More specifically, Japheth's father was a sachem, or traditional ruler. Although sachems ruled through consent, the position was usually inherited on the island, and nonruling members of royal families had a higher social status than other community members or resident nonmembers (Marten, *Wampanoags in the Seventeenth Century*, 19). The Hannit family provides one of the many examples from Martha's Vineyard of how sachems and royal families preserved their social status and power on the island by becoming ruling members of the Indian churches.

This *Pamchannit* and his Wife having buried their first five Children succes-
sively,[35] every one of them within ten Days of their Birth, notwithstanding all
their Use of the *Pawwaws* and Medicines to preserve them, had a sixth (a Son)
born to them, the same whom I am here speaking of, a few Years before the
*English* first settled on the said *Vineyard*.

The Mother[36] being then greatly distressed with fear that she should lose
this Child as she had done the former, and utterly despairing of any Help from
such Means had been formerly try'd without any Success, as soon as she was
able, which was within ten Days after his Birth, she with a sorrowful Heart
took him up and went out into the Field, that she might there weep out her
Sorrow. But while she was there musing on the Insufficiency of human Help,
she found it powerfully suggested to her Mind, that there is one *Almighty
God*[37] who is to be prayed to; that *this* God hath created all things that we see;
and that the *God* who had given Being to herself and all other People, and had
given her Child to her, was able to preserve and continue his Life.

On this she resolved that she would seek to God for that Mercy, and did
accordingly; the Issue[38] was that her Child lived, and her Faith (such as it was)
in him who had thus answered her Prayer, was wonderfully strengthened; and
the Consideration of *God's Goodness* herein manifested to her, caused her to
dedicate this Son of hers to the Service of that God who had thus preserved
his Life: Of her doing of which she early informed him, and did, as far as as[39]
she could, educate him accordingly. But this she did yet more vigorously, and to
better Purpose prosecute, when a few Years after she was by the preaching of
the Gospel, instructed in the way of Salvation by a Redeemer, and by the Grace
of God enabled truly to believe in *Jesus Christ* our only Saviour.

*Japheth's* Father being also about this time converted, and so becoming a
serious and godly Man, this [*sic*] his Son had the Advantage of a Christian
Education, while he was but a Child, not only living in a Family where *God* was
daily worshipped, but was himself taught to call on the Name of that God to
whose Service he had been devoted: and when there was a School set up for
the *Indians* on the Island in the Year 1651, his Father sent him to it, and he then

---

35. Epidemics were common on the island throughout the colonial period, and infant mortality rates were high. Kathleen Bragdon estimates that one of these epidemics killed 90 percent of the
Algonquian population in New England between 1616 and 1619 (*Native People*, 26).

36. This was Wuttunohkomkooh, who died circa 1675 (E. Mayhew, *Indian Converts*, 135–37).

37. Wampanoags were not usually monotheistic before the arrival of the Puritans. They traditionally worship a variety of manitou (spirits, gods, nonhuman forces that permeate the world [Bragdon,
*Native People*, 184–86]).

38. This is a pun: *Issue* means both "result" and "offspring."

39. The repetition of the word *as* appears in the original.

learned to read both in the *English* and *Indian* Tongue, and also to write a very legible Hand, and was then also well instructed in his Catechism.[40]

How he behaved himself while he was a Youth, I have no particular Account; however I never understood that he was viciously inclined.

After he was grown up, he marry'd a Daughter[41] of a very godly Man, named *Keestumin*,[42] whom I shall afterwards mention; and she prov'd a very pious Person, and did *him Good and not Evil all the Days of her Life.*[43]

When the first *Indian* Church was here gathered in the Year 1670, our *Japheth* was, as he himself told me, in a most distressed Condition for not being of the number of them who first confederated to walk together as a Church of Christ, according to the Order of the Gospel: he on the *one hand* greatly lamented his not being of that happy number, as he esteemed them; and on the *other*, at the same time fear'd to offer himself to the Society of God's People, lest he should be unqualified for the Privileges to which they were admitted.

But tho *Japheth* could not at this time enter into a solemn Covenant to serve the Lord, in an Attendance on all the Duties incumbent on particular Churches; yet it was not long after this, before he made a publick Profession of Repentance towards God,[44] and Faith towards our Lord *Jesus Christ*, and join'd as a Member in full Communion to the Church which he before long'd to be one of: in which Relation he from time to time behaved himself as became a good Christian.

He was not after this presently called to the Work of the Ministry, but was for a considerable time imployed in Offices civil and military, being first made a *Captain* over a Company of his own *Nation*, and also a *Magistrate*[45] among

40. Catechism involves "sending out questions and listening for the echo, the answer that fixes the depth of knowledge and understanding" (Van Dyken, *Rediscovering Catechism*, 11). Although catechism was popularized in late antiquity by St. Augustine and Erasmus, during the Reformation Martin Luther, John Calvin, and others brought catechism back to the forefront as a means of educating and saving souls (ibid., 14).

41. She was Sarah Hannit, neé Sarah Mensoo of Chappaquiddick (E. Mayhew, *Indian Converts*, 74, 166–70, 232).

42. He was the first deacon of the first Wampanoag-Puritan Church on the island, established in 1670. Mayhew describes him as a "Person of a very blameless Conversation, undoubted Piety, and an excellent Spirit" (E. Mayhew, *Indian Converts*, 74) Sarah Hannit was his only known child (ibid., 87, 166).

43. This passage outlines the qualities of a good wife (Prov. 31:12).

44. For an example of a "profession" given by an Algonquian man at Natick, see Ponampam's Confession (Eliot, *Further Account*, 54–57).

45. To be an Indian magistrate entailed the power to enforce white colonial legislation on Native communities. Native magistrates, like their white counterparts, adjudicated suits for sums under twenty shillings and punished drunkenness, swearing, lying, theft, contempt toward ministers, and absence from church (Kawashima, *Puritan Justice and the Indian*, 29). In this sense magistrates usurped, at least in part, the power and prerogative of the sachems and *ahtaskoaog* (principal men, nobles) to

them; in both which Places of Trust he behaved himself well, and to the Acceptation of both the *English* and *Indians*: and in the time of that War betwixt them, which began in the Year 1675, and was commonly call'd *Philip's War*,[46] good *Japheth* was very serviceable to both those of his *own Nation* and *ours* on this Island: for being firmly set, if possible, to maintain and preserve Peace betwixt the *English* and *Indians* here; and, being an *Indian* Captain, as has been already said, he was imployed by the *English* to observe and report how things went among the *Indians*: and to his Faithfulness in the Discharge of this Trust, I conceive that the Preservation of the Peace of our Island was very much owing, when the People on the Main were all in *War* and *Blood*.

*Japheth's* Fidelity to the *English* in this Affair gained him a high Esteem, and kind Treatment among them, he being generally look'd on as a godly and discreet Man by them; and being well accounted of among the *Indians* also, they not long after this called him to the Work of the Ministry among them. His Office of a Captain he now laid down, but that of a Magistrate he still sustain'd for some Years after he began to preach, none else being thought so fit for that Trust. The Place he preached at was that wherein he liv'd and dy'd, being join'd in that Work with his Uncle *Janawonit*,[47] before mentioned in Example the fifth.

Being called to the Work of the Ministry, he was very faithful and diligent in it, and was esteemed the best qualified of any *Indian* on the Island not yet in the Pastoral Office. He was therefore by *John Tackanash*[48] Pastor of the *Indian* Church here, in the time of his last Sickness, nominated as a fit Person to succeed him in the Office which he then expected a Discharge from; and the said *Tackanash* dying in *January* 1683–4, and being interred on the 23d of the same Month, the pious *Japheth*, who much lamented his Death, made a grave Speech

govern and make decisions for the Wampanoag community. Some of the early Indian magistrates, like Japheth, came from noble families and hence may have seen the position of magistrate as a way of continuing their families' traditional role in island life. Others, however, came from less notable families.

46. King Philip's War took place from 1675 to 1676. Mayhew's emphasis on Japheth's loyalty to the British during this conflict stands in opposition to negative portraits of Christian Indians by Puritans with respect to the war, including criticism by Mary Rowlandson, who harps on the unregenerate conduct and propensity for violence among Indian converts (Rowlandson, "True History of the Captivity," 37). Many Indian converts were bitterly mistreated during the war: Some were imprisoned on Deer Island in Boston Harbor without proper food or shelter (Lepore, "When Deer Island," 16, 19).

47. Janwannit (who died in 1686) was formerly the minister at Nashaukemuck (Chilmark) and is the younger brother of Japheth's father, the sachem Pamchannit (E. Mayhew, *Indian Converts*, 20–21).

48. John Tackanash was the first teacher of the Indian Church and later a pastor (ibid., 14–16). The office of teacher complemented that of minister: Teachers were to "attend to doctrine," administer the seals of covenant, and censure congregants (Cremin, *American Education*, 138). Some of the most famous ministers in New England, including John Cotton, held the office of teacher.

at his Funeral, some of the Heads whereof being by my Father, who heard part of it, preserved in Writing, and now before me, I shall here insert them, and they are as followeth.

> We ought, *said he,* to be very thankful to God for sending the Gospel to us, who were in utter Blindness and Ignorance, both we and our Fathers. Our Fathers Fathers, and their Fathers, and we, were at that time utterly without any means whereby we might attain the Knowledge of the only true *God.* That People also which knew the Ways of God, were some thousands of Miles distant from us; some of whom, by reason of Difference among themselves about their Way, removed into this Land but it was God that sent them, that they might bring the Gospel to us. Therefore, I say, we have great reason to be thankful to God; and we have reason to be thankful to them also, for that they brought the Gospel to us: but most especially we ought to thank God for this, for tho they taught us, it was God that sent them, and made choice of them for this Work, of instructing us in the Ways of the Lord.
>
> Before we knew God, when any Man dy'd, we said the Man is *dead;* neither thought we any thing further, but said he is *dead,* and mourned for him, and buried him: but now it is far otherwise; for now this good Man being dead, we have Hope towards God concerning him, believing that God hath received him into everlasting Rest.
>
> Now therefore we ought to improve the Benefit which we have by the Gospel. And first, such of us as had like not to have received this Kindness, I mean such of us as were grown up when the Gospel came to us, so that it only found us in being, such are strongly obliged to improve the same, since they scarcely received it, or were in danger not to have enjoyed it. Secondly, There are others of us that have been born, under the Gospel, and we that were so, ought duly to improve the same, inasmuch as we have received so wonderful a Benefit. And now tho this Man that went before us, leading us in the Way of God according to the Gospel, be deceased, and helps us no more, yet his Doctrine remaineth still for us to improve; nor ought we to forget him, but should remember him by his Wife and Children, whom he hath left among us.

Thus far *Japheth's* Speech, which savoureth of the Piety of the Man by whom it was uttered.

Good *John Takanash* being thus laid in his Grave, Mr. *Japheth* was the next *Spring* called to succeed him in the same Place and Office; and in the Fulfilment of the Ministry thus committed to him, he continued about 28 Years, *viz.* till the Year 1712. He was faithful and diligent in the Work of God, unto which he was called, preaching the Word in season and out of season, reproving, rebuking, and exhorting, with all Long-suffering and Doctrine, and used frequently to catechise the Children of his Flock in publick.

He maintained a good Discipline in the Church over which the Holy Ghost had made him Overseer, knew, how to *have Compassion* on those whose Case called for it, and how *to save others with Fear*.[49] In difficult Cases that occurred, he was careful to take the best Advice he could get. He was not at all inclined to *lord it over his Flock*,[50] but willing in Meekness to instruct them. And when there was danger of Discord among his Brethren, he would not side with any Party of them, but would in such Case make most winning and obliging Speeches to them all, tending to accommodate the Matters about which they were ready to fall out; and so wonderful an Ability had he this way, that he seldom failed of the End he aimed at.

He frequently visited the Families under his Care and Charge, especially when they were under Affliction by Sickness, or otherwise; and in the Visits he made them, he usually entertained them with serious and profitable Discourses, and I have heard him tell how very advantageous that kind of Visits had proved to some of his People.

He very often performed the Work of an Evangelist, in carrying of the Gospel into other Places, and endeavouring to promote the Kingdom of Christ in those of his own Nation; and God gave considerable Success to his Endeavours to do Good in this Way.

Tho his sermons were not very accurate, yet were they very serious, and had a great deal of good Matter in them, and he seem'd to me to do best when he did not try to oblige himself to any strict Method in them.

In Prayer he was very fervent, frequently praying with much Enlargement and Affection. On Sacrament Days[51] I have more especially observed that he has done so; and God did sometimes shew a gracious regard to the Petitions by this his Servant put up to him. One instance whereof has been formerly published in Dr. *Mather's* History of *New-England*,[52] Book VI. *pag.* 63. But in nothing was he this way more highly favoured than in God's helping of him against a Temptation, with which for some time conflicting, and crying earnestly to God for Deliverance from it, he obtained the Mercy he sought to him for.

He was fully resolved that he and his House should serve the Lord with them therefore he constantly prayed, and frequently sang Praises to God: he also read the Holy Scriptures in his House, and often gave serious Exhortations to all that were about him.

He was much given to Hospitality:[53] for being frequently visited, both by

---

49. Jude 1:23.

50. 1 Pet. 5:3.

51. Sacrament refers to baptism and communion.

52. The reference is to Mather, *Magnalia Christi Americana*.

53. The meaning of *hospitality* was different in British and Algonquian society. At its most basic level, hospitality was, for Mayhew, a Christian virtue. Hospitality was also related to social hierarchies,

Neighbours and Strangers, they were always kindly and generously entertained in his House with the best he had, or could readily procure.

He well understood, and steadily adhered to the Truths of our holy Religion in which he had been instructed, and would not be *driven about by every Wind of Doctrine.*[54]

One Instance of his Stability in the Truth, I think it may not be amiss here to give my Reader: A godly *Englishman,*[55] who had formerly been a Schoolmaster to the *Indians* here, and had taught *Japheth* and many others to read and write, and had also learned them their Catechisms, and instructed them in the Principles of Religion, having unhappily imbibed the Errors of the *Antipedobaptists,*[56] thought himself obliged to endeavour to bring Mr. *Japheth* over to his Persuasion: To this End he therefore visited him at his House, took much Pains to convince him that theirs was the right Way, and that ours of baptizing Infants, and sprinkling in Baptism, was very wrong: But none of the Arguments used by the Man, could convince *Japheth* of what they were brought to prove; at length being just about to go away, *Japheth* told him he would only say one thing more to him before he went.

> You know, Sir, *said he,* that we *Indians* were all in Darkness and Ignorance before the *English* came among us, and instructed us, and that your self are one of those *English* Men by whom we have been taught and illuminated. You taught us to read, and instructed us in the Doctrines of the Christian Religion, which we now believe, and endeavour to conform our Practices to. And when, Sir, you thus instructed us, you told us, that it may be there would shortly false Teachers

---

however: For Algonquians, giving hospitality conferred status on the giver and receiver; British colonists, however, often understood the hospitality of Algonquians as conferring status on the receiver alone.

54. Eph. 4:14.

55. The reference is to Peter Folger (1617–1690), who, according to Mayhew, was a forerunner of the Baptist Church on the island.

56. The term means literally "against-infant-Baptism." Members of this sect of Baptists were also called Anabaptists. Puritans throughout Massachusetts publicly beat, fined, and imprisoned Baptists. New England Baptists began as a splinter group that broke off from Roger Williams's Congregational Church, but their theology and practice differed from Puritanism in several important ways (Schaff, *America,* 170). First, they believed in admitting unsaved persons into church membership. Second, Anabaptists, such as those on Martha's Vineyard, believed in the complete separation of church and state and complete religious liberty, convictions that resulted in Williams's banishment from Massachusetts Bay Colony in 1636. To the Puritans, these were literally "damnable errors," that is, mistakes that jeopardized the authority and holiness of the community. With this is mind, it becomes clearer why the schoolmaster Peter Folger was run off the island in 1662 when he began to preach these Anapaptist heresies (Silverman, "Conditions for Coexistence," 119). In spite of these cautionary measures, the Baptist creed took hold on the island. The Wampanoag Baptist Church at Gay Head (now Aquinnah) is the oldest Native American Protestant church in continuous existence in British North America.

come among us, and endeavour to pervert us, or lead us off from our Belief of the things wherein we had been instructed; but you then advised us to take heed to our selves, and beware that we were not turned aside by such Teachers, so as to fall into the Errors into which they would lead us. And now, Sir, I find your Prediction true; for you your self are become one of these Teachers you cautioned us against: I am therefore fully resolved to take your good Counsel, and not believe you, but will continue stedfast in the Truths wherein you formerly instructed me.

This Speech of *Japheth's* put an End to the Disputation.

As for *Japheth's* Morals, he was generally and justly esteemed, as well by the *English* as *Indians*, a Person of a good Conversation: nor did he discover any such Infirmity in his Life, or Deportment in the World, as was inconsistent with such an Esteem; or which thro' Prayer, and the Supply of the Spirit of Jesus Christ, he did not obtain a compleat Victory over, being only privately admonished of a Failure, which some began to be offended at.

As he was generally by the *English* esteemed a truly godly Man, so being a Person of a very genteel and obliging Conversation, and one who went clean and neat in his Apparel, he was every where courteously received and entertained by them, the best Gentleman on the Island not scrupling to invite him to sit at their Tables with them;[57] and speaking *English* considerably well, Strangers that came to the Place took Delight in conversing with him. And once a Master of a Vessel[58] discoursing with him, on the Morrow after the *Sabbath*, facetiously asking him, whether he prayed for him yesterday or not? *Japeth* readily reply'd, *Sir, I prayed for all God's People, and if you be one of them, I consequently prayed for you.*

Persons have sometimes had Premonitions of their own Death, and something of this Nature our *Japheth* did experience, as he did in the time of his last Sickness declare, together with the Influence the same had on his Life; an Account of which, with some of his dying Speeches, &c. his honest Son in law, *Job Soomannah*,[59] who was frequently with him in his Sickness, having written

---

57. The status conferred to Japheth and to Wampanoag ministers on the island should be compared to a case mentioned in the diary of Samuel Sewall. Sewall recounts that when the Indian minister John Neesnummin visited him in Boston in 1708, Sewall could find no one willing to lodge Neesnummin: In part, colonists feared the "contagion" of housing an Indian, but they also feared the lowered status that would accompany hosting such an apparently undistinguished guest. Even the boardinghouses refused him, and Sewall was finally forced to lodge the minister in his study (Kawashima, *Puritan Justice and the Indian*, 108; Sewall, *Diary of Samuel Sewall*, 2:212–13).

58. *Vessel* means "ship."

59. Job Soomannah, who died in 1718 (E. Mayhew, *Indian Converts*, 110–13), was the husband of Jerusha Job(e) (Pierce and Segel, *Wampanoag Genealogical History*, 126).

in *Indian*, communicated to me soon after *Japheth's* Death: An Extract of which Account I shall here in *English* insert, and it is as followeth.

He said, that about a Year before he was taken sick, he went out of his House, and walked alone in the Woods,[60] and there it was by God revealed to him, that he had but a little time to live in this World; and that being thereupon much concerned in his Mind, he did immediately set himself on doing all that he could to prepare for his approaching End, as taking it for a Truth that his End was now very near, and looking Day and Night for it: but he said, he still misliked[61] himself, or reckoned that he came short.

Thus it was with him till *April* the 2d, 1712, which being a Day of Thanksgiving,[62] he went and preached thereon; but as with his Wife he returned home in the Evening, before they had gotten to their House he felt a Pain in his Side, and was never able after this to go to God's House of Prayer, his Sickness gradually encreasing on him from that time forward.

And having been sick about ten Weeks, he sent for the Brethren of the Church, and said to them as follows, viz. *That it did often distress him in his Heart, and cause him to weep, when he saw the miserable Estate of all the People by reason of their Sins; but especially how unapt the generality of the Church were to the Duties incumbent on them, and how often they did fall by reason of one kind of Infirmity or another, to which they were subject, tho he had very often instructed them in their Duty.*

*I have,* said he, *often wished for your sakes, that you might still enjoy*[63] *me; but now I am willing to die: however, as to this, let the Will of God be done. But do you go on to pray to God, and worship him both stedfastly and fervently.*

To his own Family, and such others as attended on him, he afterwards, not long before his Death, said, *Be not feeble in your Minds, I'm hitherto stedfastly*

---

60. For Algonquians, the woods were not an unusual venue for receiving visions or encountering the divine: As William Simmons notes, Native New Englanders often encountered manitou (spirits) "at night 'in the most hideous woods and swamps' in the shapes of Englishmen, Indians, animals, inanimate objects, and mythical creatures" (Simmons, *Spirit of the New England Tribes*, 39). Visions were also part of the popular religious practice that the colonists brought with them to New England (Hall, *Worlds of Wonder*, 86–87).

61. *Mislike* is defined as "to be displeased at; to disapprove of; to dislike" (*Oxford English Dictionary*).

62. Feasts and thanksgiving days were important rituals for both the Wampanoags and the British colonists. As the Wampanoag Tribe of Gay Head points out, "In addition to daily thanks there have always been set times for celebration that coincided with changes of season and harvest times. Our New Year comes at the Spring planting time. Summer is celebrated with Strawberry Thanksgiving, at the time when the first wild berry ripens. Green Bean Harvest and Green Corn Harvest come at mid-summer. Cranberry Harvest celebrates the ripening of the last wild berry. A ceremony is held around the time of Winter solstice as well. The harvest celebrations are held after the work has been completed" ("Wampanoag Celebrations").

63. In this sense, *enjoy* means "to have the use or benefit of, have for one's lot" (*Oxford English Dictionary*).

*resolved that I will love the Lord my God.*[64] I shall, said he, *now quickly go my last Journey, as others have done before me. Now I shall quickly set out. Thus it has been wont to be, when a Thing has here no further Use to be made of it. But Oh, what sweet Melody is there now in Heaven!* To his Son in law, the Writer hereof, he then said, *My Son, be thou of good Courage, and fail not to lay hold of the heavenly Salvation, for the sake of the things of this World.*[65] *But as for me*, said he, *I need to have my Mind further strengthened, and encouraged; for I think I shall now quickly leave you.*

The 28th of *July* 1712, was the last Day he lived in the World; for the Night following it, a little after Midnight, having desired those that were with him to praise God, by singing the 13th Psalm, and then by Prayer to commit both him and themselves to God, his Breath failed, and he resigned up his Spirit to God who gave it.

Thus far *Job Soomannah's* Memoirs of his good Father in law.

As I was well acquainted with *Japheth* in his Life, so I frequently visited him in the time of his last Sickness; and on the whole of my Acquaintance with him, I cannot but think, that he was a very serious and godly Man, and a Man of great Moderation and Prudence. His Discourse in the time of his last Sickness, when I was with him, was very pious and savoury.[66] He then expressed a humble Sense of the Sin of his Nature and Life, and yet his Hopes of eternal Salvation thro' the infinite Mercy of God, and Merits of his Son Jesus Christ. He then also expressed a Readiness and Willingness to resign himself and all that the [sic] had into the Hands of God, his faithful Creator, and merciful Redeemer. I remember also that he told me, that God had in the latter Part of his Life given him a more effectual Sense of the Evil of Sin, than formerly he had had; and that he had also enabled him with more Vigilance and Industry, to endeavour the Mortification of the Corruptions of his Heart.

Among other *Evidences* of the *real Piety* of this good Man, the Grief of his Heart for the Sins of his Countrymen, especially those who had been under his own Care and Charge, together with his Care and Concern for their Reformation, may justly be reckoned as *one*; for besides what of this Nature was discovered by him, in what is above-said, he a few Days before his Death, with his

---

64. The commandment "Love the Lord thy God" is invoked repeatedly in Deuteronomy and appears in Joshua as well.

65. One of the most important theological doctrines for Puritans was the "doctrine of weaned affections." This concept argued that the individual must learn to wean himself or herself away from earthly loves (husband, children, grandchildren, material possessions) and focus instead on God. Puritans feared that those who appreciated the sensual beauty and relationships of this world might forget the everlasting beauty of the world of the spirit (Tolles, "Of the Best Sort but Plain," 485).

66. *Savoury* is a (now obsolete) religious term meaning "full of spiritual 'savour'; spiritually delightful or edifying" or "having the savour of holiness; of saintly repute or memory" (*Oxford English Dictionary*).

feeble and dying Hand wrote an affectionate Address to the People of his own Charge, which he desired might be communicated to them: which Writing of his being now by me, I shall render into *English*, and here insert, and with that conclude my Account of the Person that penned it. It is then as followeth:

Is it not a most desirable thing for Persons in this Life certainly to know, that they shall go to Heaven when they leave this World?

Therefore now take heed, and consider well what you do, and do not cast away such Hopes as these for nothing, nor for a little of the Pleasure of this World: for it is certain, that your carnal and worldly Actions can't give you Rest. Moreover, by these you do bring all sorts of Misery on your selves; yea, and not only so, but you do thereby trouble others also, so long as you remain unconverted.

Thus you trouble such as are Magistrates to rule and govern you, and by their penal Laws to punish you.

Next, you trouble such as are *Pastors* or *Ministers*, while you hate to hear, believe, and practice their Doctrine. While your Sin and Misery is great, their Trouble and Sorrow is so too here in this World.

You do also trouble the common People by your Sins, by bringing on them various Sicknesses and pestilential Diseases, and all other divine Chastisements.

You do also hereby hinder and disturb the holy Peace of God's praying People among the Churches, and make those ashamed that are religious; and you who are still ungodly laugh at it.

Alas! Oh Lord, how very heavy is my Grief on the account hereof? seeing we now hear the Gospel preached to us, and have the Light of God's Word shining on us, and he in Peace giveth his *Sabbaths* to us.

God is constantly calling of us to Repentance, and has often repeated his Chastisements on us, by grievous Sicknesses; but, this notwithstanding, how full of Wickedness has he seen all our Towns? for both Men and Women, young Men and Maids, do all delight in Sin, and do things therein greatly grievous.

People should all of them now forsake their Sins, and turn to God; and they should come to their Ministers, and make penitential Confessions of their Transgressions to them, and entreat them to pray to God for them: then would God forgive their Iniquities, and teach them to do that which is right all the Days of their Lives.

Then also would God teach them to know Jesus Christ, and believe in him: and then they should receive Remission of all their Sins, and should be caused to walk according to the Word of God to the End of their Lives. Whoso heareth this, Oh let it put him on Consideration! These are my last Words to you. Now fare you all well. *Amen.*

## Chapter III. Example XV

*SARAH, formerly the Wife of Master JAPHETH HANNIT, who died March 1716–17.*

THE *Sarah* of whom I here speak, was the Daughter of a godly Man, named *Kestumin*,[67] mentioned in *Chap*. I. the same being afterwards Deacon[68] of the Church whereof good *Hiacoomes*[69] was Pastor. She was married to *Japheth* whilst she was but young, was a good Wife to him as long as he lived; and like another *Sarah*,[70] did reverence her Husband and obey him.

Tho she carried her self soberly and well when she was first married, yet she did not, until several Years after, make a publick and solemn Profession of Religion, and join as a Member in full Communion to the Church of Christ, whereof her own Husband became afterwards the Pastor.

Her Conversation was from first to last very blameless and exemplary: She never was, that I have heard of, guilty of any Fault that was just matter of Offence to *God's People*, from the time she first joined to the Church of Christ till she died. She was *chaste, a keeper at home, that minded her own Business*, and meddled not with what belong'd to others; and so no Busy-body, or Tale-bearer.[71]

She was one of those *wise Women that builded the House*, and not of *the foolish ones that plucked it down with their Hands*;[72] for the fair and large *Wigwam*[73] wherein she with her Husband lived, was a great part of it her own Work; the Matts, or platted Straw, Flags and Rushes with which it was covered, being

---

67. E. Mayhew, *Indian Converts*, 45, 74, 87.

68. Deacons were laymen who assisted the minister. An important social role of the deacon was to serve on the seating committee that mapped out the social hierarchy of the congregation: The closer the person sat to the minister, the higher his or her social (and presumably spiritual) status (Archer, *Fissures in the Rock*, 60). When Mayhew notes that someone was a selectman, town clerk, magistrate, or deacon, he is helping his readership mentally place the individual within the community's spiritual seating plan.

69. Hiacoomes was the first Christian Indian on Martha's Vineyard and later an important minister (E. Mayhew, *Indian Converts*, 1–12).

70. The reference is to Sarah, the biblical matriarch and wife of Abraham (Gen.).

71. Titus 2:5. Many Puritan conduct books cautioned people, particularly women, on the importance of governing the tongue.

72. Prov. 14:1.

73. The wigwam was the traditional Wampanoag house. Wampanoags in colonial New England tended to build two types of wigwams: a smaller "round house" (*puttuckakuan*), and a larger arbor-like "longhouse" (the *neesquttow*, or "house with two fires"). Thomas Mayhew Jr.'s description of the island wigwams explains that they are "made with small poles like an arbor covered with mats, and their fire is in the midst, over which they leave a place for the smoak to go out at" (Nanpashamet, "The Wetu"; J. F. Scott, *Early Colonial Houses*, 50–52). For a sketch by the Reverend Ezra Stiles of a typical eighteenth-century wigwam and a list of its contents, see Plane, *Colonial Intimacies*, 107–9.

wrought by her own Hands; and those of them that appeared within side the House, were neatly embroidered with the inner Barks of Walnut-Trees artificially softned, and dyed of several Colours for that end: so that the generality of *Indian* Houses were not so handsome as this was; neither was it inferior to those the chief Sachims lived in.

The House thus built was kept clean and neat, all thing [*sic*] in it being in their proper Places; the Clothing of the Family being also clean and whole, as by many has been observed: And in particular, this virtuous Woman's Husband was constantly so well clothed, and his Linen kept so clean and white, that he was always fit to go into the best Company, *and was known in the Gates when he sat amongst the Elders of his People.*[74]

When these good People had much Company at their House, as being given to Hospitality they frequently had, they were entertained with the best, and that ordered after the best manner, which their Circumstances would allow of; the good Woman and her Daughters serving chearfully on such Occasions, and shewing no Discontent.

But the Prudence and Industry of this Woman, in ordering her outward Affairs, tho it were very commendable, yet was not the best part of her Character; for tho she served with *Martha*, yet was she not so careful and troubled about many things, as not with *Mary* to chuse the one thing needful, even that good Part not to be taken away from her.[75]

We are told in the Description of a virtuous Woman, which we have in *Proverbs chap.* 31. *A Woman that feareth the Lord she shall be praised*; and such a one, the *Sarah* of whom I here speak was justly thought to be, by him who from that Text preached her Funeral Sermon when she was interred.

Her sincere Piety has been in part discover'd, in what has been already said of her; but this will be yet more conspicuous in what may be further related concerning her.

She then carefully remembered the Sabbath Day to keep it holy,[76] constantly and seriously attending the Worship and Ordinances of *God* in his House on that Day.

She was careful to uphold the Worship of God in her Family, praying constantly her self when her Husband was absent, (as on necessary Occasions he often was) unless there was some other Person present for whom it might be

---

74. Prov. 31:23.

75. John 11:1–20; Luke 10:38–42. Cotton Mather references this allusion in the preface to his conduct book for women, *Ornaments for the Daughters of Zion*. Mather's conduct book provides one of the standards for female behavior to which the women in Mayhew's *Indian Converts* are held.

76. Exod. 20:8.

more proper; she also frequently retired to pray in secret, as was supposed by those that observed her.

Tho she could not read very well, yet she was not discourag'd from making the best use of Books she was capable of, reading frequently in such Books as she could make the most Advantage by: and Mr. *Perkins's six Principles of Religion,*[77] having been translated into the *Indian* Tongue, was what she took great delight in reading of.

She was careful to bring up her Children[78] in the Nurture and Admonition of the Lord, frequently gave them good Instructions, and would faithfully reprove them when they did amiss; and did also frequently exhort them to the great Duties of Religion, and particularly of that of secret Prayer to God.

She was taken sick of a Fever on the second Day of the Week, and died on the Saturday next following. She told her eldest Daughter[79] then with her, that she was apprehensive that the Sickness with which she was seiz'd would be her last; and withal, expressed such a Submission and Resignation to the Will of God with respect to her own Life, and all her temporal Concernments, as did become a true Saint.[80]

She then also expressed her Desire to see and speak with her other two Daughters before she died; who being come, she expressed to them all a very deep Sense of the many Sins and Failures of her Life; but told them, that what she now most especially blamed her self for, was her not having taken so much Care for her eternal Good as she ought to have done: *for tho,* said she,

> *I have sometimes instructed and exhorted you, yet I should have done this more earnestly and pressingly than I have, and should even have commanded you to love and serve the Lord your God: But having fallen far short of my Duty herein in times past, I must now be the more earnest with you, being now about to leave the World and you.*

And she did accordingly now, in the most affecting and pressing Language of a dying Mother, urge and command these her Children to love the Lord their God with all their Hearts and Souls, Mind and Strength;[81] and did even

---

77. Perkins, *Foundation of Christian Religion.*

78. Her children are Bethia Escohana (E. Mayhew, *Indian Converts,* 102–3), Jerusha Job(e) (wife of Job Soomannah [51–52, 105, 110–13], Jedidah Hannit (232–34), Jeremiah Hannit (223–24), Joshua Hannit (224), and Hannah Tobe (wife of Elias Wauwompuque [70]). See also Pierce and Segel, *Wampanoag Genealogical History,* 126–27, 245, 338–39.

79. Bethia Escohana was her eldest daughter (E. Mayhew, *Indian Converts,* 102–3; Pierce and Segel, *Wampanoag Genealogical History,* 126).

80. Puritans used the term *saint* to refer to one of God's elect rather than to refer to those officially canonized by the church.

81. Deut. 6:5.

intreat them to avoid and abstain from those Sins which she thought them most inclined to, and all other Sins whatsoever.

She had, in times past, frequently discoursed of the woful Condition, into which, by the Sin of our first Parents, Mankind were fallen;[82] but now she seemed with more than ordinary Earnestness, to endeavour to affect her own Heart, and the Hearts of all about her, with the deepest Sense of the Guilt and Corruption whereinto all the Posterity of the first *Adam* had, by his Apostacy, been plunged; and among other things, she then said, that we who were created in the Image of God, or made like to him, did, by *Adam's* Sin and Fall, lose that *Image* with which we were indued,[83] and became like Devils for Wickedness.

This being said, she proceeded to magnify the Riches of God's Grace, in finding out and providing that Way for the Salvation of Sinners which is revealed in the Gospel, declaring in general Terms what that Way was, *viz.* that of Redemption by the Blood of *Christ*, the only Son of *God*.

She then declared, that as to her self she had hopes thro' the Mercy of God in *Jesus Christ*, the only Saviour of sinful Man, she should, notwithstanding all her Sin and Guilt, obtain everlasting Life and Happiness in the World to come; and having thus professed her own Hopes of everlasting Mercies, she exhorted all about her to have continual recourse to the Blood of *Christ* for cleansing from all Sin. She told them they could never wholly cease from committing Sin as long as they lived in this World, and therefore had need constantly to apply to the Blood of Christ for Pardon and Cleansing; and this she declared her own Intentions to do as long as her Life continued.

After she had thus discoursed, she said but little to any but God, to whom she was frequently heard pouring out her Soul; and she also desired some that came in to pray for her. The last Words that ever she was heard to say were, *O Lord I beseech thee to save my Soul.*

---

82. The doctrine of Original Sin was fundamental to New England theology and the Puritan missionary activities. As the New England primer put it, "In Adam's fall, we sinned all." Learning to overcome natural human depravity was the first step for every child and convert, whose entire life was expected to be a preparation for salvation (Cooke, "Theories of Education [XV]," 420). For Mayhew's own discussion of how man's spiritual death began with Adam, see E. Mayhew, *Grace Defended*, 5.

83. *Endue* (here spelled "indue") means "to posses or to be invested with a power or quality" (*Oxford English Dictionary*).

## Chapter IV. Example VII

*JEDIDAH HANNIT, who died in Chilmark October the 14th 1725,*[84] *being about seventeen Years old.*

*Jedidah Hannit,* of whom I here speak, was a Daughter of Master *Japheth Hannit,* and *Sarah* his Wife. She was religiously educated while she was a Child; and it is very probable that the Spirit of God did make good Impression on her Soul some Years before that in which she died. She was very obedient to her Parents, was very apt and willing to learn her Catechism,[85] and delighted much in reading her Book.[86] Nor was she much inclined to go into such vain Company as many young People delight in: And her Friends sometimes found her praying in secret Places, where she intended that none but God should see or hear her.

In the Night on which she was taken with the Sickness whereof she died, she dreamed, as she in the time of her Sickness declared, that there was a very dark and dismal time shortly coming on the *Indian* Nation; with which Dream being much distressed, she waked out of her Sleep, and had such an Impression made on her Mind, that what she had so dreamed would come to pass, and of the Dreadfulness of the thing so apprehended, that she immediately prayed earnestly to God, that she might not live to see the thing feared, but that she might be removed out of the World before it came to pass. After this, having again fallen asleep, she after some time awaked very sick: and the Sickness whereof she was so seized, did in a few Days put an end to her Life.

The Distemper[87] with which she was thus taken being a Fever, with a Pain in her Side, was so very violent from the beginning of it, that she was neither able to say much to her Friends, or do much for the Safety or Welfare of her Soul, if that Work had not been done already by her. Her Illness still increasing, she in a little time appeared to be dying, and her Friends were grieved and surprized at what was coming so suddenly on them. But having lain for some little time wholly speechless, and to appearance senseless, and almost breath-

---

84. The death date of 1725 is clearly an error, since Japheth lived only until 29 July 1712 and Sarah until March 1716/17, yet Jedidah spoke to "her Father and Mother" when her death approached, and her father made a speech as Jedidah's end neared. I am grateful to my student Mackenzie Cole (Reed College, 2006) for pointing out this discrepancy.

85. Catechism was part of the child's (and convert's) daily life in Puritan New England. Even children of only four or five years were expected to repeat it precisely at home, and after the age of seven or eight, they were expected to repeat it in front of the entire congregation (P. Ford, *New England Primer,* 81–83; Axtell, *School upon a Hill,* 37–38).

86. The reference is to the Bible.

87. *Distemper* here means "disease."

less, she began to revive, breathed better, and was in a short time able to speak, and that sensibly, and remained so for several Hours together; nor was her Pain so violent as it had before been: Being thus revived, she said she seemed to her self to have been in a Dream; but whether she were so or not, she could not determine. However, she said she was going to a Place which she much desired to be at, and was exceedingly delighted with the thoughts of her going to it; but she then thought that her Brother-in-Law, naming him, came after her, and called her to come back again, telling her that her Father and Mother and other Friends would be exceedingly troubled, if she went away so suddenly and left them.

While she seemed to be dying, as is above related, her Brother-in-Law,[88] by whom she thought she had been called back from her Journey, as is above-said, went out of the House; and not long after him, her Father also; and the last mentioned of these Persons walking by the side of an Hedge-Fence, not far from the House, overheard the other, on the other side of the Hedge, pleading most earnestly with God, that his Sister might not be so suddenly taken away from her Friends, as to appearance she seemed likely to be: Soon after this, the Father of the Maid returning to the House, found her revived, as has been declared, and was told what she had said before he came in; and soon after her said Brother came in also, and to his great Comfort saw her, as one in a manner raised from the Dead.

But lest the Relations of this young Woman, and particularly her Brother-in-Law mentioned, should be too much transported at the sudden Alteration which they saw in her, Mr. *Japheth* made a very grave and seasonable Speech to them, telling them that they should by no means conclude from his Daughter's being thus revived, that God designed to recover her from this present Sickness; but think it sufficient, that God had so far heard Prayers for her, as not to take her so suddenly away as they feared he would have done, and had given her and them a further Opportunity to speak one to another before she died and left them: and to this purpose he more particularly addressed himself to his Son-in-Law, who had prayed for his Daughter, as has been declared.

However, the Maid thus far revived, had now a further Opportunity to look up to God for his Mercy, and let her Friends understand that she did not leave the World without committing the Care of her Soul to Jesus Christ, her only

---

88. This was probably Job Soomannah. The reference to her brother-in-law again points to the error in the Mayhew's death date for Jedidah, since all of Jedidah's known brothers-in-law died before 1723, and Jedidah's illness is said to have come upon her suddenly in 1725. Her known brothers-in-law are Job Soomannah (who died in 1718), the husband of Jerusha Job(e); Elias Able (who died in 1723), the husband of Hannah Tobe; and Nicodemos Skuhunnan (who died in 1710), the husband of Bethia Escohana (Pierce and Segel, *Wampanoag Genealogical History*, 126–27, 261).

Saviour. Having such Opportunity, she now declared, that she did no longer set her Mind upon any of her worldly Enjoyments, but was willing to die and leave them. *There is*, said she, *but one thing that I am now concerned about. I am now troubled for my Sins against my God, and my not keeping his Commandments as I ought to have done. I have made Promises to him, and have not duly performed them. I desire that God's People would pray to him for me.*

After this she said, *I believe in Jesus Christ, that he is my only Saviour*; and then praying, called thus upon him, *O my God, thou who takest away the Sins of the World, forgive my Sins, I beseech thee, and save my Soul for ever.*

She also took her leave of her Relations and others in Words to this Effect: *Farewel all ye my beloved Friends! Farewel all ye young People, fear ye God greatly, pray earnestly to him, sanctify his Sabbath, and be sober on that Day in his Fear.*

As for me, said she, my Days are cut off, and I groan by reason of the Pain which I endure; but I am willing to die, because I believe in Christ that he is my Salvation.

~:~

# Tradition and Innovation in a Colonial Wampanoag Family from Martha's Vineyard

## LAURA ARNOLD LEIBMAN

When Kenneth Lockridge wrote *Literacy in Colonial New England* in 1974, he felt relatively safe in his argument that signatures on wills reflected literacy rates.[89] Since the late 1980s, however, literacy has increasingly been used to mean cultural and moral literacy rather than just the ability to read and write: That is, literacy refers to a mastery of a "a supposed body of shared knowledge" as well as to the understanding of the character traits that were "preached, if not practiced."[90] In the past, Experience Mayhew's 1727 biographies of the seventeenth- and eighteenth-century Wampanoags on Martha's Vineyard have been used to measure the degree to which Algonquians in colonial New England read and wrote.[91] Mayhew's *Indian Converts* is an equally important resource, however, for understanding Wampanoag cultural and moral literacy on Martha's Vineyard. The Hannit family biographies from *Indian Converts* portray how Wampanoags and missionaries used reading, writing, cultural literacy, and moral literacy as both "a weapon and shield."[92]

---

89. Lockridge, *Literacy in Colonial New England*, 7.
90. Blot and Collins, *Literacy and Literacies*, 2.
91. Monaghan, "She Loved to Read Good Books," 492–521.
92. Blot and Collins, *Literacy and Literacies*, 5–7, 122, 136.

Mayhew's biographies of the Hannit family represent a microcosm of Mayhew's larger work. Unlike previous records, Mayhew's *Indian Converts* not only accounts for the "Indian Ministers" and "Good Men" on the island but also contains extensive chapters on "Religious Women," and "Pious Children." Like the larger volume, the biographies of the Hannit family included here present the lives of four generations of Wampanoag converts. The selections are also representative of *Indian Converts* more generally in that they include not only translations of Wampanoag sermons, dying speeches, and testimonies but also information that Mayhew collected from English printed works and manuscripts. Mayhew's Wampanoag translations supplement the large range of archival materials authored or signed by Wampanoags on the island, such as wills, deeds, church records, and biblical marginalia. The Hannits, for example, appear numerous times in island deeds and court records.[93] One of the most important families on the island, the Hannits combined the authority of a "royal" lineage with leadership in a Wampanoag-led church. The focal point of the family is the patriarch, Japheth Hannit, an early and one of the most important ministers on the island. Japheth's biography reveals the importance of a dual lineage: He is the descendant of a petty sachem, but because of his parents' early emphasis on a Puritan education, he also emerges as a leader of his community. Like many prominent converts, Japheth secured his position in the Christian hierarchy by marrying the daughter of the first "Deacon of the Church whereof good *Hiacoomes* was Pastor": Sarah (née Sarah Mensoo of Chappaquiddick). Sarah, like many female converts, played a crucial role in educating her children about how to lead a Christian life. She appears to have been successful: Of her six known children, all (or their spouses) are mentioned as religious figures in *Indian Converts*.

The Hannit family's ability to read and write contributed to the leadership role of its members among the new Christian aristocracy. As Richard Blot and James Collins attest, literacy is linked to social power, whether that power is manifested by working within or against the colonial bureaucracy. Literacy is both "a weapon and shield."[94] Literacy, for example, allowed Wampanoags to manipulate the court system.[95] In the Hannit family, Japheth was able to read and write both English and Wampanoag; his wife, Sarah, and daughter Jedidah could read; and Japheth's son-in-law Job Soomannah could also read

---

93. For a list of documents about the Hannit family, see Pierce and Segel, *Wampanoag Genealogical History*, 126–27.

94. Blot and Collins, *Literacy and Literacies*, 5–7, 122, 136.

95. Silverman, "*Conditions for Coexistence*," 220–73.

and write.[96] The pattern of literacy within the family is typical of Wampanoag literacy rates and educational practices on Martha's Vineyard more generally. Schools such as the one attended by Japheth in 1651 educated children to read and write English and Wampanoag, with a clear emphasis on reading. As Jennifer Monaghan points out, of the 128 adults and children covered in *Indian Converts*, 60 are identified explicitly as being able to read and 9 as being able to write. Of the 9 who could write, 5 were men, 1 was a woman, and 3 were children.[97] *Indian Converts* also provides information about Mayhew's ability to read and write Wampanoag. Unlike most New England missionaries, Mayhew was not a dilettante in Wampanoag society: As a fourth-generation missionary on the island, Mayhew spoke Wampanoag fluently and had known most of his subjects or their families his entire life.

Schools such as the one attended by Japheth and his descendants not only taught pupils how to read and write but also strove to make them culturally and morally literate. Norman Earl Tanis provides a glimpse into John Eliot's curriculum, which was used throughout the "praying towns" of Massachusetts. Schools used a tutorial method to train future teachers. In addition to reading and writing, students were instructed in Calvinist theology, logic, carpentry, masonry, farming, and weaving, and children often worked as servants as part of their education. Pupils were encouraged to "attend the sessions of the Indian Magistrate so that they might learn about Massachusetts law." Advanced students might go on to study Greek and Latin.[98] The ultimate goal of learning to read and write was to reach salvation through a knowledge and acceptance of the Bible; thus, in Mayhew's version of Japheth's life, formal instruction is followed closely (textually if not temporally) by Japheth's marrying a pious woman, entering into "a solemn Covenant to serve the Lord," and serving on the side of the British during King Philip's War.[99] Books such as Experience Mayhew's *Indian Primer* (*Indiane primer asuh Negonneyeuuk* [1720]) and John Eliot's *Logic Primer* (1672) were effective only insomuch as they helped pupils reach the divine by training the students' thinking to be in line with divine logic and Puritan theology. Puritan schools sought to familiarize students with not only the expectations of the genres in which they wrote but also their social standing in colonial society: The letters of Eleazar Wheelock's pupils, for ex-

---

96. Japheth's mother, Wuttununohkomkooh, and father, Pamchannit, are not explicitly mentioned as being able to read or write; this is not surprising, however, since they were already well into adulthood when the English arrived.

97. Monaghan, "She Loved to Read Good Books," 496, 502–3.

98. Tanis, "Education in John Eliot's Indian Utopias," 317.

99. E. Mayhew, *Indian Converts*, 45–46.

ample, carefully mimic not only the English but also the style and content of eighteenth-century letter manuals. The students are artistically fluent in how to address social "superiors" and how to manipulate these "superiors" for their own benefit. The letters, which also repeatedly insist on the students' awareness of Puritan codes of moral behavior, reveal Algonquians' mastery of not only reading and writing but also the cultural and moral literacy of eighteenth-century New England.

Along with documents from Wheelock's Indian school, Mayhew's *Indian Converts* provides some of the best information we have about education and literacy among Algonquian women and children in the seventeenth and eighteenth centuries. As in Wheelock's school, both Wampanoag girls and Wampanoag boys were taught to read and write on Martha's Vineyard. Although Mayhew comments that Sarah "could not read very well," she still frequently read "such Books as she could make the most Advantage by: and Mr. *Perkins's six Principles of Religion*, having been translated into the *Indian* Tongue, was what she took great delight in reading of." Sarah was also literate in the Bible and in Puritan theology, as on her death bed she spoke about Original Sin as well as the "Riches of God's Grace" and the possibility of "Redemption by the Blood of *Christ*, the only Son of *God*." Her daughter Jedidah was even more proficient than her mother: She "was very apt and willing to learn her Catechism, and delighted much in reading her Book." As her dying speech makes clear, not only had she memorized the catechism but she was also able to apply it to her own life.

The Wampanoag texts embedded in Mayhew's biographies reveal a similar Algonquian mastery of the "master's tools," as well as a distinct rebellion against "the imposition of Western forms."[100] Japheth's sermon at the funeral of John Tackanash (January 1683/4) exposes Japheth's manipulation of the Puritan funerary genre. Along with other Puritan burial practices, funeral sermons helped the mourner envision the deceased as part of a new community of the eternally saved. Like Japheth's sermon, Puritan funerary sermons for leading members of the community emphasized the departed's partaking of a new eternal life that ideally, one day, the mourner himself or herself would join. Puritans often contrasted the optimistic nature of their funerals with the loud, emotional mourning practices of Algonquians.[101] Indeed funerary rites among the Native peoples of New England more often presented the dual nature of death as destructive and regenerative. This duality is reflected in the Massachusett word for death: *Amit* was linked to the idea of exceeding, going beyond,

---

100. Collins and Blot, *Literacy and Literacies*, 122.
101. Bragdon, *Native People of Southern New England*, 233.

rotting, on one hand, and the idea of *m'anit*, a "sacred, spiritual force, god." on the other.[102] In contrast, Japheth's sermon is almost unmitigatedly optimistic: Rather than emphasize loss, it harps on the eternal life gained by Tackanash and the salvation gained by the Wampanoags more generally through the arrival of the missionaries. Yet even by Puritan standards, Japheth's sermon fails, perhaps, in an *excess* of optimism: Puritan funerary rites reflected the delicate Puritan balance between belief in salvation and damnation. The burials helped console the mourners with the knowledge that the deceased was in the hands of God[103] but also reminded the living of their own need to repent. At least in the section quoted by Mayhew, Japheth preaches atonement (Christ dies for sinners) rather than Calvinism's *limited* atonement (Christ dies only for the elect). Indeed, this may be what Mayhew refers to when he says that Japheth's "sermons were not very accurate." We will probably never know whether Japheth's theological adaptation of Calvinism was due to a misunderstanding or a willful reenvisioning of the main tenets of Calvinism. It is important to note that by the time of his own death, he has "mastered" the genre fully: In Japheth's dying speech, recorded by his son-in-law Job Soomannah, he carefully balances belief in God and fear of damnation, and he urges his kin and friends to repent.

Just as Mayhew's *Indian Converts* testifies to the Wampanoags' cultural and moral literacy, it also testifies to Mayhew's own literacy in the Wampanoag language and Wampanoag storytelling. Certainly Mayhew's success as a missionary depended on his ability not only to speak the dialect of Massachusett spoken on the island but also to refine previous translations of Puritan documents by Eliot in order to make them resonate with the community on Martha's Vineyard. Perhaps more interesting, however, is Mayhew's "literacy" within the Native American oral tradition, both in terms of language and the motifs, characters, events, and elements that characterized precontact genres. I have argued elsewhere that Roger Williams displayed a similar sort of literacy within the Narragansett oral tradition: Williams mastered not only stories from the oral tradition but also an oral style.[104] In the Spanish colonies, missionaries such as Fray Bernardino de Sahagún went to great lengths to become conversant with Native American genres. Scholars have tended to assume, however, that Puritans did not consciously adapt either their theology or style to meet Algonquian needs or to represent Algonquian converts. Indeed, in Mayhew's account it is difficult to ascertain whether he includes the motifs, characters, events, and elements that characterized precontact genres intentionally or they

102. Trumbull, quoted in ibid., 235.
103. Stannard, *The Puritan Way of Death*, 100.
104. Arnold, "Cultures in Contact," 15–58.

are inserted inadvertently when Mayhew translates written and oral testimony by Wampanoags.

Perhaps the most crucial of the Wampanoag oral genres for Mayhew's project is the *memorate*: a concrete account of a personal encounter with the supernatural.[105] The *memorate* shares some important features with the standard Puritan conversion narrative: Like conversion narratives, *memorates* can be told in the first person or retold by someone who was not involved in the incident.[106] Just as conversion narratives were often told to gain church membership, *memorates* by *pneise* and *powwows* were told as part of the rite of passage to become a spiritual leader, advisor, or practitioner.[107] Unlike conversion narratives or experiences, *memorates* frequently came in the form of a dream or vision, often deliberately induced through a "difficult ordeal" or "loss of sleep, fasting, and drinking mixtures that may have been hallucinogenic."[108] Also unlike Puritan conversion experiences, which involved an encounter with Jesus or God, the principal deity who appeared in Algonquian visions and dreams was Hobbamock (Chepi), "whose name was related to words for death, the deceased, and the cold northeast wind."[109] Hobbamock was also associated with night, black, and liminal spaces such as "hideous woods and swamps." He could appear "in the shapes of Englishmen, Indians, animals, inanimate objects, and mythical creatures."[110] The conversion narratives told by Wampanoags in *Indian Converts* often reference the motifs, characters, events, and elements of the *memorate* tradition. For example, the conversion story told by Japheth's mother occurs in a liminal space and after a "difficult ordeal." Her granddaughter Jedidah continues this family visionary tradition. As Plane has argued about Mayhew's use of dream visions, the overlap between the *memorate* and conversion story provided a way for Wampanoags to express themselves that is both "fully Christian and fully native."[111] It is debatable to what extent Mayhew understood the Wampanoag resonances of these events; however, for those who wish to see Mayhew's use of Wampanoag tropes as conscious, we

---

105. William Simmons proposes that Wampanoag oral tradition can be divided into four genres: *memorate*, legend, myth, and folktale (*Spirit of the New England Tribes*, 6).

106. Ibid.

107. Ibid., 39–41.

108. Ibid., 39. Anne Marie Plane has called attention to the Wampanoag tradition of dream visions and dream interpretation embedded in Mayhew's text. As Plane observes, both Puritans and Wampanoags had a rich tradition of dream visions and dream interpretation, and both colonists and Wampanoags believed that dreams were a possible source of divine revelation and had a potential predictive significance ("Falling 'Into a Dreame,'" 86–87). Puritans were not as likely to try to induce their visions, however, or include them as part of the stories told to gain church membership.

109. Simmons, *Spirit of the New England Tribes*, 39.

110. Ibid.

111. Plane, "Falling 'Into a Dreame,'" 96.

might point to his frequent disclaimers that he does not know how to interpret these events: This may be an indication that Mayhew recognizes when he has recorded something potentially unusual or suspect within the Puritan context.

Literacy has often been expanded to include inscriptions and nonalphabetic record-keeping systems. Mayhew includes references to such traditions and emphasizes their worth by showing how they mesh with Puritan values. For example, Japheth's wife, Sarah, is known for her ability to weave and decorate house "Matts." Although this form of "writing" was not found among Puritans, weaving was an important Wampanoag textual tradition. Wampanoag women were esteemed New England weavers: Up to and throughout the nineteenth century, Algonquian women were able to make a (sometimes precarious) living as itinerant craftspeople who produced a range of woven goods, from baskets to chair bottoms, brooms, and mats.[112] Although some of the women in *Indian Converts* make baskets to raise money for their impoverished neighbors, Sarah Hannit uses her weaving abilities to embellish and strengthen her home. Although Mayhew emphasizes that the "Matts" that Sarah plaits and embroiders made her wigwam one of the most handsome on the island, they also contributed to climate control in both winter and summer. Sarah's "Matts" probably also honored her family heritage: House mats were often "dyed in shades of red and black in traditional family designs that were handed down from one generation to the next," as Linda Coombs (associate director of the Wampanoag Indian Program at Plimoth Plantation) remarks.[113] This tradition was carried on by Sarah's son-in-law Job Soomannah, who was also a weaver, an occupation that allowed him to provide "comfortably" for his family despite his physical disabilities.[114]

The Hannit family, like many of the families mentioned in *Indian Converts*, reflects the range of degrees of literacy found among Wampanoags on Martha's Vineyard. Not only did the ability to read and write vary between generations and between men and women; cultural and moral literacies varied as well. If literacy is associated with power, it was an ambiguous power in the Hannit family: With literacy came new ways to compose and recompose social and private identities to advance within a new society and to preserve old lifeways.

---

112. Wolverton, " 'A Precarious Living,' " 342.
113. Coombs, "Ancient Technology."
114. E. Mayhew, *Indian Converts*, 111.

# 6 · Intertribal Conversations

THE TEXTS in Chapters One to Five of this anthology are grouped according to tribal affiliation. We hope that this organization helps readers to understand literacy issues within particular cultural contexts—especially important, since the cultures that produced our anthologized texts are still vital parts of New England today.

We believe that it is important to recognize not only the significance and the persistence of tribal identities but also that individual tribal histories tell only part of the story of New England as an "Indian world."[1] Literacy practices, particularly the adoption of alphabetic literacy, cut across tribal identities and linked Native peoples of New England during the early colonial period.

This chapter takes seriously Ann McMullen's contention that we should not view the development of a pan-Indian perspective as a loss of cultural identity, that we should view "regionalism and regional cultures as survival rather than cultural disintegration."[2] Indeed, as McMullen points out, regional cultures predated the arrival of Europeans, and colonial-era alliances and intertribal conversations such as those in the Massachusetts Bay Colony might well be viewed as the successful adaptation of old ways of relating across tribal groups. This approach can incorporate Lisa Brooks's notion of the "common pot"[3] as a metaphor for how different Native spaces look when we focus not on Europeans but on Natives and their attempts to create balance and unity among and between communities.

Historians have uncovered various intertribal affiliations and conflicts throughout the period represented herein. Both before and after the arrival of the English, groups came together in defensive alliances, agreed on or disputed land use, traded, and intermarried. We have touched on some of these developments in the headnotes to the chapters. In terms of literacy, intertribal conversations have been significant: Katherine Garret and Sarah Pharaoh spoke to Indians, not just to Pequots or Narragansetts. Of course, the Wampanoag and Natick experiences with print literacy influenced their own communities

---

1. This phrase is taken from the Montaukett petition included in this chapter.
2. McMullen, "What's Wrong with This Picture?" 123.
3. L. Brooks, "The Common Pot."

deeply, but well into the eighteenth century the Massachusett-language texts that their translators and printers produced were widely distributed, read, argued about, and cherished by Indians across New England. In addition, as we discussed in the introduction and in the headnote to Chapter One ("The Mohegans"), intertribalism was a hallmark of such nativist movements as the one that led to the founding of Brotherton. Intertribalism was especially important to the prominent Mohegan writer Samson Occom, who appears once again in this chapter.

The three essays in this section illustrate the range of uses to which intertribalism and literacy were put in the eighteenth century. Joanna Brooks discusses the successful deployment of traditional language in a petition that protests the appropriation of Montaukett land by New York. The petition reflects a specific partnership—that between Occom and the Montaukett Tribe. This connection—built on not only kinship ties forged through marriage but also a common political understanding—allowed for a powerful critique of colonial policies. Sandra Gustafson's essay examines another agent for intertribal conversations: Hendrick Aupaumut, who served as a go-between in U.S. negotiations with more westerly Indians. Unlike the authors of the Montaukett petition, he could not, as a U.S. agent, be pointedly critical of white colonization; very much like the authors of the petition, however, he mobilized indigenous communicative practices within traditional Western print literacy. Heidi Bohaker's essay, in turn, serves as a reminder both of the ways that nonalphabetic literacy was employed after colonization and the artificial limits that this consideration of early Native literacy in New England imposes on its subject: The iconographic signatures that she examines—although written by people from northern rather than southern New England—were inscribed and archived in Boston, as a symbol of the Wabanaki agreement with Bay Colony officials. We contend that they number among the examples of early Native literacy in New England. Although we must not forget the assymetrical power relationships that were in place in 1725 (which required Penobscot representatives to travel from Maine to Boston), inscribed images of turtles and beavers, crayfish and thunder beings remind us that, even in colonial strongholds, seemingly English spaces were part of a wide Indian world. All three primary texts in this section demonstrate the ways that, as Joanna Brooks argues herein, Indians in the eighteenth century "viewed their literacy as a tool in the service of American Indian communities."

## Suggested Reading

McMullen, "What's Wrong with This Picture? Context, Coversion, Survival, and the Development of Regional Native Cultures and Pan-Indianism in Southeastern New England." In *Enduring Traditions: The Native Peoples of New England*, edited by Laurie Weisenstein, 123–50. Westport, Conn.: Bergin and Garvey, 1994.

Lisa Brooks. "The Common Pot: Indigenous Writing and the Reconstruction of Space in the Northeast." Ph.D. diss. Cornell University, 2004.

# Pictograph Image on a 1725 Treaty

These pictographs were inscribed by the Native American signatories to the "Treaty with Delegates of the Eastern Indians at the Council Chambers in Boston," dated December 15, 1725. The pictographs appear on the bottom right corner of the larger document that includes the full treaty text and the signatures of New England government officials. The verso contains another treaty text which renews and confirms the original on the recto: "Treaty Renewed with the Penobscots at Falmouth, Casco Bay; August 5, 1726." The parchment on which these texts appear is large and visually striking, measuring in total 34.25 inches high by 24.75 inches wide. The excerpt represented above measures 6 inches high by 6.75 inches wide. The ink of the script on the entire parchment is brown; the lines on the page are red. There were originally four seals on the document, but they are no longer attached. Red wax remnants remain. The document is part of the Massachusetts Archives Collection (vol. 34, p. 2). The Massachusetts Archives Collection comprises state papers assembled by the Reverend Joseph Felt in the 1830s and 1840s and is held at the Massachusetts State Archives in Boston. The documents were gathered from their offices of origin or deposit between the years 1836 and 1845. Jennifer Fauxsmith of the Massachusetts State Archives was most helpful in the preparation of both the digital image and this headnote.

# Reading Expressions of Identity on a 1725 Peace and Friendship Treaty

HEIDI BOHAKER

Any examination of Native literacies would be incomplete without an appreciation of the rich ways in which Native peoples used symbolic and iconic imagery to communicate. Long before Europeans introduced their alphabetic writing systems to the North American continent, Native peoples had developed their own elaborate means of textual expression through a range of media. They employed culturally distinct nonalphabetic semiotic systems to transmit meaning, from writer to reader, for a broad range of public and private com-

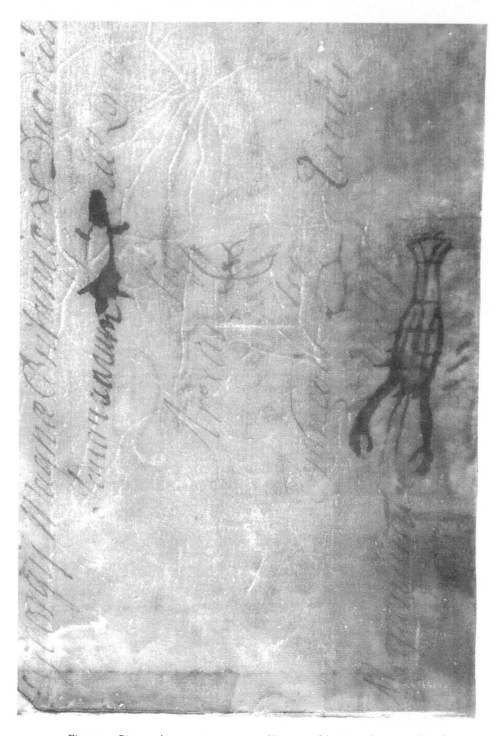

Figure 6-1. Pictograph image on a 1725 treaty. (Courtesy of the Massachusetts Archives.)

municative purposes.[4] They tattooed their bodies, painted their canoes, carved images on war clubs, left messages for travelers, and kept important records on beaded wampum belts and incised bark scrolls. The arrival of Europeans threatened these communication and record-keeping systems, as sixteenth- and seventeenth-century epidemics dramatically reduced the population. Ultimately, however, it was nineteenth- and twentieth-century programs of assimilation that had the more catastrophic impact. Compulsory schooling that promoted English-language literacy greatly reduced Native Americans' knowledge of their semiotic systems. In addition, many records have been severed from their reading communities—wampum belts, incised objects, and bark scrolls lie silent in museum vaults, and the more ephemeral tattooing practices and traveling messages have been preserved only in the descriptions recorded by visiting Europeans.[5] However, expressions of Native symbolic and iconic imagery also appear on treaties, letters, and other documents, alongside and as part of texts written by Europeans and early American settlers.

The treaty text discussed here illustrates just one example of the Native American practice of signing documents with pictographic images. In this case, the "eastern Indian" signatories were Penobscot, living in what is now the state of Maine.[6] They came to Boston in November 1725 as "Heads or Representatives" on behalf of their own people and on behalf of the Norridgewock (Kennebec), St. John (Passsamaquoddy), Cape Sable (Mi'kmaq, often spelled Micmac), and unspecified "other tribes" to discuss a "cession of hostilities" with representatives of the Massachusetts government and the British Crown.[7] Together with the Abenaki and Wolastoqiyik (Maliseet), these peoples were loosely allied across a region that stretched east to west from the Atlantic to Lake Champlain and north to south from the St. Lawrence River to just north

---

4. For example, in *African Writing and Text*, Simon Battestini argues that when studying non-Western societies, scholars should rethink what constitutes writing. He distinguishes between alphabetic and nonalphabetic semiotic systems and disputes notions of alphabetic semiotic systems as particularly privileged. Battestini legitimates the expansion of our definition of literacy and the reading of Native American authored images as text. These images are clearly a means of preserving memories and ideas and transmitting these ideas and memories through time and space.

5. In 1609 the French explorer Samuel de Champlain observed the practical use of this communication system along the Richelieu River, south of the St. Lawrence River, on his way to Lake Champlain: "Besides when they go to war they ... reconnoitre along the rivers and see whether there is any mark or sign to show where their enemies or their friends have gone. This they know by certain marks by which the chiefs of one nation designate those of another, notifying one another from time to time of any variations of these" (*Works*, 85).

6. See Calloway, Introduction, 2.

7. Samuel Stacy confirmed the arrival of the delegates in his correspondence with the acting governor of Massachusetts, Lt. Governor William Dummer, in his "Letter—Samuel Stacy to Lt. Governor Dummer, Nov 15, 1725" (see Baxter, *Documentary History of the State of Maine*, 4:352).

of Boston. Present-day descendants describe this region as Wabanakia and the people of the region as Wabanaki.[8]

The treaty in question had its roots in unresolved issues following the signing of the Treaty of Utrecht in 1713, when French Acadia was ceded to the English. Later that year, at the Treaty of Portsmouth, the English promised the Wabanaki not to molest or interfere with their "hunting, fishing, fowling and all other [of] their lawful liberties and privileges."[9] The pressures of an ever-encroaching English population, however, soon drew various Wabanaki communities into skirmishes with the English. In 1722 the situation became so explosive that Massachusetts declared war against the Wabanaki. As the conflict raged on, it took an increasingly heavy toll on all parties.[10] According to English reports, by 1725 the Penobscots had had enough. They approached Massachusetts about negotiating for peace and agreed to discuss the matter with their allies as well.[11]

After nearly a month of discussions, four Penobscot delegates entered the Council Chamber in Boston on 15 December 1725 and agreed to initial "articles of pacification" with representatives of the governments of Massachusetts Bay, New Hampshire, and Nova Scotia. On the document that purportedly recorded the agreement, Sanguaarum (alias Loron) drew a beaver, Arexis drew a thunder being (a powerful manitou represented as a bird with outstretched wings), François Xavier drew a turtle, and Meganumbe drew a crayfish.[12] The parties agreed to organize a formal, public ratification of the terms at Falmouth in Casco Bay in May 1726 and shortly thereafter at Annapolis Royal in Nova Scotia. The remaining Norridgewocks, Wawenocks, and Arasagunticocks from Canada who had missed the 1726 ceremonies ratified the agreement the following summer in July 1727. Together, the documents signed on these occasions are known as Dummer's Treaty.[13]

---

8. Nash, "Abiding Frontier," 1; Wiseman, *Voice of the Dawn*, 79.

9. The full text of this treaty is included in Kidder, *Abenaki Indians*, 25–31.

10. This conflict is well covered in Morrison, *Embattled Northeast*, 165–90. Calloway makes a convincing case that the western Abenaki involvement in this conflict should be discussed separately "as Grey Lock's War, after the warrior chief who dictated its pace and character" (*Western Abenakis of Vermont*, 113; see also 114–31).

11. Morrison, *Embattled Northeast*, 187–89; Calloway, *Western Abenakis of Vermont*, 127.

12. At first glance, Meganumbe's image appears be a lobster, but at the New York State Historical Association Ostego Institute Conference (Creation and Scholarship in Native American Art: The Past in the Present) at the Fenimore Art Museum in June 2005, Jonathan Holstein pointed out the distinctive features (including claw size relative to the length of the front pair of legs) that conclusively identified the image as a crayfish. My subsequent comparison of crayfish and lobster morphology agrees with Holstein's observation. The identification of Arexis's thunderbird is based on the widespread North American representation of thunder as a bird. See, for example, such imagery on a range of material culture presented in J. C. H. King, *First Peoples, First Contacts*.

13. Calloway, *Dawnland Encounters*, 111.

Although pictographic images by the Native American signatories appear on the manuscript originals, in printed reproductions or primary-source collections, the images are often deleted without comment or with the notation "totem" in brackets.[14] With no scholarly framework available for more word-oriented historians and literary scholars to approach the study of such images, it is not surprising that there has been virtually no debate over what these images might mean or how scholars could or should make use of them. Writers and commentators in previous centuries have attempted to describe the extent of Native writing practices (including the use of pictographs on different media) from continental and broadly comparative perspectives; there is now new interest in grounding the use of pictographs in their specific cultural and historic contexts.[15] The purpose of this essay is therefore to provide the initial scaffolding for a framework for future inquiry. For scholars of American literature and literacy, the pictographic signatures of Loron, Arexis, François Xavier, and Meganumbe offer a different and intriguing kind of evidence, one that challenges us to rethink not only definitions of literacy but also relationships between authority (authoring) and power. The images also offer the opportunity to reflect on Native American communicative practices and, through those practices, to reflect on the expression of individual and collective identities.

An initial reading of these images can take a textual or an aesthetic approach. The textual approach aims to determine what the pictograph was intended to signify. Images inscribed by Loron, Arexis, François Xavier, and Meganumbe are all iconic and proved relatively straightforward to identify and describe. Other pictographs on treaties and deeds signed by members of the Wabanaki peoples, however, appear to be symbolic—that is, the relationship between the

---

14. In some primary-source collections, such as Baxter, *Documentary History of the State of Maine*, the images are copied. There are but a scattered few examples in Baxter's collection, indexed under "marks" (see "Deed of Nanaadconitt et al to Francis Neale et al, August 4th 1672," 4:407–9; "Covenant of ye Indians made at Wells, 1691," 5:233–35; "Submission of the Eastern Indians, 1691," 10:7–11; "Letter of Wunungenit, Chief Sachem of Penobscot, 1726," 10:365–66; "Letter Chiefs of Norridgewock et al to Dummer, 1727," 10:400; "Chiefs of the Penobscot to Dunbar, 1729," 10:446–47). Since the nineteenth century, Europeans have referred to these images on treaty documents as totems or totemic signatures. See Theresa Schenck's concise discussion of the anthropological use of the term *totem* as a descriptor for everything from kinship networks to religious practices to objects ("Algonquian Totem and Totemism," 341–53). See also Bohaker, "*Nindoodemag*," 23–52.

15. Schoolcraft, *Historical and Statistical Information*, 411–20; L. H. Morgan, *Ancient Society*; Mallery, *Introduction to the Study of Sign Language*. Search the digital library of the *Early Canadiana Online* website for the phrase "picture writing" to see other antiquarian and public texts on this subject. For more recent works, see Joan Vastokas's excellent study "History without Writing," 48–64; Warkentin, "In Search of the Word of the Other," 1–27; Guillaud, Delâge, and d'Avignon, "Les signatures amérindiennes," 21–43; and Bohaker, "*Nindoodemag*."

sign and the signified could well be arbitrary.[16] It is also possible, however, that what appears to the untrained eye as a symbol is in fact an icon. For example, Great Lakes Anishinaabe (Ojibwe) people sometimes employed a track mark to indicate their identity as a crane, caribou, or heron. To the uninitiated, these images at first appear incomprehensible. Conclusive identification is best made through comparative study. Through the use of database and visual-imaging technology, researchers can take a digital photograph of each manuscript original and, from that digital image, crop out the pictographs. The resulting images can be stored in a database, with appropriate cross-references to the source documents, communities, dates, and associated names. In this way, a dataset can be constructed that permits comparison between individuals, across communities and over time.[17] Interpretation will most likely be enhanced through the study of the ecological, zoological, botanical, and cultural knowledge that Wabanaki peoples historically acquired as part of their education as hunters, fishers, and gatherers.

The aesthetic approach to reading these images draws from an understanding of art. The people who drew the images were artists who made individual or collective decisions about the representations of their identities. We can discuss the images in terms of their aesthetic quality, the use of minimalism or exaggeration, differences in motifs and styles, and the invocation of a sense of whimsy or playfulness. Loron's beaver is shaded at the head and tail. Meganumbe's crayfish is anatomically accurate, whereas François Xavier's turtle is a study in simplicity. Arexis's thunder being violates Western expectations of "right side up." Researchers might also consider the possibility that these images functioned as references (metaphorical or other) to legends or stories. Certainly beavers, thunder beings, turtles, and crayfish all figure in the rich corpus of oral tradition in the region.[18] An aesthetic/artistic approach also invites inquiry into the authorship of these images. Did each of the named signatories in fact draw his own pictograph? Or were other individuals charged with this task? Given the stylistic similarities, it is possible that one author/artist drew the pictographs for Loron and Meganumbe and that another drew the images for François Xavier and Arexis. Research into Native American pictographs

---

16. See for example, "Deed to Richard Wharton of Lands on the Androscoggin River," 365.

17. This methodology and the resulting identifications are discussed in greater detail in Bohaker, "Nindoodemag," 146–99. The methodology was derived from a model developed by Patricia Kennedy (of Library and Archives Canada) in "Treaty Texts: When Can We Trust the Written Word?" 1–25, and was developed in Guillaud, Delâge, and d'Avignon, "Les signatures amérindiennes," 21–26.

18. See Simmons, *Spirit of the New England Tribes*. See also Leland, *Algonquin Legends of New England*; Parkhill, *Weaving Ourselves into the Land*; and Whitehead, *Stories from the Six Worlds* and *The Old Man Told Us*. For a more general discussion, see Vecsey, *Imagine Ourselves Richly*.

must bring together these two concepts of reading that Western disciplinary analytical structures have generally kept apart.

To undertake research in this field, a first essential step is a thorough reading of the appropriate ethnohistorical literature. The works of Colin Calloway, Gordon Day, David Ghere, Evan Haefeli and Kevin Sweeny, Andrew Miller, Kenneth Morrison, and Alice Nash all contribute to a richer understanding of Wabanaki history, providing crucial contexts for Wabanaki-English conflicts and Wabanaki–French alliances—potential sites of treaty and deed signing practices.[19] Given French alliances and the Wabanaki presence in Canada, French-Canadian historiography must also be consulted.[20] Native Americans traveled widely: St. Francis residents traveled to Boston and Casco Bay, some members of the Passamaquoddy and Penobscot Tribes relocated temporarily to St. Francis, and the Mi'kmaq and Wolastoqiyik people traveled along the New England coast. In 1701 Wabanaki delegates attended the Great Peace of Montreal (which resulted in a treaty signed with pictographs). In 1721 nineteen pictographs were affixed to a letter (written in French) to the "Grand Capitaines des Anglois" (Massachusetts governor Samuel Shute). The signatories included the Narragansetts, the Mi'kmaqs, the Passamaquoddys, the Iroquois of the Sault from Montreal, the Algonquins from the Ottawa River, and the Montagnais from the northern shore of the St. Lawrence River. In 1764 Native American representatives from Nova Scotia joined delegates from the Sioux, the Dakotas, and the western Great Lakes Anishinaabegs (Ojibwas, Mississaugas, and Ottawas) at Niagara for an explanation and the ratification of the Proclamation of 1763.[21] Researchers must therefore search extensively to locate potential sources of these images and avoid limiting their inquiry to a particu-

19. Calloway, *Western Abenakis of Vermont*; idem, *Dawnland Encounters*; idem., *After King Philip's War*; Day, *In Search of New England's Native Past*; Ghere, "Abenaki Factionalism, Emigration and Social Continuity" and "Mistranslations and Misinformation," 3–26.; Miller, "Abenakis and Colonists in Northern New England"; Nash, "Abiding Frontier;" Haefeli and Sweeney, *Captors and Captives*; and Morrison, *Embattled Northeast*. Researchers are also referred to the individually named tribal entries in Hoxie, *Encyclopedia of North American Indians*.

20. Sévigny, *Les Abénaquis*. See also articles in the *Recherches Amérindiennes au Québec* (33, no. 2 [2003]), dedicated to the history of the Abenaki in Canada and the French–Abenaki alliance.

21. With respect to 1701, see Havard, *Great Peace of Montreal*. Unfortunately, the only surviving copy of this treaty is a clerk's copy. See "Ratification de la Paix." Mescwadoue signed for the "Abenakis of Acadia" with a quadruped. With respect to 1721, see "Eastern Indian tribes. Letter to Richard Phillips 'Grand Capitaine des Anglois,'" written in French. With respect to 1764, see Borrows, "Wampum at Niagara." While wampum belts were exchanged, no treaty or other document is known to have been signed at this meeting. However, some chiefs who had missed the July meeting met with Colonel John Bradstreet at Detroit in September to hear the terms of the agreement. That meeting produced a document signed with pictographs. See Bradstreet, "Transactions of a Congress held with the Chiefs of the Ottawas and Chippewas Nations" (September 7, 1764).

lar ethnic or tribal group. Because the pictographs appear on treaties and deeds as part of intertribal and intercultural conversations, they must be evaluated within these larger contexts.

The second crucial step involves the context of the document creation. In keeping with the colonists' long-standing practices of document management, the treaty documents at the Boston signing ceremony would have been prepared by Massachusetts Bay officials. For the signing ceremony, treaty documents—whether for peace and friendship or for the sale of land—were most often prepared in triplicate (and always at least in duplicate). The parties each kept one of the originals, and in the case of the French and British Crown one original was also sent back to the appropriate colonial office.[22] The pictograph example included here is from a manuscript original residing in the Massachusetts State Archives. Contemporary copies of this document, as well as copies and originals of related agreements, are also on file at the Public Record Office of the United Kingdom, the Nova Scotia Provincial Archives, and other regional repositories.

Private deeds, letters, and speeches signed with pictographs present their own challenges. In some cases only one copy of a document was signed, which was then given to a clerk to transcribe at the time of registration. When Emerson Baker examined seventeenth-century Maine deeds, he found that seventy deeds (dating from 1639) survived, but they were all clerks' copies. King Philip's War, King William's War, and fire (a great risk with wooden structures) resulted in the loss of many deeds. Some deeds have also proved to be forgeries.[23] Although archive staff may encourage scholars to begin by consulting microfilm copies (an important first step in verifying the presence of pictographs), it is crucial that researchers request access to manuscript originals. In the example included here, Meganumbe's crayfish was cut off and both the thunder being and the turtle were barely visible in the microfilm copy.

On initial examination, these images appear to be similar in function (if not in form) to the signatures of Europeans, but we must also consider the relationship between authorship and authority. European-style signatures were intended to identify the individual uniquely and to convey the authority of the individual as a party bound to or a witness of the document signed. Europeans also had conventions for making contracts with illiterate people—they had them sign with a (duly witnessed) mark, sometimes an X. Would the Penobscot delegates have even understood the written signatures as a separate feature of the document, distinct from the text itself? They most likely recognized what

---

22. Kennedy, "Treaty Texts," 1.
23. Baker, "'A Scratch with a Bear's Paw,'" 235–56.

appeared as a powerful symbol of representational authority on document after document: the seals of the French and English governors in right of their Crowns. In our highly literate society, although seals continue to be employed in marking legal and state documents as originals and therefore continue to function as markers of authenticity, they are viewed as a quaint oddity. The practice of affixing seals to documents, which began in Europe in the Middle Ages, was originally intended to represent the presence of an individual who could not attend the actual signing ceremony.[24] Moreover, since the seals of European monarchs consisted of the family heraldic image, they not only represented the individual but also affirmed the family identity. These pictographs might also serve as more than signatures, then; the images in Figure 6-1 might be viewed as functional equivalents to the European seals. Even if that is the case, however, there is still the question of what authority they represent. In this particular case, study of the historical context strongly suggests that Loron, Arexis, François Xavier, and Meganumbe signed as delegates, to confirm their presence at the conference not their ratification of or agreement with the treaty terms.

Additional information about the authority represented by the signatories can often be gleaned from supporting documents—such as council minutes— associated with signing events. For Dummer's Treaty, the accompanying text on the 1725 document speaks of the "submission" of the signatories to the king of England and contains clauses concerning the right of the English to the land they had settled. But Loron later protested those clauses, pointing out, "These writings appear to contain things that are not so." Loron noted that it was not the Penobscots but the English who initiated the peace. Loron rejected the notion of submission, saying, "Yes, I recognize him King of all his lands; but I rejoined, do not hence infer that I acknowledge thy King as my King, and King of my lands." Finally, Loron clarified the rationale for the November and December meetings that had led to the signing of the "treaty document" in 1725. The delegates had gone there, in Loron's words, "merely to tell the English that all my Nation approved of the cession of hostilities, and the negotiations of peace, and even then we agreed on the time and place of meeting to discuss it."[25]

The presence of these images also raises questions about political identities in Native communities. Although historians have grown increasingly concerned with the manner in which Native American political communi-

---

24. See, for example, Bedos-Rezak, "Mediaeval Identity," 1489–1533.

25. "Indian Explanation of the Treaty of Casco Bay," 115–18. Ghere discusses these clashing interpretations in "Mistranslations and Misinformation." For other records of the negotiations, see Maine Historical Society, "Indian Treaties," 377–447.

ties are identified, they continue, by necessity, to rely on the names that were recorded in the primary sources. This approach does not, however, apply the categories by which people defined their own communities, their place within those communities, and the relationships of those communities to the wider world. What is apparent in the example included here, and in the many other documents that bear these images, is the lacking correspondence between the recorded names in the written text of the document and the marks purported to be the signature, seal, or mark that conveys the authority of the individual or the community.[26] For instance, each delegate belonged to the Penobscots, yet each signed with a different pictograph. Moreover, the images themselves do not correspond to the ethnonyms recorded in the treaty text: "Penobscot, Norridgewalk, St. John's or Cape Sable." It is entirely possible that these images represent identity in a clan or kinship network, or a family identity. Indeed, a French enumeration of 1736 identified the St. Francis Abenakis as possessing this type of clan identity.[27] Like the pictographs of the signatories of the Iroquois Confederacy on the Great Peace of Montreal, these pictographs might also refer to a village-level identity.[28]

The images also invite research into Native expressions of individual identity. It is likely that none of these signatories was able to read or write English or recognize his phonetically spelled handwritten name. Individual names were not lifetime constants for many Algonquian-speaking peoples. An individual could experience a name change at puberty or at adoption into another community. Loron, also known as Sangaaruum, introduced himself as Panouamskeyen in his testimony about the Treaty of Casco Bay.[29] His pictograph, however, remained that of a beaver.[30] Leaders (sagamores or sachems) would sometimes receive the name of a deceased person on assuming the mantle of his political office. In these contexts, the pictograph as signature provides a check against

26. Bruce J. Bourque has addressed this problem directly in "Ethnicity on the Maritime Peninsula, 1600–1759," 257–84. Scholars in many other indigenous cultural and historical contexts have also wrestled with the problem of ethnonyms. See, particularly, Jan Vansina's efforts to unpack the written legacy of colonialism in *Paths in the Rainforest* and Sean Hawkins's analysis of the role of naming and writing by colonists and agents of empire in constructing indigenous ethnicities, *Writing and Colonialism in Northern Ghana*.

27. In "Dénombrement des nations sauvages," the anonymous author listed turtle, partridge, otter, and bear as "Abenaki" families. The anthropologist Frank Speck suggests that although the Penobscots in particular clearly had "family names" associated with specific animals or beings and had a practice of inscribing this identity on birch bark as a boundary marker, they did not claim descent from a common apical ancestor, either animal or human, that would meet the current-day anthropological definition of clan ("Abenaki Clans—Never!" 528–30).

28. Havard, *Great Peace*, 185–89.

29. See "Indian Explanation" in Calloway, *Dawnland Diplomancy*, 115.

30. "Chiefs of the Penobscot to Dunbar," 446–47.

which scholars can confirm both individual and family identity. Individuals also changed names when they converted to Christianity, as in the case of François Xavier. His name alone is strong evidence of his baptism as a Catholic; yet he made his mark as a turtle.[31]

Study of these images can also provide scholars with deeper access to a Native American worldview and spirituality. In an indigenous northeastern North American landscape, human beings were (and are), as Olive Dickason has described, part of a "transcendent universal system," directly contrasting the belief that emerged in early modern European societies that "humans were not only the centre of the universe but were its controlling force."[32] The allies who constituted the Wabanaki confederacy, along with their other Algonquian- and Iroquoian-speaking neighbors, all shared their world with a variety of other-than-human beings—who in turn could be kin with humans. With the single exception of the Christ figure fathered by God, Western sensibilities have been and continue to be unsettled by the notion of descent from other-than-human beings. This has posed neither a philosophical nor a physiological problem for Aboriginal peoples of North America, who were (and many of whom still are) entirely comfortable with metamorphoses, transformation, and more fluid categories of existence. From the earliest encounter texts, scholars can read the incredulity of Europeans concerning stories of "jugglers" or "sorcerers" who possessed the power to change shape, transforming into another being or form. Yet these transformations are an important theme in Native oral tradition.[33] Indeed, one way for chiefs to earn the respect of their people was to demonstrate their ability to move between forms. The signatories Loron, Arexis, François Xavier, and Meganumbe would have been familiar with and would have aspired to the exercise of this power. Because Westerners view such powers as supernatural, Western scholars, thoroughly trained in rationalism, have dismissed these assertions of authority. Yet if we as scholars are truly interested in the indigenous side of the story, we must venture outside our comfort levels and attend to these very clear assertions. An eighteenth-century Algonquian reader viewing the images included here would have immediately noted the broader spiritual connections of each, especially with reference to sacred stories.

As researchers work to incorporate an understanding of Native American spirituality into their readings of pictographic images, they must be mindful of the need to historicize and localize writing practices. In the eastern Great Lakes region, for example, the frequency and distribution of pictographic signatures

---

31. Bohaker, "*Nindoodemag*." My own study of Anishinaabe kinship networks in the Great Lakes Region indicated that conversion to Christianity did not affect the use of this identity.

32. Dickason, *Canada's First Nations*.

33. See, among others, Vecsey, *Imagine Ourselves Richly*.

change depending on whether the document is a peace and friendship agreement or a land sale. Moreover, there were clearly documented changes to both the type and number of images used. In the early eighteenth century, a single image might represent an entire community, but by the late eighteenth century, a single image was used to represent a father and sons or related men. By the early nineteenth century, British officials had worked to change the practice to ensure that a pictograph corresponded to each named individual.[34] These distinctions and transformations must be thoroughly contextualized in Wabanaki contexts as well.

To use these images as historical sources requires extending the definition of what constitutes historical evidence and, by extension, what constitutes the practice of literacy. Such changes in practice have been difficult for historians and literacy scholars to implement. The date of contact between Europeans and Aboriginal peoples of North America has served as a conceptual boundary separating North American Native "orality" from the "literacy" brought by Europeans to the New World. Nonindigenous scholars have customarily classified the indigenous peoples of northeastern North America prior to contact as preliterate and their past as prehistory. As a result, the iconic and symbolic imagery of Native North Americans has not been included in our evidentiary base. As a consequence of the belief that Aboriginal peoples did not leave written records, even ethnohistorians—who have genuinely attempted to bridge the academic divide—have often found themselves limited to narratives of cultural encounter and narratives of relationships between Aboriginal peoples and settler societies. A fuller telling of the Native American histories—including indigenous historical experiences and motivations for historical actions—has, to date, appeared to be out of reach. Study of Native authored/drawn pictographs, however, can inspire us to cross the great disciplinary divide. We can write richer histories by stepping away from a rigid definition of literacy and considering a broader one instead—one that embraces the use of alternative, yet highly sophisticated and deeply nuanced, semiotic systems. This is a fascinating field of study in which much work remains to be done.

34. Bohaker, "*Nindoodemag.*"

# Montaukett Petition, 1788

This unsigned, undated draft petition on two pages of letter paper, in the handwriting of Samson Occom, is housed among the Samson Occom Papers at the Connecticut Historical Society in Hartford, Connecticut.

To the Great and Most Excellent Governor, and to all the Great Men Ruling in the State of New York in North America.—

We who are known by the Name, Mmeeyautanheewuck or Montauk Indians, Humbly Send Greeting

We are very Glad and Rejoice with you that you have at last got your Freedom Liberty and Independence, from under the heavy and Gauling Yoke of Your Late King, who has tryed very hard to make you Slaves, and have kill'd great many of You, but by Your Steadiness, Boldness, and Great Courage, you have broke the Yoke and the Chain of Slavery; —Now, God Bless You, and Make you very great and good forever

We Montauk Indians, have Sot Still and have not Intermedled in this Family Contention of Yours, because we had no Business with it, and we have kept our Young men quiet as we Coud, and the People on both Sides have Usd us well in general[35]

Now, great and good Gentlemen, we humbly Intreat your Condescention and Patience to hear us a little Concerning ourselves.—

The Great and good Spirit above, Saw fit in his good pleasure, to plant our Fore-Fathers in this great Wilderness but when and how, none knows but himself, —and he that works all things Acording to his own Mind, Saw it good to give us this great Continent & he fill'd this Indian World, with veriety, and a Prodigious Number of four footed Beasts, Fowl without number and Fish of all kinds great and Small, fill'd our Seas, Rivers, Brooks, and Ponds every where, —And it was the Pleasure of him, Who orders all things acording to his good Will, he that maketh Rich, and maketh poor, he that kills, and that maketh alive, he that raiseth up whom he will, and pulleth down whom he

---

35. Montauketts did, in fact, participate in the American War of Independence, both on the loyalist and the patriot side (Strong, *Montaukett Indians*, 78–79; Ales, *History of the Indians*, 59). Occom actively advocated Native neutrality during the war, and after the war he observed critically that the chaos of war added significantly to the hardships of Indians and other poor people. See his letters "To the Oneida Tribe," 1775; "To John Bailey," [June or July] 1783; and "To John Bailey," [1784] (reprinted in J. Brooks, *Collected Writings of Samson Occom*, 111–12, 118–20, and 121–23, respectively).

will; Saw fit, to keep us in Poverty, Only to live upon the Provisions he hath made already at our Hands—Thus we livd, till it pleased the great and good Governor of the World, to Send your Fathers into these goings down of the Sun, and found us Naked and very poor Destitute of every thing, that your Fathers injoyd, only this that we had good and a Large Country to live in, and well furnished with Natural Provisions, and there was not a Letter known amongst them all in this Boundless Continent. —But your Fore Fathers Came With all the Learning, Knowledge, and Understanding, that was Necessary for Mankind to make them Happy, and they knew the goodness of our Land, and they Soon began to Settle and Cultivate the land, Some they bought almost for nothing, and we suppose they took a great deal without Purchace. And our Fathers were very Ignorant and knew not the value of Land, and they Cared nothing about it, they Imagin'd, they Shoud allways live by Hunting Fishing and Fowling, and gathering Wild Fruits—But alas at this age of the World, we find and plainly see by Sad experience, that by our Fore Fathers Ignorance and Your Fathers great Knowledge, we are undone for this Life—Now only See the agreeament, your Fathers and our Fathers made, —We hope you wont be angry with us in telling the [word missing]. The[y] agreed that we Shoud have only two Small necks of Land to plant on, and we are not allowd to Sow Wheate, and we as a Tribe are Stinted to keep only 50 Head of Cattle, and 200 Swine and three Dogs,[36] —Pray gentlemen take good Notice, dont this discover a profound Ignorance in our fore Fathers, indeed we Suspect, Some Times, that what little understanding they had was Drowned with hott Waters before they made these Shameful agreements, and on the other hand, don't this Show, that the English took advantage of the Ignorance of our Fore Fathers Woud they be Willing to be Servd so by us? Were we Cababale to use them So? —We fare now harder than our Fore Fathers—For all our Hunting, Fowling, and Fishing is now almost gone and our Wild Fruit is gone, What little there is left the English would Ingross or take all to themselves—and our Wood is gone and the English forbid us of geting any, where there is Some in their Claim—and if our Hogs happen to root a little the English will make us pay Damages, and they freequently Count our Cattle and Hogs, —Thus we are Usd by our English Neighbours—Pray most Noble Gentlemen Consider our Miserable Case and for God's Sake help us; For we have no where to go now, but to your Excellence for help; If we had but 150 head of Cattle and some [Sheep?] and a few more Hogs we Shoud be Contented and thankful

---

36. These restrictions on swine and cattle keeping reflect the terms of the 1703 agreements. A law passed in 1712 restricted the tribe to only three dogs (Ales, *History of the Indians*, 52). Historical records show that on at least two recorded occasions—in 1727 and 1742—colonial trustees sent agents to kill all dogs at Montauk except the permitted three (Strong, *Montaukett Indians*, 73).

This is all we have to Say at this Time, and Shall now wait to See your Pleasure Concerning Us—

## "This Indian World"

### A Petition/Origin Story from Samson Occom and the Montaukett Tribe

JOANNA BROOKS

When Samson Occom, a Mohegan, first came to Montauk in 1749 as a missionary and schoolteacher, he helped to renew traditional kinship, social, linguistic, and economic networks critical to the welfare of the Montauk, Mohegan, Niantic, Tunxis, Shinnecock, and Groton Indian communities of the Long Island Sound. In 1751 Occom married Mary Fowler, the daughter of Betty Pharaoh Fowler (Montaukett), a member of the powerful Pharaoh family and a descendant of the seventeenth-century sachem Wyendanche and James Fowler (Shinnecock). Their union openly defied colonial policies established in 1719, which prohibited "stranger Indians" from marrying into the Montauk community.[37] It also accorded Occom a place of political prominence in the community, which he acknowledged by learning traditional Montaukett lifeways, including herbal medicine.[38] Occom maintained close ties with the traditional Montauk community, even after many Christian Montauketts, including Occom's brothers-in-law David and Jacob Fowler, moved to upstate New York to join the intertribal Brotherton settlement in the 1770s and 1780s. Occom and the Montaukett Tribe of Long Island composed the petition to the governor of New York together, probably when Occom visited Montauk in April 1788.[39] This document shows how Occom used his literacy to help the Montauketts craft a political statement grounded in their understanding

---

37. Ales, "History of the Indians," 52; Strong, "How the Montauk Lost their Land," 91; Strong, *Montaukett Indians*, 70–71.

38. An autobiographical narrative written by Occom in 1768 notes that he and Mary Fowler Occom lived among the Montauketts in a traditional wigwam and that he served as a tribal scribe and judge, maintained his family by fishing and planting his own crops, and studied traditional lifeways, including herbal medicine, which he learned from a Montaukett man named Ocus. See Occom's "Autobiographical Narrative, Second Draft [17 September 1768]," reprinted in J. Brooks, *Collected Writings of Samson Occom*, 52–58, and Rabito-Wyppensenwah and Abiuso, "Montaukett Use of Herbs."

39. See the entries for 14–18 April 1788 in the Samson Occom diary (reprinted in J. Brooks, *Collected Writings of Samson Occom*, 396–97).

of the world, the land, proper ways of being, and the rights and responsibilities of indigenous people. Together, Occom and the Montaukett Tribe adopted the written form to tell an origin story asserting Montaukett sovereignty.

From the seventeenth century on, English colonists usurped Montaukett territorial meadowlands and beaches on eastern Long Island, threatening the survival of the Montaukett people and heavily impacting traditional agricultural and aquacultural practices, including fishing, whale harvesting, game hunting, grass and fruit gathering, and planting. A century of English encroachment culminated in 1703 with controversial agreements that affirmed that the colony held exclusive legal title to traditional Montaukett lands and established strict regulations for Montaukett land use, requiring Montauketts to fence in their landholdings, permitting English livestock to graze Montaukett planting fields, capping Montaukett livestock holdings at 250 hogs and 50 head of cattle or horses, and requiring the Montauketts to establish permanent residences at one of two sites—North Neck or Indian Fields—rather than migrate seasonally as was their custom.[40]

In their quest to obtain desirable Montaukett lands, English colonists took advantage of intertribal political intrigues, socioeconomic pressures, and the illiteracy of seventeenth-century Montaukett tribal leaders. They sought to entrap the Montauketts financially by levying heavy fines on the tribe when individual members violated colonial rules, and colonial agents provided alcohol for treaty negotiations and signings. Colonists also strategically manipulated sharp differences between Native American and English concepts of land rights. Montaukett people understood (and still understand) themselves to be originally, intimately, and ineradicably connected to their Long Island territory; to their minds, land was not something to be owned, bought, partitioned into individual plots, or sold. Tribal leaders may well have viewed their early land agreements with English settlers not as outright land sales that terminated Native land rights but as leases that granted the English rights of access and use.[41] Moreover, according to a Native worldview in which gift giving confirmed relationships of power and status, the Montauketts may have viewed the act of granting the English permission to use the land as a confirmation of their own authority and sovereignty. Conversely, the rather small sums of money and trade goods offered by the English in these land agreements were probably understood by the Montauketts not as the price of purchase but as a tribute or gratuity.[42]

---

40. "Agreement between the Trustees and the Indians," 69; Strong, *Montaukett Indians*, 57–58.
41. Strong, *Montaukett Indians*, 16.
42. On contrasting colonist and Native views of land, see Cronon, *Changes in the Land*, 54–81.

Eighteenth-century leaders of the Mohegans, the Montauketts, and other tribes used petitions to voice their grief over the loss of traditional lands and to reassert their territorial rights. Their adoption of the petition form marks not only a new level of English-language literacy in Native communities but also a widening perspective on the extensive damage wrought by English colonization. In a compelling study of petitions by such Mohegan leaders as Oweneco, Mahomet, Samson Occom, Samuel Ashpo, and Henry Quaqua-quid, Abenaki scholar Lisa Brooks observes the importance of the petition as an early Native American literary form. She writes, "The petition presents the communal remembrance of a world in which balance was the aim, even if not always achieved, a world which had systems in operation for dealing with scar-city, conflict, and individual desire, in striking contrast with the community's experience of the world they inhabit now, a 'time' within native space marked by seemingly insurmountable imbalance."[43] Mired in protracted court battles and colonial power struggles, Native American leaders used petitions to assert their authority and interject their own voices, perspectives, and beliefs into an often unfair and imbalanced legal process. In this way, Lisa Brooks suggests, early Native petitions effect "a translation of the unique nature of indigenous land tenure within the discursive territory of English property law."[44]

In 1764 Montaukett leader Cyrus (or Silas) Charles signed his mark to a petition that alleged that Long Island colonists had negotiated Montauk land agreements in bad faith. The petition asserted that since the Montauketts had become "not only civilized, but christianized" and "willing to behave as good subjects to his majesty King George the third," the colony should honor their property rights as British subjects.[45] The petition co-crafted by Occom and the Montauketts in 1788 adopts a dramatically different political strategy, forcefully asserting the rights of the tribe not as "civilized," "christianized" British subjects but as indigenous people who had inhabited Long Island since the beginning of time. This is an important, fundamental shift in argumentation, one that rhe-torically resituates the contest over Long Island land and resources in Native terms and on Native grounds. Occom and the Montauketts use the petition as a venue for a collective tribal voice and for the telling of tribal narratives.

To this end, the petition is written from the standpoint of the collective "we." Earlier petitions at Montauk had been written in the deferential third person. For example, the 1764 statement by Cyrus Charles represented the claims of "your Petitioner and his Associates." By speaking from a collective

43. "The Common Pot," 107.
44. Ibid., 123.
45. Petition of the Montauk Indians, 70.

first-person "we" rather than an indirect third-person "your Petitioner," the Occom–Montaukett petition asserts the legal subjectivity of the tribe as a united whole. The collective legal standing of the tribe as a self-determining body is an important tenet of Native American land tenure and Native American sovereignty.

By crafting the petition in the first-person "we," Occom also subsumed his individual authorship within the collective authority of the tribe. This indicates that English-language-literate American Indians such as Occom historically viewed their literacy as a tool in the service of American Indian communities. Occom first sought to become English-language literate after his appointment as a tribal counselor to sachem Ben Uncas II in 1742; when he began to study with the Reverend Eleazar Wheelock in 1743, the Mohegan Tribe was embroiled in a bitter land dispute (known as the Mason Case) with the colony of Connecticut.[46] After witnessing some of the proceedings and the disappointing 1773 conclusion of the Mason Case in favor of the colony, Occom bitterly criticized radical assymmetries of power between colonists and Indians: "I am afraid the poor Indians will never stand a good chance with the English in their land controversies, because they are very poor, they have no money. Money is almighty now-a-days, and the Indians have no learning, no wit, no cunning: the English have it all."[47] Occom taught Native people at Montauk to read and write. In his *Sermon at the Execution of Moses Paul* (1772), Occom encouraged his Native audience members to exercise their "rational powers" in defense of their survival, and he used his own literacy to help the Montauk, Mohegan, and Brotherton Indians and other tribal groups press their claims on the government.[48] In these petitions especially, he did not assert his own standing or reputation among whites as a celebrated Native American preacher; rather, he used his position of authority as a voice for the collective, including the Montauketts who chose not to migrate to Brotherton. This petition thus presents an early example of what Jace Weaver (Cherokee) has identified as an ethic of "communitism"—a "sense of community and commitment to it"—which defines Native American literature.[49]

Occom and the Montauketts designed this petition to change the balance of power in land disputes between the tribe and the colonists through an act

46. On the Mason Case, see Conroy, "Defense of Indian Land Rights;" St. Jean, "Inventing Guardianship;" and L. Murray, *To Do Good*, 33–39.

47. "To Samuel Buell," 1773, reprinted in J. Brooks, *Collected Writings of Samson Occom*.

48. See "Sermon, Preached at the Execution of Moses Paul" and "Brotherton Tribe to United States Congress," [1785?], reprinted in J. Brooks, ed., *Collected Writings*, 176–95 and 148–50, respectively.

49. Weaver, *That the People Might Live*, 43.

of storytelling: narrating the history of Long Island from a Montaukett point of view. "The Great and good Spirit above," begins the narrative, "Saw fit in his good pleasure, to plant our Fore-Fathers in this great Wilderness but when and how, none knows but himself.—and he that works all things Acording to his own Mind, Saw it good to give us this great Continent." The petition describes American Indians as having been "planted" by God from time immemorial in "this great Continent"; the language of "planting" asserts Native peoples' natural preeminence on the land. It also uses a theological language that reflects both the influence of Christianity on Native northeastern communities and the ways in which Native people used the Christian religion for their own purposes. In this case, Occom and the Montauketts use the doctrine of the sovereignty of God to bolster the sovereignty of the tribe. Note, especially, the description of God as an all-powerful being who "works all things Acording to his own Mind." Prominent eighteenth-century theologians such as Jonathan Edwards believed that the mind of God directed human history. Occom, who knew Edwards's writings,[50] argues that God first intended this land for Native peoples. According to the doctrine of divine sovereignty, God also allowed for suffering to enter the world. This is how the petition portrays the coming of the English, as an event permitted by a God who "maketh Rich, and maketh poor, he that kills, and that maketh alive, he that raiseth up whom he will, and pulleth down whom he will."

The petition remembers how Native people understood and inhabited the land before colonization. America was an "Indian world," a "Boundless Continent," "well furnished with Natural Provisions": "a Prodigious Number of four footed Beasts, Fowl without number and Fish of all kinds great and Small, fill'd our Seas, Rivers, Brooks, and Ponds every where." Occom and the Montauketts emphasize the superabundance of their environment, the numberless variety and quantity of its flora and fauna. Amid this natural bounty, indigenous people lived, according to an ethic of balanced existence, a life of humble subsistence: They "Imagin'd, they Shoud allways live by Hunting Fishing and Fowling, and gathering Wild Fruits." The description of America as "Boundless Continent" is a trope coined by Occom to invoke a Native sense of geography.[51] Native Americans of the Northeast occupied traditional territories defined by geo-

---

50. Occom owned a copy of Jonathan Edwards's *A Careful and Strict Enquiry into the Modern Prevailing Notions of that Freedom of the Will* (1754), which is now housed at the East Hampton Public Library.

51. For instances of this trope, see Occom's "To John Bailey," [June or July] 1783; "Brotherton Tribe to United States Congress," [1785?]; and "'To All the Indians in this Boundless Continent' (1784)," reprinted in J. Brooks, *Collected Writings of Samson Occom*, 118–20, 148–50, and 196–97, respectively.

graphical and ecological features and by tribal histories and sacred stories. In contrast, the English viewed land as empty, homogenous space to be organized into individually owned, fenced plots. This petition remembers the land from a tribal perspective as "Boundless" and forever Indian, despite English efforts to erect boundaries against Native land use by engineering legal agreements and building fences. The petition belongs to what Lisa Brooks has identified as a colonial Native New England tradition of using literature to re-create a Native sense of space.

English colonization is represented as introducing a destructive spirit of greed, want, and guile into the people's relationship with the land. Occom and the Montauketts openly accuse the English of negotiating in bad faith. "Some [land] they bought almost for nothing," they state, "and we suppose they took a great deal without Purchace." Citing the terms of the controversial agreement of 1703, which stripped the Montauketts of crucial land rights, the petition demands:

> Take good Notice, dont this discover a profound Ignorance in our fore Fathers, indeed we Suspect, Some Times, that what little understanding they had was Drowned with hott Waters before they made these Shameful agreements, and on the other hand, don't this Show, that the English took advantage of the Ignorance of our Fore Fathers. Woud they be Willing to be Servd so by us? Were we Ca[p]abale to use them So?

This passage demonstrates that the Montauketts recognized the English exploitation of both traditional assumptions about the nature of land rights and their ancestors' individual weaknesses. "Thus we are Usd by our English Neighbours," Occom and the Montauketts protest, indicting the English failure to live up to the biblical maxim to "love thy neighbor as thyself." Advantage taking, imbalance, and hypocrisy rather than fairness, reciprocity, and honor characterize the English quest for land.

The dishonorable conduct of the English constricts the natural plenty of the land, according to the Montauketts. Compare the description of the original "Boundless" nature of America as an "Indian World" and the animal and plant life "without number" to the Montaukett account of their current "Stinted" circumstances: "We . . . have only two Small necks of Land to plant on, and we are not allowd to Sow Wheate, and we as a Tribe are Stinted to keep only 50 Head of Cattle, and 200 Swine and three Dogs." Any transgression of these rules would result in the punishment of the entire tribe with fines, thus plunging the Montaukett community into perpetual indebtedness. These already difficult legal circumstances are compounded by the greed of individual English colonists. "All our Hunting, Fowling, and Fishing is now almost gone and our Wild Fruit is gone," the tribe protests. "What little there is left the English would Ingross or take all to themselves." Colonization creates unnatural conditions of scarcity that threaten Montaukett survival.

At times, the petition presents Occom and the Montauketts in what appears to be a posture of supplication. The tribe appeals to the "Condescention" of the New York government and regrets the "profound Ignorance" of its "fore Fathers." It is undeniable that Occom and Montaukett tribal members absorbed the rhetoric of colonial agents and missionaries who repeatedly charged Native communities with being backward, degenerate, and incapable of self-governance. It is also possible to read the apparently humble tone of this petition as a strategic appeal to Euro-American rhetorical customs or as a manipulation of the trope of the poor Indian, which was a mainstay of Anglo-American colonial discourse. As scholars David Murray, Jace Weaver (Cherokee), and Lisa Brooks (Abenaki) observe, early Native American authors such as Occom sometimes adopted and redirected the trope of the poor Indian to deliver sharp criticisms of the colonial regimes that created conditions of poverty for Native peoples.[52]

This petition is most powerful not as an appeal to the New York government for pity but as an act of storytelling. It uses a traditional Euro-American rhetorical form to present a collective, tribe-centered narrative that asserts that this land belonged first to American Indians, that colonists have entrapped Native peoples and dishonestly taken Native lands, and that this has resulted in conditions of scarcity in this once abundantly fruitful place. Weaver writes, "Storytelling. At base that is what American Indian authors and poets are doing—storytelling."[53] As so many contemporary Native American authors— from Leslie Marmon Silko (Laguna Pueblo) to Thomas King (Cherokee)— teach us, stories have the power to enact new realities, create communities, and effect new power relationships.[54] They often function in Native American communities to help listeners remember their responsibilities to the land and the community or to help them learn proper conduct. Although the story of how the first peoples of the Americas were invaded by European colonists and impacted by imperialist greed may now seem familiar to some contemporary audiences, it is important to remember how very rarely such criticisms of colonization found public expression in the eighteenth century. Through this

---

52. Weaver, *That the People Might Live*, 51; D. Murray, *Forked Tongues*, 53, and *Indian Giving*, 27–29; L. Brooks, *The Common Pot*, 213–14.

53. Weaver, *That the People Might Live*, 3.

54. See especially Silko, "Language and Literature," and T. King, *Truth about Stories*.

petition—a written vehicle for an oral tradition—Occom and the Montauketts asserted themselves, their perspective, and their story into the public record. In so doing, the Montauketts remember and remind Anglo-American colonists of Native peoples' ineradicable rights to the land.

# A Short narration of my last Journey
## to the western Contry

### Hendrick Aupaumut

Aupaumut's *Short Narration* exists in both a manuscript and a printed format. The manuscript, which is 6.5 inches by 8.25 inches, is bound in a burgundy morocco cover. The end papers appear to be old legal documents; one of them may be an indenture. The title page, written in a different hand, identifies the manuscript as "Journal of a Mission to the Western Tribes of Indians by Hendrick Aupaumut 1791." Authenticating documents from Timothy Pickering are bound at the head of the volume. Aupaumut numbered his pages from 1 to 102. (Page numbers of the selections printed here are those of the first printed version of the text.) He titled his text *A Short narration of my last Journey to the western Contry.* The handwriting is generally legible. The ink has faded to brown, and there is considerable spotting, crossing out, and interlineation of words in what appears to be Aupaumut's hand. Aupaumut divided the *Short Narration* into sections by drawing lines across the page. The speeches that he includes are readily identifiable through the textual features that he employs, particularly the manner in which he indicates the addresses (e.g., "Grandfathers attend—") and aligns his text along the right margin when wampum is delivered. On page 85, Aupaumut inserts the text of the "Message to the U.S. delivered by Mkhequeh Posees, or Big Cat, Sachem of Wenaumie or Delaware," which is a separate document. It is preceded by a rough map of the encampments along the river (probably the Maumee River) where the negotiations took place. Aupaumut signed his manuscript with an elaborate flourish.

The printed narrative as edited by Dr. Benjamin H. Coates appears as "A Narrative of an Embassy to the Western Indians, from the Original Manuscript of Hendrick Aupaumut" in *Memoirs of the Historical Society of Pennsylvania,* vol. 2 (Philadelphia, 1827). Coates includes authenticating prefatory remarks along with those of Pickering. The transcription is fairly accurate, apart from Coates's more standardized capitalization and punctuation. One major exception is Coates's decision to excise the discussion of poison in Selection 6.

## Selection 1 (pages 76–77)

[*Aupaumut opens his narrative with an account of his reasons for accepting the commission from the Washington administration.*]

Having agreed with the great men of the United States, to take a tour, with their Message of peace to the hostile nations—which enterprise some of the principal Chiefs of the five Nations did oppose—Alledged that it would be folly for the United States to send me on that Business—(says they,) Western Nations will not regard the voice of one Nation but the business ought to be negotiated by the five Nations & the british. But on my part, I have hitherto had a persuasion on my mind that if the western nations could be rightly informed of the desires of the United States, they would comply for peace and that the informer should be an Indian to whom they look upon as a true friend, who has never deceived or injuried them.

When I come to reflect in the path of my ancestors, the friendship & connections they have had with these Western Tribes, and my own feellings towards them, I conclude that I could acquaint them my best knowledge with regard of the dispositions, desires, and might of the United States, without partiallity—and without groundless opinion I could be more useful in that particular Embassage than those who have been opposing my undertaking, &c.

Before I proceed in the business I am upon, I think it would be necessary to give a short sketch what friendship and connections our forefathers & we have had with the western Tribes.

The Delawares, who we calld Wenaumeew, are our Grand Fathers according to the ancient Covenant of their & our Ancestors, to which we adhere without any devition in these near 200 years past, to which Nation the five Nations & British, (after finding themselves incapaple of completeing a Union of all who has one colar,) have commit the Whole business. For this Nation had the greatest influence with the Southern, Western, and Northern nations.

The Shawannese, who we calld Weshauwonnoow, are our Younger brothers, according to ancient Covenant between our forefathers—For our ancestors, near 200 years ago rescued them from the mouth of many nations, as well as of the five nations who were ready to swallow my younger brother Shawany, for which kind deliverance they ever have felt themselves under the greatest obligation to obey our voice—and many nations had knowledge of this.

✦   ✦   ✦

*[Aupaumut identifies several other tribes with whom the Mahicans had historic ties, including the Miamies, the Monthees, the Wyondots, the Ottawas, and the Chepawas (Chippewas).]*

It was the business of our fathers to go around the Towns of these nations to renew the agreements between them, and tell them many things which they discover among the White people in the east, &c

## Selection 2 (pages 87–89)

*[Aupaumut describes his first meeting with the grand council of western nations on the Miami River after his arrival there on 14 July. Here he exchanges speeches with the Delaware sachem Tautpuhqtheet, following the Iroquois condolence ritual.]*

Accordingly they came in our Camp. Then the Sachem Named Tautpuhqtheet begin to speak to us, on the following words.

My grandchildren, attend—

Here we meet together—the great good Spirit has thought & have fixed this day that we should meet together.

Grandchildren—

You have come from great way off to see and visit us—You have seen many dismal objects for which your tears droping down. Our good ancestors did hand down to us a rule or path where we may walk. According to that rule I now wipe off your tears from your Eyes & face that you may see clear. And since there has been so much wind on the way that the dust and every evil thing did fill your Ears, I now put my hand & take away the dust from your Ears, that you may hear plain—And also the heavy burden on your mind I now remove, that you may feel easy, and that you may contemplate some Objects without burden.

Grandchildren—Here you find your poor Grandfather which has met with many difficulties—Yet I am rejoiced to see you. You have waded thro many miry places & Briers on your Journey. I now wash your legs & wipe them clean, and I pull all briers which stick on your legs & feet—and then I take the nicest weesqui, which contains the pure oil, and put the same on your legs and feet that you may feel Easy.

This all I have to say—four white strings of wampom 3 feet long deliverd.

Then they arose & shake our hands, to confirm their friendship to us.

Few minutes after this—

Then I rehears his speech and then deliver a congratulatory speech as answer, to manifest my friendship to them as they did to us, on the following words.

Grandfather, Attend—I am happy to reflect how that the great good Spirit has so ordered that our forefathers have found the way to maintain such friendship between them—and that we met each this day, and that on your part you have manifested your kindness to us.

Grandfather—Here we meet together in a dismal State, and you have put a great comfort on my mind, for which I heartily thank you.

Grandfather—

As I come to you, when I beheld your face, I saw your tears flowing down, for the reason of much difficulties and crosses. I now put my hand on your face and wipe off your tears, so that you may see things clear, and that to a great distance.

Grandfather—

Since there is so much wind, and much dust flying about, your Ears are Stop'd, you are almost deaf. But I now stretch my hand and take away all the dust from your ears, that you may now hear. And I also put my hand and clean your throat, and take away all heavy burdens which hangs on your mind, and cast it away, that you may now understand what is good for your Children, and that you may have comfort.

Grandfather—

When I beheld your Garments, I saw blood by reason of war, which I now wipe away. Also your beds, I clean them that you may set with ease.

Six white strings of wampom delivered.

After this, the Sachem heartily thanked us. Then says he, I should be glad to hear some news from the east. And then I informd him that my nation live in peace—and that the great men of the United States wished to live in peace with all Indians—and that there is some wars among the great people over the great waters—and that Negroes also have cut off many of their masters—which the Indians glad to hear—and I tell them that I would inform them further, as soon as they can all meet together.

## Selection 3 (pages 92–95)

[Here Aupaumut turned to the main purpose of his mission: delivering the message of the Washington administration. He first explained the history of his mission.]

I then faithfully deliver the Message of the United States. In the first place I begin with an introductory speech, on the follow words.

My friends—

In order to have you to understand our business, I will acquaint you some things of our situation, lest you may have wrong apprehension. Since the British & Amaricans lay down their hatchets, then my Nation was forgotten. We never have had invitation to set in Council with the white people—not as the 5 Five Nations & you are greatly regarded by the white people but last winter was the first time I had invitation from the great man of the United States to attend Council in Philladelphia. According to that invitation I went—and after we arrived at Philadelphia, I find that the business was for the wellfare of all nations—and then I was asked whether I would carry a Message of peace to you here. I then reply that I would—for I know that it would look unfriendly to you, had I refuse to bring good Tidings, and so for the sake of our good friendship, and for peace I was willing to take this long Journey, &c.

Then I begin with the Message, and take up the Seven Strings of Wampom, on the following words.

Sachems and Head Warriors of Delawares, and the whole of the Confederate Nations.

Brothers attend—

We the 15 Sachems of the United States will now in one voice speak to you—we speak from our hearts—where there is a burden of sorrow.

It is very uncertain thing how our voice of peace may reach your ears—It has been feared that our word of peace has not reached your ears, but has fallen & been burried under ground, or gone into the air by means of malignant birds.

Brothers—

We the 15 sachems, do now send our Message of peace, by your own colar, & friend of Muhheaconnuk who we trust will faithfully delivered to you, and will impartially acquaint you, according to his best knowledge with regard to the dispositions of the United States—

Brothers—

You the sachems of the whole confederacy will not regard the voice of flying birds—be it known to you, that we the 15 Sachems have never believed such, although we have seen & heard Various kinds, which have had different heads—

And further you the Sachems of the confederacy have never consultd together and agreed with an intend of speaking to some other nation deceitfully—brothers, be assured that the 15 United Sachems have never done such, for we scorn to speak from the lips only.

> Seven strings of white and purple wampom delivered, near 4 feet long.

Then I take up the belt & begin with these words—

Brothers of the while [whole] Confederacy—

We have informed you that we speak from our hearts & in sorrow—because there are difficulties subsisting between you and the big knifes—

Brothers—be it known to you all, that we the 15 Sachems have no desire to quarrel with you—but on the contrary we sincerely wish to have lasting peace established.

Brothers—

We have tender effections for our Children, women, young men and old parents. We wish to promote their happiness. You likewise brothers, have great regard for your children, women, young men, and old parents—you wish them many good mornings and evenings—in this we are alike.

Brothers—

We, the United Sachems, now Stretch our hand to reach your hand and lead you at the first place, Fort Jefferson, where you will meet one of our great man, that you there may agree where you will chose to have a treaty on Ohio—where we may use our utmost endeavours to establish happiness for our Children.

Brothers—

As we have not believed the various reports of many birds, we still look to you—when you speak to us we will attend. If the Big Knifes have done any injuries to you, you must manifest it to us. Or if our servants have wrongd you in any matter, or have defraud you with regard to your Lands, you must inform us the same. Then we shall endeavour to remove these burdens from your minds that you may rejoice.

Brothers—

Had we not used means to remove all difficulties so as to put an end to the war, the great Nations over the great waters would find fault with us. You likewise brothers, if you do not regard or comply with what we now offer to you. The great Nations, who resides behind you, will afterwards blame you.

Brothers—

As soon as you comply with terms of peace the forts which stands on your Lands shall fall—and if you are disirous for peace you must instandly call in all your war parties. With respect to the big knifes, they are not to be compared to our least fingure [finger]. We will hold them fast, and they shall not stir untill we let them lose.

Brothers—

We have now speaken so much to you—we will stop—and listen—when after all patience, we could not hear a word from you—Then we thought or conclude the reports of many Birds are certainly true.

> A large belt of wampom delivered, which contains 15 rows, and in the middle there is 15 square marks, which denote 15 United

sachems, and path of peace goes thro the marks—the belt is purely white, except the marks and the path—near 4 feet long.

Then I say—Grandfathers & all friends—

I have deliverd you a great Message in your hands, and you must exert yourselves, and consider it seriously—and do remember our children, women, young men, and old people, and take the wisest part; and as I am here with you, I will endeavour to assist you as far as I can.

Then Hobakon, or Pipe-Sachem of Delawares, speak to us, & said Grand-children—You have brought to us a great good Message from the great people, for which we heartily thank you—and you may rest assured that we will exert ourselves to promote peace, and tomorrow you shall hear us again—we will consult among ourselves today & tomorrow, &c.

## [Selection 4 (pages 98–101)

[*On 2 August, Aupaumut met with the Delaware chief Big Cat, hoping to win his support for the negotiations, which were threatened by reports of encroachments by the Big Knifes.*]

Early in the morning of the 2ⁿᵈ inst. my Uncle sent a runner to inform the Chiefs that we were arrived and will meet them in Council. My business was to comfort Big Cat for the Death of his Brother who died last Spring; he was the Chief Sachem of the Delawares; also Pukonchehluh for the Death of his Son. According to the ancient Custom in such cases, long as they are not comforted they are not to Speak in Public and this Ceremonie of comforting each other is highly esteemed among these Nations.

Then we met them in council after drawing the smoak thro our nostrils. Then I got up & begin on the following words: —

Grand Father attend—

It is by the goodness of the great good Spirit we are meet together—so many of us the remnant of our ancesstors, to smoak our pipes & to put each other in mind of our ancient friendship. We are in a dismal State; we can only pity each other, at the same time we can rejoice to see each other. I have met with some difficulties on the way; one of my Counsellors is taken sick, who I left at the forks with the other two of my Companions.

I am not waiting the motions of other nations in doing the business, which I will perform this time.

Grandfather—

We the poor remnant of our ancestors are met together. Our good fathers have left good Customs, & path to go by. So that in all occasions we are to put each other in remembrance of the ancient Customs of our fathers as well as the friendship.

Grandfather—

Here you have meet with many troubles; in this we are all alike.

Grandfather—

You have meet great losses; your great Sachem is fallen, and also some of your principal young men. The sound of which stopd your Eyes & Ears; your tears flowing down, and that continually; and for which reason you could not look up.

Grandfather—

Having seen you in such a situation, I without delay arise & come, and now put my hand to your face & wipe off your tears and open your Eyes, so that you may now see the sun when it rises, also when it sets down, and also other things, and that you could see your Grand Children in a Clear Light; also I clean your Ears, that you may hear distinctly. And I clean your throat also, and losen your Tongue that you may now speak and that freely. And there is such a weight of Sorrow causes your heart to hang upside down, but I now remove these burdens, and set your heart aright, that you may contemplate the welfare of your Children, and that with pleasure.

Six strings of white wampom delivered.

Grand Father—

Many troubles has attended us. You have lost your great Sachem; also some honourable young men, who have fallen, and lay under the Earth ever since last Spring. I now remember what our good ancestors used to teach us their Children. And I now gather the bones of these deceased, and put them together, and take up the lasting Plank and put it over the Graves, that the heat of the Sun may not penetrated and that the rain may not flow into them.

(Nunneh *this is all.*) A belt delivrd, contains 10 rows, has three marks across, near three feet long.

This nation had delivered speach to my nation twice before—as a query whether my nation would accept the plan of Union. At this time I deliverd an answer.

Grandfather, once more attend—

As you have always paid great regard to our friendship—You have spoken to me with regard of Union, whether I would take hold of it—with respect to this, my Grandfather, I now speak to you.

It is a happy thing that we should maintain a Union. But to us it is not a new thing. For our good Ancestors (who used to have compassion to each other) many, many years ago, have agreed to this. And we who are of their desendance should not hisitate, or as it were ask one another, whether we should like it. But we must always remind each other how our Ancestors did agree on this Subject, that we may never forgo that.

## Selection 5 (pages 111–113)

[*Aupaumut's opponents in the negotiations included the anti-American border warrior Simon Girty, the British officer Colonel Alexander McKee, Mohawk leader Joseph Brant, and Brant's nephew Tawalooth. They or their messengers began arriving at the Forks encampment in late August and soon crystalized the emergent opposition to Aupaumut's diplomacy.*]

On the 12th of September a Message of Colonel M'Kee brought at the forks, which he sent by his Son and Nephew from the rapids, was interpreted in the language of Shawanny. The Substance of it is this.

My friends who resides at the forks attend—You seem to begin to be weary of doing your business. But I now exhort you to consider seriously what is best for you & your children.

My friends I now gave you a caution—there is Muhheconneew [i.e., Aupaumut] talking continually among you at the forks. Do not mind what he says, for he is sent by the Big knifes. If you do believe him, then you will be a miserable people, for then you will forfeit every thing—if the Muhheconneew had business other than from the big knifes, we could have heard it &c.

My friends—

I am coming, I shall now assist you, as I have promised three years ago. I did say at that time, that whatever the great [British] King directed that I will do; now I have received his orders, every thing is ready for you, Guns and Amunition, & Cloathing, that you may stand strong against your enemies.

Then I said to my friends, that I could convince M'Kee that I have a Lawful Business with you here—which his Masters will not forbid.

On the 13th Brant's messengers arrived, 11 in number. The Head of them called Tawalooth.

On the 14th inst. This Tawalooth Brant's nephew, and now Messenger, deliverd a Speech in a council. He informd the Shawannese & others that he is now come with ten men to assist these nations in war &c.

Then he delivered Brants Message to these Nations.

The substance of it is this. My friends of the whole Confederate nations, who has one colar, attend—

I now send my voice to you, to let you know that I have wonderfully got thro from here to Congress & back again. I am much concernd for you but am lame & could not go at present—But will go & see you as soon as may be. My friends—

I now tell you do not believe what Message the Muhheconneew brought to you, neither believe what he says, if you do you will be greatly deceived. I have myself seen Washington, and see his heart and bowels; and he declared that he claims from the mouth of Miamie to the head of it—thence to the head of Wabash river, and down the same to the mouth of it; and that he did take up dust, and did declare that he would not restore so much dust to the Indians, but he is willing to have peace with the Indians, &c.

Previous to this M'Kee had informed the Indians that he received a letter from Captain Brant. In this letter says M'Kee, Brant enquird of me, whether it is safe for him to come among you. Then I sent answer to let him know that it was my opinion there is no danger.

Brant as it were felt guilty for going alone to Congress, Contrary to what he recommended to those nations, that no individual nation or person should go to speak to the Big knifes, that if any do this they or he must be abandoned.

This Tawalooth could speak the Shawany Tongue, also some other Languages, and he told many lies against us. Among other things he told the Indians that Muhheconneew have sent letters to the Big knifes, to inform them that they have gained the attention of so many Nations—that the Big knifes may now come & fall upon these Indians unexpectedly. This he told to frustrate peace, and that we may be hated or killed. He is a proper Liar or Emmissary of the Devil. He did hurt the feelings of many Indians, and greatly hurt the Message of the U.S. (by delivering his uncle's Message) & by his own artful lies.

## Selection 6 (pages 122–25)

[*After Aupaumut's mission failed, Big Cat and other Delaware leaders sympathetic to his diplomatic effort asked Aupaumut to write a speech explaining the outcome.*]

My friends who are for peace, have sometime ago declared that if treaty could not take place this fall yet they will send their voice to the U.S. that the U.S. may know what were the obsticles in the path of peace.

On the 18th inst. Big Cat & some of his heroes came to us by order of the Council, to desire me to write their speech to the U.S. Then the Sachem begins on the following words. Although we well know that Shawannese & Wyondots do not speak from the heart to the 5 Nation respecting a treaty next spring, yet we who are for peace will bring them to it, &c.

Then he begin to deliver their Message to the U.S. which I have put in other paper, &c.

The Substance of a Message to the U.S. delivered by Mkhequeh Posees, or Big Cat, Sachem of Wenaumie or Delaware.[55]

Brothers attend—

We speak to you, and to acquaint you that your good Message was deliverd to us last summer by our friends of Muhheconnuk, and also to acquaint you what were the reasons that we could not meet your great man.

You may remember that you have some people among you who have and will oppose the work of peace. We likewise unavoidably have such. In your Message you have told us that you have some doubts with regard of your Messengers of peace, whether they reachd to us, that we may hear your Voice of peace.

Brothers—

You have a reason to Doubt, for we have among us, foolish & obstinate young men—of such went out early last Spring to hunt, and come cross your Messengers, and have killed them; it was not out of our desire nor Custom to kill such—

Brothers—

When we heard your Message of peace, it gladen our hearts and did take a hold of it immediately; then we exhort our Sachems to forwarded to the Wyondots first & to the greater Nations, (to wit) the Ottawas, Chepawas, and Potawatommees, who we knew would glad to hear such Message, & would readily accepted; our intention was this, that the Message should go around to these greater nations, and that it will come to us with these nations (at the forks). Then we was to repeat & declare that we have received such Message and did taken hold of it (that is, we so many nations comply with it.) Then the Shawannese would Oblige to Submit. Then we was to send an escort to fort Jefferson to make our conclusions known.

Our Sachems without any delay did forward the Message to the above mentioned nations and they the Wyondots sent runners to invite the Sachems & Head warriors of Ottawas, Chepawas, & Potawatommees to meet such a place, at the same time gave them notice that they have received such a Message of the U.S. for which they must meet together. According to this invitation, the Sachems of these nations meet in council for the good Message. But before they come to conclusion, an alarming voice reachd their ears that the Big knifes come on their way to fight against the nations, and have killed three of the

---

55. The text of the message that follows is in a separate document that Aupaumut incorporated into his *Short Narration*.

Delawares who went to see whether it was true that the big knifes are come. Brothers this terrible voice was the first reason or obsticle for which the war party have occasion to oppose the work of peace, and for which the Sachems & Head warriors of the four nations cover the Belt in a blanket.

Brothers—

The second reason is this that before we could remove the first obsticle the voice of the 5 Nations reached our ears and did not speak agreeable to your good Message, which Strengthen the arguments of the enticers to war.

Brothers—

The third reason is this, that immediately after the second reason, the Message of Brant reachd to our ears by his Nephew. A Prohibitory & Cautionary Message that the Confederacy should not listen nor believe what Message the Muhheconneew brought neither to what he say, for if you do believe you will be greatly deceived. And further says he, I have seen the great men of the U.S. they speak good words to Muhheconnuk but they did not speak so well to the 5 Nations, and they speak contrary to the Big knifes, that the big knifes may prepare for war & fall upon the Indians unawares; and the Presidend [sic] of the U.S. did declare that he claim from the mouth of Miamie River on Lake Erie to its head from thence to the head of Wabash river, and down the same to the mouth of it, and that he will by no means restored to the Indians.

Brothers—The fourth reason is, that by our spies we do understand that the Big knifes does truely preparing for war, and have strengthen the fort Jefferson.

Brothers—

The fifth reason is, that Col. M'Kee's son brought a letter from Detroit. That one of the Americans arrived there with an intelligence that the Big knifes have brought a Large quantity of Goods and Liquors in the forts, which they will send with the army, and that before they will come to battle against the Indians, they will put a Poison in the Goods & Liquors, and that after a little fight they will retreat and leave the Goods & Liquors, by which means many of the Indians will die.[56]

Brothers—

These are the principal reasons or obsticles which enrage the hostile party, and when we come to Debate their arguments are stand in force, and we could not convince them otherwise.

Brothers—

Now the matter is laid before you. If you discourage we will also discour-

---

56. The printed text of this paragraph omits the discussion of poisoning included in the manuscript.

aged. But if you will lengthen your patience, and manifest your power in withdrawing the Big knifes from the forts which stands on our Land—then repeat your Message of peace to us. Then we will arise immediately and exert ourselves to promote peace. Then we can assure the back nations that you have a power to govern the hostile big knifes, and that you mean to have peace. Then the back nations will never regard the voice of these hostile Nations here. Then the war party will be speechless.

## Selection 7 (pages 128–31)

*[Aupaumut's conclusion stresses his good-faith efforts to make peace between the western nations and the United States.]*

And here I will also mention the Substance of my Speech to these Nations, deliverd immediately after Brants Prohibitory & Cautionary Message deliverd. And after the Indians been informd by some Emmissaries, that I and my Companions were sent by the Big knifes to number the Indians, and was to return again with the information that the White people may Judge how many men will be sufficient to fall upon the Indians, &c.

I begin with these words—Grandfathers & brothers and friends attend—

As we have acquaint to each other many things, and as we have agreed that we would set together in council to manifest our sentiments to each other, I will now speak. We have heard various reports of many birds, for which occasion I will now speak. The Prohibitory Voice of the Mohawks has reachd your ears. That you should not believe the Message I deliver to you, nor to what I say, that I was to deceive you, &c.

My Grandfathers Brothers & friends—

Let us consider the meaning of this Brants Message—by the sound of it he point at me as a deceiver or roag [rogue], that every nation must be warned. But let us now look back in the path of our forefathers, and see whether you can find one single instance wherein, or how my ancestors or myself have deceived you, or led you one step astray. I say Let us look narrowly, to see whether you can find one Bone of yours lay on the ground, by means of my deceitfulness. And I now declare that you cannot found such instance. And further, you may reflect, and see wherein I have speak deceitfully since I come here, that Mohawks should have occasion to stop your Ears. But you look back and see heaps of your Bones, wherein the Mauquas have deceived you repeatedly. I think I could have good reason to tell you not to believe the Message or words of the Mohawks, for they will deceive you greatly as Usual. But I forbear.

Another information reached your ears, that I and my men were sent on purpose to number your nations &c. This also is a Dark Lye, for if you only consider whether I ever ask any of you how many warriors have you, you could easyly know whether I was sent on this Business.

My friends—I now tell you that the white people well knew your numbers not only your warriors, but your women & Children too. (How come they know you would say) because in every fall you gave your numbers to the whites therefore they knew it—now consider, and think whether there is any need on the part of the Whites to sent me to number your nations, &c.

Six strings of wampom delivered.

After this—then they talk among themselves, and then rehearse my speech and heartily thank me for the same.

And the Sachem of Delaware speak and said—

Grand Child—

It is true all what have said, we could not found any instance wherein your ancestors have deceived our fathers, and we cannot find any fault with your words since you meet us in this country &c. But on the other hand, our Uncles [the Mohawks] have injured us much these many years; and now after they divided, now they wanted to divide us also. And further, it is true we have gave our numbers to the English every year &c.

I have not mention Several Speeches with wampom delivered by these Indians to me while I was with them, and my last speech to Shawany &c. and many other affairs.

I have now occasion to say that I have been endeavouring to do my best in the business of peace and according to my best knowledge with regard of the desires of the United States, I have press in the minds of friends in the westward repeatedly.

But since I arrived at home I understand that my Character is darkend by envious Indians who stayed but few days in Miamie. But for my conduct I will appeal to the nations whom I had Business with last summer, that is if any of my Brothers should doubt of my faithfulness. But this one thing every wise men well knew, that to employ an enemy or half friend will never speak well, &c.

With regard to myself, I think it is easy matter to find out whether I was not faithful with the United States in the late war, and whether I have not been faithfull in the work of peace according to abilities in these near two years. I have as it were sacrifice all my own affairs, and my family, for the sake of peace, and this last time have gone from home better than Eleven months, and have gone thro a hazardous Journeys, and have sufferd with sickness & hunger, and have left my Counsellors with the nations who are for peace, to promote peace and forward every means of peace while I am absent—not only so But I have

been pleading and Justifying the Conduct of these people, for which they were well received at their arrival at Miamie. Notwithstand of all this, they brought my Name at Nought. The occasion of my speaking this sort, because of many evil and false reports sounded in the Ears of my friends—and I am ready to answer any thing that may be asked respecting to the different Tribes of Indians, &c.—
HENDRICK AUPAUMUT

# Historical Introduction to Hendrick Aupaumut's *Short Narration*

### SANDRA M. GUSTAFSON

During the 1790s[57] Hendrick Aupaumut participated in at least two U.S. diplomatic missions to the western Indian nations on the Ohio frontier, where he represented the Washington administration in its efforts to end the warfare that erupted with increasing frequency and violence in the region. These battles were typically sparked by the actions of the Big Knifes, the white settlers who violated official U.S. policy by unlawfully occupying Indian land. A crucial question arose among the Native people whose lands were being taken: Were the Big Knifes truly acting against George Washington's wishes? Or were they, as Joseph Brant implied, fulfilling a secret mandate from the U.S. president, carrying out a covert effort that directly undermined Washington's stated policy of limiting westward expansion and respecting Native claims to the western territories? It was this uncertainty that Aupaumut's mission was intended to address, and it was this uncertainty that led to his failure to establish a peaceful relationship between the western Indian nations and the U.S. government.

When Washington asked Aupaumut to negotiate on behalf of his administration in 1792, he may have hoped that by embracing the Native diplomatic traditions that the United States had previously spurned he would have better success at a peaceful settlement. The indigenous communities of the Northeast had developed diplomatic traditions with the British over the previous two

---

57. The dating of Aupaumut's *Short Narration* has been the source of some confusion. In his text, Aupaumut does not identify the year of his journey. Moreover, he appears to have conducted at least two missions to the western Indian nations. The manuscript text is entitled "Journal of a Mission to the Western Tribes of Indians by Hendrick Aupaumut 1791." On the basis of internal evidence and documentation found in *American State Papers* and confirmed by Hilary Wyss and others, I have identified the year of his journey as 1792 and date the *Short Narration* between 1792 and 1793.

centuries. British negotiating practices followed the forms of Native diplomacy, notably the use of the Iroquois Condolence Ritual as a central component of diplomatic oratory. At first the U.S. government, hoping to consolidate its power by imposing its own diplomatic practices, refused to employ these traditional forms. Eventually, government officials came to realize that this strategy was counterproductive, particularly since the ongoing British presence in the West made the U.S. approach appear strident and hostile.

Washington chose Aupaumut as an ambassador for the United States because of the weight that his Native background would bring to the U.S. government suit for peace. In a March 1792 speech to the Iroquois delegation that Aupaumut accompanied to Philadelphia (then the capital of the nation), Washington promised peace "between the United States and all the natives of this land . . . founded upon the principles of justice and humanity."[58] Peace on the Ohio frontier seemed especially urgent at this time. The early 1790s was a period of considerable turmoil on many fronts: on the western frontier, within the United States itself, and in the larger Atlantic world. Republican ideals and the success of the American Revolution had inspired revolutionary movements in France and Haiti, events that, in turn, sparked opposition within the United States to the Washington presidency. Washington sought peace with the western coalition because he had numerous political and military opponents, both inside and outside U.S. borders. Had Aupaumut's mission succeeded, it might have proved a turning point in U.S.–Native relations, and at several points Aupaumut's narrative reflects his awareness of both this reality and the implications of his failure. (See his opening explanation for conducting the mission in Selection 1, included herein.)

Aupaumut left Philadelphia on 10 May 1792, shortly after the meeting with Washington. He and his brother traveled first to western New York, where they collected a diplomatic party of five counselors and young men for the trip west. Aupaumut also took this opportunity to retrieve his "bag of peace" filled with "ancient wampom," a diplomatic tool containing records of prior agreements among these Native communities. Aupaumut needed this wampum to "manifest" the truth of his claims about historic alliances among the nations.[59]

The group proceeded to Canandaigua to meet with the representatives of the Five Nations, or Iroquois. There Aupaumut encountered Brant, the Mohawk leader allied with the British to resist U.S. expansion. Brant, who emerges later in the narrative as Aupaumut's nemesis, here urged Aupaumut to send the diplomatic message of the U.S. government to the western Indian nations

58. Lowrie and Clarke, *American State Papers*, 229.
59. Aupaumut, "A Narrative of an Embassy to the Western Indians," 78.

through British representatives: "For, says he, the Indians will hear quicker by the English.""I gave him no answer," Aupaumut observed.[60]

Aupaumut and his party continued on to Buffalo Creek, where, on 13 June, the Iroquois confederacy held a general council "that all may hear news from the United States." Aupaumut exchanged speeches with the Seneca leaders, telling them of his mission and emphasizing, "This message is very urgent" and must "go with all speed."[61] The Iroquois leaders planned to send their own diplomatic party west to participate in the negotiations, and Aupaumut apparently feared that they would insist on preceding him. On the morning of 15 June, however, the Iroquois received word that Iroquois warriors had killed two members of the influential western Delaware community. The Iroquois leaders, worried that their diplomats would be attacked in retaliation, agreed to let Aupaumut's party go before them.

First, however, the Seneca leader Farmer's Brother called on Aupaumut to "write his speech [for him] and deliver it to the western Delawares." In this speech, which Aupaumut later delivered as requested, Farmer's Brother apologized for the murder of the two men. Echoing the phrases of the Iroquois Condolence Ritual, he concluded, "I now wipe of your tears which runs down your cheeks—we all very sorry with you."[62] Farmer's Brother then delivered five strings of wampum to confirm the spoken words and their written representation.

After further exchanges of speeches, including several with the famous Seneca orator Red Jacket, Aupaumut left Buffalo Creek for the West on 18 June. Traveling along the northern side of Lake Erie, his party confronted high winds and bad weather for several days. As he sojourned, Aupaumut collected news, including reports that Brant's nephew Tawalooth had been in the region spreading rumors that the Iroquois were preparing to send warriors to the western Indian nations to join in an alliance against the Big Knifes. Finally, on 14 July, they arrived at a camp on the Miami River, where a grand council of the western Indian nations was about to convene.

There the Delaware sachem Tautpuhqtheet and Aupaumut exchanged speeches following the protocols of the Condolence Ritual. Afterward Aupaumut shared his news, which included his report of the revolutionary turmoil in Europe and Haiti (see Selection 2). Later Aupaumut exchanged speeches with the Shawnee leaders and delivered oral and written messages from the Five Nations. He then addressed his central task, delivering the message from the Washington administration (see Selection 3).

---

60. Ibid., 78.
61. Ibid., 80.
62. Ibid., 81.

The council meeting continued until 18 July. On that day it concluded on a positive note: Aupaumut's message was embraced by the assembled leaders as a "pure message" and "the Life of all our Nations." The prospect of a peaceful settlement loomed large, as the final council speaker promised, "Every Nation will declare that they have received such Message and accepted of it." Then the reluctant Shawnees would be brought into the fold, either willingly or "if not, then every nation must teach them, and chastise them; if that will not do, then they will be abandoned."[63] Aupaumut's mission seemed to be nearing fulfillment.

Immediately after this promising conclusion, however, disturbing rumors began to circulate among the assembled nations. On 30 July, Aupaumut reported that two "Cherekes brought Alarming Voice yesterday that the Big Knifes are discovered near fort Jefferson," and on 1 August sixteen warriors were sent "to see whether the terrible Voice yesterday is true."[64] At this tense moment in the negotiations, Aupaumut met with Big Cat, the Chief sachem of the Delawares, who he hoped would be his ally. Aupaumut believed that Big Cat embraced the customs of alliance and peacemaking that their peoples shared. He began his speech with a Condolence Ritual for Big Cat's brother, who had died the previous spring (see Selection 4).

Aupaumut continued to meet informally with Big Cat and other sympathetic leaders, even as he battled ill health, negotiated for costly provisions, and confronted more rumors of aggression by the Big Knifes. The Shawnee leaders meanwhile continued to make the case for war, noting particularly the greediness and violence of the Big Knifes. In these days, Aupaumut observed, "these nations seemed much stupified by reason of a thousand stories. By this time the hostile party begin to lift up their heads."[65] Aupaumut struggled to keep the negotiations on track, but he faced mounting resistance. First, the British officer Colonel Alexander McKee sent a message warning that Aupaumut was "sent by the Big Knifes." Then on 13 September Brant's nephew Tawalooth arrived at the head of a party of messengers. Four days later, Tawalooth delivered to a Shawnee council Brant's message accusing Aupaumut of deception (see Selection 5).

From this point on Aupaumut's efforts at diplomacy rapidly came unraveled. Individuals continued to debate the risks and benefits of war, but these private discussions were superseded by the public displays showing evidence of past alliances among the tribes in their effort to resist westward pressure

---

63. Ibid., 96–97.
64. Ibid., 98.
65. Ibid., 105.

by white settlers. The arrival of the Five Nations representatives, including Aupaumut's old friend Red Jacket, gave Aupaumut's cause a temporary boost. A central point of dispute during the negotiations involved the novel Shawnee practice of giving precedence to their warriors over their sachems. The Iroquois leaders reprimanded the Shawnee in council, saying, "Our Sachems used to set before the Head warriors, but now you set before your Sachems. . . . Now let your Sachems set before you—for they are the proper managers of publick affairs." Ultimately, the Iroquois were pressured into acknowledging their prior alliances, concurring with the Shawnee proposal that "the United States have laid these troubles, and they can remove these troubles. And if they take away all their forts and move back to the ancient line, then we will believe that they mean to have peace, and that Washington is a great man—then we may meet the U.S. at Sandusky, or kausaumuhtuk, next spring." [66]

In the end, the negotiations turned on the nature of the alliances that already existed among the Native tribes whose representatives gathered at the Maumee Rapids. Aupaumut repeatedly stressed the history of alliances for peace among the tribes, arguing on this basis that the allies should accept the U.S. condition that they call in their war parties as a prerequisite to the dismantling of U.S. forts on tribal lands and governmental restraint of the Big Knifes. The Shawnee leadership responded by emphasizing intertribal treaties that promised a shared commitment to mutual protection in the face of encroachments by white settlers. The Shawnee head warrior, Puckonchehluh, scolded the Iroquois: "In our publick council you tell us, we whose [sic] are one colar, now have one heart and one head. If any Nation strikes us, we must all feel it. Now you must consider whether this is true what you told us." [67] The Shawnee leaders refused to stop the fighting until the forts on Indian lands were removed, and ultimately the Iroquois delegation fell into line. The Shawnees and Wyondots declared for war on 11 October, and that evening Brant arrived at the council site. After the council meeting concluded, Aupaumut observed as a party of two hundred warriors left for the frontier—presumably to strike at the Big Knifes at Fort Jefferson.

Before Aupaumut departed for the East, Big Cat and others sympathetic to his cause asked him to write a speech explaining the outcome of the failed mission from their perspective (see Selection 6). Aupaumut, too, felt the need for explanation. He concludes his narrative with the speech that he gave in

---

66. Ibid., 118, 121.
67. Ibid., 117.

response to Brant. His final words convey his ongoing sense of embattlement and a need to defend himself against "many evil and false reports sounded in the Ears of my friends." The written narrative is a material embodiment of his own story, intended to counter those "evil and false reports" (see Selection 7).

# Hendrick Aupaumut and the Cultural Middle Ground

### SANDRA M. GUSTAFSON

Hendrick Aupaumut played a significant role in the history of Native America—that of the cultural mediator, or go-between, who attempted to integrate Native communicative practices into European and Euro-American cultural and political institutions. Aupaumut was one of a number of early Native leaders who endeavored to occupy an important piece of cultural terrain whose very existence was contested, one that had analogies on the actual territorial frontier: a "middle ground" (to adapt a term from historian Richard White)[68] that could be occupied by both indigenous Americans and white settlers on terms of relative equality. On this cultural middle ground, Native traditions carried authority and weight comparable to, and indeed sometimes dominant over, traditions inherited from Europe. Cultural traditions are sometimes portrayed today as all-or-nothing propositions. Either we are fully ethnic and determined to resist accommodation to a hegemonic power or we are assimilationists who contribute to the destruction of our "authentic" culture. A similar insistence on cultural purity is evident in earlier times as well. For Aupaumut, the wartime context of his diplomacy made his efforts to claim the cultural middle ground especially challenging. Yet he hoped it would offer him an alternative to the "us or them" model of identity that frontier warfare created.

Today this cultural middle ground is often occupied by Native American novelists and poets such as Leslie Marmon Silko, Louise Erdrich, Sherman Alexie, and Simon Ortiz, who use Western media (i.e., writing and print) and forms (e.g., the novel and the lyric) to give new shape to Native cultural traditions and to share them with diverse audiences. In Aupaumut's lifetime, this territory was not inhabited by literary writers—there were no Native writers who would usefully be described as "literary" in the eighteenth century, and the

---

68. White, *Middle Ground.*

category "literature" was not employed, as it is today, to mean primarily fiction, poetry, and plays. Rather, well into the nineteenth century, the cultural middle ground was populated by Native ministers (notably Samson Occom and William Apess) and by political leaders and diplomats such as Aupaumut himself. The resources of Native tradition provided them with the means to sustain their own and their communities' indigenous identities, even as they embraced certain European cultural practices. Communicative traditions were central to the establishment of living Native identities on this cultural middle ground.

Aupaumut was a member of the Mahican Nation, an indigenous people with a rich historical tradition of serving as diplomats and mediators among the tribes of the Northeast. Asked to negotiate on behalf of George Washington's administration, Aupaumut believed that by employing Mahican traditions to represent the U.S. government, he could incorporate these communicative practices into U.S. society. Early in the narrative of his diplomatic mission, Aupaumut explained its history: "It was the business of our fathers to go around the Towns of these nations to renew the agreements between them, and tell them many things which they discover among the White people in the east." He hoped to use the forms of Mahican diplomacy, which he regarded with pride, to prevent frontier violence in order to benefit both indigenous Americans and the new U.S. government.

Born in 1757 in Stockbridge, Massachusetts, Aupaumut grew up in a "blended" community. Stockbridge was a mission town where the eminent theologian Jonathan Edwards had once briefly held the pulpit. A number of Native communities in the vicinity coexisted with the white population. Raised in the Christian faith, Aupaumut was also well acquainted with the traditional practices of his community. In the early 1790s he wrote an autoethnography called "History of the Muh-he-con-nuk Indians," in which he sketched his people's precontact modes of life; outlined their social organization, governmental structure, and communicative practices; and described their historical relationships with other Native communities, including their role as mediators and diplomats.

During these years of the early 1790s, Aupaumut was clearly preoccupied by his Native identity and his place in the United States. He had fought on the American side during the Revolutionary War, a relatively rare circumstance, since most of the Native Americans who fought sided with the British. Aupaumut believed that accommodation was the best way for Native communities to survive. The emergent pan-Indian resistance movement later led by the Shawnee warrior Tecumseh he viewed as suicidal for indigenous peoples and even—as his repeated descriptions of the pan-Indian leaders as "Emmisar[ies] of the Devil" suggest—as demonically inspired. Yet as his writings make clear, accommodation for Aupaumut did not mean wholesale assimilation, and it did not mean overlooking the very real oppressions that Native peoples suffered. In his narrative he complains of deceptive practices with respect to land sales and other forms of mistreatment by the white settlers. Aupaumut hoped to use his diplomatic status to influence the U.S. government on behalf of the Mahicans and other indigenous groups. Had Aupaumut been successful in establishing a treaty between the western nations and the U.S. government, pan-Indianism might have taken a different shape, with diplomacy rather than war at its center. We will never know whether negotiated settlements would have resulted in a more equitable, less exploitive (and often deadly) outcome for indigenous communities. The juggernaut of westward expansion was already on the move when Aupaumut came on the scene, and there is little reason to suppose that anything could have stopped it. Our principal interest in Aupaumut lies in his recognition of the importance of preserving and valuing a broad range of indigenous communicative practices.

Communicative practices were central to the role that Aupaumut envisioned for the Mahicans within American society. Aupaumut was trained in the forms of alphabetic literacy as a youth at the Stockbridge mission school. His education emphasized the importance of reading and writing as essential skills. The disciplinary and restrictive nature of reading and writing were particularly exigent in mission schools, where literacy, Christianity, and civilization were linked in opposition to "savage" life.[69] Aupaumut resisted such oppositional thinking. Even as he developed a firm grasp of the communicative practices organized by alphabetic literacy, Aupaumut came to value and, by comparison, better understand the oral modes and material expressive practices of Mahican society.[70] Instead of accepting Western hierarchies that set writing and print above indigenous textual forms, imagining that literate modalities would ultimately replace the oral and material modes of indigenous communication, Aupaumut imagined a role in the United States for such media as wampum, oratory, and the Iroquois Condolence Ritual. These expressive forms would not simply persist locally in indigenous societies as so-called residual forms. In Aupaumut's vision they would become key media of the U.S. government, employed in diplomatic negotiations with Native communities.

---

69. The relationship between literacy, Christianity, and civilization has been well explored. For a recent review, see Wyss, *Writing Indians*, 8. On Aupaumut's literacy training, see ibid., 106. More generally, see Wyss's analysis of Aupaumut's writings in ibid., 105–21.

70. See the discussion of oral modalities in Aupaumut's "History of the Muh-he-con-nuk Indians" in Gustafson, *Eloquence Is Power*, 258–59. Aupaumut's "History" can be found in Peyer, *The Elders Wrote*, 25–33. My analysis of Aupaumut here focuses on the range of communicative practices in his narrative, which are set in a more detailed historical context in *Eloquence Is Power*, 257–64.

Aupaumut projected an American culture that included indigenous textual practices as equal alternatives to script and print. In his manuscripts we can see anticipation of current postcolonial scholarship on textual media that pursues the project of "indigenizing the page." To indigenize the page means to connect discussions of print culture and history of the book to "Aboriginal oral, glyphic, artefactual modes, and conceptualizations of communication"; the phrase also refers to indigenous uses of the page in ways that reorient its meaning.[71] Aupaumut's skilled use of a range of oral, script-based, and material practices of communication anticipates such indigenous approaches to textuality. The pages of Aupaumut's manuscripts deliberately highlight his appreciation for and strategic use of diverse, multicultural media. In this sense, they are indigenized pages. They point the way toward an inclusive and comparatist approach to communicative practices and modes of textuality.

The parties at the council meetings described in Aupaumut's *Short Narration* disputed their points through competing displays of written speeches, wampum, and other material artifacts such as pipes and tobacco. These materializations of past agreements represented different versions of history and allegiance that were fundamentally contested at the treaty council. Were the parties to the negotiations bound by the "ancient wampum" that Aupaumut carried, which represented the historical role of the Mahicans and the agreements to peaceful cooperation that the tribe had sustained among the nations? Aupaumut insisted on this historical role in a council speech in which he argued that a "Union" was a "happy thing" but "not a new thing." Rather, he said, the union was established out of compassion for one another's burdens by "our good Ancestors . . . many, many years ago"; therefore, it was their duty to sustain it. To this ancestral union Aupaumut sought to add the elaborate belt from the "15 Sachems" of the United States representing the path of peace, so that if the war parties were called in and the nations sent a deputation to Fort Jefferson, the U.S. would rein in the predatory Big Knifes and endeavor "to establish happiness for our Children." Alternatively, the Shawnee leaders displayed wampum and a pipe to represent a commitment between the western confederation and the Five Nations in the establishment of a pan-Indian "Union" of tribes for the common defense. These competing models of union—ancestral and peace oriented, pan-Indian and resistance oriented—were the major points of contention in the negotiations.

Because the rituals of the Iroquois Condolence Council provided a major

---

71. See Battiste, "Indigenizing the Page: Part 1," 111–23, quotation on 121; and Findlay, "Indigenizing the Page: Part 2," 125–41.

structuring device for Native diplomacy in the Northeast, they can be considered a communicative practice. The language of the Condolence Ritual appears in many of the speeches that Aupaumut records in the narrative. By the seventeenth century, the Condolence Ceremony, which was probably developed as a ritual of symbolic kinship to first establish and then solidify the Iroquois Confederacy, had become the model for treaty protocol among Native communities and between Native communities and European colonial governments. As the word *condolence* suggests, the ritual is rooted in the importance of recognizing grief and compensating for human losses in the process of establishing or maintaining peace. Restoration of social equilibrium and the creation of compensatory bonds are central components of the Condolence Council. The paradigm of the ritual, as described by the anthropologist William N. Fenton, moves through the stages of arrival and greeting, the acknowledgment of deaths that must be compensated, offers of material reimbursement and its acceptance, the signing of a treaty or reaching of an agreement, and the feast and exchange of gifts. The ritual is conducted primarily through the exchange of formal oratory, which has a number of characteristic metaphors. Bodily metaphors are common, particularly in references to wiping away tears, cleaning ears, and otherwise purging the senses. Often a path or way must be made clear by eliminating obstacles such as logs or brambles. Kinship terms are important for defining and establishing relationships. Wampum belts and other material mnemonics are incorporated into the Condolence Council to represent treaties or messages. The ritual paradigm offered guidelines rather than a fixed or mandatory framework for the components of the Condolence Council. In Aupaumut's narrative, elements of the Condolence Ritual are introduced particularly when there are deaths that require acknowledgment and compensation.[72]

Wampum served a particularly significant function in the diplomatic process. The ethnologist Michael K. Foster describes wampum as a material embodiment of the message that it represents—although the images woven into the belts do not represent specific meanings, it is believed that the wampum literally "carries" the message that the messenger utters. A messenger first hears the message that the chiefs wish to communicate and then repeats it while holding the wampum; it is believed that this repetition—rather than improve the messenger's memory—increases the power of the wampum. According to Foster, "Wampum is regarded as a kind of recording device, somewhat in

---

72. The most comprehensive study of the Condolence Ritual is Jennings et al., *History and Culture of Iroquois Diplomacy*. For Fenton's essay "Structure, Continuity, and Change in the Process of Iroquois Treaty Making," see ibid., 3–36.

the way we conceive of the function of a tape recorder."[73] Wampum calls to mind previous agreements, and thus has a retrospective function. It also has a prospective function in that it structures future events, organizing the flow of exchange at a council meeting as one party responds to an offering of a speech and an offering of wampum with a reciprocal speech and wampum. There are similarities to writing here, but there are also important differences. Writing has a retrospective function in that it offers a specific representation of words spoken or agreements reached. Whether a written document has a prospective function depends on the content of the text or the situation in which the text is used.

Native diplomats sometimes carried written speeches on the same missions for which they carried wampum. It is sometimes assumed—and, indeed, it was often assumed by Aupaumut's white contemporaries—that Indians preferred to negotiate via oral recitation and wampum rather than via written documentation. As Aupaumut's narrative shows, the situation was considerably more complex. Written speeches were sent not only between Native leaders and the U.S. government but also among Native leaders themselves. At the request of the Seneca sachems, Aupaumut transcribed a speech that he later delivered to the western Delawares. It appears that writing was the preferred medium in this instance, perhaps because Aupaumut was not a Seneca and may not have been fully trusted as a messenger. Written messages were often backed by wampum. On this same mission Aupaumut carried a large wampum belt from the United States, or "15 United sachems," which he used when he delivered his speech on their behalf. After Aupaumut's mission failed, the Delaware leader Big Cat asked him to transcribe a speech to the U.S. government explaining the reasons for that failure. Writing seems to have been the generally preferred medium for dealing with the U.S. government, although again (as with the Seneca message) because Aupaumut did not represent the Delawares, perhaps he could not rely on wampum alone. Aupaumut later bound this Delaware speech into the manuscript of his narrative.

In addition to wampum, other physical tokens were commonly used to confirm the truth of a message or signal a historic agreement. Such messages and signs of alliance took a range of concrete material forms. Late in the negotiations a Shawnee speaker referred to speeches that "I now have in my hand" and displayed a pipe used to ratify an earlier agreement. The Senecas pulled out "a tin case, which contained a map and all the speeches of Colonel Pickering delivered to the Senecas at Philadelphia." As the "voices" of rumor grew louder and the negotiations began to fall apart, Aupaumut demanded that

---

73. Foster, "Another Look at the Function of Wampum in Iroquois–White Councils," 105.

even informal verbal messages be accompanied by material objects that would confirm the truth of the words. He told one messenger who conveyed a demand that Aupaumut attend a meeting, "I have not seen any token or message in strings of wampom, or writing, nor Tobacco," and so "I will not go." There are many similar instances when speech is defined in relationship to material objects or is itself imagined as a material object. Of the "voice of Shawannese," Aupaumut notes, "I put it under my feet, I do not regard it." Later a Delaware chief, again conveying the sense of voice as a material object, asks whether "you would . . . put your voice with ours." A message from the Wyondots also observes, "I sent our Tobacco to reach your hand and lead you here, for we wish to hear you further."[74] The frequency with which passages stress the material embodiments of verbal messages is related to the repeated call for the negotiating parties to "manifest" their sentiments or opinions. In a situation rife with competing rumors and potential violence, the need to make intentions clear and to produce stable marks of meaning (whether wampum, tobacco, or writing) became increasingly urgent.

The historian Gregory Evans Dowd notes the potency of rumor on the frontier. "Even among long-term allies, and during periods of relative peace, the lack of reliable information about one another could create extreme anxiety," he writes in a description of an earlier episode of white–indigenous conflict. "Rumors are, by definition, unauthorized, and their source, even if cited, is unreachable. They are, in that sense alone, groundless." *News* is the correlative to the term *rumor*. News bearing and news gathering were major activities for Aupaumut throughout his journey, as he sought to communicate his own mission and collect information about regional events that might affect the outcome. Yet news was often impossible to distinguish from rumor. Dowd notes the frequent metaphors of birds and flight in descriptions of rumor on the frontier and observes, "Groundlessness and flight suggest not only lack of authorization but also speed and power."[75] Similar metaphors punctuate Aupaumut's *Short Narration*; for instance the speech that he delivers from the Washington administration complains that "the voice of flying birds" has disrupted the prospects for peace. The message from the government was clear: The account of Washington's bad intentions circulated by Brant and his followers was, they claimed, inaccurate; it was an unauthorized and groundless rumor designed to prevent peaceful reconciliation.

---

74. Aupaumut, "A Narrative of an Embassy to the Western Indians," 116–17, 121, 106, 107, 109, 110.

75. Dowd, "The Panic of 1751," 527, 547.

The text of Aupaumut's narrative describes a broad range of indigenous communicative practices: formal oratory; the forms of the Condolence Ritual; wampum; written speeches; news and rumor; materializations of speech, such as tobacco, pipes, or maps. The *Short Narration* is, in this sense, a description of the cultural middle ground and an instance of the indigenized page. Yet the physical manuscript itself is literally bound up with Western written media. The end papers of the volume are legal papers unrelated to the *Short Narration*. The authenticating apparatus around the manuscript and printed versions of the *Short Narration* highlight the framing context that the written and printed words put around Aupaumut's text. A testimonial letter from Pickering dated 1826 witnesses to Pickering's acquaintance with Aupaumut, noting that Aupaumut "was intelligent, and spoke the English language familiarly, and with so much correctness, as to be easily and distinctly understood; and he wrote a legible hand." He observes, "If Hendrick's manuscript is correct in spelling and grammar, his draft must have been corrected, perhaps by Mr. Sargent." In a subsequent statement, Pickering confirms that the handwriting in the narrative matches other specimens that he has of Aupaumut's script. Further, Pickering reports on the history that Aupaumut relates, filling in the context. The printed text of the narrative appeared in the 1827 *Memoirs of the Historical Society of Pennsylvania*, to which Benjamin Coates attached prefatory remarks of his own, in addition to printing Pickering's commentary. Like Pickering, Coates comments on Aupaumut's handwriting and literacy, noting, "The narrative is freely interlined with corrections in grammar and expression; not indeed sufficient to render it perfectly admissible as an English composition, but appearing to have been aimed at the more obvious faults." Coates's interest in the content of the narrative focuses on its unique portrayal of "the history of an Indian negociation, as recorded by the negociator, himself an Indian." He continues, "We know of no instance, as yet, in which the history of the wars and diplomacy of our native predecessors has ever been committed to print, as prepared by one of their own race and character." The written and printed records are here given clear precedence over other forms of diplomatic record, such as wampum. Coates focuses too on the role of the Delawares as leaders and peacemakers and offers a defense of the "venerable [John] Heckewelder,"[76] the Moravian ethnologist whose description of the Delawares influenced James Fenimore Cooper's portrayal in *The Last of the Mohicans*, which appeared in 1826. Aupaumut's *Short Narration* thus became a piece of evidence in a debate

---

76. Aupaumut "A Narrative of an Embassy to the Western Indians," 70, 71, 64, 63.

prompted by Cooper's novel. Emphasizing the literate and literary context for Aupaumut's *Short Narration*, neither Pickering nor Coates recognized the significance of the work for a broader, comparative understanding of indigenous communicative practices on the cultural middle ground and its importance as an instance of "the indigenized page." We can read Aupaumut's *Short Narration* today for the content that Pickering and Coates overlooked or suppressed: the wide range of indigenous oral, textual, and material practices that it depicts.

# Bibliography

Adams, Eliphalet. *A Sermon Preached on the Occasion of the Execution of Katherine Garret, an Indian-Servant . . . Together with her Dying* WARNING *and* EXHORTATION. New London, Conn.: T. Green, 1738.

"Agreement between the Trustees of East Hampton and the Indians of Montauk (1702–1703)." In Stone, *The History and Archeology of the Montauk,* 69.

Ales, Marion Fisher. "A History of the Indians on Montauk, Long Island." In Stone, *The History and Archeology of the Montauk,* 5–66.

Amory, Hugh. "The Trout and the Milk: An Ethnobibliographical Talk." *Harvard Library Review* 7, no. 1 (Spring 1996): 50–65.

Anderson, Virginia DeJohn. "Chickwallop and the Beast: Indian Responses to European Animals in Early New England." In Calloway and Salisbury, *Reinterpreting New England Indians and the Colonial Experience,* 24–51.

Andreski, Stanislav. *Syphilis, Puritanism and Witch Hunts.* New York: St. Martin's Press, 1989.

Apess, William. *On Our Own Ground: The Complete Writings of William Apess, a Pequot.* Ed. Barry O'Connell. Amherst: University of Massachusetts Press, 1992.

"Aquinnah Cultural Center." Wampanoag Tribe of Gayhead website. Available at http://www.wampanoagtribe.net/. Accessed 10 May and 30 June 2006.

Archer, Richard. *Fissures in the Rock: New England in the Seventeenth Century.* Hanover, N.H.: University Press of New England, 2001.

Arnold, Laura. "Cultures in Contact." Ph.D diss. University of California at Los Angeles, 1995.

Aupaumat, Hendrick. "A Narrative of an Embassy to the Western Indians, from the Original Manuscript of Hendrick Aupaumut." Edited by Benjamin Coates. *Memoirs of the Historical Society of Pennsylvania,* vol. 2, 76–131. Philadelphia: M'Carty and Davis, 1827.

Avery, David. "A Valedictory Address Delivered to the Indians at Kananawarohare," 22 June 1772. Manuscript. Wheelock Papers, 772370. Rauner Special Collections Library, Dartmouth College, Hanover, N.H.

Axtell, James. *The School upon a Hill: Education and Society in Colonial New England.* New Haven, Conn.: Yale University Press, 1974.

Backus, Isaac. *A History of New England, with Particular Reference to the Denomination of Christians Called Baptists.* 3 vols. Boston, 1777.

Baker, Emerson W. "'A Scratch with a Bear's Paw': Anglo-Indian Land Deeds in Early Maine." *Ethnohistory* 36, no. 3 (Summer 1989): 235–56.

Baldwin, Thomas W., comp. *Vital Records of Natick, Massachusetts to the Year 1850.* Boston: Stanhope Press, 1910.

Bangs, Jeremy Dupertuis. *Indian Deeds: Land Transactions in Plymouth Colony, 1620–1691*. Boston: New England Historic Genealogical Society, 2002.

Banks, Charles Edward. *The History of Martha's Vineyard: Dukes County, Massachusetts*. Boston: G. H. Dean, 1911–25.

Banner, Stuart. *The Death Penalty: An American History*. Cambridge, Mass.: Harvard University Press, 2002.

Barsh, Russell L. "Behind Land Claims: Rationalizing Dispossession in Anglo-American Law." *Law and Anthropology* 1 (1986): 15–50.

Battestini, Simon. *African Writing and Text*. Ottawa: Legas, 2000.

Battiste, Marie. "Print Culture and Decolonizing the University: Indigenizing the Page: Part 1." In *The Future of the Page*, edited by Peter Stoicheff and Andrew Taylor, 110–23. Toronto: University of Toronto Press, 2004.

Baxter, James, ed. *Documentary History of the State of Maine*. Vol. 4. Portland: Lefavor-Tower, 1907.

Baxter, James, ed. *Documentary History of the State of Maine*. Vol. 10. Portland: Lefavor-Tower, 1907.

Bedos-Rezak, Brigitte Miriam. "Medieval Identity: A Sign and a Concept." *American Historical Review* 105, no. 5 (December 2005): 1489–1533.

Benard, Akeia. "An Ethnohistoric Perspective on Native American Childrearing." Manuscript. Department of Anthropology, University of Connecticut, n.d.

Bercovitch, Sacvan. *The American Jeremiad*. Madison: University of Wisconsin Press, 1978.

Bhabha, Homi, K. *The Location of Culture*. 1994. Reprint, London: Routledge, 2001.

———. "Of Mimicry and Man: The Ambivalence of Colonial Discourse." *October* 28 (Spring 1984): 125–33.

———. "Sly Civility." *October* 34 (Fall 1985): 71–80.

Blake, S. Leroy. *The Later History of the First Church of Christ, New London, Conn.* New London, Conn.: Press of the Day Publishing Company, 1900.

Blodgett, Harold. *Samson Occom*. Hanover, N.H.: Dartmouth College, 1935.

Blot, Richard, and James Collins. *Literacy and Literacies: Texts, Power, and Identity*. Cambridge: Cambridge University Press, 2003.

Bohaker, Heidi. "*Nindoodemag*: Anishinaabe Identities in the Eastern Great Lakes Region, 1600–1900." Ph.D. diss. University of Toronto, 2006.

Boone, Elizabeth H., and Walter D. Mignolo, eds. *Writing without Words: Alternative Literacies in Mesoamerica and the Andes*. Durham: Duke University Press, 1994.

Borrows, John. "Wampum at Niagara: The Royal Proclamation, Canadian Legal History and Self-Government." In *Aboriginal and Treaty Rights in Canada*, edited by Michael Asch, 155–72. Vancouver: UBC Press, 1997.

Boston, Patience. *Faithful Narrative of the Wicked Life and Remarkable Conversion*. Boston: S. Kneeland and T. Green, 1738.

Bourque, Bruce J. "Ethnicity on the Maritime Peninsula, 1600–1759." *Ethnohistory* 36, no. 3 (Summer 1989): 257–84.

Bradley, James W. *Evolution of the Onondaga Iroquois: Accommodating Change, 1500–1655.* Syracuse, N.Y.: Syracuse University Press, 1987.

Bradstreet, John. "Transactions of a Congress held with the Chiefs of the Ottawas and Chippewas Nations with several others." September 7, 1764. Manuscript copy. Amherst MSS, U1350 O48/4. Centre for Kentish Studies, Maidstone, Kent County, United Kingdom.

Bragdon, Kathleen. "Emphatical Speech and Great Action: An Analysis of Seventeenth Century Native Speech Events Described in Early Sources." *Man in the Northeast* 33 (1987): 101–11.

———. *Native People of Southern New England, 1500–1650.* Norman: University of Oklahoma Press, 1996.

Brooks, Joanna. *American Lazarus: Religion and the Rise of African-American and Native American Literatures.* New York: Oxford University Press, 2003.

———, ed. *The Collected Writings of Samson Occom, Mohegan: Literature and Leadership in Eighteenth-Century Native America.* New York: Oxford University Press, 2006.

———. "Six Hymns by Samson Occom." *Early American Literature* 38, no. 1 (2003): 67–87.

Brooks, Lisa. "The Common Pot: Indigenous Writing and the Reconstruction of Native Space in the Northeast." Ph.D. diss. Cornell University, 2004.

Bross, Kristina. *Dry Bones and Indian Sermons: Praying Indians in Colonial America.* Ithaca, N.Y.: Cornell University Press, 2004.

———. "Dying Saints, Vanishing Savages: 'Dying Indian Speeches' in Colonial New England Literature." *Early American Literature* 36, no. 3 (December 2001): 325–52.

Brumble, H. David, III. *American Indian Autobiography.* Berkeley and Los Angeles: University of California Press, 1988.

Caldwell, Patricia. *The Puritan Conversion Narrative: The Beginnings of American Expression.* New York: Cambridge University Press, 1983.

Calloway, Colin, ed. *After King Philip's War: Presence and Persistence in Indian New England.* Hanover, N.H.: University Press of New England, 1997.

———. *Dawnland Encounters: Indians and Europeans in Northern New England.* Hanover, N.H.: University Press of New England, 1991.

———. *The Western Abenakis of Vermont, 1600–1800: War, Migration and the Survival of an Indian People.* Norman: University of Oklahoma Press, 1990.

Calloway, Colin, and Neal Salisbury, eds. *Reinterpreting New England Indians and the Colonial Experience.* Boston: Colonial Society of Massachusetts, 2003.

Campisi, Jack. "The Emergence of the Mashantucket Pequot Tribe, 1637–1975." In *The Pequots in Southern New England: The Rise and Fall of an American Indian Nation,* edited by Laurence M. Hauptman and James D. Wherry, 117–40. Norman: University of Oklahoma Press, 1990.

———. *The Mashpee Indians: Tribe on Trial.* Syracuse, N.Y.: Syracuse University Press, 1991.

Castiglia, Christopher. *Bound and Determined: Captivity, Culture-Crossing, and White Womanhood from Mary Rowlandson to Patty Hearst.* Chicago: University of Chicago Press, 1996.

Castillo, Susan, and Ivy Schweitzer. *The Literatures of Colonial America: An Anthology.* Malden, Mass.: Blackwell Publishers, 2001.

Caulkins, Frances Mainwaring. *History of New London, Connecticut.* 2 vols. 1895. Reprint, Bowie, Md.: Heritage Books, 2000.

Cave, Alfred A. *The Pequot War.* Amherst: University of Massachusetts Press, 1996.

Champlain, Samuel de. *The Works of Samuel de Champlain.* Vol. 2. Toronto: University of Toronto Press, 1971.

Channing, Edward. *The Narragansett Planters: A Study of Causes.* Johns Hopkins University Studies in History and Political Science, 4th ser., no. 3. Baltimore: Johns Hopkins University Press, 1886.

Channing, Henry Trevett. *God Admonishing His People of Their Duty.* New London, Conn.: T. Green, 1738.

Cheyfitz, Eric. *The Poetics of Imperialism: Translation and Colonization from The Tempest to Tarzan.* Exp. ed. Philadelphia: University of Pennsylvania Press, 1997.

"Chiefs of the Indians of Penobscot to Col. Dunbar, Nov. 14 1729." In *Documentary History of the State of Maine,* edited by James Baxter, vol. 10, 446–48. Portland: Lefavor-Tower, 1907.

Cohen, Charles. "Conversion among Puritans and Amerindians: A Theological and Cultural Perspective." In *Puritanism: Transatlantic Perspectives on a Seventeenth-Century Anglo-American Faith,* edited by Francis Bremer, 233–56. Boston: Massachusetts Historical Society, 1993.

Cohen, Daniel. *Pillars of Salt, Monuments of Grace: New England Crime Literature and the Origins of American Popular Culture, 1674–1860.* New York: Oxford University Press, 1993.

Connecticut (Colony). *The Public Records of the Colony of Connecticut, from April 1636 to October 1776.* 15 vols. Hartford, Conn.: Brown and Parson, 1850–1890. Reprint, New York: AMS Press, 1968.

Conroy, David W. "The Defense of Indian Land Rights: William Bollan and the Mohegan Case in 1743." *Proceedings of the American Antiquarian Society* 103, no. 2 (1993): 395–424.

Cook, James. *Captain Cook's Journal during His First Voyage round the World Made in H.M. Bark "Endeavour" 1768–71: A Literal Translation of the Original MSS.* Ed. Captain W. J. L. Wharton. London: Elliot Stock, 1893. Reprinted in *Australiana Facsimile Editions* no. 188. Adelaide: Libraries Board of South Australia, 1968.

———. *A Journal of a Voyage round the World in H.M.S. Endeavour, 1768–1771.* London, 1771. Reprint, New York: De Capo Press, 1967.

Cooke, Jacob Ernest, ed. "Theories of Education (XV)." In *Encyclopedia of the North American Colonies,* vol. 3, 417–34. New York: Charles Scribner's Sons, 1993.

Coombs, Linda. "Ancient Technology: Building a Wampanoag Home of the Seventeenth Century." Plimoth Plantation website. Available at http://www.plimoth.org/discover/wampanoag-life/wampanoag-home.php. Accessed 17 September 2007.

Crain, Patricia. *The Story of A: The Alphabetization of America from the New England Primer to the Scarlet Letter.* Stanford, Calif: Stanford University Press, 2000.

Cremin, Lawrence Arthur. *American Education: The Colonial Experience, 1607–1783.* New York: Harper and Row, 1970.

Cronon, William. *Changes in the Land: Indians, Colonists, and the Ecology of New England.* New York: Hill and Wang, 1983.

Currie, Douglas, and Kevin A. McBride. "Respect for the Ancestors: New Approaches for the Recovery and Analysis of Native American Burials." In *Human Remains: Conservation, Retrieval and Analysis*, edited by Emily Williams, 32–43. BAR International Series, no. 63. Oxford, England: Archaeopress, 2001.

Cushman, Robert. "Reasons and Considerations Touching the Lawfulness of Removing out of England into the Parts of America." In *A Journal of the Pilgrims at Plymouth: Mourt's Relation*, edited by Dwight B. Heath, 88–96. New York: Corinth Books, 1963.

Danforth, Samuel. *The Cry of Sodom Enquired Into.* Cambridge, Mass.: Marmaduke Johnson, 1674.

———. *The Woful Effects of Drunkenness.* Boston: B. Green, 1710.

Danforth, Samuel, and Rawson Grindal. "Account of an Indian Visitation, A.D. 1698." *Massachusetts Historical Society Collections*, 1st ser., vol. 10, 129–34. Boston, 1809.

Day, Gordon M. *In Search of New England's Native Past: Selected Essays by Gordon M. Day*, edited by Michael K. Foster and William Cowan. Amherst: University of Massachusetts Press, 1999.

Dayton, Cornelia Hughes. "Taking the Trade: Abortion and Gender Relations in an Eighteenth-Century New England Village." *The William and Mary Quarterly* 48, no. 1 (January 1991): 19–31.

———. *Women before the Bar: Gender, Law, and Society in Connecticut, 1639–1789.* Chapel Hill: University of North Carolina Press, 1995.

"Deed to Richard Wharton of Lands on the Androscoggin River. In *Documentary History of the State of Maine*, edited by James Baxter, vol. 7, 365. Portland: Lefavor-Tower.

Deforest, John W. *History of the Indians of Connecticut from the Earliest Known Period to 1850.* Hartford, Conn.: William James Hamersley, 1852.

"Dénombrement des nations sauvages, 1736." Archives Nationales de France (ANF), Paris. Fondes des Colonies, series C11A, Vol. 66, folio 236–56v.

DenOuden, Amy. "Against Conquest: Land, Culture, and Power in the Eighteenth-Century Histories of the Native Peoples of Connecticut." Ph.D. diss. University of Connecticut, 2001.

Dexter, Franklin B., ed. *Extracts from the Itineraries and Other Miscellanies of Ezra Stiles, D.D., LL.D., 1755–1794.* New Haven, Conn.: Yale University Press, 1916.

Dickason, Olive Patricia. *Canada's First Nations: A History of Founding Peoples from Earliest Times.* 3rd ed. Toronto: Oxford University Press, 1999.

Dom Rex v. Kate an Indian Woman (Nov. 1737), New London Superior Court Files, RG 003, box 13, folder 18, no. 62, Connecticut State Library.

Dowd, Gregory Evans. "The Panic of 1751: The Significance of Rumors on the South Carolina–Cherokee Frontier." *William and Mary Quarterly,* 3rd ser., no. 53 (1996): 527–60.

Early Canadiana Online website. Canadian Institute for Historical Microreproductions. Available at http://www.canadiana.org. Accessed 15 March 2006.

"Eastern Indian tribes. Letter to Richard Phillips 'Grand Capitaine des Anglois.'" 28 July 1721. Massachusetts Archives Collection, Boston. Vol. 31, Indian: 1705–1750, series 2042, folio 101–5.

Eisinger, Chester E. "The Puritan Justification for Taking the Land." *Essex Institute Historical Collections* 84 (1948): 131–43.

Eliot, John. *The Dying Speeches of Several Indians.* Cambridge, Mass., 1685.

———. *A Further Account of the Progress of the Gospel amongst the Indians in New England.* London: J. Macock, 1660.

———. *The Logic Primer.* 1672. Reprint, Cleveland: Burrows Brothers, 1904.

Eliot, John, and Thomas Mayhew, Jr. "Tears of Repentance: Or, A Further Narrative of the Progress of the Gospel amongst the Indians in New-England." 1653. Reprinted in *Tracts Relating to the Attempts to Convert to Christianity the Indians of New England.* Massachusetts Historical Society Collections, 3rd ser., vol. 4. Boston, 1834.

Elliott, Michael. "'This Indian Bait': Samson Occom and the Voice of Liminality." *Early American Literature* 29 (1994): 233–53.

Fawcett, Jayne G., and Gladys Tantaquidgeon. "Symbolic Motifs on Painted Baskets of the Mohegan-Pequot." In McMullen and Handsman, *A Key into the Language of Woodsplint Baskets,* 94–101.

Fawcett, Melissa Jayne [Melissa Tantaquidgeon Zobel]. *The Lasting of the Mohegans.* Uncasville, Conn.: Mohegan Tribe, 1995.

———. *Medicine Trail: The Life and Lessons of Gladys Tantaquidgeon.* Tucson: University of Arizona Press, 2000.

Feder, Kenneth L. "'The Avaricious Humour of Designing Englishmen': The Ethnohistory of Land Transactions in the Farmington Valley." *Bulletin of the Archaeological Society of Connecticut* 45 (1993): 29–40.

Findlay, L. M. "Print Culture and Decolonizing the University: Indigenizing the Page: Part 2." In *The Future of the Page,* edited by Peter Stoicheff and Andrew Taylor, 125–41. Toronto: University of Toronto Press, 2004.

Fish, Joseph. Letter to Andrew Oliver, 5 November 1757. Miscellaneous Bound. Massachusetts Historical Society, Boston.

Fitzpatrick, Tara. "The Figure of Captivity: The Cultural Work of the Puritan Captivity Narrative." *American Literary History* 3, no. 1 (1991): 1–26.

Ford, John W., ed. *Some Correspondence between the Governors and Treasurers of the New England Company.* New York: Burt Franklin, 1970.

Ford, Paul Leicester, ed. *The New England Primer: A History of Its Origin and Development with a Reprint of the Unique Copy of the Earliest Known Edition*. New York: Columbia University Press, 1962.

Foster, Michael K. "Another Look at the Function of Wampum in Iroquois–White Councils," in Jennings et al., *The History and Culture of Iroquois Diplomacy*, 99–114.

Frasier, Isaac. *A Brief Account of the Life, and Abominable Thefts, of the Notorious Isaac Frasier, Who Was Executed at Fairfield, Sept. 7th, 1768*. New London, Conn.: T, Green, 1768.

Ghere, David L. "Abenaki Factionalism, Emigration and Social Continuity in Northern New England, 1725–1765." Ph.D. diss. University of Maine, 1988.

———. "Mistranslations and Misinformation: Diplomacy on the Maine Frontier, 1722–1755." *American Indian Culture and Research Journal* 8 (1984): 3–26.

Goddard, Ives, and Kathleen J. Bragdon, eds. *Native Writings in Massachusett*. 2 vols. Philadelphia: American Philosophical Society, 1988.

Guillaud, Yann, Denys Delâge, and Mathieu d'Avignon. "Les signatures amérindiennes: Essai d'interprétation des traits de paix de Montréal de 1700 et de 1701." *Recherches Amérindiennes au Québec* 31, no. 2 (2001): 21–43.

Gussman, Deborah. "The Politics of Piety in Pequot Women's Conversion Narratives." In *Studies in Puritan American Spirituality: Literary Calvinism and Nineteenth-Century American Women Authors*, edited by Michael Schuldiner, 101–24. Lewiston, Canada: Edwin Mellen Press, 1997.

Gustafson, Sandra. *Eloquence Is Power: Oratory and Performance in Early America*. Chapel Hill: University of North Carolina Press for the Omohundro Institute of Early American History and Culture, 2000.

Haefeli, Evan, and Kevin Sweeney. *Captors and Captives: The 1704 French and Indian Raid on Deerfield*. Amherst: University of Massachusetts Press, 2003.

Hall, David. *Worlds of Wonder, Days of Judgment: Popular Religious Belief in Early New England*. New York: Alfred A. Knopf, 1989.

Hallam, Nicholas. Affidavit. Presented to the Privy Council, 12 January 1704. Privy Council Records, CO 5/1290. Public Records Office, London.

———. Memorial Relating to the Complaints of the Mohegan Indians. Presented to the Privy Council 3 December 1703. Privy Council Records, CO 5/1290. Public Records Office, London.

*Harper American Literature*, vol. 1. Ed. Donald McQuade. New York: HarperCollins College, 1996.

Harris, Sharon. *Executing Race: Early American Women's Narratives of Race, Society and the Law*. Columbus: Ohio State University Press, 2005.

Harvey, Tamara. "'Taken from Her Mouth': Narrative Authority and the Conversion of Patience Boston." *Narrative* 6, no. 3 (1998): 256–70.

Havard, Gilles. *The Great Peace of Montreal of 1701: French–Native Diplomacy in the Seventeenth Century*, translated by Phyllis Aronoff and Howard Scott. Montreal: McGill-Queen's University Press, 2001.

Hawkins, Sean. *Writing and Colonialism in Northern Ghana: The Encounter between the LoDagaa and "the World on Paper."* Toronto: University of Toronto Press: 2002.

*Heath Anthology of American Literature: Colonial Period to 1800*, vol. A. Ed. Paul Lauter. New York, Houghton Mifflin, 2005.

Herndon, Ruth Wallis, and Ella Wilcox Sekatau. "The Right to a Name: The Narragansett People and Rhode Island Officials in the Revolutionary Era." *Ethnohistory* 44, no. 3 (1997): 433–62.

Hinton, Leanne, and Ken Hale. *The Green Book of Language Revitalization in Practice.* San Diego: Academic Press, 2001.

Hoffer, Peter, and N. E. H. Hull. *Murdering Mothers: Infanticide in England and New England, 1558–1803.* New York: New York University Press, 1981.

Holmes, Abiel. *A Discourse, Delivered before the Society for Propagating the Gospel among the Indians and Others in North America at their Anniversary Meeting in Boston, November 3, 1808.* Boston, 1808.

Hoxie, Frederick E., ed. *Encyclopedia of North American Indians: Native American History, Culture, and Life From Paleo-Indians to the Present.* Boston: Houghton Mifflin, 1996.

Hull, N. E. H. *Female Felons: Women and Serious Crime in Colonial Massachusetts.* Urbana: University of Illinois Press, 1987.

"Indian Explanation of the Treaty of Casco Bay." In Calloway, *Dawnland Encounters,* 115–18.

Jennings, Francis. *The Invasion of America: Indians, Colonialism and the Cant of Conquest.* New York: W. W. Norton, 1975.

Jennings, Francis, William N. Fenton, Mary A. Druke, and David R. Miller, eds. *The History and Culture of Iroquois Diplomacy: An Interdisciplinary Guide to the Treaties of the Six Nations and Their League.* Syracuse, N.Y.: Syracuse University Press, 1985.

Jones, Brian D., and Kevin A. McBride. "Indigenous Archaeology in Southern New England: Case Studies from the Mashantucket Pequot Reservation." In *Native Peoples and Archaeology in the Northeastern United States,* edited by Jordan Kerber, 265–80. Lincoln: University of Nebraska Press, 2006.

Julian. *The Last Speech and Dying Advice of Poor Julian.* Boston: T. Fleet, 1733.

Kawashima, Yasuhid. *Puritan Justice and the Indian: White Man's Law in Massachusetts, 1630–1763.* Middletown, Conn.: Wesleyan University Press, 1986.

Kellaway, William. *The New England Company, 1649–1776: Missionary Society to the American Indians.* New York: Barnes and Noble, 1962.

Kelleter, Frank. "Puritan Missionaries and the Colonization of the New World: A Reading of John Eliot's *Indian Dialogues* (1671)." In *Early America Re-explored: New Readings in Colonial, Early National, and Antebellum Culture,* edited by Fritz Fleischmann and Klaus H. Schmidt, 71–106. New York: Peter Lang, 2000.

Kendall, Thomas. *Diary and Account Book, 1772–1774.* Manuscript. Eleazar Wheelock Papers, 772900.3. Rauner Special Collections Library, Dartmouth College. Hanover, N.H.

Kennedy, Patricia. "Treaty Texts: When Can We Trust the Written Word?" *Social Sciences and Humanities Aboriginal Research Exchange.* 3, no. 1 (Spring/Summer 1995): 1–25.

Kerber, Jordan E., ed. *Cross-Cultural Collaboration: Native Peoples and Archaeology in the Northeastern United States.* Lincoln: University of Nebraska Press, 2007.

Kidder, Frederic. *The Abenaki Indians, Their Treaties of 1713 & 1717, and a Vocabulary: With a Historical Introduction.* Portland: Brown Thurston, 1859.

King, J. C. H. *First Peoples, First Contacts: Native Peoples of North America.* London: British Museum Press, 1999.

King, Thomas. *The Truth about Stories: A Native Narrative.* Toronto: Anansi Press, 2004.

Krupat, Arnold. *Ethnocriticism: Ethnography, History, Literature.* Berkeley and Los Angeles: University of California Press, 1992.

———. *For Those Who Come After: A Study of Native American Autobiography.* Berkeley and Los Angeles: University of California Press, 1985.

LaFantasie, Glen W., ed. *The Correspondence of Roger Williams.* 2 vols. Hanover, N.H.: Brown University Press, 1987.

Leibman, Laura Arnold, ed. *Experience Mayhew's* Indian Converts: *A Cultural Edition.* Native Americans in the Northeast. Amherst: University of Massachusetts Press, 2008.

LeJeune, Philipe. *On Autobiography.* Minneapolis: University of Minnesota Press, 1989.

Leland, Charles. *The Algonquin Legends of New England: Or, Myths and Folk Lore of the Micmac, Passamaquoddy, and Penobscot Tribes.* Boston: Houghton Mifflin, 1884.

Lepore, Jill. *The Name of War: King Philip's War and the Origins of American Identity.* New York: Alfred A. Knopf, 1998.

———. "When Deer Island Was Turned into Devil's Island." *Bostonia Magazine,* Summer 1998, 14–19.

Little, Elizabeth. "Indian Horse Commons at Nantucket Island, 1660–1760." Paper presented to the American Society for Ethnohistory, Charleston, S.C., 1986.

———. "Sachem Nickanoose and the Grass Contest, Part I." *Historic Nantucket* 23 (1976): 14–21.

———. "Sachem Nickanoose and the Grass Contest, Part II." *Historic Nantucket* 24 (1976): 22–30.

———. "Three Kinds of Indian Land Deeds at Nantucket, Massachusetts." In *Papers of the Eleventh Algonquian Conference,* edited by William Cowan, 61–70. Ottawa: Carleton University Press, 1980.

Lockridge, Kenneth. *Literacy in Colonial New England.* New York: W. W. Norton, 1974.

London, William. *A Catalogue of the Most Vendible Books in England, Orderly and Alphabetically Digested.* 1658. Reprint, London: Gregg-Archive, 1965.

Love, William DeLoss. *Samson Occom and the Christian Indians of New England.* 1899. Reprint, Syracuse, N.Y.: Syracuse University Press, 2000.

Lowrie, Walter, and Matthew St. Claire Clarke, eds. *American State Papers: Documents, Legislative and Executive, of the Congress of the United States . . . , Class II, Indian Affairs, IV* (Washington D.C: Gales and Seaton, 1832.

Maclure, David. *Diary of David McClure, Doctor of Philosophy, 1748–1820.* Ed. Franklin B. Dexter. New York: Knickerbocker, 1899.

Mallery, Garrick. *Introduction to the Study of Sign Language among the North American Indians: As Illustrating the Gesture Speech of Mankind.* Washington, D.C.: General Printing Office, 1880.

Mandell, Daniel R. *Behind the Frontier: Indians in Eighteenth-Century Eastern Massachusetts.* Lincoln: University of Nebraska Press, 1996.

Marten, Catherine. *Wampanoags in the Seventeenth Century: An Ethnohistorical Survey.* Plimoth Plantation, Occasional Papers in Old Colony Studies, no. 2. Plymouth, Mass.: Plimoth Plantation, 1970.

Martin, Calvin. *Keepers of the Game: Indian–Animal Relationships and the Fur Trade.* Berkeley and Los Angeles: University of California Press, 1978.

Massachusetts-Bay Province. *The Acts and Resolves, Public and Private, of the Province of the Massachusetts-Bay.* 21 vols. Boston: Wright & Potter, 1869–1922.

Mather, Cotton. *Magnalia Christi Americana: Or, The Ecclesiastical History of New England.* 2 vols. Hartford, Conn.: S. Andrus, 1853.

———. *Ornaments for the Daughters of Zion: Or, The Character and Happiness of a Vertuous Woman.* Cambridge, Mass.: S. Phillips, 1692.

Mayhew, Experience. *A Discourse Shewing that God Dealeth with Men as with Reasonable Creatures. With a Brief Account of the State of the Indians on Martha's Vineyard, . . . 1694 to 1720.* Boston: B. Green for Samuel Gerrish, 1720.

———. *Experience Mayhew's Indian Converts: A Cultural Edition.* Ed. Laura Arnold Leibman. Native Americans in the Northeast. Amherst: University of Massachusetts Press, 2008.

———. *Grace Defended.* Boston: B. Green for D. Henchman, 1744.

———. *Indian Converts: Or, Some Account of the Lives and Dying Speeches of a Considerable Number of the Christianized Indians of Martha's Vineyard in New England.* London, 1727.

———. *The Indian Primer or The First Book: By Which Children May Know Truely to Read the Indian Language.* Boston: B. Green, 1720.

Mayhew, Matthew. *The Conquests and Triumphs of Grace: Being a Brief Narrative of the Success Which the Gospel Hath Had among the Indians of Martha's Vineyard (and the Places Adjacent) in New-England.* London: N. Hiller, 1695.

———. Letter to Wait Winthrop, 24 October 1702. Winthrop Papers. Massachusetts Historical Society, Boston.

McBride, Kevin. "'Ancient and Crazie': Pequot Lifeways during the Historic Period." In *Algonkians of New England: Past and Present,* edited by Peter Benes, 63–75. Boston: Annual Proceedings of the 1991 Dublin Folklife Seminar, Boston University, 1993.

McCallum, James Dow. *The Letters of Eleazar Wheelock's Indians*. Hanover, N.H.: Dartmouth College Publications, 1932.

McClure, David. Letter to Eleazor Wheelock, 8 May 1777. Wheelock Papers, 777308.2. Rauner Special Collections Library. Dartmouth College. Hanover, N.H.

McKenzie, D. W. *Bibliography and the Sociology of Texts*. Cambridge: Cambridge University Press, 1999.

McMullen, Ann. "Looking for People in Woodsplint Basketry Decoration." In McMullen and Handsman, *A Key into the Language of Woodsplint Baskets*, 102–23.

———. "What's Wrong with This Picture? Context, Coversion, Survival, and the Development of Regional Native Cultures and Pan-Indianism in Southeastern New England." In *Enduring Traditions: The Native Peoples of New England*, edited by Laurie Weisenstein, 123–50. Westport, Conn.: Bergin and Garvey, 1994.

McMullen, Ann, and Russell G. Handsman, eds. *A Key into the Language of Woodsplint Baskets*. Washington, Conn.: American Indian Archeological Institute, 1987.

*Memoirs of the Historical Society of Pennsylvania II*. Philadelphia: Carey, Lea & Carey, 1827.

Merrell, James H. "Some Thoughts on Colonial Historians and American Indians." *William and Mary Quarterly* 46 (1989): 94–119.

Miller, Andrew. "Abenakis and Colonists in Northern New England, 1675–1725." Ph.D. diss. Johns Hopkins University, 2005.

Monaghan, E. Jennifer. *Learning to Read and Write in Colonial America*. Amherst: University of Massachussets Press, 2005.

——— "Literacy Instruction and Gender in Colonial New England." In *Reading in America: Literature and Social History*, edited by Cathy N. Davidson, 53–80. Baltimore: Johns Hopkins University Press, 1989.

——— "'She Loved to Read in Good Books': Literacy and the Indians of Martha's Vineyard, 1643–1725." *History of Education Quarterly* 30 (1990) 493–521.

Montaukett Petition, 1788[?]. Occom Papers, Connecticut Historical Society. Reprinted in Brooks, *The Collected Writings of Samson Occom*, 150–52.

Moodey, Samuel. *Summary Account of the Life and Death of Joseph Quasson*. Boston: S. Gerrish, 1726.

Morgan, Edmund S. *Visible Saints: The History of a Puritan Idea*. New York: New York University Press, 1963.

Morgan, Lewis Henry. *Ancient Society*. New York: Holt, 1877.

Morrison, Dane. *A Praying People: Massachusett Acculturation and the Failure of the Puritan Mission, 1600–1690*. New York: Peter Lang, 1995.

Morrison, Kenneth. *The Embattled Northeast: The Elusive Ideal of Alliance in Abenaki–Euramerican Relations*. Berkeley: University of California Press, 1984.

Mowatt, Linda, Howard Morphy, and Penny Dransart, eds. *Basketmakers: Meaning and Form in Native American Baskets*. Oxford, England: Pitt Rivers Museum, 1992.

Mulford, Carla, Angela Vietto, and Amy Winans. *Early American Writings*. New York: Oxford University Press, 2002.

Murray, David. *Forked Tongues: Speech Writing and Representation in North American Indian Texts*. Bloomington: University of Indiana Press, 1992.

———. *Indian Giving: Economies of Power in Indian–White Exchanges*. Amherst: University of Massachusetts Press, 2000.

Murray, John E., and Ruth Wallis Herndon. "Markets for Children in Early America: A Political Economy of Pauper Apprenticeship." *Journal of Economic History* 62 (2002): 356–82.

Murray, Laura J. ' "Pray Sir, Consider a Little': Rituals of Subordination and Strategies of Resistance in the Letters of Hezekiah Calvin and David Fowler to Eleazar Wheelock." In *Early Native American Writing: New Critical Essays*, edited by Helen Jaskoski, 15–41. New York: Cambridge University Press, 1996.

———, ed. *To Do Good to My Indian Brethren: The Writings of Joseph Johnson, 1751–1776*. Amherst: University of Massachusetts Press, 1998.

Murray, Laura, and Karen Rice, eds. *Talking on the Page: Editing Aboriginal Oral Texts*. Toronto: University of Toronto Press, 1999.

Naeher, Robert James. "Dialogue in the Wilderness: John Eliot and the Indian Exploration of Puritanism as a Source of Meaning, Comfort, and Ethnic Survival." *New England Quarterly* 62, no. 3 (September 1989): 346–68.

Nahaton, William (alias Quaanan) et al. Letter to Daniel Fisher and others, 14 April 1680. In *Ancient Deeds from the Indians to the Town of Dedham*, edited by William Hill, n.p. Edward Ayer MSS, 279. Newberry Library, Chicago, 1881.

Nanpashamet. "The Wetu or Native House." Plimoth Plantation website, 2000–2001. http://www.plimoth.org/Museum/Hobbamock/wetu.htm. Accessed 2 February 2003; no longer available.

Narragansett Indian Tribe website. Available at http://www.narragansett-tribe.org/. Accessed 30 June 2006.

Nash, Alice. "The Abiding Frontier: Family, Gender, and Religion in Wabanaki History, 1600–1763." Ph.D. diss. Columbia University, 1997.

Nelson, Dana. " '(I Speak Like a fool but I Am Constrained)': Samson Occom's Short Narrative and Economies of the Racial Self." In *Early Native American Writing: New Critical Essays*, edited by Helen Jaskoski, 42–65. New York: Cambridge University Press, 1996.

Noley, Homer. "The Interpreters." In *Native American Religious Identity: Unforgotten Gods*, edited by Jace Weaver, 48–60. Maryknoll, N.Y.: Orbis Books, 1998.

*The Norton Anthology of American Literature, Seventh Edition*, Vol. A, *Beginnings to 1820*. Ed. Nina Baym. New York: W. W. Norton, 2007.

O'Brien, Jean. *Dispossession by Degrees: Indian Land and Identity in Natick, Massachusetts, 1650–1790*. New York: Cambridge University Press, 1997.

Occom, Samson. *The Collected Writings of Samson Occom, Mohegan: Literature and Leadership in Eighteenth-Century Native America*. Ed. Joanna Brooks: New York: Oxford University Press, 2006.

———. "Temperance and Morality Sermon." Edited by Heather Bouwman, Margret Aldrich, Nicole Brudos Ferrara, Keri Henkel, Sara Hoffmann, and Marilyn Paulson. Early Americas Digital Archive website. Available at http://www.mith2.umd.edu/eada/. Accessed 20 September 2007.

Original Indian Record Book. Morse Institute Public Library. Natick, Mass.

*Oxford English Dictionary.* New York: Oxford University Press, 1989–2004. Online version available at www.oed.com.

Parkhill, Thomas. *Weaving Ourselves into the Land: Charles Godfrey Leland, "Indians," and the Study of Native American Religions.* Albany: State University of New York Press, 1997.

Peabody and Badger Records, Church of Natick, 1725–1795. Typescript. Massachusetts Historical Society, Boston.

Perkins, William. *The Foundation of Christian Religion Gathered into Six Principles and It Is to Be Learned of Ignorant People That They May Be Fit to Hear Sermons with Profit, and to Receive the Lords Supper with Comfort.* Boston: Samuel Green, 1682.

Peyer, Bernd. *The Tutor'd Mind: Indian Missionary-Writers in Antebellum America.* Amherst: University of Massachusetts Press, 1997.

———, ed. *The Elders Wrote: An Anthology of Early Prose by North American Indians, 1768–1931.* Berlin: Reimer, 1982.

Pierce, R. Andrew, and Jerome D. Segel. *The Wampanoag Genealogical History of Martha's Vineyard, Massachusetts.* Baltimore: Genealogical Publication, 2003.

Pitkin, Timothy. *A Sermon, Delivered at . . . the Execution of John Jacobs.* Hartford, Conn.: Green and Watson, 1768.

Plane, Ann Marie. *Colonial Intimacies: Indian Marriage in Early New England.* Ithaca, N.Y.: Cornell University Press, 2000.

———. "Customary Laws of Marriage: Legal Pluralism, Colonialism, and Narragansett Indian Identity in Eighteenth-Century New England." In *The Many Legalities of Early America,* edited by Christopher L. Tomlins and Bruce H. Mann, 186–87. Chapel Hill: University of North Carolina Press for the Omohundro Institute of Early American History and Culture, 2001.

———. "Falling 'Into a Dreame': Native Americans, Colonization, and Consciousness in Early New England." In Calloway and Salisbury, *Reinterpreting New England Indians and the Colonial Experience,* 84–105.

———. "Putting a Face on Colonization: Factionalism and Gender Politics in the Life History of Awashunkes, the 'Squaw Sachem' of Saconet." In *Northeastern Indian Lives, 1632–1816,* edited by Robert S. Grumet, 140–65. Amherst: University of Massachusetts Press, 1996.

Porter, Frank W., III, ed. *The Art of Native American Basketry: A Living Legacy.* New York: Greenwood Press, 1990.

Pratt, Mary Louise. "Arts of the Contact Zone." In *Ways of Reading,* edited by Donald Bartholomae and Anthony Petrosky, 582–95. 5th ed. Boston: Bedford/St. Martins.

Rabito-Wyppensenwah, Philip, and Robert Abiuso. "The Montaukett Use of Herbs: A Review of the Recorded Material." In Stone, *The History and Archeology of the Montauk,* 585–88.

"Ratification de la Paix . . . ," 4 August 1701. Archives Nationales de France (ANF), Paris. Fondes des Colonies, series C11A, vol. 19, folio 41–44.

Richardson, Leon Burr. *An Indian Preacher in England.* Hanover, N.H.: Dartmouth College Publications, 1933.

Richmond, Trudy Lamb. "Spirituality and Survival in Schaghticoke Basket-Making." In McMullen and Handsman, *A Key into the Language of Woodsplint Baskets*, 127–43.

Ronda, James P., and Jeanne Ronda. "The Death of John Sassamon: An Exploration in Writing New England Indian History." *American Indian Quarterly* 1 (1974): 91–102.

Rowlandson, Mary. "A True History of the Captivity and Restoration of Mrs. Mary Rowlandson" [1682], edited by Amy Schrager Lang. In *Journeys in New Worlds: Early American Women's Narratives*, edited by William Andrews, 11–66. Madison: University of Wisconsin Press, 1990.

Rubertone, Patricia E. *Grave Undertakings: An Archaeology of Roger Williams and the Narragansett Indians.* Washington, D.C.: Smithsonian Institution Press, 2001.

Ruppert, James. "The Old Wisdom: Introducing Native American Materials." In *Teaching the Literatures of Early America*, edited by Carla Mulford, 11–26. New York: Modern Language Association of America, 1999.

*R. v. Sarah Pharaoh*, March 1730. Records of the Superior Court of Judicature (Rhode Island). Supreme Court Judicial Records Center, Pawtucket, R.I.

Salisbury, Neal. Introduction to *The Sovereignty and Goodness of God*, by Mary Rowlandson, 1–60. Boston: Bedford Books, 1997.

———. *Manitou and Providence: Indians, Europeans, and the Making of New England: 1500–1643.* New York: Oxford University Press, 1982.

———. "Red Puritans: The 'Praying Indians' of Massachusetts Bay and John Eliot." *The William and Mary Quarterly* 31 (1974): 27–54.

St. Jean, Wendy. "Inventing Guardianship: The Mohegan Indians and their 'Protectors.'" *New England Quarterly* 72, no. 3 (1999): 362–87.

Schaff, Philip. *America: A Sketch of Its Political, Social, and Religious Character.* Cambridge, Mass.: Harvard University Press, 1961.

Schenck, Theresa. "The Algonquian Totem and Totemism: A Distortion of the Semantic Field." In *Papers of the Twenty-eighth Algonquian Conference*, edited by David H. Pentland, 341–53. Winnipeg: University of Manitoba Press, 1997.

Schoolcraft, Henry Rowe. *Historical and Statistical Information, Respecting the History, Condition and Prospects of the Indian Tribes of the United States.* Vol. 3. Philadelphia: Lippincott, Grambo, 1851.

Scott, James C. *Domination and the Arts of Resistance: Hidden Transcripts.* New Haven, Conn.: Yale University Press, 1990.

Scott, Jonathan Fletcher. "The Early Colonial Houses of Martha's Vineyard." Ph.D. diss. University of Minnesota, 1985.

Seeman, Erik. "Reading Indians' Deathbed Scenes: Ethnohistorical and Representational Approaches." *Journal of American History* 88 (2001): 17–47.

Sergeant, John. *Letter to Dr. Colman.* Boston: Rogers and Fowle, 1743.

"1727 Ratification of the Treaty of 1725 for Ratification at Casco Bay." Indian Treaties Collection, Nova Scotia Archives, ref. no. 513. Halifax.

Sévigny, André. *Les Abénaquis: Habitat et migrations, 17e et 18e siècles.* Montréal: Bellarmin, 1976.

Sewall, Samuel. *Diary of Samuel Sewall, 1674–1729.* 3 vols. Massachusetts Historical Society Collections, 5th ser., vols. 5–7. Boston: Massachusetts Historical Society, 1878–82.

Shurtleff, Nathaniel B., ed. *Records of the Governor and Company of the Massachusetts Bay in New England.* 5 vols. Boston, 1853–54.

Silko, Leslie Marmon. "Language and Literature from a Pueblo Indian Perspective." In *English Literature: Opening up the Canon,* edited by Leslie Fiedler, 54–72. Baltimore: Johns Hopkins University Press, 1981.

Silverman, David J. "Conditions for Coexistence, Climates for Collapse: The Challenges of Indian Life on Martha's Vineyard, 1524–1871." Ph.D. diss. Princeton University, 2000.

———. "Deposing the Sachem to Defend the Sachemship: Indian Land Sales and Political Structure on Martha's Vineyard, 1680–1740." *Explorations in Early American Culture* 5 (2001): 9–44.

———. *Faith and Boundaries: Colonists, Christianity, and Community among the Wampanoag Indians of Martha's Vineyard, 1600–1871.* Studies in North American Indian History. New York: Cambridge University Press, 2005.

Simmons, William, S. *Cautantowwit's House: An Indian Burial Ground on the Island of Conanicut in Narragansett Bay.* Providence, R.I: Brown University Press, 1970.

———. "The Great Awakening and Indian Conversion in Southern New England." In *Papers of the Tenth Algonquian Conference,* edited by William Cowan, 25–36. Ottowa: Carleton University, 1978.

———. "Narragansett." In *Handbook of North American Indians,* vol 15, *Northeast,* edited by Bruce G. Trigger, 190–197. Washington, D.C.: Smithsonian Institution, 1978.

———. *Spirit of the New England Tribes: Indian History and Folklore, 1620–1984.* Hanover, N.H.: University Press of New England, 1986.

Simmons, William S., and Cheryl L. Simmons, eds. *Old Light on Separate Ways: The Narragansett Diary of Joseph Fish, 1765–1776.* Hanover, N.H.: University Press of New England, 1982.

Smith, Sidonie, and Julia Watson. *Women, Autobiography, Theory: A Reader.* Madison: University of Wisconsin Press, 1998.

Snyder, Gary. *Myths and Texts.* New York: Totem Press, 1960.

Spalding, Joshua. *A Sermon Delivered . . . Previous to the Execution of Isaac Coombs.* Salem, Mass.: Dabney and Cushing, 1787.

Speck, Frank G. "Abenaki Clans—Never!" *American Anthropologist,* n.s., 37, no. 1 (July–September 1935): 528–30.

Speck, Frank G., and Jesse Moses. *The Celestial Bear Comes Down to Earth*. Scientific Publications, no. 7. Reading, Pa.: Reading Public Museum and Art Gallery, 1945

———. *Eastern Algonkian Block-Stamp Decoration*. Trenton, N.J.: Archeological Society of New Jersey, 1947.

———. "Native Tribes and Dialects of Connecticut: A Mohegan-Pequot Diary." In *Forty-Third Annual Report of the Bureau of American Ethnology*, 199–288. Washington, D.C.: Smithsonian Institution, 1928.

———. "Some Mohegan-Pequot Legends." *Journal of American Folklore* 17, no. 66 (1904): 183–84.

Stannard, David E. *The Puritan Way of Death: A Study in Religion, Culture, and Social Change*. New York: Oxford University Press, 1977.

Stevens, Laura. "The Christian Origins of the Vanishing Indian." In *Mortal Remains: Death in Early America*, edited by Andrew Burstein and Nancy Isenberg, 17–30. Philadelphia: University of Pennsylvania Press, 2003.

Stone, Gaynell, ed. *The History and Archeology of the Montauk—Readings in Long Island Archeology and Ethnohistory*, 2nd ed. Vol. 3. Stony Brook, N.Y.: Suffolk County Archeological Association, 1993.

Strong, John. "How the Montauk Lost Their Land." In Stone, *The History and Archeology of the Montauk*, 77–120.

———. *The Montaukett Indians of Eastern Long Island*. Syracuse, N.Y.: Syracuse University Press, 2001.

Szasz, Margaret Connell. *Indian Education in the American Colonies, 1607–1783*. Albuquerque: University of New Mexico Press, 1988.

Tanis, Norman Earl. "Education in John Eliot's Indian Utopias, 1646–1675." *History of Education Quarterly* 10, no. 3 (Fall 1970): 308–23.

Tansur, William. *American Harmony; or Royal Melody Complete*. Newburyport, Mass. D. Bailey, 1769.

———. *A New and Complete Introduction to the Grounds and Rules of Musick*. Newburyport, Mass.: D. Bailey, 1764.

Tantaquidgeon, Gladys. "Notes on Mohegan-Pequot Basketry Designs." *Indians at Work* 2 (1935): 43–46.

Taylor, Alan. "Captain Hendrick Aupaumut: The Dilemmas of an Intercultural Broker." *Ethnohistory* 43, no. 3 (Summer 1996): 431–57.

Thacher, Peter. *Brief Account of the Society of the Propagation of the Gospel among the Indians and Others in North America*. Boston: S. Hall, 1798.

Thomas, Halsey M., ed. *The Diary of Samuel Sewall, 1674–1729*. 2 vols. New York: Farrar, Straus and Giroux, 1973.

Tolles, Frederick B. "'Of the Best Sort but Plain': The Quaker Esthetic." *American Quarterly* 11, no. 4 (Winter 1959): 484–502.

Tooker, William Wallace. *John Eliot's First Indian Teacher and Interpreter, Cockenoe-de-Long Island*. New York: F. P. Harper, 1896

Trigger, Bruce G., ed. *Handbook of North American Indians*. Vol 15, *Northeast*. Washington, D.C.: Smithsonian Institution, 1978.

Turnbaugh, Sarah Peabody, and William A. Turnbaugh. *Indian Baskets*. West Chester, Pa.: Schiffer Publishing, 1986.

———. "Weaving the Woods: Tradition and Response in Southern New England Splint Basketry." In McMullen and Handsman, *A Key into the Language of Woodsplint Baskets*, 77–93.

Ulrich, Laurel Thatcher. *The Age of Homespun: Objects and Stories in the Creation of an American Myth*. New York: Alfred A. Knopf, 2001.

———. *Good Wives: Image and Reality in the Lives of Women in Northern New England, 1650–1750*. New York: Oxford University Press, 1982.

———. *A Midwife's Tale: The Life of Martha Ballard, Based on Her Diary, 1785–1812*. New York: Alfred A. Knopf, 1990.

———. "Of Pens and Needles: Sources in Early American Women's History." *Journal of American History* 77 (1990): 200–207.

Van Dyken, Donald. *Rediscovering Catechism: The Art of Equipping Covenant Children*. Phillipsburg, N.J.: P&R Publishing, 2000.

Vansina, Jan. *Paths in the Rainforest: Toward a History of Political Tradition in Equatorial Africa*. Madison: University of Wisconsin Press, 1990.

Vastoka, Joan. "History without Writing: Pictorial Narratives in Native North America." In *Gin Das Winan: Documenting Aboriginal History in Ontario*, edited by Dale Standen and David McNab, 48–64. Occasional Papers of the Champlain Society, no. 2. Toronto: Champlain Society, 1996.

Vaughan, Alden T. *New England Frontier: Puritans and Indians 1620–1676*. Boston: Little, Brown, 1965.

Vecsey, Christopher, ed. *Imagine Ourselves Richly: Mythic Narratives of North American Indians*. New York: Harper Collins, 1991.

"Wampanoag Celebrations." Wampanoag Tribe of Gay Head website. Available at http://wampanoagtribe.net/education/celebrat.htm. Accessed 10 August 2007.

Warkentin, Germaine. "In Search of the Word of the Other: Aboriginal Sign Systems and the History of the Book in Canada." *Book History* 2 (1999): 1–27.

Warrior, Robert Allen. "A Native American Perspective: Canaanites, Cowboys, and Indians." In *Voices from the Margin: Interpreting the Bible in the Third World*, edited by R. S. Sugirtharajah, 277–85. 2nd ed. New York: Orbis Books, 1997.

Washburn, Wilcomb E. "The Moral and Legal Justification for Dispossessing the Indians." In *Seventeenth-Century America: Essays in Colonial History*, edited by James Morton Smith, 22–25. New York: W. W. Norton for the Institute of Early American History and Culture, 1959.

Weaver, Jace. "From I-Hermeneutics to We-Hermeneutics: Native Americans and the Post-Colonial." In *Native American Religious Identity: Unforgotten Gods*, edited by Jace Weaver, 1–25. Maryknoll, N.Y.: Orbis Books, 1998.

———. *That the People Might Live: Native American Literatures and Native American Community*. New York: Oxford, 1997.

Wheeler, Rachel. "Hendrick Aupaumut: Christian-Mahican Prophet." *Journal of the Early Republic* 25 (2005): 187–220.

Wheelock, Eleazar. *A Plain and Faithful Narrative of the Original Design, Rise, Progress and Present State of the Indian Charity School at Lebanon, in Connecticut.* Boston: R. and S. Draper, 1763.

White, Richard. *The Middle Ground: Indians, Empires, and Republics in the Great Lakes Region, 1650–1815.* New York: Cambridge University Press, 1991.

Whitehead, Ruth Holmes. *The Old Man Told Us: Excerpts from Micmac History, 1500–1950.* Halifax: Nimbus, 1991.

——— *Stories from the Six Worlds: Micmac Legends.* Halifax: Nimbus, 1988.

Williams, Daniel. *Pillars of Salt: An Anthology of Early American Criminal Narratives.* Madison, Wis.: Madison House, 1993.

Williams, Roger. *A Key into the Language of America.* 1643. Reprint edited by Howard M. Chapin. 5th ed. Providence: Rhode Island and Providence Plantations Tercentenary Committee, 1936.

Winslow, Edward. *The Glorious Progress of the Gospel amongst the Indians in New England, 1649.* Reprinted in *Tracts Relating to the Attempts to Convert to Christianity the Indians of New England.* Massachusetts Historical Society Collections, 3rd ser., vol. 4. Boston, 1834.

Wiseman, Frederick Matthew. *The Voice of the Dawn: An Autohistory of the Abenaki Nation.* Hanover, N.H.: University Press of New England, 2001.

Withey, Lynne. *Voyages of Discovery: Captain Cook and the Exploration of the Pacific.* New York: William Morrow, 1987.

Wolverton, Nan. "'A Precarious Living': Basket Making and Related Crafts among New England Indians." In Calloway and Salisbury, *Reinterpreting New England Indians and the Colonial Experience,* 341–68.

Wong, Hertha Dawn. *Sending My Heart Back across the Years: Tradition and Innovation in Native American Autobiography.* New York: Oxford University Press, 1992.

Wyss, Hilary E. *Writing Indians: Literacy, Christianity, and Native Community in Early America.* Amherst: University of Massachusetts Press, 2000.

# Contributors

HEIDI BOHAKER is an assistant professor of Aboriginal history in the Department of History at the University of Toronto. Bohaker's research interests include Aboriginal writing systems and literacies, treaties and treaty-making practices, and the political significance of kinship networks. Her article "*Nindoodemag*: Algonquian Kinship Networks and Cross-Cultural Alliances in the Eastern Great Lakes Region, 1600–1700" was published in *William and Mary Quarterly*, 3rd series, 63, no. 1 (January 2006): 23–52.

HEATHER BOUWMAN is an associate professor of English at the University of St. Thomas in St. Paul, Minnesota. She specializes in colonial and early American literature. Recently, she and nine graduate students published two Samson Occom sermons at the Early Americas Digital Archives (http://www.mith2 .umd.edu/eada/). In addition, Bouwman has published poetry and essays on teaching and academic life. Her first novel (set in North America in the late 1700s) is scheduled for publication in 2008.

JOANNA BROOKS is an associate professor of English at San Diego State University and the author of *American Lazarus: Religion and the Rise of African-American and Native American Literatures* (New York: Oxford University Press, 2003), which received the 2003 Modern Language Association William Sanders Scarborough Prize as an outstanding work in African-American literary criticism. Brooks is editor of *The Collected Writings of Samson Occom, Mohegan: Leadership and Literature in Eighteenth-Century Native America* (New York: Oxford University Press, 2006).

KRISTINA BROSS is an associate professor of English and American studies at Purdue University. Her reviews and essays have been published in *Common-Place* and *Early American Literature*, and she is the author of *Dry Bones and Indian Sermons: Praying Indians in Colonial America* (Ithaca, N.Y.: Cornell University Press, 2004).

STEPHANIE FITZGERALD (Cree) is an assistant professor of English and Indigenous Nations Studies at the University of Kansas. Among her works on Native women's writings is *Keepers of the Morning Star: An Anthology of*

*Native Women's Theater* (Los Angeles: UCLA American Indian Studies Center, 2003), co-edited with Jaye T. Darby.

Sandra M. Gustafson is an associate professor of English at the University of Notre Dame. She is the author of *Eloquence Is Power: Oratory and Performance in Early America* (Chapel Hill: University of North Carolina Press for the Omohundro Institute of Early American History and Culture, 2000). She has published numerous reviews and essays and currently serves as the book review editor for the journal *Early American Literature*.

Laura Arnold Leibman is an associate professor of English and humanities at Reed College in Portland, Oregon. She is the academic director of *American Passages: A Literary Survey* (Annenberg Foundation/Corporation for Public Broadcasting) and the lead advisor for *Artifacts & Fiction* (Annenberg Foundation). She has published essays on colonial American and Native American literature and is the editor of a forthcoming cultural edition of Experience Mayhew's *Indian Converts* (University of Massachusetts Press). Her current research project is on the Sephardic community in eighteenth-century Newport, Rhode Island.

Kevin A. McBride is an associate professor of anthropology at the University of Connecticut and the director of research for the Mashantucket Pequot Museum and Research Center, where he oversees field study programs on the reservation for graduate students and directs all ongoing archaeological excavations and ethnohistorical research for the tribe. His research interests include the prehistory and ethnohistory of eastern North America, the historic archaeology of Euro-Americans, settlement systems, and paleoethnobotany.

David Murray is a professor of American literature and culture in the School of American and Canadian Studies at the University of Nottingham in England. Among his writings on American poetry and culture are *Forked Tongues: Speech, Writing, and Representation in North American Indian Texts* (Bloomington: Indiana University Press, 1991 ), *Indian Giving: Economies of Power in Indian-White Exchanges* (Amherst: University of Massachusetts Press, 2000), and *Matter, Magic and Spirit: Representing Indian and African American Belief.* (Philadelphia: Pennsylvania University Press, 2007). His current projects include an anthology of essays on jazz as related to other African American arts.

Laura J. Murray is an associate professor of English at Queen's University. She is the editor of *To Do Good to My Indian Brethren: The Writings of Joseph*

*Johnson, 1751–1776* (Amherst: University of Massachusetts Press, 1998) and, with Keren Rice, the co-editor of *Talking on the Page: Editing Aboriginal Oral Texts* (Toronto: University of Toronto Press, 1999). In addition, she has written articles on Native American studies for such journals as *American Quarterly*, *American Literary History*, and *New England Quarterly*. Her current research concerns the history and public policy of copyright law in American, Canadian, and Aboriginal contexts.

JEAN M. O'BRIEN (Ojibwe) is an associate professor of history at the University of Minnesota, where she is also affiliated with the Department of American Indian Studies and the Department of American Studies. Her publications include numerous articles on colonial Algonquian communities and the book *Dispossession by Degrees: Indian Land and Identity in Natick, Massachusetts, 1650–1790* (New York: Cambridge University Press, 1997).

ANN MARIE PLANE is an associate professor of history at the University of California at Santa Barbara. She is the author of *Colonial Intimacies: Indian Marriage in Early New England* (Ithaca, N.Y.: Cornell University Press, 2000), and her essays on early Native American studies have been published in the journals *Law and Social History*, *Ethnohistory*, and *Major Problems in American Women's History*.

PHILLIP H. ROUND is an associate professor of English and the former coordinator of American Indian and Native studies at the University of Iowa. He is the author of *By Nature and by Custom Cursed: Transatlantic Civil Discourse and New England Cultural Production, 1620–1660* (Hanover, N.H.: University Press of New England, 1999). His essays have been published in *Early American Literature*, *American Indian Quarterly*, and *American Literary History*.

JODI SCHORB is an assistant professor of English at the University of Florida. Her articles have been published in *The Puritan Origins of American Sex: Religion, Sexuality, and National Identity in American Literature*, edited by Tracy Fessenden et al. (London: Routledge, 2000) and such journals as *Tulsa Studies in Women's Literature*. She is currently working on a book-length project that evolved from her doctoral dissertation on the role of race, gender, and sexuality in early American criminal captivity narratives.

DAVID J. SILVERMAN, who received his doctoral degree from Princeton University in 2000, is an associate professor of history at George Washington University. He is the author of *Faith and Boundaries: Colonists, Christianity, and Community among the Wampanoag Indians of Martha's Vineyard, 1600–1871* (New York: Cambridge University Press, 2005). An article from that project won the Lester J. Cappon Award for best essay of 2005 in the *William and Mary Quarterly*. His current projects include a book about the Brothertown Indian community and the evolution of Indian race consciousness.

HILARY E. WYSS is an associate professor of English at Auburn University. She is the author of *Writing Indians: Literacy, Christianity, and Native Community in Early America* (Amherst: University of Massachusetts, 2000). She has also published numerous articles about colonial Native American writing. Among her current projects is *English Letters: Native American Literacies, 1750–1850*, a book-length study of Native American education in the colonial and early national period.

# Index

Adams, Eliphalet, 142, 150
adultery, 61, 70, 109
aesthetic approach, 205–7
alcohol, 24, 155, 216. *See also* drunkenness
ale-wives, 119
Algonquian peoples, 2–7, 78, 84, 175n35, 179n53, 182n60, 191, 194–95, 211
Allen, Christopher, 86–87, 89, 90
alphabetic literacy, 3, 4–5, 6–11, 82, 105–6, 168, 198
*amit* (death), 194–95
Anne, Queen of England, 19–20, 24
anthropologists, 132, 152
Apess, William, 130–31, 148, 159–60, 243
Aquinnah (Gay Head, Mass.), 162–64, 167
archaeologists, 132
"as told to" narratives, 151–52
autobiographies, Indian, 152–53, 160–61

balance, spiritual, 137, 198, 217, 219
baptism, 142, 145, 180, 211
barn, 89, 144, 150
basketry, 4n5, 12, 51–56. *See also* weaving; *madu'a*
bears and bear paws, 133, 135–36, 140
Bhabha, Homi, 69–70, 116n20, 117n22
Bible, 7, 20, 25, 101, 115, 133–34, 138, 143, 194; Indian, 7, 77–79, 106, 112, 118, 136–37, 168; King James version, 114–15, 132, 136
Big Knifes, 145, 228, 231–32, 234, 237, 239–41
boarding schools, 9, 11, 97–98
book history, 6, 7
Boston, 48, 75, 106, 136, 199, 203, 207
Boston, Patience, 146n41, 148, 149, 152n52, 160
Bragdon, Kathleen, 2, 6. *See also* Goddard, Ives, and Kathleen Bragdon
Brant, Joseph, 235, 237–39, 240–42, 248
Brooks, Lisa, 5, 198, 217, 220–21
Brotherton (Brothertown), N.Y., 10–11, 15, 43, 50, 65, 68, 82–83, 199, 215, 218
burial rites, 78, 194–95

Calvin, Hezekiah, 10, 104n38
Canonicus, 84

captivity narratives, 156
catechism, 7, 34, 168, 176, 180, 189n85, 194
Cautantowwit, 84, 130, 135
Chappaquiddick, Mass., 162–63
Charles II, King of England, 20, 25
Charlestown, R.I., 84–85, 98
Cheepi, 84, 130. *See also* Hobbamock
children, 9–10, 30, 42, 45, 59, 82, 91, 97, 101, 110, 112, 133, 135–36, 143, 168, 175, 187, 193–94
Chilmark, Mass., 167
Christian Indians, 7, 44, 49, 70, 105–6
Christianity, 5–7, 42, 44, 158–59, 219. *See also* Christian Indians; Praying Indians
clans, 210
Cochituate Pond, 127, 129
coffins, 147
Cohanit, 108
Cohen, Charles, 111
Colchester, Mass., 20
communitism, 218
conversion narratives: Indian, 7, 159, 196; Puritan, 196
Cook, Captain James, 60, 63–64
courts, judicial, 20n10, 24, 86, 90–91, 119, 124, 126, 142, 145, 150, 155, 167
Covenant of Grace, 145
cursing, 58, 69

Dartmouth College, 10, 48
Deake, Edward, 100
Deer Island, Mass., 106
depositions, 77, 86–87, 89, 92. *See also* testimony, legal
diseases, 6, 8, 44, 59–60, 134, 138, 203. *See also* epidemics
Dongan, Thomas, 167, 171
Dorchester, Mass., 108
Dowd, Gregory Evans, 248
dreams, 48, 67n108, 103, 189, 190, 196
drunkenness, 43, 58, 64–65. *See also* alcohol
Dummer's Treaty, 204
Dutch colonists, 67, 84, 130
dying Indian speeches, 149, 181, 192, 194

273